ADVANCE PRAISE FOR *THE BOOK OF POSTFIX*

"While many technical books are little more than recycled product documentation, Koetter and Hildebrandt provide fantastic insight into the fundamentals of Postfix. After building the solid understanding for the reader, they tackle many of Postfix's more advanced features. I put the book down feeling that, if other mail programs had books like this, the technology would be better understood."

—TOM THOMAS, AUTHOR OF *NETWORK SECURITY FIRST-STEP* (CISCO PRESS)

"As Postfix grows in distribution and adds new features, it's increasingly necessary to have a comprehensive guide that administrators can consult for deploying and maintaining their Postfix installations. Patrick Koetter and Ralf Hildebrandt are experts who have been dedicated to Postfix since the very beginning, and their book answers this critical need."

—LUTZ JÄNICKE, CREATOR AND MAINTAINER OF THE TLS PATCH FOR POSTFIX

"What most impressed me about Ralf and Patrick's book was the way it makes difficult, complex concepts simple to understand. The authors clearly know their subject inside and out and present it in an easy-to-follow format. They haven't missed anything."

—TOBIAS OETIKER, INVENTOR OF ROUND ROBIN DATABASE TOOL (RRDTOOL) AND MULTI ROUTER TRAFFIC GRAPHER (MRTG)

"This book, with its many practical examples and clear explanations, is like having a Postfix expert at your side."

—DAVID SCHWEIKERT, AUTHOR OF POSTGREY (A POSTFIX GREYLISTING POLICY SERVER)

"I recommend this book for anyone using Postfix, especially those planning to integrate the AMaViS virus scanning."

—RAINER LINK, FOUNDER OF OPENANTIVIRUS.ORG

"It's a must-have resource for anybody interested in using and understanding Postfix, from the home user to the administrator of the largest mail systems today."

—DR. LIVIU DAIA, SENIOR RESEARCHER AT THE INSTITUTE OF MATHEMATICS OF THE ROMANIAN ACADEMY

THE BOOK OF™ POSTFIX

State-of-the-Art Message Transport

by Ralf Hildebrandt and Patrick Koetter

NO STARCH PRESS

San Francisco

Printed on recycled paper in the United States of America

1 2 3 4 5 6 7 8 9 10 – 07 06 05

Publisher: William Pollock
Managing Editor: Karol Jurado
Production Manager: Susan Berge
Cover and Interior Design: Octopod Studios
Developmental Editor: Brian Ward
Technical Reviewer: Brian Ward
Copyeditor: Andy Carroll
Compositor: Riley Hoffman
Proofreader: Stephanie Provines
Indexer: Kevin Broccoli

For information on book distributors or translations, please contact No Starch Press, Inc. directly:

No Starch Press, Inc.
555 De Haro Street, Suite 250, San Francisco, CA 94107
phone: 415.863.9900; fax: 415.863.9950; info@nostarch.com; http://www.nostarch.com

Library of Congress Cataloging-in-Publication Data

Hildebrandt, Ralf.
  The book of Postfix : state-of-the-art message transport / Ralf Hildebrandt and Patrick Koetter.
       p. cm.
  ISBN 1-59327-001-1
1. Postfix (Computer file). 2. Electronic mail systems--Computer programs. 3. Internet. I. Koetter,
Patrick. II. Title.
   TK5105.74.P66H55 2005
   005.7'13--dc22
                                        2003017563

To those who like good software

ABOUT THE AUTHORS

Ralf Hildebrandt and Patrick Koetter are active and well-known figures in the Postfix community. Hildebrandt is a manager technics for T-Systems, a German information and communications technology (ICT) solutions company. Koetter is an information architect running his own company consulting and developing corporate communication for customers in Europe and Africa. Both have spoken about Postfix at industry conferences and hacker conventions and contribute regularly to a number of open source mailing lists.

ACKNOWLEDGMENTS

There are a lot of people we need to thank for this book, so we'll each give our lists.

Ralf Hildebrandt

One thing I noticed while writing this book was how little I knew about how Postfix works "under the hood." I knew how it behaved, but not exactly why, at least not in every single component and corner-case. In some cases I didn't know much, in other areas I found my knowledge (or lack thereof) to be wrong. I had to RTFM and ask a lot of questions on the helpful postfix-users mailing list to get the details. This book will not be able to replace the experience of running Postfix for more than five years, but it will lead you closer to mastering it.

Admittedly, when I started with Unix in '94, the Internet was a much safer place than it is now. There wasn't any spam! I only got to know Postfix because Sendmail kept crashing on me. After a brief interlude with qmail, I found Postfix and stuck with it. I never looked back.

When Bill approached me and asked if I wanted to write a book about Postfix, I hesitated at first. I needed a co-author, since the sheer amount of work to be done was far too much for one person. At that time, Patrick was cursing SASL on the list and vowed to write a SASL-HOWTO if he ever got it working. He did, and I read the HOWTO, liked it, and asked him for his co-authorship.

As it turns out, the amount of work was too much even for two people, so Brian Ward joined us as a technical editor, adding valuable experience in areas where we lacked it.

Without the help of Wietse Venema, Vi(c|k)tor Duchovni, Lutz Jänicke, Andreas Winkelmann, and Peter Bieringer, this book would have never reached its present state, so they're in for a free copy. Not that they need it, but it sure makes a great gift. A big thanks and love go to my wife Constanze who endured my frequent "But I still have to write a chapter now!" excuses and thus made it possible to finish the book instead of letting it become vaporware. Oh yeah, and when reading Patrick's comments, please keep in mind that I'm only slightly crazy.

Patrick Koetter

Years will pass before the Internet provides us with all the services we want it to have. Just as with any other new medium, the immediate impulse of those who provide services is to push growth, especially in the quantity of content and services. The quality of the service and its functionalities usually has to stand back—at least until the service starts to pay off. In the meantime it is exposed to people who like to abuse and destroy things rather than promote and expand them.

This has happened to email and this is where Postfix comes in, and really does provide a new dimension of quality.

When I went out to get myself an SMTP server, I was shocked that Sendmail seemed to require a diploma of some sort, especially to figure out the macros. So I looked around for other software. To cut it short: I fell in love with Postfix.

Postfix showed me that it's possible to have complex software configured with a simple, clear, and structured syntax. If you know SMTP, you already know most of the important details of configuring Postfix. I didn't really know SMTP when Ralf asked me to write the book with him. This book required me to learn more than I had expected and to correct misunderstandings.

I am very proud that this book gives me the opportunity to hand over what I know about computers and email today. Hopefully this book will get you well on your way to using Postfix creatively. Creativity grows the best when there is knowledge.

This book would not have seen the light without the knowledge, curiosity, and support of Wietse Venema, Vi(c|k)tor Duchovni, Liviu Daia, Lutz Jänicke, Florian Kirstein, Walter Steinsdorfer, Roland Rollinger, Tom Thomas, Alexey Melnikov, Andreas Winkelmann, Eric "cybertime hostmaster," and the users of the Postfix mailing list; their questions and problems told us what was missing when we thought everything had been said.

Most importantly, I need to thank Ralf, whose knowledge about Postfix is outclassed only by his sassy use of computers. He's like a duck taking to water in this respect. It was Ralf who chose me to be his companion on this adventure called *The Book of Postfix*, and I'm indebted to this crazy guy who became a close friend as we wrote this book.

The book has been a great challenge, not only to me, but also to my wife Birgit; her trust in me carried me through the countless lines of this book. It's a great privilege to be asked to do something that you've set your heart on. It's a godsend to have somebody like Birgit at your side when you finally do it.

BRIEF CONTENTS

About This Book
xxv

Chapter 1
An Introduction to Postfix
1

Part I: Basics

Chapter 2
Preparing Your Host and
Environment
7

Chapter 3
Mail Server for a Single Domain
17

Chapter 4
Dial-up Mail Server
for a Single Domain
29

Chapter 5
Anatomy of Postfix
35

Part II: Content Control

Chapter 6
A Postmaster's Primer to Email
55

Chapter 7
How Message Transfer
Restrictions Work
69

Chapter 8
Using Message Transfer
Restrictions
81

Chapter 9
How Built-in Content
Filters Work
111

Chapter 10
Using Built-in Content Filters
117

Chapter 11
How External Content
Filters Work
129

Chapter 12
Using External Content Filters
141

**Part III: Advanced
Configurations**

Chapter 13
Mail Gateways
169

Chapter 14
A Mail Server
for Multiple Domains
189

Chapter 15
Understanding SMTP
Authentication
217

Chapter 16
SMTP Authentication
247

Chapter 17
Understanding
Transport Layer Security
267

Chapter 18
Using Transport Layer Security
279

Chapter 19
A Company Mail Server
313

Chapter 20
Running Postfix in a chroot
Environment
369

Part IV: Tuning Postfix

Chapter 21
Remote Client Concurrency
and Request Rate Limiting
379

Chapter 22
Performance Tuning
387

Appendices

Appendix A
Installing Postfix
407

Appendix B
Troubleshooting Postfix
419

Appendix C
CIDR and SMTP Standards
Reference
435

Glossary
441

Index
449

CONTENTS IN DETAIL

ABOUT THIS BOOK   xxv

Additional Resources xxvi
    Postfix Documentation, How-tos, and FAQs xxvi
    Mailing Lists xxvi
Conventions Used in This Book xxvii
Domains and Names Used in This Book xxvii
    The Local Domain.. xxviii
    Our Provider.. xxviii
Scripts xxviii
Comments xxviii

1
AN INTRODUCTION TO POSTFIX   1

PART I: BASICS

2
PREPARING YOUR HOST AND ENVIRONMENT   7

Hostname 8
Connectivity 8
    TCP Port 25 8
System Time and Timestamps 9
Syslog 10
Name Resolution (DNS) 11
DNS for Mail Servers 13
    A Records 13
    PTR Records 14
    MX Records 15

3
MAIL SERVER FOR A SINGLE DOMAIN   17

The Minimum Configuration 17
Configuring Postfix 18
    Setting the Hostname in the smtpd Banner 18
    Setting the Domain Mail Is Accepted For 19
    Setting the Domain to Be Appended to Outgoing Messages 20
    Mapping Mail Sent to root to a Different Mailbox 21
    Starting Postfix and Testing Mail Delivery to root 22
    Mapping Email Addresses to Usernames 25
    Setting Permissions to Make Postfix Relay Email from Your Network 26

4
DIAL-UP MAIL SERVER FOR A SINGLE DOMAIN 29

Disabling DNS Resolution 31
Adjusting Relay Permissions 31
Setting the ISP Relay Host 32
Deferring Message Transport 32
Triggering Message Delivery 33
Configuring Relay Permissions for a Relay Host 34
    POP-before-SMTP 34
    SMTP Authentication 34

5
ANATOMY OF POSTFIX 35

Postfix Daemons 37
Postfix Queues 42
Maps 43
    Map Types 44
    How Postfix Queries Maps 47
External Sources 47
Command-Line Utilities 48
    postfix 48
    postalias 48
    postcat 48
    postmap 48
    postdrop 49
    postkick 49
    postlock 50
    postlog 50
    postqueue 50
    postsuper 51

PART II: CONTENT CONTROL

6
A POSTMASTER'S PRIMER TO EMAIL 55

Message Transport Basics 55
    Why Do You Need to Know This? 56
Controlling the SMTP Communication (Envelope) 57
Controlling the Message Content 61
    Headers 63
    Body 64
    Attachments 65

7
HOW MESSAGE TRANSFER RESTRICTIONS WORK 69

Restriction Triggers 70
Restriction Types 71
    Generic Restrictions 71
    Switchable Restrictions 72
    Customizable Restrictions 72
    Additional UCE Control Parameters 73
    Application Ranges 74
Building Restrictions 74
    Notation 74
    Moment of Evaluation 75
    Influence of Actions on Restriction Evaluation 75
    Slowing Down Bad Clients 77
Restriction Classes 79

8
USING MESSAGE TRANSFER RESTRICTIONS 81

How to Build and Test Restrictions 81
    Simulating the Impact of Restrictions 82
    Making Restrictions Effective Immediately 83
Restriction Defaults 84
Requiring RFC Conformance 84
    Restricting the Hostname in HELO/EHLO 85
    Restricting the Envelope Sender 87
    Restricting the Envelope Recipient 88
Maintaining RFC Conformance 91
    Empty Envelope Sender 92
    Special Role Accounts 92
Processing Order for RFC Restrictions 93
Antispam Measures 94
    Preventing Obvious Forgeries 94
    Bogus Nameserver Records 95
    Bounces to Multiple Recipients 97
    Using DNS Blacklists 98
    Verifying the Sender 103
    Restriction Process Order 107
Uses for Restriction Classes 108

9
HOW BUILT-IN CONTENT FILTERS WORK 111

How Do Checks Work? 112
Applying Checks to Separate Message Sections 112
    What's So Special about These Parameters? 113
When Does Postfix Apply Checks? 114
What Actions Can Checks Invoke? 115

10
USING BUILT-IN CONTENT FILTERS 117

Checking Postfix for Checks Support 118
    Building Postfix with PCRE Map Support 118
Safely Implementing Header or Body Filtering 119
    Adding a Regular Expression and Setting a WARN Action 119
    Creating a Test Pattern 119
    Does the Regular Expression Match the Test Pattern? 119
    Setting the Check in the Main Configuration 120
    Testing with Real Mail 120
Checking Headers 120
    Rejecting Messages 121
    Holding Delivery 122
    Removing Headers 122
    Discarding Messages 122
    Redirecting Messages 123
    Filtering Messages 123
Checking MIME Headers 124
Checking Headers in Attached Messages 125
Checking the Body 126

11
HOW EXTERNAL CONTENT FILTERS WORK 129

When Is the Best Moment to Filter Content? 130
    Filters and Address Rewriting 131
content_filter: Queuing First, Filtering Later 132
    Filter-Delegation Daemons 134
    The Basics of Configuring content_filter 135
smtpd_proxy_filter: Filtering First, Queuing Later 137
    Considerations for Proxy Filters 139
    The Basics of Configuring smtpd_proxy_filter 139

12
USING EXTERNAL CONTENT FILTERS 141

Appending Disclaimers to Messages with a Script 142
    Installing alterMIME and Creating the Filter Script 143
    Configuring Postfix for the Disclaimer Script 145
    Testing the Filter 146
Scanning for Viruses with content_filter and amavisd-new 148
    Installing amavisd-new 149
    Testing amavisd-new 150
    Optimizing amavisd-new Performance 154
    Configuring Postfix to Use amavisd-new 157
    Testing the Postfix amavisd-new Filter 160
Scanning for Viruses with smtpd_proxy_filter and amavisd-new 163
    Configuring Postfix to Use amavisd-new with smtpd_proxy_filter 164

PART III: ADVANCED CONFIGURATIONS

13
MAIL GATEWAYS 169

Basic Setup 170
    Setting Gateway Relay Permissions 170
    Setting a Relay Domain on the Gateway 171
    Setting the Internal Mail Host on the Gateway 171
    Defining Relay Recipients 171
Advanced Gateway Setup 172
    Improving Security on the Mail Gateway 173
    Using Postfix with Microsoft Exchange Server 174
    Configuring Exchange and Postfix Communication 185
NAT Setup 187

14
A MAIL SERVER FOR MULTIPLE DOMAINS 189

Virtual Alias Domains 189
    Setting the Virtual Alias Domain Name 190
    Creating a Recipient Address Map 190
    Configuring Postfix to Receive Mail for Virtual Alias Domains 191
    Testing Virtual Alias Domain Settings 191
    Advanced Mappings 192
Virtual Mailbox Domains 194
    Checking Postfix for Virtual Delivery Agent Support 195
    Basic Configuration 195
    Advanced Configuration 199
Database-Driven Virtual Mailbox Domains 203
    Checking Postfix for MySQL Map Support 204
    Building Postfix to Support MySQL Maps 205
    Configuring the Database 205
    Configuring Postfix to Use the Database 208
    Testing Database-Driven Virtual Mailbox Domains 212

15
UNDERSTANDING SMTP AUTHENTICATION 217

The Architecture and Configuration of Cyrus SASL 218
    Which Approach Is Best? 220
SASL: The Simple Authentication and Security Layer 221
    Authentication Interface 222
    SMTP AUTH Mechanisms 223
    Authentication Methods (Password-Verification Services) 225
    Authentication Backends 225
Planning Server-Side SMTP Authentication 226
    Finding Clients and Their Supported Mechanisms 226
    Defining the Authentication Backend and Password-Verification Service 228

Installing and Configuring Cyrus SASL 229
    Installing Cyrus SASL 229
    Creating the Postfix Application Configuration File 230
    Configuring Logging and the Log Level 231
    Setting the Password-Verification Service 231
    Selecting SMTP AUTH Mechanisms 232
    Configuring saslauthd 232
    Configuring Auxiliary Plug-ins (auxprop) 236
    Testing the Authentication 242
The Future of SMTP AUTH 245

16
SMTP AUTHENTICATION   247

Checking Postfix for SMTP AUTH Support 247
Adding SMTP AUTH Support to Postfix 248
Server-Side SMTP Authentication 249
    Enabling and Configuring the Server 250
    Testing Server-Side SMTP AUTH 254
    Advanced Server Settings 258
Client-Side SMTP Authentication 259
    AUTH for the Postfix SMTP Client 260
    Testing Client-Side SMTP AUTH 263
    The lmtp Client 265

17
UNDERSTANDING TRANSPORT LAYER SECURITY   267

TLS Basics 268
    How TLS Works 269
Understanding Certificates 270
    How to Establish Trust 270
    Which Certification Authority Suits Your Needs? 271
Creating Certificates 271
    Required Information 271
    Creating the CA Certificate 272
    Distributing and Installing the CA Certificate 273
    Creating Your Server's Certificate 276
    Signing Your Server's Certificate 277
    Preparing Certificates for Use in Postfix 278

18
USING TRANSPORT LAYER SECURITY   279

Checking Postfix for TLS Support 279
Building Postfix with TLS Support 281
    Building and Installing OpenSSL from Source Code 282
    Building Postfix with TLS 282

Server-Side TLS 283
    Basic Server Configuration 284
    Server Performance Tuning 290
    Server-Side Measures to Secure the SMTP AUTH Handshake 292
    Server-Side Certificate-Based Relaying 298
    Tightening the TLS Server 302
Client-Side TLS 302
    Basic Client Configuration 303
    Selective TLS Use 307
    Client Performance Tuning 308
    Securing Client SMTP AUTH 309
    Client-Side Certificate-Based Relaying 309
    Tightening Client-Side TLS 311

19
A COMPANY MAIL SERVER   313

Conceptual Overview 314
The LDAP Directory Structure 315
    Choosing Attributes in a Postfix Schema 316
    Branch Design 317
    Building User Objects 318
    Creating List Objects 319
    Adding Attributes for the Remaining Servers 320
Basic Configuration 321
    Configuring Cyrus SASL 321
    Configuring OpenLDAP 322
    Configuring Postfix and LDAP 325
    Configuring Courier Maildrop 333
    Configuring Courier IMAP 343
Advanced Configuration 348
    Expanding the Directory 349
    Adding Authentication to Servers 350
    Protecting Directory Data 356
    Encrypting LDAP Queries 358
    Enforcing Valid Sender Addresses 365

20
RUNNING POSTFIX IN A CHROOT ENVIRONMENT   369

How Does a chroot Jail Work? 370
    Basic Principles of a chroot Setup 370
    Technical Implementation 371
How Does chroot Affect Postfix? 371
    Helper Scripts for chroot 372
    chrooted Daemons 372
    chroot Libraries, Configuration Files, and Other Files 374
Overcoming chroot Restrictions 375

PART IV: TUNING POSTFIX

21
REMOTE CLIENT CONCURRENCY AND REQUEST RATE LIMITING 379

The Basics of Rate Limiting 379
Gathering Rate Statistics 380
    Running the anvil Daemon 381
    Changing the anvil Log Interval 381
Limiting Client-Connection Frequency 382
    Testing Client-Connection Rate Limits 382
Restricting Simultaneous Client Connections 384
    Testing Simultaneous Client-Connection Limits 384
Exempting Clients from Limits 386

22
PERFORMANCE TUNING 387

Basic Enhancements 387
    Speeding Up DNS Lookups 388
    Confirming That Your Server Is Not Listed as an Open Relay 389
    Refusing Messages to Nonexistent Users 390
    Blocking Messages from Blacklisted Networks 391
    Refusing Messages from Unknown Sender Domains 391
    Reducing the Retransmission Attempt Frequency 392
Finding Bottlenecks 392
    Incoming Queue Bottlenecks 393
    Maildrop Queue Bottlenecks 395
    Deferred Queue Bottlenecks 396
    Active Queue Bottlenecks 397
    Asynchronous Bounce Queue Congestion Inequality 399
    Using Fallback Relays 401
Tuning for Higher Throughput 402
Configuring an Alternative Transport 403

APPENDICES

A
INSTALLING POSTFIX 407

The Postfix Source Code 407
    Applying Patches 408
    Building and Installing from Source Code 408
    Starting and Stopping Postfix 409

Installing Postfix on Debian Linux 410
    Installing Postfix 410
    Starting and Stopping Postfix 411
    Installing an Update 411
    Building from a Debian Source Package 411
Installing Postfix on Red Hat Linux 413
    Getting Postfix for Red Hat Linux 413
    Building an RPM from an SRPM 414
    Switching to Postfix 417
    Removing the Sendmail MTA 417
    Starting and Stopping Postfix in Red Hat Linux 417

B
TROUBLESHOOTING POSTFIX 419

Problems Starting Postfix and Viewing the Log 419
Connecting to Postfix 423
    Checking the Network 423
    Verifying the Listening Process 424
Getting Postfix to Use Your Configuration Settings 425
Reporting Postfix Problems 425
Getting More Logging Information 426
    Client-Specific Logging 426
    Logging and qmgr 427
Other Configuration Errors 427
Intricacies of the chroot Jail 428
Solving Filesystem Problems 428
Library Hell 429
Daemon Inconsistencies 429
    Fork Hell 430
Stress-Testing Postfix 430
    Disk I/O 432
    Too Many Connections 433

C
CIDR AND SMTP STANDARDS REFERENCE 435

Subnets in CIDR Notation 435
Server Response Codes 437

GLOSSARY 441

INDEX 449

Using words to describe magic is like using a screwdriver to cut roast beef.
—Tom Robbins

ABOUT THIS BOOK

This book is a step-by-step guide to Postfix. You start as a beginner, and when you make it to the end, you'll hopefully be an expert. The individual chapters come in three types: tutorials, theory, and Postfix practice. The tutorials are primers that help you understand the subject before you try to implement a solution in Postfix. Theory-oriented chapters tell you how Postfix deals with the subject. Practice chapters show you exactly how to go from theory to a working installation.

We have split the book into four parts that separate major steps in learning how to run Postfix:

Basics

Part I of the book shows you the basics of Postfix. You will learn how to configure Postfix for a single domain and for a dial-up server. You'll also see the anatomy of Postfix from a distance and find out what tools it provides.

Content Control

Postfix allows you to significantly control the message flow on your system. Part II starts out by showing you how SMTP communication works and explains the format of email. From there, you'll see how Postfix can control the various aspects of message handling.

Advanced Configurations

Postfix often interacts with other third-party applications, such as SQL servers, Cyrus SASL, OpenSSL, and OpenLDAP. The chapters in Part III show you how to do it.

Tuning Postfix

Configurable software always leaves room for tuning. Part IV helps you find bottlenecks in your installation and provides hints that will help you increase the mail system's overall performance.

Additional Resources

In addition to *The Book of Postfix* and the documentation that comes with Postfix, there are two other resources that you can turn to when looking for information or help.

Postfix Documentation, How-tos, and FAQs

The Postfix website (http://www.postfix.org/docs.html) has a page that covers Postfix documentation, how-tos, and FAQs written by the Postfix community.

Mailing Lists

Wietse Venema runs several mailing lists that serve the Postfix community. You can find information about how to subscribe to the following lists at the Postfix Mailing Lists page (http://www.postfix.org/lists.html):

postfix-announce@postfix.org

A list for announcements of Postfix releases and updates.

postfix-users@postfix.org

General discussions about experiences with the Postfix mail system. Postings are unmoderated and for members only.

postfix-users-digest@postfix.org

A daily mailing of articles that were sent out via the `postfix-users` mailing list.

postfix-devel@postfix.org

A low-traffic list for people interested in Postfix development.

The Postfix community discusses concepts, problems, errors, patches, and many other topics on the `postfix-users@postfix.org` list. When you experience a problem or want to know about anything else related to Postfix, chances are that you will find the answer browsing through the mailing-list archives. Several organizations or people host `postfix-users@postfix.org` archives that can be accessed with a web browser. A comprehensive list of archives can be found at the Postfix Mailing Lists page (`http://www.postfix.org/lists.html`).

Conventions Used in This Book

`Monospace` type is used for

- Filenames and path names
- Mailing list names and Internet addresses, such as domain names, URLs, and email addresses
- Daemons, commands, parameter names and values, environment variables, and command-line options

`Monospace italic` is used for

- Parameters and placeholders that should be replaced with the appropriate value for your system
- Comments in sample command lines and code examples

`Monospace bold` is used for

Command lines and options to be typed into a shell window

`Monospace bold italic` is used to

Highlight specific lines referred to in the discussion

NOTE   *The $ character represents the regular prompt in command lines; the # character is the superuser's shell prompt.*

Domains and Names Used in This Book

Because this book is about mail services, we will talk a lot about message delivery and transport, and we will need to include names of domains, senders, and recipients in examples. The names that we'll normally use are as follows.

The Local Domain

Throughout the book, we'll claim the domain example.com as our own. The mail server will presumably accept (or at least consider) messages for local users anyuser@example.com and anyuser@mail.example.com. When following examples to build your own Postfix server, you will need to replace example.com with the name of your domain.

NOTE   *Of course, we don't really own the example.com, example.org, and example.net domains. The Internet Assigned Numbers Authority (IANA) has reserved them for use in documentation.*

Our Provider

Throughout the book, we'll use the example-isp.com domain as our ISP's domain name.

Scripts

You can find supporting scripts and other helpful information, such as errata, at http://www.postfix-book.com.

Comments

If you find an error or want to send some other feedback, please send your comments to comments@postfix-book.com.

1

AN INTRODUCTION TO POSTFIX

Postfix is a message transport agent (MTA) that transports messages from a mail user agent (MUA, or mail client) to a remote mail server with SMTP. An MTA also accepts messages from remote mail servers to relay them to other MTAs or deliver them to local mailboxes. After transmitting or delivering a message, Postfix's job ends. Other servers are responsible for getting the message to the end user. For example, MTAs, such as POP3 or IMAP servers, hand the message to an MUA like Mutt, Outlook, or Apple Mail, where the user can read it.

At first glance, the MTA's job seems fairly simple, but it isn't. A message transport agent is special because it must communicate across network borders—they transmit content to other networks and accept content for their own network. Common sense now dictates that anyone running a network must take precautions to protect their servers and data from attacks, and there is a widespread belief that all you need to do is install a firewall that controls connections in both directions between local and remote networks. This is a myth: a firewall is not an application; it's a concept.

The most popular part of a common firewall implementation is an application that monitors and restricts connections. Unfortunately, firewalls normally have no way of evaluating the content exchanged between two hosts; they control the hosts, ports, and transport layer protocols that are used in data communication, but they do not restrict communication based on its content. Analyzing content is a much harder job that must be done by specialized applications that can decide what to do with the content and determine whether it is harmful or not. MTAs perform this task for email. In addition, modern MTAs must be fast, reliable, and secure because they transport the most popular data on the largest network on the planet: email.

There are many MTAs to choose from, but most of them fall short in one way or another. For example, one has a brilliant security model, but its developer base is no longer a small core team, and this is an invitation to failure and opens doors for security problems. A second MTA is widespread because it is part of a popular groupware package, but it appears that the development team spent too much time on the groupware functionality and forgot to keep up with Internet standards and new challenges from spam and malicious attackers. Finally there's an MTA that easily copes with the standards and has no problems with servicing many users at the same time, but it has a security record so terrible that you need an expert who can take the necessary counteractive measures between fixes in order to run it safely.

You don't need to be an expert to run Postfix; it tries to run as safely as possible out of the box. Postfix security is rooted in its default configuration settings. If the basic configuration of an application is safe and complete enough that you don't need to change anything, it's easy to run a safe MTA. Better still, if you need to change something, Postfix has such a clear, structured syntax for parameters and options that it is rather easy to change the default behavior successfully. Furthermore, the Postfix application design is modular, with each module running at the lowest possible privilege level required to get the job done. Postfix was designed with security in mind, starting at a higher level than the code itself.

Postfix performs admirably because it is focused on the core tasks of mail transport; it doesn't reinvent the wheel with functionality that other applications on the system already provide. Postfix gives you the means to plug in external applications when a related task is outside of the message transport area. In addition, Postfix uses the full power of Unix to do its work. This tight integration with the operating system not only makes it easier to access external applications, but also improves performance.

A look at the modern tasks of mail transport and handling reveals Postfix to be the very heart of a mail transport suite. In Figure 1-1, you can see that Postfix is surrounded by specialized applications and tools to help control content, connections, and relaying.

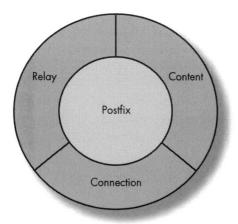

Figure 1-1: Postfix: The very heart of a mail transport suite

This book shows you how to configure Postfix for use in a small network, as a mail relay, as a virus filter, and as a company mail server integrated into a modern IT architecture. As you progress through the chapters, you will find theory and tutorials that go far beyond the online manuals, helping you get the most out of this excellent package.

PART I

BASICS

The first part of this book covers the basics of Postfix, starting with the operating system prerequisites and how to set up a mail server for a single domain. These chapters will help you become familiar with the Postfix configuration file syntax and some of Postfix's component programs and utilities.

Here is an overview of the four chapters in this part of the book:

Preparing Your Host and Environment

Before installing Postfix, you should always verify that your server host can handle an SMTP server. Chapter 2 shows you how to configure the operating system so that you can get the most out of Postfix.

Mail Server for a Single Domain

The first step in any new Postfix installation is to create a configuration that can receive mail for a single domain. In Chapter 3, you will see how to verify that the system works and how to create a basis for more complicated setups.

Dial-up Mail Server for a Single Domain

You don't need to significantly modify the single-domain setup to get a working dial-up configuration. Chapter 4 shows you these small but important changes.

Anatomy of Postfix

Wietse Venema says that "Postfix is actually a router," one that routes messages instead of IP packets. In Chapter 5, you'll get the big picture of how the Postfix innards interact.

2

PREPARING YOUR HOST AND ENVIRONMENT

At first there was nothing. God said, "Let there be light!" Then there was still nothing, but you could see it.—Ignacio Schwartz

You're probably pretty excited because you just got this book and you can't wait to start working with Postfix. However, there is one thing you should know before you start.

Postfix was built by Wietse Venema, who really knows Unix, and the Postfix design does not include functionality that Unix provides by default. Therefore, Postfix expects your system to be set up properly and will only perform as well as the underlying system.

Don't skip this chapter because it seems like kiddie stuff. Take the time to go through the following sections to ensure that your system is in order. Postfix will reward you for this effort with fast, reliable, and secure services.

Here is the system checklist for Postfix:

☐ Set your hostname correctly

☐ Verify your host's connectivity

☐ Maintain a reliable system time

- ☐ Make sure that the syslog service can record Postfix diagnostics
- ☐ Configure name resolution for the client
- ☐ Configure domain name service (DNS) records for the mail server

Hostname

A mail server must have a fully qualified domain name (FQDN; see RFC 821, ftp://ftp.rfc-editor.org/in-notes/rfc821.txt) such as mail.example.com to interoperate reliably with other systems. Postfix automatically uses the hostname that you assign to the server when greeting remote mail clients and servers, unless you manually configure another name.

A fully qualified domain name is also important because Postfix does more than accept mail from clients—when in client mode, Postfix also transports messages to other mail servers. Many mail servers check the hostname that the client announces and do not accept messages if the client does not provide a fully qualified domain name, and some servers even check that the FQDN resolves in DNS.

Your operating system sets your system's hostname at boot time. To see whether your system already has an FQDN, log in and enter hostname:

```
$ hostname -f
mail.example.com
```

If this command does not return a fully qualified domain name, find out how your system sets the hostname and fix it. However, if your system already has an FQDN hostname, but you would like Postfix to use a different one, leave your system's setting as it is. You'll override the default using the myhostname parameter instead.

NOTE *The -f option to hostname doesn't work on Solaris, with the GNU hostname command, and in some other environments. If your hostname doesn't work as described here, try omitting the -f option. If that doesn't work, consult your manual.*

Connectivity

Verify that your machine can reach its network and that hosts on the network can talk to it. The first part should be easy—if your machine can go online and access web pages, it is connecting to a network. Incoming connections are trickier. To test them, you need a client in the network that typical clients will connect from. If Postfix offers services to the entire Internet, you should verify connectivity from a host that is completely independent of your server.

TCP Port 25

Make sure that nothing blocks your server's TCP port 25. If you have a firewall, make sure that the firewall policy allows incoming and outgoing connections on port 25. Keep in mind that some Internet service providers

(ISPs) block outgoing connections to port 25 on the entire Internet on their routers unless you ask them to lift the restriction. Some ISPs may refuse to lift the restriction, preferring that you relay through their mail servers using a system such as SMTP authentication, described in Chapter 16.

The reason that TCP port 25 must be kept open is that Postfix and other mail servers listen for connections on it. It is the official IANA port assignment for SMTP (see http://www.iana.org/assignments/port-numbers for a full list). The IANA is the central registry for assigned numbers in the Internet Protocol, such as ports, protocols, enterprise numbers, options, codes, and types.

System Time and Timestamps

Having the correct system time is important when you are tweaking features and weeding out problems. When you need to go beyond the boundaries of your system to work out mail problems with other postmasters, a correct timestamp might be exactly what you need to link actions on your mail servers with those on servers that you do not control.

Postfix keeps careful track of its actions in mail headers. For example, have a look at this header:

```
Received: from mail.example.net (mail.example.net [192.0.34.166])
        by mail.example.com (Postfix) with ESMTP id 6ED90E1C65
        for <recipient@example.com>; Sat,  7 Feb 2004 10:40:55 +0100 (CET)
Reply-To: sender@example.net
From: Sender <sender@example.net>
To: Recipient <recipient@example.com>
Subject: Keep correct system time
Date: Sat, 7 Feb 2004 10:42:01 +0100
```

Postfix also makes date-related notes in the mail log. Here are some sample log messages:

```
Feb 7 2004 10:40:55 mail postfix/pickup[32610]: 6ED90E1C65: uid=501 from=<sender>
Feb 7 2004 10:40:55 mail postfix/cleanup[398]: 6ED90E1C65:
        message-id=<20040416020209.7D62343F30@mail.example.com>
```

Therefore, you should ensure that you get the best time you can. Don't trust your system's built-in timer; not only does the time kept by the Unix kernel drift over time, but the chips that motherboard manufacturers use in their battery-backed clocks are cheap and also drift from the real time. You cannot expect a local time source to be in sync with the times on other mail servers.

There are two ways to get an accurate clock. You can use NTP (Network Time Protocol) to get the time over the network, or use a GPRS (worldwide) or DCF-77 (in most of Europe) time device to get the time over radio. However, if you don't have access to these solutions, you can try using

clockspeed (http://cr.yp.to/clockspeed.html) as a last resort. This application
uses a hardware tick counter to compensate for a persistently fast or slow
system clock. Given a few time measurements from a reliable source, it
computes and compensates for the clock skew.

NOTE *To use an NTP server, you must run an NTP client on your system (such a client comes
with practically every operating system). To use NTP, you must allow incoming and
outgoing User Datagram Protocol (UDP) packets on port 123 on your firewall. If you
don't know how to configure your NTP client, visit the NTP website (http://
www.ntp.org) for more information.*

Syslog

One of the most important places to look for diagnostic messages is the
mail log. Postfix uses the standard Unix logging utility, called syslogd. You
normally configure syslogd through the /etc/syslog.conf file. Here's a sample
configuration:

```
# Log anything (except mail) of level info or higher.
# Don't log private authentication messages!
*.info;mail.none;authpriv.none;cron.none -/var/log/messages
# The authpriv file has restricted access.
authpriv.* -/var/log/secure
# Log all the mail messages in one place.
mail.*        -/var/log/maillog
# Log cron stuff
cron.*        -/var/log/cron
# Everybody gets emergency messages, plus log them on another
# machine.
*.emerg       *
# Save mail and news errors of level err and higher in a
# special file.
uucp,news.crit    -/var/log/spooler
# Save boot messages also to boot.log
local7.*          /var/log/boot.log
```

First, take a look at the first entry, which contains mail.none to keep mail
messages out of /var/log/messages. This is important because you do not want
mail log messages to clutter your general system messages. You can see that
the mail log gets its own entry and file (/var/log/maillog). The hyphen in
front of the filename indicates that syslogd should write the messages to the
file asynchronously, rather than try to force a write to the disk every time a
new log message arrives.

Unfortunately, there are several things that can go wrong with syslogd.
If you don't seem to be getting any log messages, the very first thing you
should do is make sure that syslogd is actually running. The following
example shows how to run the ps command to look for the daemon.

```
# ps auxwww | grep syslog
root    15540  0.0  0.0  1444  524 ?      S    May21  18:20 syslogd -m 0 ❶
root    22616  0.0  0.0  1444  452 pts/0  R    18:09   0:00 grep syslog
```

❶ The first line of output here shows that syslogd has been running since May 21.

In addition, make sure that the log files exist and are writable before you instruct syslogd to write to them. Some implementations of syslogd do not automatically create files and fail silently if there is a problem with the log file. The Solaris syslogd is notorious for this.

A very common error is to use spaces instead of tabs to separate the log type and the log file in the /etc/syslog.conf file. Your syslog.conf should be written like this:

```
mail.*<TAB>-/var/log/maillog
```

Yet another syslogd.conf problem is logging to another network host. Watch out for an entry like this:

```
mail.* @loghost
```

In this case, syslogd is sending all of its logs to loghost, so you should check the logs on that host instead of the mail server. Make sure that you actually have such a host. It's all too common to have logs going to an unintended host (or into a black hole) due to an errant syslogd.conf file entry.

Name Resolution (DNS)

Before a mail server such as Postfix can transport a message to a remote destination, it must locate that destination. On the Internet, you find remote resources with the domain name service (DNS). A nameserver returns the IP address of a hostname, and conversely the hostname that corresponds to an IP address.

Well-functioning DNS is critical to MTA performance. The sooner Postfix can resolve a target IP address, the sooner it can start to communicate with the remote mail server and transport a message.

NOTE   *Poor hostname lookup performance can become a major bottleneck on large mail hubs. If your server runs into problems, a caching nameserver can help. Set up a caching nameserver for large mail systems. Be aware that antispam measures can increase the number of DNS queries that your mail server performs by several factors.*

Before you attempt to improve name-resolution performance on your system, be sure that your operating system correctly resolves remote hostnames by asking your nameserver for the MX record (see the "MX Records" section, later in this chapter) of postfix-book.com. Try this command:

```
$ dig postfix-book.com MX
```

The output should look like this:

```
; <<>> DiG 9.2.2-P3 <<>> postfix-book.com MX
;; global options:  printcmd
;; Got answer:
;; ->>HEADER<<- opcode: QUERY, status: NOERROR, id: 23929
;; flags: qr rd ra; QUERY: 1, ANSWER: 1, AUTHORITY: 2, ADDITIONAL: 2
;; QUESTION SECTION:
;postfix-book.com.               IN      MX
;; ANSWER SECTION:
postfix-book.com.       86400   IN      MX      10 mail.postfix-book.com. ❶
;; AUTHORITY SECTION:
postfix-book.com.       86400   IN      NS      ns3.ray.net. ❷
postfix-book.com.       86400   IN      NS      ns.state-of-mind.de.
;; ADDITIONAL SECTION:
mail.postfix-book.com.  86400   IN      A       212.14.92.89
ns.state-of-mind.de.    81566   IN      A       212.14.92.88
;; Query time: 58 msec
;; SERVER: 212.18.0.5#53(212.18.0.5)
;; WHEN: Sat Apr 17 03:56:47 2004
;; MSG SIZE  rcvd: 145
```

❶ This line indicates that mail.postfix-book.com is the mail server that accepts mail for recipients within the postfix-book.com domain.

❷ These two lines show that ns3.ray.net and ns.state-of-mind.de are the authoritative nameservers for postfix-book.com.

NOTE *The dig (Domain Information Groper) command is not standard on some outdated platforms. You can get dig with the BIND distribution at ISC (http://www.isc.org). If you can't install dig, you can probably still run the preceding query with host or nslookup; the latter command is now deprecated.*

If the lookup query is successful, Postfix can (in theory) resolve hostnames correctly. If the request is not successful and no hostnames can be resolved, you need to get DNS sorted out immediately.

One common problem with name resolution is for it not to work when the server tries to query unavailable nameservers. Check your /etc/resolv.conf file. Let's say that it looks like this, where the machine queries a nameserver on localhost (127.0.0.1), and upon failure it queries 134.169.9.107:

```
nameserver 127.0.0.1
nameserver 134.169.9.107
```

It's fine to query localhost if you're running a caching nameserver. However, if you don't have one, this request will take a while to time out.

If you find out later that nameserver queries with dig work, but Postfix cannot find the host (for example, if you see no route to host in the log), then it's likely that you're running Postfix chrooted, and therefore, it looks at a different configuration file to determine settings for name resolution. For example, if your chroot jail is /var/spool/postfix, Postfix will then look at /var/spool/postfix/etc/resolv.conf. Make sure that the files are consistent by running **cp -p /etc/resolv.conf /var/spool/postfix/etc/resolv.conf**, and then stop and start Postfix.

DNS for Mail Servers

You need to configure your nameserver to tell the rest of the world that your server is the one that can deliver mail to your domain. Ask your hostmaster (the person responsible for running the nameserver of your domain) to set the following entries:

A record

Your mail server must have a fully qualified hostname so that clients can find out where your server is. An A record maps an FQDN to an IP address.

PTR record

Your system's hostname should be reverse-resolvable. Mail servers that learn your server's hostname from SMTP communication should be able to find out if your server is really the one speaking to them.

MX record

MX records let clients know that your server is responsible for mail delivery for a domain or a certain host.

A Records

The domain name system has different types of records to tell hosts about resources on the Net. One of the most important is the A record, which maps hostnames to addresses. A client that sends a hostname to a nameserver should get the IP address of the host as a response. The following is an example session that shows that www.example.com is mapped to 192.0.34.166.

```
$ dig www.example.com A
; <<>> DiG 9.2.1 <<>> www.example.com
;; global options:  printcmd
;; Got answer:
;; ->>HEADER<<- opcode: QUERY, status: NOERROR, id: 30122
;; flags: qr rd ra; QUERY: 1, ANSWER: 1, AUTHORITY: 2, ADDITIONAL: 0
;; QUESTION SECTION:
;www.example.com.                IN      A
```

```
;; ANSWER SECTION:
www.example.com.          172627  IN    A      192.0.34.166
;; AUTHORITY SECTION:
example.com.              21427   IN    NS     b.iana-servers.net.
example.com.              21427   IN    NS     a.iana-servers.net.
;; Query time: 1 msec
;; SERVER: 127.0.0.1#53(127.0.0.1)
;; WHEN: Sat Apr 17 16:43:40 2004
;; MSG SIZE  rcvd: 97
```

PTR Records

The counterpart to the A record is the PTR record, which maps addresses to hostnames. When the client sends an IP address to a nameserver, the response should be the hostname corresponding to the address, as in this example:

```
$ dig -x 192.0.34.166
; <<>> DiG 9.2.1 <<>> -x 192.0.34.166
;; global options:  printcmd
;; Got answer:
;; ->>HEADER<<- opcode: QUERY, status: NOERROR, id: 37949
;; flags: qr rd ra; QUERY: 1, ANSWER: 1, AUTHORITY: 5, ADDITIONAL: 0
;; QUESTION SECTION:
;166.34.0.192.in-addr.arpa.     IN      PTR
;; ANSWER SECTION:
166.34.0.192.in-addr.arpa. 21374 IN     PTR     www.example.com.
;; AUTHORITY SECTION:
34.0.192.in-addr.arpa.    21374   IN    NS     ns.icann.org.
34.0.192.in-addr.arpa.    21374   IN    NS     svc00.apnic.net.
34.0.192.in-addr.arpa.    21374   IN    NS     a.iana-servers.net.
34.0.192.in-addr.arpa.    21374   IN    NS     b.iana-servers.org.
34.0.192.in-addr.arpa.    21374   IN    NS     c.iana-servers.net.
;; Query time: 1 msec
;; SERVER: 127.0.0.1#53(127.0.0.1)
;; WHEN: Sat Apr 17 16:44:39 2004
;; MSG SIZE  rcvd: 201
```

CAUTION   *Now that spammers plague the Internet, reverse-resolution of A records with PTR records is more important than ever. Many postmasters configure their mail servers to accept mail only if a reverse lookup for the connecting client succeeds.*

However, just because other mail servers reject mail based on reverse lookups doesn't mean that you should. This often causes problems because many ISPs do not delegate reverse name lookup to their customers' nameservers and will not provide proper information on their server.

MX Records

A nameserver can do more than resolve resources; it can also tell clients about services offered in a domain. The mail server responsible for a domain is one of these services. You can configure an MX record to point to the A record of your mail server.

CAUTION   *DNS also has a CNAME, an alias that can point to an A record. For example, you could configure a CNAME record that points www.example.com at srv01.example.com. Clients that ask for www.example.com would get srv01.example.com as a response.*

Do not have your MX record point to one of these aliases. The most common mail transport protocol (SMTP) requires that the domain name in an email address be either an A or an MX record. In the preceding example, you could not point an MX record at www.example.com, but because srv01.example.com has an A record, you could point it there.

You may specify more than one MX record, and you can also prioritize mail servers so that clients try servers in a specific order. Here's an example:

```
$ dig m-net.de MX
; <<>> DiG 9.2.1 <<>> m-net.de MX
;; global options:  printcmd
;; Got answer:
;; ->>HEADER<<- opcode: QUERY, status: NOERROR, id: 3133
;; flags: qr rd ra; QUERY: 1, ANSWER: 3, AUTHORITY: 2, ADDITIONAL: 0
;; QUESTION SECTION:
;m-net.de.                    IN      MX
;; ANSWER SECTION:
m-net.de.             7200    IN      MX      50 mail-in.m-online.net. ❶
m-net.de.             7200    IN      MX      100 mx01.m-online.net. ❷
m-net.de.             7200    IN      MX      100 mx02.m-online.net.
;; AUTHORITY SECTION:
m-net.de.             7200    IN      NS      ns2.m-online.net.
m-net.de.             7200    IN      NS      ns1.m-online.net.
;; Query time: 27 msec
;; SERVER: 127.0.0.1#53(127.0.0.1)
;; WHEN: Sat Apr 17 17:07:05 2004
;; MSG SIZE  rcvd: 140
```

❶ mail-in.m-online.net has the highest priority because it has the lowest number (50). Clients will try to deliver mail to this mail server first.

❷ mx01.m-online.net and mx02.m-online.net have the second-highest priority (100) by number. Clients will try either one of these if the highest-priority mail exchanger is unavailable.

3

MAIL SERVER FOR A SINGLE DOMAIN

Configuring Postfix for a single domain takes a matter of minutes. No matter what configuration you plan to set up, starting with the following single-domain configuration should always be your first production step; it will prove that Postfix works in its most simple setup.

This chapter will introduce you to the minimum configuration parameters that Postfix needs in order to run, and it will show you how to map long email addresses to short usernames in a single domain setup.

The Minimum Configuration

We will set up Postfix to accept email for a single domain, and Postfix should deliver emails with different mail addresses within this domain to different mailboxes.

Postfix should handle mail for this one domain only, and we'll show the minimum set of configuration changes that need to be applied against a vanilla installation. A typical network architecture for a minimum configuration is shown in Figure 3-1.

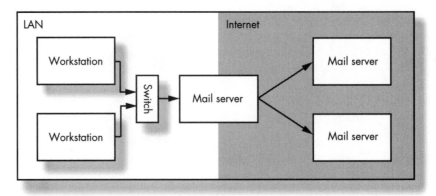

Figure 3-1: A single-domain Postfix network

The mail server is connected permanently to the Internet and has a static IP address. Forward (A record) and reverse DNS records that match the IP address of the mail server have been provided.

A basic setup has basic requirements. Make sure you have properly configured your host, as described in Chapter 2.

Configuring Postfix

In this chapter, we will configure Postfix to receive mail for a single domain. Our machine will be named `mail.example.com`, and our domain is `example.com`. We will follow these steps:

1. Configure Postfix to greet mail clients with the correct hostname.
2. Configure Postfix to accept mail for the domain `example.com`.
3. Configure Postfix to append `example.com` to mail sent with a bare username.
4. Configure Postfix to deliver mail addressed to `root` to a different mailbox.
5. Configure Postfix to deliver mail sent to email addresses to the appropriate usernames.
6. Set permissions to make Postfix relay email from your network.

Setting the Hostname in the smtpd Banner

When mail clients and servers meet, they greet each other with their DNS hostnames. The first thing we do is to configure the name that Postfix will use when it introduces itself to a mail client. If your hostname is the same as the name you want Postfix to use to greet mail clients, then you are lucky: there is nothing to change. On the other hand, if your system's hostname is set to www.example.com, and you run Postfix on the same machine and want it to greet mail clients with mail.example.com as the hostname, you can easily achieve that.

CAUTION *When Postfix transports messages to other mail servers, it acts as a mail client. While introducing itself to the mail server, it uses the myhostname parameter as the HELO name by default. Some mail servers are configured to reject mail if the HELO name and the reverse-resolvable FQDN of the server do not match. Either make sure that the hostname you set for Postfix matches the hostname of your server's IP, or set smtp_helo_name to match your official FQDN in the DNS namespace.*

There are two ways to achieve a different hostname, either by setting the myhostname parameter or by setting the mydomain parameter.

Setting myhostname

Setting myhostname is done by editing /etc/postfix/main.cf. Use your favorite editor to open the file and search for myhostname. Then add your intended hostname as the FQDN hostname:

```
myhostname = mail.example.com
```

As soon as you have set myhostname, Postfix is able to automatically derive mydomain. Postfix simply strips off everything up to and including the first dot. Because we have set myhostname to be mail.example.com, Postfix will derive mydomain to be example.com—just what we need.

Setting mydomain

Instead of setting myhostname, you can set only mydomain. This alternative can be very handy if you have a configuration that needs to be copied to multiple machines.

```
mydomain = example.com
```

As soon as you have set mydomain, Postfix is able to create myhostname by concatenating the output from the uname -n command of this specific host with mydomain. This means that if your main.cf only sets mydomain explicitly, and you copy the file to another host within the same domain (example.com in our example), Postfix will complete the correct hostname by itself.

Setting the Domain Mail Is Accepted For

Postfix will relay host for local clients, meaning it will accept mail for domains for which it is not configured as final or relay destination. In a single-domain setup, all you need to do is to set the mydestination parameter. (Procedures for setting Postfix up to relay mail for more than one domain are discussed in Chapters 13 and 14.)

NOTE *When you set* `mydestination`, *you can hard-code the destination (for example,* `mydestination = mail.example.com`) *or you can use the values from parameters that have already been set in Postfix using the* `$parameter` *notation. Hard-coding makes it awkward to change configurations because there are many parameters to edit, and considering typos and other potential human errors, this is a failure-prone setup. We do not recommend hard-coding.*

Our goal in this chapter is to make Postfix accept any mail that is destined for `example.com`. Because we already have provided this value in `mydomain`, we can simply refer to it when we set `mydestination` in `main.cf`:

```
mydestination = $mydomain
```

If you want to take this further and you want Postfix to accept mail for the hostname you have set in `myhostname`, then you simply add that parameter to `mydestination`:

```
mydestination = $mydomain, $myhostname
```

As you can see, values are added in a comma-separated list, and the list ends without a comma. To take this another step further, you can also add `www.example.com` and `ftp.example.com` by expanding the list with a combination of host and `$mydomain`:

```
mydestination =
    $mydomain,
    $myhostname,
    www.$mydomain,
    ftp.$mydomain
```

This example also introduces another form of notation. If you need to add many values to a parameter, you can set each on a separate line, but each subsequent line must start with some whitespace (otherwise Postfix will not recognize the value). You can verify this in a shell window by checking the output of `postconf mydestination`, just to be sure.

This format can be used for any parameter within Postfix that takes more than one value.

Setting the Domain to Be Appended to Outgoing Messages

When a local service, such as `cron` or `at`, or a command-line mail client sends mail, it usually does not supply a complete sender or recipient address, but just bare usernames. Although this is okay as long as the recipient is local, it becomes a problem when the message is sent off to another host. It takes quite some time to track which host the mail came from, and the receiving mail server will not be able to bounce the mail back if the mail's recipient does not exist on the target host.

Postfix provides a parameter whose value is appended to senders or recipients that are specified in a non–fully qualified form: `myorigin`. Again, we can reuse parameters that already have been set within `main.cf`:

```
myorigin = $mydomain
```

As soon as you have enabled this setting, Postfix will append the value in `mydomain` to any address that has not been fully qualified. For example, a message produced by a cron job and sent as root would be set to `root@$mdomain`, which in our case would become `root@example.com`.

If you do not set `myorigin` manually, it will default to `myhostname`, which comes in handy if you run various hosts whose root messages should be delivered to one role account at a central server. This way you will always know the hostname the message came from; a cron job sent as root, for example, would be modified by Postfix to be sent as `root@$myhostname`, which in our case would be `root@mail.example.com`.

Mapping Mail Sent to root to a Different Mailbox

Postfix will deliver mail to any local user directly, even root, but Postfix won't give root privileges to *external* programs during delivery. This means you cannot use local delivery agents (LDAs) such as procmail or maildrop to deliver mail for root, because Postfix won't run those programs as root, but instead will run them with `default_privs`, which default to the privileges of the user `nobody`. This is a security precaution designed to never compromise the superuser account by running a vulnerable external program as root. This does not mean that it is impossible to deliver mail that is meant for root, though. The solution is to create a different user on your machine with normal, low privileges, and have mail meant for root delivered to this account instead.

In our examples we use `admin` as the account from which we start administration of our host.[1] To make Postfix deliver mail for root to `admin`, simply open `/etc/postfix/aliases`, which the Postfix installation installs by default,[2] and change `postfix` to `admin` so that it reads as follows:

```
root:    admin
```

NOTE   *If you choose to use admin for this purpose, you must also delete the aliases file entry that sends admin mail to root. Otherwise you will create a loop.*

---

[1] Just recently a virus/worm used the sender address `admin@$mydomain` to spread itself through the Internet. The name `admin` may not be a good choice for a user account.

[2] The aliases file that comes along with Postfix contains all the addresses that are required by various RFCs on a mail server. The aliases file itself will give you hints about where to find more information on these requirements.

Once you have edited /etc/postfix/aliases[3] and added the username you prefer, you must create an indexed version, usually /etc/postfix/aliases.db, in order to speed up the lookup process for Postfix. This is done by running either postalias on the /etc/postfix/aliases or newaliases without parameters. To get used to the tools that Postfix brings along, run this command:

```
# postalias hash:/etc/postfix/aliases
```

CAUTION   *Postfix will not use any changes in your aliases file until you have updated the indexed version, as it only reads from that file.*

Starting Postfix and Testing Mail Delivery to root

It's time to run the first tests. In the previous sections we added or changed a number of settings, and if we go further without verifying that things are okay to this point, we will probably have trouble if we need to trace an error.

Start Postfix

Before we start sending mail, we must start Postfix. All you need to enter is **postfix start** and Postfix will reply with the following message:

```
# postfix start
postfix/postfix-script: starting the Postfix mail system
```

If you get the following message, then Postfix was already up and running:

```
# postfix start
postfix/postfix-script: fatal: the Postfix mail system is already running
```

If Postfix was running when you made changes to its configuration, those changes won't have been noticed by Postfix. You could stop and start Postfix to make it reread the configuration, but there is a far more elegant way of doing this. Simply type **postfix reload**:

```
# postfix reload
postfix/postfix-script: refreshing the Postfix mail system
```

This way, Postfix reloads only the configuration, which takes less time and will not interrupt Postfix's service to the clients.

---

[3] The input and output file formats are expected to be compatible with Sendmail version 8 and to be suitable for use as NIS maps.

Send Test Mail

Now that Postfix is started, we can run the first test: deliver mail sent to root to its mailbox. There are two very simple ways to do this: send mail from the command line, or send mail from a telnet session. Both approaches have the advantage of excluding the influence of other applications, such as complex GUI mail clients, and letting you focus on Postfix, in case an error turns up.

Sending Mail Using Postfix's sendmail Binary

The most simple, reliable test is to use sendmail to test basic functionality, because no components outside of Postfix will be involved. This command-line utility is called sendmail for backward compatibility—many applications on Unix systems that send email have the path to the sendmail binary, /usr/sbin/sendmail or /usr/lib/sendmail, hard-coded in them. This is also where Postfix puts its own sendmail binary, in order to offer a smooth switch transition from Sendmail to Postfix.[4]

Type the following command to send mail to root:

```
# echo foo |  /usr/sbin/sendmail -f root root && tail -f /var/log/maillog
```

This will send the text foo to root with an envelope sender of root, and it will open your mail log to check on its delivery status:

```
Aug 20 21:56:42 mail postfix/pickup[5160]: 848AD7247: uid=0 from=<root>
Aug 20 21:56:42 mail postfix/cleanup[5340]: 848AD7247:
    message-id=<20030820195642.848AD7247@mail.example.com>
Aug 20 21:56:42 mail postfix/nqmgr[5161]: 848AD7247:
    from=<root@mail.example.com>, size=306, nrcpt=1 (queue active)
Aug 20 21:56:42 mail postfix/local[5343]: 848AD7247:
    to=<admin@mail.example.com>, orig_to=<root>, relay=local, delay=0,
    status=sent (mailbox)
```

As you can see from the mail log, Postfix was able to send the message to the mailbox. You can check this by running **less /var/mail/admin**:

```
From root@mail.example.com  Wed Aug 20 21:56:42 2003
Return-Path: <root@mail.example.com>
X-Original-To: root
Delivered-To: admin@mail.example.com
Received: by mail.example.com (Postfix, from userid 0)
        id 848AD7247; Wed, 20 Aug 2003 21:56:42 +0200 (CEST)
Message-Id: <20030820195642.848AD7247@mail.example.com>
Date: Wed, 20 Aug 2003 21:56:42 +0200 (CEST)
From: root@mail.example.com (root)
To: undisclosed-recipients:;

foo
```

[4] There's one hook: If you migrate from Sendmail to Postfix, you may end up with two sendmail binaries: The one that Postfix installed and the one that's left over from the real Sendmail. You must only use the one Postfix installed.

NOTE *If you are unsure where to look for the mailbox, type* `postconf mail_spool_directory`. *This will tell you where Postfix delivers the mail.*

So far so good. Postfix is able to deal with its own applications.

Sending Mail from the Command Line

Next we will verify that we are able to send mail from an MUA on localhost to root. This is the second-simplest test case there is:

```
# mail admin
Subject: Test from command line
This is a test mail from command line.
.
```

TIP *In case you are not familiar with the mail program, here's how to use it:*

1. *Enter* **mail** *on the command line.*

2. *Enter the name of the account that you want to send mail to, and press RETURN.*

3. *When prompted, enter a subject and press RETURN.*

4. *Enter the text of the message.*

5. *To send the message, start a new blank line, enter a single period (.), and press RETURN.*

To verify that the mail was sent, run **less /var/mail/admin** once more:

```
# less /var/mail/admin
From root@mail.example.com  Wed Aug 20 20:55:11 2003
Return-Path: <root@mail.example.com>
X-Original-To: admin
Delivered-To: admin@mail.example.com
Received: by mail.example.com (Postfix, from userid 0)
        id 37DE07247; Wed, 20 Aug 2003 20:55:11 +0200 (CEST)
To: admin@mail.example.com
Subject: Test from command line
Message-Id: <20030820185511.37DE07247@mail.example.com>
Date: Wed, 20 Aug 2003 20:55:11 +0200 (CEST)
From: root@mail.example.com (root)

This is a test mail from command line.
```

The message was delivered, and we have proven that local users can send mail to other local users. Now it's time to check whether mail can be sent to admin from a remote user.

Sending Mail through a Telnet Session

The simplest mail client is a telnet client that connects to the SMTP port (port 25). We'll be doing it the hard way, because we want to exclude side effects that might be introduced by other more comfortable (and more buggy) mail clients. Here's how you send a mail message with telnet.

```
# telnet mail.example.com 25
Trying 172.16.0.1...
Connected to mail.example.com.
Escape character is '^]'.
220 mail.example.com ESMTP Postfix
HELO client.example.com
250 mail.example.com
MAIL FROM: <test@client.example.com>
250 Ok
RCPT TO: <root@example.com>
250 Ok
DATA
354 End data with <CR><LF>.<CR><LF>
Test mail from a telnet session.
.
250 Ok: queued as 69F1A7247
QUIT
221 Bye
```

And for the last time, check delivery with **less /var/mail/admin**:

```
From test@client.example.com  Wed Aug 20 21:25:16 2003
Return-Path: <test@client.example.com>
X-Original-To: root@example.com
Delivered-To: admin@mail.example.com
Received: from client.example.com (mail.example.com [172.16.0.1])
        by mail.example.com (Postfix) with SMTP id 2D89A7251
        for <root@example.com>; Wed, 20 Aug 2003 21:24:59 +0200 (CEST)
Message-Id: <20030820192459.2D89A7251@mail.example.com>
Date: Wed, 20 Aug 2003 21:24:59 +0200 (CEST)
From: test@client.example.com
To: undisclosed-recipients:;

Test mail from a telnet session.
```

This message was delivered too, and we have proven that Postfix accepts messages that are sent from remote users to local users and that Postfix is able to deliver them.

Mapping Email Addresses to Usernames

Now that we have successfully set up the basics, it is time to configure email addresses that are a little more sophisticated. By default, Postfix will only deliver email to usernames on your mail server. However, usernames (such as y0000247), which are also often used for authentication when a user wants to retrieve mail, rarely match the names people use when they communicate with each other (such as john.doe@example.com). To make Postfix receive and deliver email for names used in the real world to existing accounts, you need to create aliases that point to the destinations Postfix is to deliver the messages to.

Creating Aliases

Let's assume that you have a new colleague at Example Inc. whose name is John Doe, and it's your job to provide him with an email account. John works in the sales department, and he is supposed to receive mail addressed to john@example.com, john.doe@example.com, and doe@example.com in one mailbox, as well as any mail that is sent to sales@example.com, where he works together with Silvia and Karol, who both receive any mail that goes to <sales@example.com>. John already has been provided the account john, with which he can access his files.

What you must do now is map these alias names (john@example.com, sales@example.com, and so on) to his local username. This is done by creating entries in /etc/postfix/aliases. In John's case, you only have to create three entries, although four mappings are required. The one you don't have to create is <john@example.com>, as any mail that is sent to that address will be delivered to the username john, which is John's account. You would need to add the following entries to /etc/postfix/aliases:

```
# users
john.doe:      john
doe:           john
# groups
sales:         silvia, karol, john
```

To complete your task, you will need to run either **postalias hash:/etc/postfix/aliases** or **newaliases** to update your aliases.db file.

NOTE *From the preceding listing, you can see that you must specify a* localpart *on the left side, followed by a colon and the username on the right side (the localpart of an email address is everything before the @ sign). Every alias entry can consist of one or more values separated by commas. You may specify either usernames or email addresses. Email addresses can point to other users on different hosts, which means that you could accept mail for a user at your mail server and have it delivered to a totally different address. Further information can be found in the aliases file itself, or you can run* **man 5 aliases**.

Once you have added as many aliases as you need, it is time to run tests for those mailboxes, just like the test we made before.

Setting Permissions to Make Postfix Relay Email from Your Network

Open relays are a postmaster's nightmare. Any Postfix installation is relay safe by default. In its default configuration, Postfix will relay only messages from IP addresses inside your network. Postfix knows what the IP addresses of your network are by checking the interfaces you have configured for your server.

NOTE *On a Linux server, Postfix will trust all the subnets the machine's interfaces are in. Run* **ifconfig** *on Linux to get a list of all subnets Postfix will trust by default.*

The default settings work as long as your server and the hosts that use Postfix on it are within the same network range. Chances are that you will need to alter these settings when your network grows or gets more complex. You could, for example, decide to run Postfix in a DMZ within an IP range that differs from the one your internal hosts use. In that situation, Postfix likely would not allow your clients to relay mail to foreign destinations, and you would need to configure it to establish correct relay permissions.

Expanding or restricting relay permissions can be done either generically, by choosing a mynetworks_style that suits your network topography, or individually, by manually specifying a list of IP addresses or ranges in Classless Inter-Domain Routing (CIDR) notation (see Appendix C) for mynetworks.

Both methods require you to change the configuration in main.cf manually. The administration effort is reasonable for static IP ranges, because they do not change often.

NOTE *The manual administration effort is not reasonable if you want to permit relaying for hosts with dynamic IP addresses, which change their IP address regularly. Applying changes manually quickly becomes a tedious task. Chapter 16 explains and shows how to automate this process.*

Generic Network Relay Permissions

Generic relay permissions are set with mynetworks_style by choosing the class, subnet, or host option.

class

The class option will make Postfix expand relay permissions to the whole IP class A/B/C networks the server was configured for. For example, if you ran Postfix on a machine with the IP address 192.0.34.166, and you enabled mynetworks_style = class, Postfix would trust the whole class C network, 192.0.34.0/24, and would permit relaying for hosts within this range.

subnet

The subnet option will make Postfix restrict relay permissions to exactly the subnetworks for which you configured the server's network interfaces. For example, if you ran Postfix on a machine with the IP address 192.0.34.166/30, and you enabled mynetworks_style = subnet, Postfix would trust all the hosts exactly within this range.

host

The host option will make Postfix restrict relay permissions to the server you run Postfix on. For example, if you ran Postfix on a machine with the IP addresses 192.0.34.166/30 and 127.0.0.1, and you enabled mynetworks_style = host, Postfix would trust the hosts only (the IP addresses 127.0.0.1 and 192.0.34.166).

Individual Relay Permissions

Individual relay permissions are set with mynetworks by creating a comma-separated list of all the hosts and networks, in CIDR notation, for which Postfix is to relay messages.

For example, if you ran Postfix in a network that connected two locations (192.168.100.0/24 and 192.168.200.0/24), and you wanted it to permit relaying for all the hosts of the DMZ it stands in (10.0.0.0/30), and also for any of its own local interfaces (127.0.0.0/8), you would specify a list like this:

```
mynetworks = 127.0.0.0/8, 192.168.100.0/24, 192.168.200.0/24, 10.0.0.0/30
```

NOTE   *If you have many IP addresses and ranges, this kind of listing can become quite complex within main.cf. Alternatively you can point mynetworks to a separate file (mynetworks = hash:/etc/postfix/mynetworks) and create the complex listing there. This file may not contain networks in CIDR notation, though. If you need CIDR notation, use mynetworks = cidr:/etc/postfix/mynetworks.*

4

DIAL-UP MAIL SERVER FOR A SINGLE DOMAIN

Setting up a mail server to use a dial-up connection requires only minor changes to a basic Postfix configuration. Dial-up access to the Internet can cost money (especially in Europe, where there are connection fees), so you may not want to run a mail server that initiates a connection for each outgoing message. Instead, you can have the server collect a certain number of messages before sending them, to make the dial-up process cost-effective.

When a dial-up connection goes active, you will want Postfix to relay the queued messages through your ISP's relay host. In addition, you may need to support SMTP authentication. You should also automatically retrieve messages that could not be delivered to local users while the server was offline.

The differences between a dial-up server and the basic Postfix configuration are as follows:

Connection

Because the mail server is only temporarily connected to the Internet, its IP address likely changes with every new connection.

DNS resolution

The server cannot look up hostnames when it is offline. Also, the server's own DNS information changes with every new connection, so correct reverse resolution might not be available.

Delivery restriction

Your ISP requires you to use its relay host, and furthermore, the relay host may only relay messages for authenticated users.

Mail retrieval

Outside mail servers cannot deliver messages directly to your server because your server isn't usually online. Your ISP should handle this with a mail server that holds your mail. When a message is sent to you, your ISP's mail server accepts and stores it until you use either a POP/IMAP client or fetchmail to retrieve the mail and hand it down to your local MTA.

NOTE *Mail retrieval with POP/IMAP and fetchmail (http://catb.org/~esr/fetchmail) is not described in this book.*

Figure 4-1 depicts a typical dial-up network. One or more machines reside in a private network, and any machine that needs to access Internet services uses your dial-up gateway, which also runs your Postfix server.

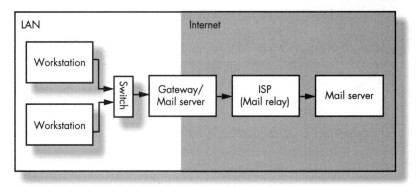

Figure 4-1: A typical dial-up network

You will need to perform the following steps to configure Postfix as a dial-up mail server for a single domain. These steps are described in the following sections.

1. Disable DNS resolution.

2. Check relay permissions.

3. Set the relay host.

4. Defer message transport.

5. Trigger message delivery.

6. Configure relay permission for the relay host.

NOTE *This scenario builds on the setup in Chapter 3. You need to configure and test your server as described in that chapter. In addition, you should have already configured your server's dial-up procedure (`http://www.ibiblio.org/pub/Linux/docs/HOWTO/ other-formats/html_single/PPP-HOWTO.html`).*

Disabling DNS Resolution

When Postfix receives a message to be delivered to a remote domain, it must look up the MX or A record for the destination domain. Name lookups on DNS servers normally involve a query leaving your network, meaning that the server must connect to the Internet.

Because you want to keep dial-up connections to a minimum, you should instruct Postfix not to look up DNS data until the server goes online. In fact, Postfix should never look up the remote domains, because you want it to send messages through your ISP's relay host, which can figure out where to send the message itself.

To prevent Postfix from looking up DNS data, set the `disable_dns_lookups` parameter in your `main.cf` file:

```
disable_dns_lookups = yes
```

This suppresses DNS MX/A lookups in the smtp(8) client, and A lookups in the lmtp(8) client; in both cases gethostbyname() is used instead. You'll need to keep this in mind when you set the relay host later in this chapter.

After setting the `disable_dns_lookups` parameter, reload Postfix to activate the change.

NOTE *This setting does* not *disable DNS for the `smtpd` server program. Parameters such as `reject_unknown_sender_domain` and `permit_mx_backup` (see Chapter 8) still work, regardless of the value of `disable_dns_lookups`.*

Adjusting Relay Permissions

A dial-up server normally has a dynamic IP address that changes whenever the server connects to the Internet. Therefore, you cannot control relay permissions for the dial-up server's network interface unless you manually set relay permissions every time your server goes online. Also, who in the Internet would want to relay through a dial-up host other than a spammer?

NOTE *Even if your host has only periodic connectivity, you should never allow relay access for the entire Internet. One of the author's dial-up mail servers received 56 (failed) relay attempts within a 30-day period. That's roughly two a day, and the machine wasn't even online 24/7! Fortunately nothing happened because it was relay safe.*

Unless you want certain users from the Internet to use your Postfix server as a relay for some bizarre reason (see Chapter 16), you should restrict relaying to your local network interface and the loopback interface in your main.cf file. Here's how you might do it if your private network were 192.168.0.0/24:

```
mynetworks = 192.168.0.0/24, 127.0.0.1/8
```

CAUTION   *Don't use* mynetworks_style = class *to control relay permissions for a dial-up server. This setting uses all IP address ranges configured for your network interfaces, including the network that your server dials in to. Therefore, every client in your ISP's network would be able to use your mail server to relay messages!*

As before, use **postfix reload** to reload the configuration.

Setting the ISP Relay Host

Before you perform this particular configuration step, you need to determine your ISP's mail relay host. Many ISPs block outgoing connections on TCP port 25 (the SMTP port) for dial-up customers, because spammers abuse dial-up service trial offers.

NOTE   *In addition to your ISP's own requirements, there are plenty of good reasons not to have Postfix deliver messages directly to the final destination. For example, because a significant amount of spam originates from dial-up machines, blacklists have started to list whole blocks of dial-up networks (analog, ISDN, and DSL) that known spammers use. Even if your message is not spam, a remote MTA might reject it on the basis of a DUL (dial-up user list), simply because your mail originates from an IP address range belonging to a dial-up pool.*

For example, if the relay host were relay.example.com, you would use this line:

```
relayhost = [relay.example.com]
```

Placing the relay host's name or address in square brackets disables MX lookups for that host.

After the customary **postfix reload**, you're ready to move on.

Deferring Message Transport

At this point, Postfix has a configuration that delivers mail to a relay host without DNS lookups, avoiding any open relay issues. However, the server still dials up the ISP any time it receives outgoing mail destined for remote networks. To stop this behavior and make Postfix queue outgoing messages instead, edit main.cf and tell Postfix to defer the SMTP transport method with the defer_transports parameter, as shown in the following example.

```
defer_transports = smtp
```

NOTE *If you use UUCP instead of SMTP, you can substitute uucp for smtp.*

As usual, execute **postfix reload** as root after after making this change. After the reload, Postfix will no longer deliver messages via SMTP until the defer_transports parameter changes or vanishes. The next section shows how to use this feature to deliver the messages when your server dials up the ISP.

Triggering Message Delivery

The only remaining task is to instruct Postfix to deliver all queued mail via SMTP when it connects to the Internet. All you have to do is automatically reconfigure Postfix when the server goes online and reverting to the original configuration afterward. You can trigger this with scripts that the system runs after establishing a connection. On a Linux system running PPP, these scripts often reside in /etc/ppp/ip-up.d.

Create a script named postfix in this directory to run *after* the script that sets resolv.conf. The postfix script looks like this:

```
## start or reload Postfix as needed
# if Postfix is running chrooted, copy resolv.conf to the resolv.conf Postfix
uses
cp -p /etc/resolv.conf `postconf -h queue_directory`/etc/resolv.conf ❶
# unset defer_transports and make Postfix note it
postconf -e "defer_transports ="
postfix reload
# Force a queue run to unload any mail that is hanging around
postfix flush
```

❶ The line involving resolv.conf is relevant only if Postfix is running in a chroot jail. It assumes that the server alters its resolv.conf file when dialing up. Postfix also needs to know the current nameservers, so this command copies the new version to the chroot jail, where Postfix can find it.

Similarly, when the machine goes offline, you want to restore the old queuing behavior. Create a script named postfix in /etc/ppp/ip-down.d to run when the connection goes down (again, the line with resolv.conf is necessary only in a chroot jail):

```
## start or reload Postfix as needed
# copy resolv.conf to the resolv.conf Postfix uses (only if Postfix is chrooted)
cp -p /etc/resolv.conf `postconf -h queue_directory`/etc/resolv.conf
# set defer_transports and make Postfix note it
postconf -e "defer_transports = smtp"
postfix reload
```

Configuring Relay Permissions for a Relay Host

Many free mail providers, especially those that offer SMTP client access along with a web mail interface, require extra validation before they permit your client to use their relay host. This is necessary because most of their users connect from other access providers (and, therefore, from other IP ranges than their own), so they cannot set relay permissions based on IP addresses. If mail providers opened their mail servers to a wide range of IP addresses, they would effectively become open relays, and it would be a matter of minutes before spammers started to use them. Therefore, mail providers require POP-before-SMTP or SMTP authentication.

POP-before-SMTP

A provider that requires POP-before-SMTP (see Chapter 15) accepts outgoing relay messages only if you retrieve incoming mail before sending any new messages. In other words, your machine must authenticate itself with the provider's POP3 or IMAP4 server before sending anything. When your host authenticates, the provider notes your current IP address and allows that IP address to send messages through its relay within a certain time window.

Postfix is an MTA; it does *not* speak POP3 and IMAP4. Therefore, Postfix cannot perform POP-before-SMTP by itself. This is not a problem, because you can easily configure fetchmail (`http://catb.org/~esr/fetchmail`) to do it for you. Fetchmail is a small command-line utility that retrieves mail from almost any kind of mail system on the Internet. To use it in a POP-before-SMTP setup, perform these steps:

1. Configure Postfix as described in this chapter.
2. Follow the instructions in the fetchmail documentation to create a working configuration.
3. Add a trigger that calls fetchmail *before* reconfiguring Postfix in your `/etc/ppp` dial-up script.

This way, your server runs fetchmail (a POP/IMAP client) at least once before running the Postfix (SMTP) dequeuing phase, so your mail provider will accept your outgoing messages.

SMTP Authentication

A provider that requires SMTP authentication allows your client or server to relay messages through their relay host only if it has authenticated itself during the SMTP dialog. To use SMTP authentication in Postfix, you don't need any extra services or programs, so it is preferable to POP-before-SMTP (especially in cases where you want to send messages but not retrieve anything).

You can find extensive information on how to configure client-side SMTP authentication for Postfix in Chapter 16.

5

ANATOMY OF POSTFIX

This chapter describes how Postfix works, what each piece of the system does, and how these components relate to each other. After going through this material, you should have an understanding of Postfix as a whole, so that you can you focus on individual goals.

Postfix consists of a small number of programs that interact with user processes (sendmail, postqueue, postsuper, and so on) and a larger number of programs that run in the background. Only the programs that run in the background are controlled by the master daemon. The master daemon's job is to determine what work there is to do and dispatch the appropriate program to do the work. This modular design allows for a higher level of security because each program runs with the lowest privilege set needed to fulfill its task.

You can think of the whole Postfix system as a router. This may sound strange at first, but remember that a router's job is to look at an IP packet, determine the destination IP address (and possibly the source), and then choose the right interface to route the packet toward its destination. Postfix does the same thing with mail (see Figure 5-1), looking at the destination of a message (the envelope recipient) and the source (the envelope sender) to determine the application that will move the message closer to its final destination.

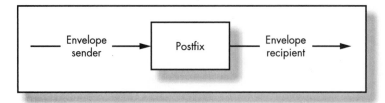

Figure 5-1: Postfix works like a router

Now let's look more closely at the system. A real router usually accepts IP packets from multiple interfaces, routing them back out through the interfaces. The same is true for Postfix; it accepts messages from multiple sources and then passes the mail on to multiple destinations. A message's origin may be the local `sendmail` binary or an SMTP or QMQP connection. The destination can be a local mailbox, outgoing SMTP or LMTP, a pipe into a program, and more. Figure 5-2 shows this view of Postfix.

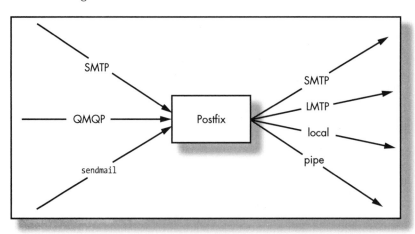

Figure 5-2: A Postfix "router" accepts and establishes all kinds of connections

The origin and destination of a message seem clear enough, but how does Postfix pick a delivery method given a destination? A router uses routing tables that match IP addresses to networks to determine a path. Postfix does the same thing with email addresses.

In Postfix, lookup tables are called *maps*. Postfix uses maps not only to find out where to send mail, but also to impose restrictions on clients, senders, and recipients, and to check certain patterns in email content. Figure 5-3 shows where the maps—to name but a few, `aliases`, `virtual`, and `transport` are shown—fit in.

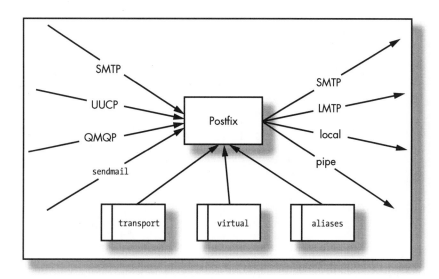

Figure 5-3: Maps are the lookup tables of the Postfix "router"

Postfix Daemons

Figure 5-4 shows an overview of the Postfix daemons and how they fit together.

NOTE   *Postfix is constantly under development. The following list of daemons is based on Postfix 2.1.*

master

The master daemon is the supervisor of Postfix, and it oversees all other Postfix daemons. The master waits for incoming jobs to be delegated to subordinate daemons. If there is a lot of work to do, the master can invoke multiple instances of a daemon. You can configure the number of simultaneous daemon instances, how often Postfix can reuse them, and a period of inactivity that should elapse before stopping an instance.

If you have ever worked with the inetd server on a Unix machine, you will find many similarities between it and the master daemon.

bounce and defer

A mail transfer agent must notify the sender about undeliverable mail. In Postfix, the bounce and defer daemons handle this task, which is triggered by the queue manager (qmgr). Specifically, the two event types that cause sender notices are unrecoverable errors and a destination that is unreachable for an extended period of time. The latter case results in a delay warning.

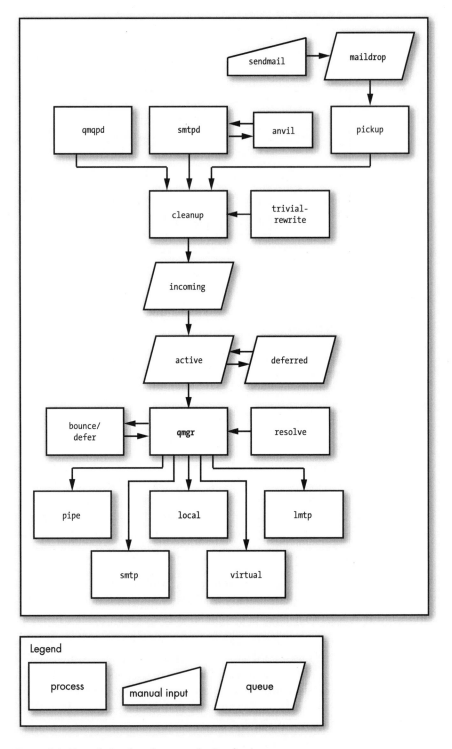

Figure 5-4: The relationships between the Postfix daemons

error

The error daemon is a mail delivery agent like local or smtp. It is a delivery agent that always causes mail to be bounced. Usually you don't use it unless you configure a domain as undeliverable by directing mail to the error delivery agent. If a mail is sent to the error daemon it will inform the bounce daemon to record that a recipient was undeliverable.

trivial-rewrite

The trivial-rewrite daemon acts upon request by the cleanup daemon in order to rewrite nonstandard addresses into the standard user@fqdn form.

This daemon also resolves destinations upon request from the queue manager (qmgr). By default, trivial-rewrite distinguishes only between local and remote destinations.

showq

The showq daemon lists the Postfix mail queue, and it is the program behind the mailq (sendmail -bp) command. This daemon is necessary because the Postfix queue is not world-readable; a non-setuid user program cannot list the queue (and Postfix binaries are not setuid).

flush

The flush daemon attempts to clear the mail queue of pending and deferred messages. By using a per-destination list of queued mail, it improves the performance of the SMTP Extended Turn (ETRN) request and its command-line equivalent, sendmail -qR destination. You can maintain the list of destinations with the fast_flush_domains parameter in the main.cf file.

qmgr

The qmgr daemon manages the Postfix queues; it is the heart of the Postfix mail system. It distributes delivery tasks to the local, smtp, lmtp, and pipe daemons. After delegating a job, it submits queue file path-name information, the message sender address, the target host (if the destination is remote), and one or more message-recipient addresses to the daemon it delegated the delivery task to.

The qmgr design is a good example of how Postfix handles jobs to avoid resource starving and to maintain stability. Two things stand out:

- qmgr maintains a small active queue, with just a few messages pending for delivery. This queue effectively acts as a limited window for the potentially larger incoming and deferred queues, and it prevents qmgr from running out of memory under a heavy load.

- If Postfix cannot immediately deliver a message, qmgr moves the message to the deferred queue. Keeping temporarily undeliverable messages in a separate queue ensures that a large mail backlog does not slow down normal queue access.

qmgr uses the bounce and error daemons to bounce mail for recipients listed in the relocated table that contains contact information for users or domains that no longer exist on the system.

proxymap

Postfix client processes can get read-only access to maps through the proxymap daemon. By sharing a single open map among many Postfix daemons, proxymap circumvents chroot restrictions and reduces the number of open lookup tables.

spawn

The spawn process creates non-Postfix processes on request. It listens on a TCP port, Unix domain socket, or FIFO connected to the standard input, output, and error streams. The only use for spawn discussed in this book is for the Postfix external content filtering system in Chapter 13.

local

As the name suggests, the local daemon is responsible for local mailbox delivery. The Postfix local daemon can write to mailboxes in the mbox and Maildir formats. In addition, local can access data in Sendmail-style alias databases and user .forward files.

NOTE *These capabilities make local the counterpart to the Sendmail mail posting agent, and they both maintain the same user interface.*

As an alternative, local can delegate mailbox delivery to a local delivery agent (LDA) that provides more advanced features, such as filtering. Two very popular LDAs are procmail (http://www.procmail.org) and maildrop (http://www.flounder.net/~mrsam/maildrop).

Postfix can run multiple instances of local.

virtual

The virtual daemon, sometimes called the *virtual delivery agent,* is a stripped-down version of local that delivers exclusively to mailboxes. It is the most secure Postfix delivery agent; it does not perform alias and .forward file expansions.

This delivery agent can deliver mail for multiple domains, making it especially suitable for hosting several small domains on a single machine (a so-called POP toaster) without the need for real system or shell accounts.

smtp

The smtp client is the Postfix client program that transports outbound messages to remote destinations. It looks up destination mail exchangers, sorts the list by preference, and tries each address until it finds a server that responds. A busy Postfix system typically has several smtp daemons running at once.

lmtp

The lmtp client communicates with local and remote mailbox servers with the Local Mail Delivery Protocol (LMTP) defined in RFC 2033 (ftp://ftp.rfc-editor.org/in-notes/rfc2033.txt). It is often used with the Cyrus IMAP server (http://asg.web.cmu.edu/cyrus/imapd).

The advantages of a setup using Postfix's lmtp client are that Postfix handles all of the queue management and one Postfix machine can feed multiple mailbox servers (which need to have an LMTP daemon) over LMTP. The opposite is also true: several Postfix machines can feed one mailbox server through lmtp. These mailbox server(s) could, for example, be running Cyrus IMAP.

pipe

The pipe mailer client is the outbound interface to other mail transport mechanisms. It invokes programs with parameters and pipes the message body into their standard input.

pickup

The pickup daemon picks up messages put into the maildrop queue by the local sendmail user client program. After performing a few sanity checks, pickup passes messages to the cleanup daemon.

smtpd

The smtpd daemon handles communication with networked mail clients that deliver messages to Postfix through SMTP. smtpd performs a number of checks that protect the rest of the Postfix system, and it can be configured to implement unsolicited commercial email (UCE) controls (local or network-based blacklists, DNS lookups, other client requests, and so on).

After accepting a message, smtpd puts it into the incoming queue, where qmgr takes over.

cleanup

The cleanup daemon is the final processing stage for new messages. It adds any required missing headers, arranges for address rewriting, and (optionally) extracts recipient addresses from message headers. The cleanup daemon inserts the result into the incoming queue and then notifies the queue manager that new mail has arrived.

sendmail

sendmail is a Postfix command that replaces and emulates Eric Allman's MTA Sendmail. Its purpose is to provide a Sendmail-compatible interface to applications that will only invoke /usr/sbin/sendmail. It interacts with the postdrop binary to put mail into the maildrop queue for pickup.

NOTE   *sendmail is the slowest way to inject mail into the Postfix queue system. If you need to send a large amount of mail at once, use SMTP instead.*

qmqpd

The Postfix QMQP server implements the Quick Mail Queuing Protocol (QMQP; see http://cr.yp.to/proto/qmqp.html) to make Postfix compatible with qmail and the ezmlm list manager.

anvil

The Postfix anvil is a preliminary defense against SMTP clients and denial-of-service attacks that swamp the SMTP server with too many simultaneous or successive connection attempts. It comes with a whitelist capability for disabling restrictions for authorized clients. anvil is not included with Postfix 2.1, but it is available in the Postfix 2.2 experimental release. anvil will stay experimental until there is enough experience with Postfix rate limiting.

Postfix Queues

Postfix polls all queues in the directory specified by the queue_directory parameter in your main.cf file. The queue directory is usually /var/spool/ postfix. Each queue has its own subdirectory with a name identifying the queue. All messages that Postfix handles stay in these directories until Postfix delivers them. You can determine the status of a message by its queue: incoming, maildrop, deferred, active, hold, or corrupt.

incoming

All new messages entering the Postfix queue system get sent to the incoming queue by the cleanup service. New queue files are created with the postfix user as the owner and an access mode of 0600. As soon as a queue file is ready for further processing, the cleanup service changes the queue file mode to 0700 and notifies the queue manager that new mail has arrived. The queue manager ignores incomplete queue files whose mode is 0600.

The queue manager scans the incoming queue when moving new messages into the active queue and makes sure that the active queue resource limits have not been exceeded. By default, the active queue has a maximum of 20,000 messages.

CAUTION *Once the active queue message limit is reached, the queue manager stops scanning the incoming and deferred queues.*

maildrop

Messages submitted with the sendmail command that have not been sent to the primary Postfix queues by the pickup service await processing in the maildrop queue. You can add messages to the maildrop queue even when Postfix is not running; Postfix will look at them once it is started.

The single-threaded pickup service scans and drains the maildrop queue periodically, as well as upon notification from the postdrop program. The postdrop program is a setgid helper that allows the unprivileged sendmail program to inject mail into the maildrop queue and notify the pickup service of message arrival. (All messages that enter the main Postfix queues do so via the cleanup service.)

deferred

If a message still has recipients for which delivery failed for some transient reason, and the message has been delivered to all the recipients possible, Postfix places the message into the deferred queue.

The queue manager scans the deferred queue periodically to put deferred messages back into the active queue. The scan interval is specified with the queue_run_delay configuration parameter. If the deferred and incoming queue scans happen to take place at the same time, the queue manager alternates between the two queues on a per-message basis.

active

The active queue is somewhat analogous to an operating system's process run queue. Messages in the active queue are ready to be sent, but are not necessarily in the process of being sent.

The queue manager is a delivery agent scheduler that works to ensure fast and fair delivery of mail to all destinations within designated resource limits.

NOTE *Although most Postfix administrators think of the active queue as a directory on disk, the real active queue is a set of data structures in the memory of the queue manager process.*

hold

The administrator can define smtpd access(5) policies and cleanup header and body checks (see Chapter 10) that cause messages to be automatically diverted from normal processing and placed indefinitely in the hold queue. Messages placed in the hold queue stay there until the administrator intervenes. No periodic delivery attempts are made for messages in the hold queue. You can run the postsuper command to manually put messages on hold or to release messages from the hold queue into the deferred queue.

Messages can potentially stay in the hold queue for a time that exceeds the queue file lifetime set by the maximal_queue_lifetime parameter (after which undelivered messages are bounced to the sender). If older messages need to be released from the hold queue, you can use postsuper -r to move them into the maildrop queue, so that the message gets a new timestamp and is given more than one opportunity to be delivered.

NOTE *The hold queue doesn't play much of a role in Postfix performance; monitoring of the hold queue is typically motivated by tracking spam and malware rather than by performance issues.*

corrupt   The corrupt directory contains damaged queue files. Rather than discarding these, Postfix stores them here so that the (human) postmaster can inspect them using postcat.

Postfix logs a warning about any corrupt files upon startup.

Maps

Maps are files and databases that Postfix uses to look up information. Maps have many different purposes, but they all have one thing in common—a left-hand side (LHS, or *key*) and a right-hand side (RHS, or *value*).

Here are a few examples of keys and values:

Key	Value
postmaster:	john
postmaster@example.com	john
192.168.254.12	REJECT
spammer@example.com	REJECT
/^Subject: your account {25}[a-z]{8}/	REJECT Mimail Virus Detected

To use a map, you specify a key and get the associated value as a result.

NOTE *The keys and values here come from various files and would not make sense in one file. The preceding list is just an illustration to show that all map entries take the same basic form.*

Map Types

Postfix can use many different kinds of maps. The formats available depend on the way Postfix was compiled on your particular system. To find out what formats your Postfix supports, run **postconf -m** on the command line. You should get a list of map types:

```
# postconf -m
btree
cdb
cidr
environ
hash
ldap
mysql
nis
pcre
proxy
regexp
sdbm
static
tcp
unix
```

Indexed Maps (hash, btree, dbm, and So On)

Indexed maps are binary databases built from regular text files with commands such as newaliases, postalias, and postmap. The binary maps have an indexed format so that Postfix can quickly retrieve the value associated with a key. As a further performance improvement, the Postfix daemons open these maps when starting up, and they do not re-read them unless they notice a change in the map files in the filesystem. To reload a map, a daemon exits and a new one is started by the master daemon.

If you have indexed maps that change frequently, the daemons using these maps will restart just as often. Under a heavy load, this can lead to performance problems.

The most common indexed maps are built from the aliases, virtual, transport, relocated, and sasl_passwd text files. You can identify a map file because its name is the original file with a suffix that also tells you the index format. For example, an aliases map file built with the postalias command is named aliases.db.

NOTE *When you create a file in order to build an indexed map from it you don't have to put keys in a specific order. The conversion tools and programs that use indexed maps do not require a specific order for input. In fact, the process of conversion removes the ordering.*

Postfix queries entries in a predefined order specified in the access(5) manual page. In other words, each map lookup actually consists of a series of single queries (derived from the original query) on single keys in the indexed map.

Linear Maps (PCRE, regexp, CIDR, and Flat Files)

Linear maps are regular text files. Postfix reads these files from top to bottom, making them different from indexed maps. This difference is quite important, because the first match in the file determines the action that Postfix will take. Postfix ignores any later entries, whether they match the query or not.

Consider the following regexp map, where a john.doe@example.com lookup returns OK, because the first line matches.

```
/john\.doe@example\.com/ OK
/example\.com/           REJECT
```

However, if you swap the lines in the regexp map, the other entry matches first, so the same john.doe@example.com lookup returns REJECT:

```
/example\.com/           REJECT
/john\.doe@example\.com/ OK
```

You do *not* need to convert linear maps to a binary form (in fact, you can't do it). The Postfix daemons read them at startup and do not notice any changes to the map until they are restarted. Typical Postfix linear maps include header_checks, body_checks, and mime_header_checks (see Chapter 9).

CAUTION *As your linear maps grow, it takes longer for the Postfix daemons to process them. This is especially true with respect to body or header checks, because the cleanup daemon needs to check every line of the body (up to body_checks_size_limit) and headers against every line of the map.*

This can cause a significant slowdown, especially if you have extensive *_checks parameters that use regexp or PCRE (Perl-compatible regular expression) type maps in *order to prevent spam from entering the system. When this happens, it's usually time to hand complex spam filtering to an external application.*

To make the Postfix daemons notice changes in linear maps, run **postfix reload**. If the timing is not critical, you can set the max_use parameter to define a time-to-live for daemons. As soon as a daemon has processed the number of tasks specified in that parameter, it quits and is restarted by master. Upon restart, it re-reads all required maps.

Databases (MySQL, PostgreSQL, LDAP)

Postfix treats a database just like an indexed map. The result of a database query is Match (along with the value returned by the query) or No match. The principal difference between a database map and an indexed map is that you do not need to restart a daemon when there is a change to the database. Postfix does not assume that the postmaster is the only person who can alter the database.

The drawback to this approach is that the database may not be able to handle the number of queries gracefully, because Postfix needs to perform at least three queries for each lookup in a map (see the "How Postfix Queries Maps" section that follows). Under heavy load, the database backend could stop working, and your mail service would be vulnerable to a self-induced meltdown or a denial-of-service attack. This possibility should not prevent you from using database backends, but you should be aware of the risk.

Database lookups can become a problem for systems with a heavy load, but this isn't the only issue to consider—latency can be another problem. Database queries have a higher latency than indexed maps because Postfix must connect to the database backend, send the query, and then wait for the result. With an indexed map, Postfix has only to consult data that is already loaded in memory.

If your database becomes a bottleneck, and you do not have an excessively large map, you can insert a map between the database and Postfix. That is, you can create an indexed map from a complete database query, and then run Postfix with that map. You need to remember to update the map as often as necessary, but the proxymap daemon can be used to significantly reduce the number of concurrent connections.

Determining the Number of Simultaneous Connections to a Database

Postfix daemons (smtpd, smtp, and so on) run with a process limit (set by default_process_limit) of 100 simultaneous processes. Running at peak load, there would be 100 concurrent smtpd daemons, each querying the database backend for one access(5) lookup (e.g., because we use a map for checking if the client is in our personal blacklist and should then by denied from sending mail to us).

Remember that one lookup results in at least three queries, so the number of simultaneous queries to the database would be at least default_process_limit * 3 (which, in the default configuration, would be 300 queries), while the number of simultaneous connections is `default_process_limit`. This is only the number of queries and connections for `smtpd` daemons; other daemons, such as `local` and `qmgr`, may be working on other jobs, adding to the number of open connections and simultaneous queries.

How Postfix Queries Maps

Maps can be used for various tasks. Postfix has table-driven mechanisms that use maps (see access(5), aliases(5), canonical(5), and transport(5)). These maps can use different lookup mechanisms (LDAP, NIS, SQL, btree, hash, regexp, cdb, cidr, pcre, and so on).

1. `<localpart@domainpart>`   Matches the specified mail address verbatim.
2. `<domainpart>`   Matches *domainpart* as the domain part of an email address. The pattern *domainpart* also matches subdomains, but only when the string `smtpd_access_maps` is listed in the Postfix `parent_domain_matches_subdomains` configuration setting. Otherwise, specify *.domainpart* (note the initial dot) to match subdomains.
3. `<localpart@>`   Matches all mail addresses with the specified user part (*localpart*), no matter what domain they belong to.
4. Fail   If the lookups don't match, Postfix will return `no match found`, and the query ends with an error.

NOTE   *It isn't possible to look up a null sender address in some lookup table types. By default, Postfix uses <> as the lookup key for the null sender address. The value is specified with the* `smtpd_null_access_lookup_key` *parameter in the* `main.cf` *file.*

This order of lookups implies that Postfix performs several lookups for each query, which isn't really a problem unless you're using high-latency maps like SQL or LDAP maps (and, of course, you should expect that a lot of lookups will need multiple queries). This is just one thing to remember before you put all your maps into LDAP and then complain on the postfix-users mailing list that "Postfix is slow. . . ."

External Sources

Postfix supports information sources that are not built on top of Postfix and that aren't even under your direct control, such as blacklists (DNSBL and RHSBL lists), DNS-based lists, and other external sources. Blacklists are almost exclusively used in `smtpd_*_restrictions` parameters in order to reject mail coming from clients or senders listed in DNSBL- or RHSBL-style lists (see Chapter 7).

As with any external query, these lookups can fail due to connectivity problems, denial-of-service attacks against the blacklist servers, and other problems. In case of a timeout or other failure, Postfix may still accept mail (bypassing a possible restriction), but it will log an appropriate warning to the mail log.

Command-Line Utilities

Postfix ships with a number of command-line utilities to assist you with administration tasks. Although they perform different functions (such as querying maps, examining queue files, dequeuing and requeuing messages, and changing the configuration), they all have one thing in common—their names start with "post."

NOTE *These commands can do much more than what is described here. We are focusing on the options that you will experience in day-to-day operation. If you don't find what you are looking for here, the first place to look is the online manual.*

postfix

The postfix command stops, starts, and reloads the configuration with the stop, start, and reload options.

postalias

The postalias command creates an indexed alias map from an alias file. It works just like the postmap command (described shortly), but it pays special attention to the notation in an alias file (where a colon separates the key and value). postalias must be used on alias files.

postcat

The postcat command displays the content of a message in a mail queue.

To read a message in a mail queue, you need its queue ID. Run **mailq** for a list of queue IDs. For example, the queue ID of the following message is F2B9715C0B3:

```
# mailq
F2B9715C0B3  2464 Mon Oct 13 15:29:39  markus.herrmann@example.com
             (connect to mail.example.com[217.6.113.151]: Connection timed out)
                                        torsten.hecke@example.net
-- 2 Kbytes in 1 Requests.
```

After obtaining a queue ID, use it as an option to postcat to see the contents of the queue file:

```
# postcat -q F2B9715C0B3
```

postmap

The postmap command's primary purpose is to build indexed maps from flat files. For example, to build /etc/postfix/virtual.db from /etc/postfix/virtual, run the following command.

```
# postmap hash:/etc/postfix/virtual
```

The `postmap` command can do more. Among its most useful features is the ability to test any kind of map that your Postfix installation supports. This is extremely helpful when debugging a configuration where lookups to the maps appear to fail, and you are unsure whether the key and value are actually visible to Postfix.

Debugging an Entry in a Lookup Table

To determine whether Postfix can find an entry in a map, use `postmap -q`. For example, the following command returns the value assigned to the key <sender@example.com> in the map /etc/postfix/sender_access (type **hash**):

```
# postmap -q sender@example.com hash:/etc/postfix/sender_access
OK
```

It's important to note that `postmap` does *not* look for the terms <sender@>, <example.com>, and <com>, even though these terms are in the access(5) manual page. You need to perform those lookups manually:

```
# postmap -q sender@ hash:/etc/postfix/sender_access
# postmap -q example.com hash:/etc/postfix/sender_access
# postmap -q com hash:/etc/postfix/sender_access
```

postdrop

The `postdrop` command reads mail from the standard input and drops the result into the `maildrop` directory. This program works in conjunction with the sendmail utility.

postkick

The `postkick` command sends a request to a Postfix daemon through a local transport channel, making Postfix interprocess communication accessible to shell scripts and other programs.

NOTE *The postkick command sends messages to Postfix daemon processes. This requires that Postfix is running.*

Requeuing a Message

The following advanced `postkick` example shows how to requeue a message for immediate redelivery:

```
# cat queueidlist | postsuper -r -
postkick public pickup W
```

This sequence of commands moves all selected messages listed in queueidlist to the maildrop queue with the postsuper -r - command, where the pickup daemon would process them like any other piece of mail. By doing this, you reset the content filter to the setting appropriate for local submission and add an extra Received: header.

The postkick command requests an immediate maildrop queue scan. Otherwise, the messages would stay in the maildrop queue for a maximum of 60 seconds. The pickup daemon submits the message to the cleanup daemon, where it gets a new queueid and is deposited into the incoming queue. The whole point is to move the message to the active queue as quickly as possible.

postlock

The postlock command gives you exclusive access to mbox files that Postfix writes, and then it runs a command while holding the lock. The lock you get from postlock is compatible with the Postfix local delivery agent. Postfix does not touch the file while your command executes. Here is an example:

```
# postlock /var/mail/user from
```

CAUTION   *Try to avoid any commands that might require a CTRL-C to terminate. Interrupting postlock does not guarantee that the lock will go away; you may need to remove a lock file to deliver to the mailbox again. To see if there is a lingering lock file, run* **postlock** *without a command. If this hangs and eventually times out, you probably have a left-over lock.*

postlog

The postlog command allows external programs, such as shell scripts, to write messages to the mail log. This is a Postfix-compatible logging interface; by default, it logs the text from the command line as a single record. Here's a very simple example:

```
# postlog This is a test
postlog: This is a test
# grep "This is a test" /var/log/mail.log
Feb 20 11:50:16 mail postlog: This is a test
```

postqueue

The postqueue command is a user interface to Postfix queues, giving you functionality that is traditionally available with the sendmail command.

- The -f parameter makes postqueue request the queue manager to deliver all queued mail (flush), regardless of destination. This is equivalent to postfix flush or sendmail -q:

```
# postqueue -f
```

- The -p parameter makes postqueue print the contents of the queue. It is equivalent to mailq:

```
# postqueue -p
```

- The -s domain parameter makes postqueue attempt to deliver all queued mail bound for domain. This is equivalent to sendmail -q domain:

```
# postqueue -s example.com
```

NOTE   *The postqueue command sends messages to Postfix daemon processes. This requires that Postfix is running.*

postsuper

The postsuper command maintains jobs inside Postfix queues. Unlike postqueue, this command is restricted to the superuser, and it can run while Postfix is down. Some postsuper features are needed to check the queue before daemon processes are started. Table 5-1 shows what the postsuper command can do.

Table 5-1: Capabilities of the postsuper Command

Option	Action
-d	Delete a message with the named queue ID from the named mail queue(s)
-h	Place a message on hold so that no attempt is made to deliver it
-H	Release mail currently on hold
-p	Purge temporary files left over from crashes
-r	Requeue messages with a named queue ID from a named mail queue
-s	Check and repair the queue structure

One of the most frequent uses of postsuper is deleting a message from the mail queue with postsuper -d queueid. Doing this manually is tedious, especially when deleting many files. The following Perl script (delete_from_mailq) makes it easier:

```perl
#!/usr/bin/perl
$REGEXP = shift || die "no email-address given (regexp-style, e.g. bl.*\
@yahoo.com)!";
@data = qx</usr/sbin/postqueue -p>;
for (@data) {
  if (/^(\w+)(\*|\!)?\s/) {
    $queue_id = $1;
  }
  if($queue_id) {
    if (/$REGEXP/i) {
      $Q{$queue_id} = 1;
      $queue_id = "";
    }
  }
```

```
  }
}
#open(POSTSUPER,"|cat") || die "couldn't open postsuper" ;
open(POSTSUPER,"|postsuper -d -") || die "couldn't open postsuper" ;
foreach (keys %Q) {
  print POSTSUPER "$_\n";
};
close(POSTSUPER);
```

Here's how you'd use it:

```
# mailq
C73A015C095     7509 Mon Oct 13 14:56:17  MAILER-DAEMON
        (connect to mx5.ancientaward.com[64.156.166.211]: Connection refused)

National_Nosepicking_Month@mx5.ancientaward.com
```

Notice that the sender is identified as <MAILER-DAEMON> here. To remove these bounces, run **delete-from-mailq** as root:

```
# delete-from-mailq MAILER-DAEMON
postsuper: C73A015C095: removed
postsuper: Deleted: 1 message
```

PART II

CONTENT CONTROL

Postfix comes with three feature sets that control how messages can enter and leave the mail system. With these features, you can manage message flow based on the SMTP dialog and message content, or you can delegate the content management to external applications. These three types of features fall into three distinct groups of configuration parameters: restrictions, checks, and filters.

A Postmaster's Primer to Email

Content control requires knowledge about the content. You have to know what must, should, and may be in an email to apply restrictions, checks, and filters effectively. Read Chapter 6 to get an insight on email content.

How Message Transfer Restrictions Work

Restrictions control SMTP communication. Chapter 7 will explain how restrictions work. Take your time reading it; it will make implementing restrictions a lot easier.

Using Message Transfer Restrictions

In Chapter 8 we show you how to bring restrictions to life. All of them can be used almost immediately.

How Built-in Content Filters Work

Checks do their work based on message content. But how do they work? Chapter 9 introduces you to checks and tells you all about the theory of checks.

Using Built-in Content Filters

Chapter 10 contains a bunch of assorted examples to get you going right away.

How External Content Filters Work

External content filters delegate SMTP communication management and content control to external applications. To understand how Postfix processes messages that go through external content filters, read Chapter 11.

Using External Content Filters

Need some examples of how to implement external content filters? Read Chapter 12 to find examples you can actually get your hands on.

6

A POSTMASTER'S PRIMER TO EMAIL

The terms *envelope, header, body,* and *attachment* all relate to some part of the data that MTAs exchange. If you know what they mean, you will understand the parts of messages that the Postfix content control parameters affect. It's also handy that the Postfix parameter names and syntax are derived from the RFCs.

This chapter is a primer to content control. Read it carefully, and take some time to let the terminology and concepts sink in. After you get a grasp of the basics, you will have no trouble attaining efficient content control.

Message Transport Basics

Message transport involves two major parts: the SMTP communication that handles the transport and the data that is transported (which most people refer to as the "email" or "message"). The terms used to describe message transport weren't invented out of the blue; they were adopted from an ancient but well-known and established system that people in earlier centuries referred to as "mail."

When dealing with the regular postal system, the terms *messenger, envelope, header, body,* and *attachment* all have well-known meanings. These terms are technical terms when referring to email. Figure 6-1 compares a regular letter to an email, and you can identify the following parts:

Messenger

In regular mail, the messenger is called the *postman* or *letter carrier.* In email, the messenger is the *client.*

Envelope

In email, just as with regular letters, the envelope serves as a wrapper that explains how the content is to be delivered. On the envelope, you find the *envelope sender* and the *envelope recipient.*

Header

The header gives you metadata (information) about a message. Just as in a real letter, the header gives you information about the sender (the From: header), the intended recipient (To:), the originating date and time (Date:), and the subject (Subject:). Furthermore, the Received: headers in an email message tell you the path of a message and how long it took to transmit.

Body

The body of an email message contains the actual content, just as in a letter.

Attachments

If there are attachments inside an email message, this fact will be noted in the body; just as it would in a real letter. Attachments are optional and can be in a variety of formats.

Why Do You Need to Know This?

This may sound a bit theoretical, so far; what does all of this have to do with running Postfix? First, there is typically more information in an email message than in a letter. You need to know what the extra pieces are, as well as in which part of the message these pieces appear. Also, Postfix has three distinct parameter groups for controlling content that relate directly to different parts of messages:

smtpd_*_restrictions

The smtpd_*_restrictions parameters control the client connection and envelope during message transport.

*_checks

The *_checks parameters oversee the header, body, and attachments.

Filters

Postfix uses filters to delegate tasks to other (external) screening applications. Filters are general-purpose; they can control every part of the message, from the envelope to attachments.

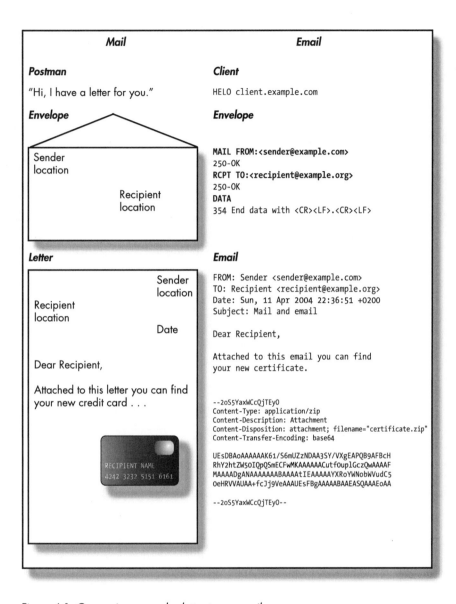

Mail	Email
Postman	**Client**
"Hi, I have a letter for you."	`HELO client.example.com`
Envelope	**Envelope**
Sender location	`MAIL FROM:<sender@example.com>`
	`250-OK`
	`RCPT TO:<recipient@example.org>`
Recipient location	`250-OK`
	`DATA`
	`354 End data with <CR><LF>.<CR><LF>`
Letter	**Email**

Letter side:

Sender location

Recipient location

Date

Dear Recipient,

Attached to this letter you can find your new credit card . . .

RECIPIENT NAME
4242 3232 5151 6161

Email side:

```
FROM: Sender <sender@example.com>
TO: Recipient <recipient@example.org>
Date: Sun, 11 Apr 2004 22:36:51 +0200
Subject: Mail and email

Dear Recipient,

Attached to this email you can find
your new certificate.


--2oS5YaxWCcQjTEyO
Content-Type: application/zip
Content-Description: Attachment
Content-Disposition: attachment; filename="certificate.zip"
Content-Transfer-Encoding: base64

UEsDBAoAAAAAK61/S6mUZzNDAA3SY/VXgEAPQB9AFBcH
RhY2htZW5oIQpQSmECFwMKAAAAACutfOup1GczQwAAAAF
MAAAADgANAAAAAABAAAAtIEAAAAAYXRoYWNobWVudC5
OeHRVVUAA+fcJj9VeAAAUEsFBgAAAAABAAEASQAAAEoAA

--2oS5YaxWCcQjTEyO--
```

Figure 6-1: Comparing a regular letter to an email

Each one of these parameters has a great number of options; if you don't know what part of a message triggers a particular parameter, your content control won't work.

Controlling the SMTP Communication (Envelope)

SMTP communication involves two components: the client (the machine that's connecting to the server providing the SMTP service), and the envelope that the client hands over. It's easiest to see this by using the telnet program on your machine to connect to your server.

Here's a sample communication. Start by connecting to port 25 of your mail server on the command line:

```
$ telnet mail.example.com 25
220 mail.example.com
```

The 220 code that is returned from the server confirms the hostname of the server. Now, introduce yourself to the server like this:

```
HELO client.example.com
250 mail.example.com
```

You can perform the handshake with a HELO (for SMTP) or EHLO (for ESMTP) command, with your client's hostname as a parameter. If the command is successful, you should get a 250 return code followed by the server's hostname.

Let's send some mail now. The MAIL command constructs an envelope, starting with the envelope's sender. If the server accepts the sender, you will get another 250 return code:

```
MAIL FROM:<sender@example.com>
250 Ok
```

The next step in building the envelope is to use the RCPT command to specify an envelope recipient. You can enter more than one recipient:

```
RCPT TO:<recipient@example.com>
250 Ok
RCPT TO:<recipient_2@example.com>
250 Ok
```

NOTE   *Keep in mind that the envelope sender and envelope recipient are often different from the sender and recipient given in the message header (which is specified as part of the DATA command sequence that you're about to see). If you confuse the various senders and recipients, your content control can fail.*

To send the actual message (including all additional headers, such as Subject, To, and Date), use the DATA command:

```
DATA
354 End data with <CR><LF>.<CR><LF>
Subject: message
...

This is the message
...
.
250 Ok: queued as 92933E1C66
QUIT
```

Here is a rundown of the things that you have just seen, as defined in the electronic mail RFCs:

Client

The client is the machine sending mail; Postfix will either log hostname and IP, or "unknown" (if the hostname cannot be determined using DNS lookups). Postfix gets the client IP address from the kernel's TCP/IP stack, and gets the name from DNS or /etc/hosts before SMTP communication takes place. This allows Postfix to impose restrictions if the client's IP address and the hostname during SMTP communication don't match.

Postfix always logs the client IP address and hostname (if available) in the mail log, and it also includes this information in the final message header.

HELO/EHLO statement

A client must introduce itself to the mail server with two pieces of information: service type and hostname.

The first part of the introduction statement is the service type that the client requests. HELO specifies normal service as defined by RFC 821 (ftp://ftp.rfc-editor.org/in-notes/rfc821.txt), and EHLO requests extended service as defined in RFC 2821 (ftp://ftp.rfc-editor.org/in-notes/rfc2821.txt).

Following the service type is the client identity. The client is supposed to submit its fully qualified hostname.

Envelope

The envelope must contain at least two different items: exactly one envelope sender and at least one envelope recipient. The client sends the envelope by transmitting the envelope sender first and follows up with the envelope recipients.

If there is more than one envelope recipient, the client must submit them one after another, beginning each envelope recipient with a new line and waiting for the server's response after each submission.[1] It's the server's job to permit delivery to some or all recipients.

Envelope sender

The envelope sender is the sender that Postfix replies to in the case of an error, such as a delay or bounce notice.

Envelope recipient

The envelope recipient specifies the message's intended recipient(s). A single message may have multiple envelope recipients (for example, a message to several subscribers of a mailing list).

A mail server requires at least one envelope recipient (otherwise it has no one to deliver the message to). Therefore, a client may not use an empty envelope recipient (<>).

---

[1] ESMTP command pipelining is the exception to this rule.

Don't look at the recipient specified in the To header when you want to restrict messages to a recipient. Messages go to the recipients defined in the envelope, not the message header.

Nearly all of the data from the preceding list can be forged, so Postfix offers ways to restrict forgery with the smtpd_*_restrictions parameters, which address the following questions:

1. Where does the client come from?
2. Who does the client pretend to be?
3. Does the client have special privileges?
4. Who is the sender?
5. Who are the recipients?

Postfix also tries to get the answers to these more difficult questions:

1. Does the client provide Postfix with information in an appropriate manner?
2. Does the client provide the information in an appropriate order?
3. Does the client provide all of the information?
4. If the client does not provide all of the appropriate information, will the client attempt to send the message?
5. Is it possible to tell whether the information is correct?
6. If it is possible, is the client lying?

Postfix can get the answers to these questions by inspecting the envelope of a message and how the SMTP dialog took place. When Postfix rejects a message with SMTP envelope restrictions, it rejects the message before it is received. Therefore, Postfix will not send an "undeliverable mail" notification to the sender address. That remains the responsibility of the client.

NOTE *If Postfix refuses a message based on an SMTP envelope restriction, Postfix does not have to bounce it because Postfix preempted the client. This helps to save system resources, keeping traffic low, and can be particularly handy if Postfix is under a heavy spam attack that would require thousands of bounces if the messages were initially accepted for further transport.*

You can learn what restrictions Postfix has and how they work in Chapter 7. Chapter 8 contains several examples that you can use in your own configuration.

Controlling the Message Content

An email message consists of a header and body. The body may also contain one or more attachments in the form of a file or another message encapsulated within the main message. Figure 6-2 shows a high-level view of a simple message with an attachment.

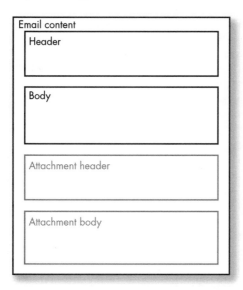

Figure 6-2: An email message with an attachment

Figure 6-3 shows a message with another message as an attachment.

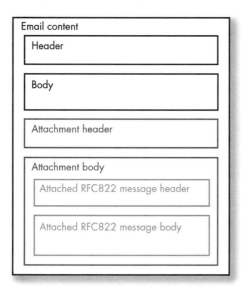

Figure 6-3: An email message with another message as an attachment

You can identify these parts by looking at the message with a plaintext viewer or editor. For example, here is a message with a file attachment:

```
Return-Path: <sender@example.com> ❶
X-Original-To: recipient@example.com
Delivered-To: recipient@example.com
Received: by mail.example.com (Postfix)
        id 9F71443F50; Mon, 26 Apr 2004 01:32:59 +0200 (CEST)
Delivered-To: recipient@example.com
Received: by mail.example.com (Postfix, from userid 500)
        id 2F23043F4F; Mon, 26 Apr 2004 01:32:59 +0200 (CEST)
Date: Mon, 26 Apr 2004 01:32:58 +0200
From: Sender <sender@example.com>
To: Recipient <recipient@example.com>
Subject: Elements of email content
Message-ID: <20040425233258.GA22383@mail.example.com>
Mime-Version: 1.0
Content-Type: multipart/mixed; boundary="/9DWx/yDrRhgMJTb"
Content-Disposition: inline
User-Agent: Mutt/1.5.4i

--/9DWx/yDrRhgMJTb ❷
Content-Type: text/plain; charset=us-ascii
Content-Disposition: inline

A blank line separates the body of a message from the headers. MIME-
encoded text and MIME-encoded attachments may appear in the body.

You may attach one or more files, including another email message.
A message within another message includes its own header and body.
Therefore, you may have nested headers.

Hope this helps,

sender

--/9DWx/yDrRhgMJTb ❸
Content-Type: application/x-zip-compressed
Content-Disposition: attachment; filename="attachment.zip"
Content-Transfer-Encoding: base64

UEsDBAoAAAAAAIILmjBOMx1uCwAAAAsAAAAOAAAAYXR0YWNobWVudC50eHRhdHRhY2htZW50
ClBLAQIUAAoAAAAAAIILmjBOMx1uCwAAAAsAAAAOAAAAAAAAAAEAIAC2gQAAAABhdHRhY2ht
ZW50LnR4dFBLBQYAAAAAAQABADwAAAA3AAAAAA=

--/9DWx/yDrRhgMJTb--
```

The parts of the email are as follows:

❶ Email headers

❷ Start of email body

❸ Start of attachment

Postfix can perform checks on each of these pieces (header_checks, body_checks, mime_header_checks) separately. To check them effectively, you need to know the required, recommended, and optional pieces that a message may contain.

Headers

The header carries meta-information about the message body, such as the character encoding and transmission date. RFC 2822 (ftp://ftp.rfc-editor.org/in-notes/rfc2822.txt) splits header elements into required and recommended categories.

NOTE *Header fields are* not *required to occur in any particular order. It is recommended, though, that if they are present, headers be sent in the order Return-Path, Received, Date, From, Subject, Sender, To, Cc, and so on. You'll find further information about headers in Reading Email Headers (http://www.stopspam.org/email/headers.html).*

Required Headers

There are two required header elements:

Date
> The date field normally specifies the date and time that the message was composed and sent. If the sender's client omits this header, Postfix adds it.

From
> This field contains the identity of the person(s) who sent this message. If the sender's client omits this header, Postfix adds it.

Recommended Headers

These are the recommended header elements:

Message-Id
> This field contains a unique identifier that refers to the current version of the current message. The client generates the message ID and guarantees its uniqueness. In addition, the message ID is intended to be read by a machine, and it may not necessarily mean anything to humans. Because a message ID corresponds to exactly one instance of a particular message, any subsequent revisions of the message should get new message IDs.
>
> If the sender's client omits this header, Postfix adds it.

To

This field contains the identity of the primary recipients of the message. If the sender's client omits this header, Postfix adds the value of the `undisclosed_recipients_header` configuration parameter.

Subject

This field should contain a very brief description of the message.

Cc

This field contains the identity of any secondary recipients of the message.

Reply-To

This field indicates where the recipient's client should send responses to the message.

Content-type

This field is defined in RFC 1049 (`ftp://ftp.rfc-editor.org/in-notes/ rfc1049.txt`), and it indicates the structure of the message body.

MIME-Version

If this header field is present, the body of the message was (supposedly) composed in compliance with RFC 1521 (`ftp://ftp.rfc-editor.org/in- notes/rfc1521.txt`).

Received

Each transport agent that encounters a message adds one of these header lines to indicate where, when, and how the message arrived. The information in these fields can be useful for tracing transport problems.

Return-Path

This header indicates the envelope sender and is used to identify a path back to the originator. The mail server inserts this field upon delivery from a local delivery agent, such as the `local` daemon.

Optional Headers (X-Headers)

X-header is a generic term for an extension header field with a name that starts with a capital X and a hyphen. X-headers are meant to be nonstandard and to provide information only, and conversely, any nonstandard informative header should be an X-header.

Here are a few sample X-headers (there are, of course, millions more):

```
X-Mailer: Ximian Evolution 1.4.3
X-Priority: 3
X-Spam-Checker-Version: SpamAssassin 2.53 (1.174.2.15-2003-03-30-exp)
X-Original-To: recipient@example.com
```

Body

The body carries the message and must occur after the header section. The body may be in plaintext or an encoded form. The body may also contain attachments encoded in a form that does not get mangled when transported across the Internet (in old days, many MTAs were not eight-bit clean; stripping off the eighth bit of a binary file corrupts it).

Attachments

Attachments are files converted into a text-only representation (printable characters only) suitable for sending as email. There are several pieces in the attachment puzzle, and they're explained in the following subsections.

MIME Encodings

MIME stands for Multipurpose Internet Mail Extensions, and it is a system for redefining the format of messages, as described in RFC 2045 (http://www.rfc-editor.org/rfc/rfc2045.txt). Two common MIME encodings for binary files are quoted-printable and base64:

quoted-printable

> The quoted-printable encoding is intended to represent data that largely consists of octets that correspond to printable characters in the US-ASCII character set. It encodes the data in such a way that the resulting octets are unlikely to be modified by mail transport.

base64

> base64 is a data-encoding scheme defined in RFC 1421 (ftp://ftp.rfc-editor.org/in-notes/rfc1421.txt) and RFC 2045 (ftp://ftp.rfc-editor.org/in-notes/rfc2045.txt) to convert binary-encoded data to printable ASCII characters. It is essentially a MIME-content transfer encoding for use in Internet email that uses only alphanumeric characters (A–Z, a–z, the numerals 0–9) and the "+" and "/" symbols, with the "=" symbol as a special suffix code. Command-line utilities for manually encoding and decoding base64 include mpack, munpack, and uudeview.

All halfway modern MUAs are MIME-aware, and attachments will usually be sent base64-encoded only.

Encoding Processor

The MUA performs the task of encoding the binary attachment, and it also automatically creates the MIME structure required to embed the mail text and the encoded attachments in a form understood by other MIME-capable MUAs. This form requires the following headers in the message:

MIME-Version

> The presence of this header indicates that the message is MIME-formatted. The value is normally 1.0, so the header usually looks like this:

```
MIME-Version: 1.0
```

Content-type

This header indicates the type and subtype of the message content. Here is an example:

Content-type: text/plain

The combination of type (text, in this example) and subtype (plain) is generally called a MIME type, so the MIME type is text/plain in this example.

A large number of file formats have registered MIME types. IANA runs an archive listing the registered types (ftp://ftp.isi.edu/in-notes/ iana/assignments/media-types). In addition, all text types have an additional optional charset parameter that indicates the character encoding. A very large number of character encodings have registered MIME charset names.

Content Types

This section lists some of the MIME types that you are likely to encounter. In addition, the multipart-mime-message MIME type allows messages to consist of several different pieces arranged in a treelike structure, where the leaf nodes have a non-multipart content type and non-leaf nodes are any of a variety of multipart types. The MIME mechanism supports the following types (among others):

text/plain

Simple text messages use text/plain; it is the default value for the Content-type header.

multipart/mixed

This type indicates text plus attachments (multipart/mixed with a text/ plain part and other non-text parts). A MIME message with an attached file generally indicates the file's original name with a Content-disposition header, so the type of file is indicated both by the MIME content type and the (usually OS-specific) filename extension.

Viruses often send themselves as files where the Content-type and the Content-disposition headers indicate different file types.

message/rfc822

This is a reply with the original message attached (multipart/mixed with a text/plain part and with the original message as a message/rfc822 part). Postfix generates bounces this way (the message/rfc822 attachment is the original message that was bounced).

multipart/alternative

This type indicates content with two alternative viewing methods, such as a message sent in both plaintext and another format, such as HTML (the same content in text/plain and text/html forms). Outlook Express uses this content type by default, because it sends mail both as HTML and plaintext at the same time.

Encoding Structure

A MIME multipart message contains a boundary, noted as boundary in the mail, in the Content-type header, and this boundary should not occur in any of the parts. Instead, it should appear between the parts, and at the beginning and end of the body of the message. The following example illustrates a sample multipart message:

```
Return-Path: <sender@example.com>
X-Original-To: recipient@example.com
Delivered-To: recipient@example.com
Received: by mail.example.com (Postfix)
        id 9F71443F50; Mon, 26 Apr 2004 01:32:59 +0200 (CEST)
Delivered-To: root@example.com
Received: by mail.example.com (Postfix, from userid 500)
        id 2F23043F4F; Mon, 26 Apr 2004 01:32:59 +0200 (CEST)
Date: Mon, 26 Apr 2004 01:32:58 +0200
From: Sender <sender@example.com>
To: Recipient <recipient@example.com>
Subject: Elements of email content
Message-ID: <20040425233258.GA22383@mail.example.com>
Mime-Version: 1.0 ❶
Content-Type: multipart/mixed; boundary="/9DWx/yDrRhgMJTb" ❷
Content-Disposition: inline
User-Agent: Mutt/1.5.4i


--/9DWx/yDrRhgMJTb ❸
Content-Type: text/plain; charset=us-ascii ❹
Content-Disposition: inline

A blank line separates the body of a message from the headers. MIME-
encoded text and MIME-encoded attachments may appear in the body.

You may attach one or more files, including another email message.
A message within another message includes its own header and body.
Therefore, you may have nested headers.
```

```
Hope this helps,

sender

--/9DWx/yDrRhgMJTb ❺
Content-Type: application/x-zip-compressed ❻
Content-Disposition: attachment; filename="attachment.zip"
Content-Transfer-Encoding: base64 ❼
```

```
UEsDBAoAAAAAAIILmjBOMx1uCwAAAsAAAAOAAAAYXROYWNobWVudC50eHRhdHRhY2htZW50
ClBLAQIUAAoAAAAAAIILmjBOMx1uCwAAAsAAAAOAAAAAAAAAAEAIAC2gQAAAABhdHRhY2ht
ZW50LnR4dFBLBQYAAAAAAQABADwAAAA3AAAAAA=
```

```
--/9DWx/yDrRhgMJTb-- ❽
```

The parts of the message are as follows:

❶ This is the MIME version header.

❷ This is the header containing the content type and the boundary string used to separate the different parts of the message.

❸ The first appearance of the boundary string. A new part of the multipart message begins here.

❹ This part is plaintext.

❺ This is the second appearance of the boundary string, indicating that the previous part is complete and a new part of the multipart message begins here.

❻ The new part is a Zip format file.

❼ The Zip file is encoded in base64 format.

❽ This is the final use of the boundary string, indicating the end of the part and message.

7

HOW MESSAGE TRANSFER RESTRICTIONS WORK

To know what can be restricted, one needs to know
what "what" is and what it should be. . . .
—Patrick, in an attempt to understand Ralf while
he explained restrictions

 This chapter explains the theory of restrictions. Restrictions allow your mail server to accept or reject incoming messages by inspecting the SMTP communication that takes place between client and server. The information gained from this dialog enables Postfix to impose or lift restrictions on the client, sender, and recipient.

Although the word "restrict" usually means that you're limiting something, the term "restriction" can also mean the exact opposite in Postfix; you can configure restrictions to explicitly allow something.

Restriction Triggers

Restrictions are powerful tools. To use them effectively, you need to understand SMTP communication and the features that Postfix provides to analyze this communication. You have already seen how SMTP communication takes place in Chapter 6. We'll look at it from a different perspective here; this time we're interested in the stages of SMTP communication as defined by the commands given by the client. Figure 7-1 outlines these stages.

```
                          $ telnet mailserver.example.com 25
                  Client { 220 mailserver.example.com ESMTP Postfix
                          HELO client.example.com
    HELO/EHLO hostname  { 250-mailserver.example.com
                          MAIL FROM:<sender@example.com>
      Envelope sender   { 250 Ok
                          RCPT TO:<recipient@example.com>
 Envelope recipient(s) { 250 Ok
                          DATA
                          354 End data with <CR><LF>.<CR><LF>
                          From: "Sender" <sender@example.com>
                          To: "Recipient" <recipient@example.com>
                          Date: Sat, 17 May 2003 15:24:43 +0200
                 DATA   {
                          Here comes the mail content . . .
                          .
                          250 Ok: queued as 0EAFFE1C65
                          QUIT
                          221 Bye
```

Figure 7-1: Stages of SMTP communication and typical client input

Each new stage in Figure 7-1 marks a moment when the Postfix smtpd daemon learns another bit of information about the client and the message that it wants to transmit. Postfix uses these stages to trigger restrictions, and each stage has its own restriction parameter named after the active daemon, the name of the stage, and purpose. That's why restriction triggers follow this template: smtpd_*stagename*_restrictions.

Here is a list of all restriction triggers and their default behavior:

smtpd_client_restrictions

This trigger applies to the client's IP address or its hostname or both. By default, Postfix allows any client to connect.

smtpd_helo_restrictions

This trigger applies to the client's HELO/EHLO argument and the client's IP address or hostname or both. The default is to allow any HELO/EHLO argument.

smtpd_sender_restrictions

This is the first trigger set that restricts parts of the envelope. Postfix applies it to the envelope sender, the HELO/EHLO argument, and the client. The default is to allow any envelope sender to send messages.

smtpd_recipient_restrictions

> This trigger applies to the envelope recipient(s), the envelope sender, the HELO/EHLO argument, and client IP address or hostname or both. The default setting in Postfix is to permit any recipient for clients that belong to the mynetworks configuration parameter, but otherwise to allow only recipient domains in relay_domains and recipient domains in mydomains. This protects Postfix from becoming an open relay.

smtpd_data_restrictions

> This trigger detects clients that send mail content before Postfix has replied to the DATA command. Postfix does this by tracing the DATA command when the client sends the command to the server. There is no restriction by default.

smtpd_etrn_restrictions

> This special trigger can restrict clients that may request Postfix to flush the mail queue. The default is to allow any client to issue the ETRN command.

Each restriction trigger corresponds to a set of restrictions; you can think of the triggers as empty boxes. To get any use out of them, you need to put stuff (restrictions) inside.

Restriction Types

Postfix has several kinds of restrictions that can be arranged into four distinct groups:

- Generic restrictions
- Switchable restrictions
- Customizable restrictions
- Additional UCE control parameters

Generic Restrictions

The first group of restrictions do not check anything in the SMTP dialog; they simply carry out a command:

permit

> Allows a request.

defer

> Defers (delays) a request.

reject

> Rejects a request.

warn_if_reject

> Assists with later restrictions; if a restriction after the warn_if_reject decides to reject a request, Postfix doesn't actually reject the message, but rather, prints a reject_warning message to the log.

reject_unauth_pipelining

Rejects the request when the client sends SMTP commands ahead of time without knowing that Postfix actually supports ESMTP command pipelining. This stops bulk mail software that improperly uses ESMTP command pipelining from speeding up deliveries.

Switchable Restrictions

The second kind of restriction works just like switches. You turn them on or off, and once activated, they see if a certain condition has been met. Here's an incomplete list:

smtpd_helo_required

This restriction requires clients to send a HELO (or EHLO) command at the beginning of an SMTP session. Both RFC 821 and RFC 2821 require the HELO/EHLO.

strict_rfc821_envelopes

This restriction adjusts the Postfix tolerance for errors in addresses given in MAIL FROM or RCPT TO commands. Unfortunately, the widely used Sendmail program permits quite a bit of nonstandard behavior, and as a result, there is a lot of software that expects to get away with it. Being strict here stops some unwanted mail, but it can also block legitimate mail from poorly written clients.

disable_vrfy_command

The SMTP VRFY command allows clients to verify that a recipient exists. This restriction allows you to disable the VRFY command.

allow_percent_hack

This restriction controls rewrites of the form user%domain to user@domain.

swap_bangpath

This restriction controls rewrites of the form site!user to user@site. This is necessary if your machine is connected to a UUCP network.

Customizable Restrictions

Customizable restrictions are maps that work like filters. In each map entry, the key is a filter and the value is the action to take if the filter matches (refer to the section "Generic Restrictions" for a list of valid actions). Here are a few kinds of customizable restrictions:

HELO (EHLO) hostname restrictions

These restrictions limit the hostnames that clients may send with the HELO or EHLO command.

Client hostname/address restrictions

These limit the clients that may establish SMTP connections to the mail server.

Sender address restrictions

These limit the sender addresses (envelope senders) that Postfix accepts for `MAIL FROM` commands.

Recipient address restrictions

These restrictions limit the recipient addresses (envelope recipients) that Postfix accepts for `RCPT TO` commands.

ETRN command restrictions

These limit the clients that may issue `ETRN` commands.

Header filtering

This filtering limits what is allowed in message headers. Patterns are applied to entire logical message headers even when a logical header spans multiple physical lines of text.

Body filtering

This filtering restricts the text that may appear in message body lines.

DNSBL-style blacklists

These blacklists restrict connections from IP addresses (clients) that appear in DNSBL blacklists.

RHSBL-style blacklists

These blacklists disallow sender domains (as part of the envelope sender) that appear in RHSBL blacklists.

Additional UCE Control Parameters

The set of additional UCE control parameters support other restrictions or features that are not part of Postfix's default functional range. Here are just a few of the restrictions available:

`default_rbl_reply`

Creates a default reply template to be used when an SMTP client request is blocked by a `reject_rbl_client` or `reject_rhsbl_sender` restriction.

`permit_mx_backup_networks`

Limits the use of the `permit_mx_backup` relay control feature to destinations whose primary MX hosts match a list of network blocks.

`rbl_reply_maps`

Specifies lookup tables with DNSBL reply templates indexed by DNSBL domain name. If no template is found, Postfix uses the `default_rbl_reply` template instead.

`relay_domains`

Instructs Postfix to accept mail for these domains, even though this server isn't the final destination.

`smtpd_sender_login_maps`

Specifies a user that is allowed to use a specific `MAIL FROM` address (envelope sender). To use this restriction, Postfix must know a username, so the client must identify itself with SMTP authentication.

Application Ranges

The key to using restrictions correctly is to understand what stage of the communication you can apply them to. Some restrictions don't make sense in certain stages. Table 7-1 lists restrictions by stage.

Table 7-1: Range of Application

Stage	Restriction
Client (IP address and/or hostname)	check_client_access reject_rbl_client reject_rhsbl_client reject_unknown_client
HELO/EHLO hostname	check_helo_access permit_naked_ip_address reject_invalid_hostname reject_non_fqdn_hostname reject_unknown_hostname
Envelope sender	check_sender_access reject_non_fqdn_sender reject_rhsbl_sender reject_unknown_sender_domain reject_unverified_sender
Envelope recipient	check_recipient_access permit_auth_destination permit_mx_backup reject_non_fqdn_recipient reject_unauth_destination reject_unknown_recipient_domain reject_unverified_recipient
DATA	reject_unauth_pipelining

Building Restrictions

Restrictions can become quite complex, and you can break your mail server in subtle (and not so subtle) ways by trying to tweak them without knowing what you're doing. Keep the following rules in mind when building your restrictions:

- Sloppy notation will render your restriction useless.
- The stage of evaluation makes a difference.
- The order of appearance within a restriction trigger is important. Preceding actions influence how further restrictions are evaluated.

Notation

As we mentioned earlier, restriction triggers are like empty boxes. However, filling them does not mean you just throw restrictions in and you're done.

```
restriction_trigger = conditional_restriction, customizable_restriction \
maptype:/path/to/the/map, general_restriction
```

Because a single restriction can easily exceed the reasonable width of a line, you can add whitespace to the beginning of each line that continues the preceding line so that Postfix will recognize the lines as a single parameter setting.

Furthermore, the commas separating the preceding restrictions are optional. Therefore, the following is equivalent to the preceding example (and much easier to read).

```
restriction_trigger =
    conditional_restriction
    customizable_restriction maptype:/path/to/the/map
    general_restriction
```

Moment of Evaluation

In general, Postfix does not evaluate and execute the restrictions based on a restriction trigger immediately after the corresponding SMTP communication step takes place. Instead, Postfix waits until the client sends the first envelope recipient. This delay exists because some mail clients keep trying to submit their message if the server rejects a command before they have finished sending at least one envelope recipient.

You can override this default by setting the smtpd_delay_reject parameter to no.

However, even though it is possible to track down these clients and build an exception list to ensure that they will not be interrupted, the best practice is to wait until all steps have been finished and set the restrictions to take effect after that. Not only do you reduce the complexity of your mail system, but you also collect more data about the mail delivery attempt.

To get an idea of how smtpd_delay_reject influences the evaluation of restrictions, have a look at Figure 7-2.

Influence of Actions on Restriction Evaluation

As described in the section "Customizable Restrictions," customizable restrictions use maps. When Postfix looks up a key in a restriction map, Postfix executes the value that corresponds to that key. A map could look like this:

```
10.0.0.1        PERMIT Private IP from VPN transfer tunnel
172.16.0        REJECT Private IP address cannot come from outside
168.100.1.3     DUNNO
192.0.34.166    OK
```

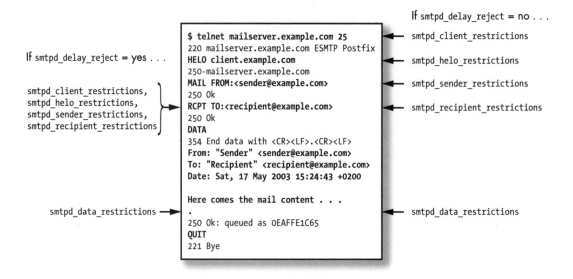

If smtpd_delay_reject = no ...

$ telnet mailserver.example.com 25 ← smtpd_client_restrictions
220 mailserver.example.com ESMTP Postfix

If smtpd_delay_reject = yes ...   HELO client.example.com ← smtpd_helo_restrictions
250-mailserver.example.com

smtpd_client_restrictions,   MAIL FROM:<sender@example.com> ← smtpd_sender_restrictions
smtpd_helo_restrictions,   250 Ok
smtpd_sender_restrictions,   RCPT TO:<recipient@example.com> ← smtpd_recipient_restrictions
smtpd_recipient_restrictions   250 Ok
DATA
354 End data with <CR><LF>.<CR><LF>
From: "Sender" <sender@example.com>
To: "Recipient" <recipient@example.com>
Date: Sat, 17 May 2003 15:24:43 +0200

Here comes the mail content . . .
smtpd_data_restrictions → .   ← smtpd_data_restrictions
250 Ok: queued as 0EAFFE1C65
QUIT
221 Bye

Figure 7-2: Influence of smtpd_delay_reject on restriction evaluation

The preceding map contains four different actions for customizable restrictions: PERMIT, REJECT, DUNNO, and OK. These values tell Postfix what to do with a client, sender, or recipient. Although there are several actions (see the access(5) manual page), these are the most common:

OK

There are no objections against the client and the message. Postfix stops evaluating restrictions in the current set of restrictions and moves to the next set.

PERMIT

Equivalent to OK.

REJECT

Reject the message immediately, ignoring any further restrictions. The message is ultimately rejected.

DUNNO

Stop evaluating the current restriction, but proceed to the next restriction in the current set of restrictions.

The order of restrictions within a set is important, because the first match that returns OK or REJECT immediately halts the evaluation of restrictions in the current set (with REJECT meaning that a client, sender, or recipient is ultimately rejected) Postfix reads and applies restrictions from top to bottom, or left to right if you write them in a single line. This is why it's easier to use the multiline notation for complicated restrictions. Imagine trying to read this restriction if it were all on one line!

```
smtpd_recipient_restrictions =
  check_recipient_access hash:/etc/postfix/recipients_restrictions,
  permit_sasl_authenticated,
  permit_mynetworks,
  reject_unauth_destination,
  reject_unauth_pipelining,
  reject_rbl_client relays.ordb.org
  permit
```

Figure 7-3 illustrates the restriction evaluation process and shows the action for each of the four values.

Slowing Down Bad Clients

Any client that causes a number of errors when talking to smtpd (for example, by triggering a REJECT in a restriction or causing a syntax error in arguments) causes smtpd to make a short pause before accepting further commands in that session. This serves as a defense against runaway client software.

You can tune this with several parameters. The smtpd_error_sleep_time parameter specifies the number of seconds to pause after each mistake (the default is one second). The smtpd_soft_error_limit parameter serves as a kind of tarpitting mechanism; when a remote SMTP client makes several mistakes, the Postfix SMTP server can insert additional delays before responding. Finally, you can abort the session based on the smtpd_hard_error_limit parameter.

These three parameters work together as follows:

- If a client causes errors and the total number of errors in the current SMTP session is below the value of smtpd_soft_error_limit, each error causes a delay of smtpd_error_sleep_time.

- If a client causes errors and the total number of errors in the SMTP session exceeds smtpd_soft_error_limit, each error causes a delay of the number of errors above the smtpd_soft_error_limit in seconds.

- If a client's number of errors exceeds smtpd_hard_error_limit, Postfix terminates the session.

For example, let's say that you configure the parameters as follows:

```
smtpd_soft_error_limit = 5
smtpd_hard_error_limit = 10
smtpd_error_sleep_time = 1s
```

If a client causes 11 errors in a single session, Postfix pauses for 1, 1, 1, 1, 1, 2, 3, 4, 5, and 6 seconds, respectively, and upon the 11th error, it disconnects.

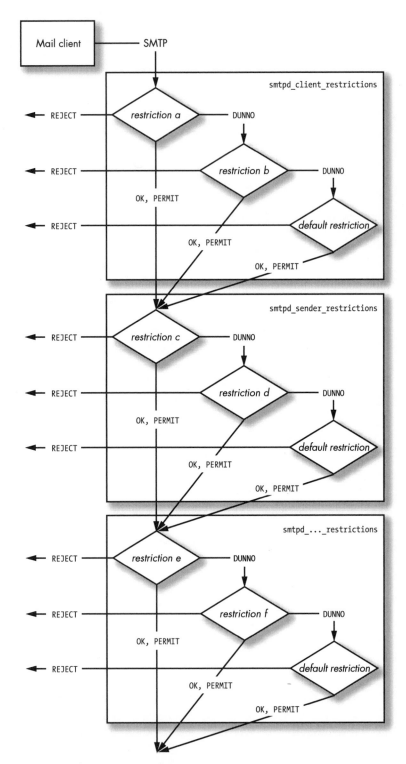

Figure 7-3: The restriction evaluation process

Restriction Classes

A restriction class is a special form of restriction trigger that is not predefined or bound to any particular stage of SMTP communication. You define them as you need them, and you trigger them by referring to them in maps of customizable restrictions.

For example, let's say that you have a customizable restriction map for checking envelope sender addresses, and you want to trigger another set of restrictions if the envelope sender matches example.com. In this case, you want to put this new set of restrictions in a new class named check_if_example.com_sender. First, declare the new class in your main.cf file.

```
smtpd_restriction_classes =
    check_if_example.com_sender
```

Now, also in main.cf, add some restrictions to your new class:

```
check_if_example.com_sender =
    check_sender_access hash:/etc/postfix/bounces
    check_sender_access hash:/etc/postfix/valid_example.com_senders
    check_sender_access regexp:/etc/postfix/nice_reject.regexp
```

As you can see, these new restrictions examine the envelope sender (although they could be anything appropriate for the current stage of the SMTP dialog).

Don't worry about the maps in these restrictions; you'll see how to define them later. We're still missing an important part, though. How do you activate check_if_example.com_sender?

To do this, you need a check_sender_access restriction in your smtpd_*_restrictions set. Let's say that you already have this set to the following map that accepts senders from foo.com and rejects those from bar.org (see the section "Influence of Actions on Restriction Evaluation" earlier in this chapter for valid actions):

foo.com	OK
bar.org	REJECT

To add the new restriction class, augment the map as follows:

foo.com	OK
bar.org	REJECT
example.com	check_if_example.com_sender

As you can see, the key to using restriction classes is finding the correct place to insert them in a customizable restriction's map.

8

USING MESSAGE TRANSFER RESTRICTIONS

Junk mail is war. RFCs do not apply.
—*Wietse Venema*

 Restrictions control the message flow, making decisions based on what the client transmits during the SMTP dialog. The number of situations in which restrictions can be used is seemingly immeasurable, so instead of listing all restrictions and all possible options available for those restrictions, this chapter describes the scenarios that frequently come up on the Postfix mailing list and in everyday use. For each scenario, we'll discuss the restrictions and options in depth to show you how to implement them and help you understand why they are implemented as they are.

How to Build and Test Restrictions

Before you start modifying the default restrictions, you should know exactly what you are trying to restrict. This isn't very difficult when you only toggle Boolean restrictions on or off, but it can get trickier if you want to restrict email from hosts that try to disguise their origin.

A common adage on the Postfix mailing list is "The log is your friend." It might seem difficult to imagine a mail log as a friend, but the log really comes in handy when gathering information for restricting email flow. Simply put, the mail log holds most of the information needed to build effective restrictions. Take a look at this series of log entries for an incoming message:

```
Apr 14 21:14:48 mail postfix/smtpd[31840]: 4F2A643F30:
  client=unknown[172.16.0.1] ❶
Apr 14 21:14:48 mail postfix/cleanup[31842]: 4F2A643F30:
  message-id=<002101c42254$792c2530$010010ac@stateofmind.de> ❷
Apr 14 21:14:48 mail postfix/nqmgr[31836]: 4F2A643F30:
  from=<test@example.com>, ❸
  size=666, nrcpt=1 ❹ (queue active)
Apr 14 21:14:48 mail postfix/smtpd[31840]: disconnect from unknown[172.16.0.1]
Apr 14 21:14:48 mail postfix/smtp[31844]: 4F2A643F30: to=<p@state-of-mind.de>, ❺
  relay=mail.state-of-mind.de[212.14.92.89], ❻
  delay=0, status=sent (250 Ok: queued as 97E70E1C65) ❼
```

The parts of the message are as follows:

❶ The client (IP and hostname) that delivered the message

❷ The Message-Id header

❸ The envelope sender (MAIL FROM command in SMTP dialog)

❹ The number of recipients

❺ The envelope recipient(s) (RCPT TO command in SMTP dialog)

❻ Where the message went

❼ The queue ID that the remote Postfix server assigned to the message

If your job is to restrict the transport of a message, and you need some more information to figure out what you're dealing with, the log is the place to get to know your "opponent."

Simulating the Impact of Restrictions

A good set of restrictions is rarely achieved on the first try. To get what you need, you typically have to go through several iterations of trial and error. To test your restrictions, you will need messages to run your restrictions against, and chances are that you do not have a test machine at your service and must develop your restrictions on the production server. Unfortunately, this presents the risk of having false positives and losing important email.

To solve this problem, Postfix has a warn_if_reject parameter for testing restrictions, which is similar to the WARN action in checks. By prepending this parameter to a restriction that you want to test, Postfix just logs the effect of the restriction, but does not reject the mail. Here's how you might use it to test reject_unknown_sender_domain.

```
smtpd_recipient_restrictions =
    permit_mynetworks
    reject_unauth_destination
    warn_if_reject reject_unknown_sender_domain
    permit
```

As soon as you set this parameter up, the mail log reports the "simulated" rejection like this:

```
Jun 25 16:10:52 mail postfix/smtpd[32511]: 8075015C02F: reject_warning: RCPT
    from sccrmhc11.comcast.net[204.127.202.55]: 550 <DickinsL@newfaces.gr>:
    Sender address rejected: Domain not found; from=<DickinsL@newfaces.gr>
    to=<example@charite.de> proto=ESMTP helo=<sccrmhc11.attbi.com>
```

After you're sure that the restriction works, you can remove the warn_if_reject parameter from your restriction. Further log entries will inform you that the restriction was successful by logging rejected messages:

```
Jun 25 16:11:23 mail postfix/smtpd[32511]: 8075015C02F: reject: RCPT from
    sccrmhc11.comcast.net[204.127.202.55]: 550 <DickinsL@newfaces.gr>: Sender
    address rejected: Domain not found; from=<DickinsL@newfaces.gr>
    to=<recipient@example.com> proto=ESMTP helo=<sccrmhc11.attbi.com>
```

Making Restrictions Effective Immediately

Postfix consists of several different daemons that load their configuration data upon startup. Some of the daemons run only for a short time and terminate in order to avoid excess resource utilization. However, other daemons do *not* restart unless you tell Postfix to do so.

These long-running daemons, qmgr and nqmgr (it's called nqmgr in older versions only, the new versions of Postfix use the new queuemanger by default, but in that case it's named qmgr—with the old queuemanager being oqmgr), play an important role in restricting email flow and will *not* notice configuration changes until the whole system restarts or you intervene manually. Therefore, you need to remember that whenever you change main.cf or master.cf, you must issue a **postfix reload** command to make the queue manager reload the configuration.

NOTE   *Theoretically, the changes will be picked up over time, because daemons will die and be reborn after max_use uses. Except, of course, in the case of qmgr, which never dies. Changes in options for qmgr always require a postfix reload. Allowing the changes to be adopted over time, however, can lead to some daemons using the old configuration while the others use the new configuration, which may not be ideal.*

Restriction Defaults

Postfix comes with a safe set of default restrictions that prevent your machine from becoming an open relay (or third-party mail relay). You can find out what the default restrictions are by telling postconf to print out the default settings for smtpd_recipient_restrictions like this:

```
# postconf -d smtpd_recipient_restrictions
smtpd_recipient_restrictions = permit_mynetworks, reject_unauth_destination
```

Postfix evaluates restrictions in the order that they're listed. In this case, if a client wants to relay a message, Postfix checks whether the connection came from a host within mynetworks. If that's the case (if the evaluation of permit_mynetworks returns OK), Postfix accepts the message for delivery.

If the client does not come from mynetworks, Postfix evaluates reject_unauth_destination. This restriction defeats relaying attempts by checking whether the message recipient is inside the final destination and relay domains that you configured for Postfix. If the recipient is not within those domains, reject_unauth_destination returns REJECT, and Postfix tells the client that it may not relay.

If Postfix feels responsible for the message destination, reject_unauth_destination returns OK, and Postfix evaluates the next restriction. However, there are no more restrictions in the list, so Postfix assumes an implied default of permit and accepts the message.

These two restrictions are the basics that protect your server from being an open relay, but they do not protect your users from spam, nor do they tell clients connecting to your server to behave properly. The rest of this chapter shows you how to make restrictions tougher.

Requiring RFC Conformance

Requiring proper behavior (conformance to the RFCs) from local and remote clients is the first step in running a tight ship. Not only does this ensure that your mail server circulates valid messages to other mail servers, but it also requires remote clients to behave properly. This can be useful in defending against spammers, who are always in a hurry, skirt the rules, and disguise identifying information.

This section shows you how to impose restrictions on the hostname, envelope sender, and envelope recipient to achieve RFC conformance.

NOTE   *The restrictions you see in here will not be used in* main.cf *in the order they are explained. This is intentional, and you'll see why in the section "Processing Order for RFC Restrictions" later in this chapter. For the moment, just add the restrictions as they appear in the example listings.*

Restricting the Hostname in HELO/EHLO

A good place to start is to have Postfix insist that clients introduce themselves properly when they want to send messages to or through your server. There are a number of restrictions that you can impose on the HELO/EHLO part of the SMTP dialog, from simply requiring that clients send a hostname to requiring that they send a valid hostname.

Requiring a Hostname

The Postfix smtpd_helo_required parameter requires all clients to issue either a HELO or an EHLO statement when starting SMTP communication. Both RFC 821 (ftp://ftp.rfc-editor.org/in-notes/rfc821.txt) and RFC 2821 (ftp://ftp.rfc-editor.org/in-notes/rfc2821.txt) mandate this handshake, but Postfix sets the parameter to no by default. Enable it by adding the following line to your main.cf file:

```
smtpd_helo_required = yes
```

After a configuration reload, Postfix will refuse messages from any client that does not introduce itself properly. You can test this by connecting to your server and trying to initiate a message transmission without the HELO statement. Here's how Postfix should interact when requiring a hostname:

```
$ telnet mail.example.com 25
220 mail.example.com ESMTP Postfix
MAIL FROM: <sender@example.com>
503 Error: send HELO/EHLO first
QUIT
221 Bye
```

Requiring an FQDN

The HELO/EHLO statement is nice, but clients are also required to submit their full hostname along with the handshake (for example, HELO client.example.com). Furthermore, the RFCs mandate that the hostname be a fully qualified domain name (FQDN).

NOTE *An FQDN does not necessarily exist in domain name service (DNS) records.*

Postfix will refuse messages from any client that does not submit an FQDN hostname if you set the reject_non_fqdn_hostname option inside smtpd_recipient_restrictions.

CAUTION *Be careful with this restriction. Some mail clients, such as Microsoft Outlook, use only the localpart of the name (e.g., client) by default, unless you configure the operating system to provide an FQDN hostname for its applications.*

When you add `reject_non_fqdn_hostname` to your list of `smtpd_recipient_restrictions`, it should look something like this in your `main.cf` file:

```
smtpd_recipient_restrictions =
  permit_mynetworks
  reject_unauth_destination
  reject_non_fqdn_hostname
  permit
```

Test the restriction by connecting to your mail server and issuing a simple hostname, as in this example:

```
$ telnet mail.example.com 25
220 mail.example.com ESMTP Postfix
HELO client
250 mail.example.com
MAIL FROM: <sender@example.com>
250 Ok
RCPT TO: <recipient@example.com>
504 <client>: Helo command rejected: need fully-qualified hostname
QUIT
221 Bye
```

Rejecting Invalid Characters in the Hostname

The RFCs say that hostnames sent with the `HELO`/`EHLO` statement should not only be FQDNs, but the characters used to build the hostnames must also obey the requirements of the domain name system. A valid domain name must contain at least the following elements:

- A top level domain (TLD), such as "com"
- A domain name, such as "example"
- A dot (.) separating the TLD and domain name

Any other hostname is not likely to resolve properly, making interaction between the client and the server difficult, if not impossible. You can tell Postfix not to speak with such clients by using the `reject_invalid_hostname` option in `smtpd_recipient_restrictions`. Here's an example of where you might put it:

```
smtpd_recipient_restrictions =
  permit_mynetworks
  reject_unauth_destination
  reject_non_fqdn_hostname
  reject_invalid_hostname
  permit
```

As before, test this by connecting from a remote host to your mail server and issuing an invalid hostname. The client introduces itself as "." in the following sample session.

```
$ telnet mail.example.com 25
220 mail.example.com ESMTP Postfix
HELO .
250-mail.example.com
MAIL FROM:<sender@example.com>
250 Ok
RCPT TO:<recipient@example.com>
501 <.>: Helo command rejected: Invalid name
QUIT
221 Bye
```

Restricting the Envelope Sender

The envelope sender must also contain an FQDN in the domain part, and
the envelope must belong to an existing domain. Envelope senders such as
sender and sender@example do not include the FQDN domain part. An example
of a complete envelope server is sender@example.com. Invalid addresses can
cause great confusion because the sender address of the message looks as if it
originated from the server. There are two things that can go wrong:

- An MTA that needs to bounce a message with an incomplete envelope
  sender would bounce to local users. The bounce wouldn't make it to the
  original sender.

- Postfix could try to "fix" the invalid address, creating an even worse situation. Because Postfix knows that the envelope sender must be an FQDN,
  it would run the trivial-rewrite daemon to canonicalize these email
  addresses by adding $myorigin to sender (resulting in sender@$myorigin)
  and $mydomain to sender@example (resulting in sender@example.$mydomain).
  Therefore, the envelope sender for messages coming from a remote
  server would be completely incorrect.

To prevent this, add the reject_non_fqdn_sender option to smtpd_recipient_
restrictions, as in this example:

```
smtpd_recipient_restrictions =
  reject_non_fqdn_sender
  permit_mynetworks
  reject_unauth_destination
  reject_non_fqdn_hostname
  reject_invalid_hostname
  permit
```

Test this by connecting from a remote machine to your mail server and
issuing an incorrect envelope sender. This example shows how the restriction will make Postfix reject messages from such a sender:

```
$ telnet mail.example.com 25
220 mail.example.com ESMTP Postfix
HELO client.example.com
```

```
250 mail.example.com
MAIL FROM: <sender>
250 Ok
RCPT TO: <recipient@example.com>
504 <sender>: Sender address rejected: need fully-qualified address
```

Mail from Nonexistent Domains

A responsible mail server does not accept messages from sender domains that do not exist, because it cannot contact the sender in the nonexistent domain if there is a delivery failure. Other configurations would cause a double bounce as soon as the MTA tried to notify the sender, and a message with a nonexistent sender domain would end up in the postmaster's mailbox.

NOTE *Mail servers have to deal with nonexistent domains because users sometimes mistype their mail addresses when configuring mail clients; spammers also use nonexistent domains to hide their origin.*

To protect recipients and postmasters from double bounces and ill-formed messages, add the reject_unknown_sender_domain option to your smtpd_recipient_restrictions configuration. For example, you can place it as follows:

```
smtpd_recipient_restrictions =
  reject_unknown_sender_domain
  permit_mynetworks
  reject_unauth_destination
  reject_non_fqdn_hostname
  reject_invalid_hostname
  permit
```

The following example shows how you might test the restriction (you're looking for the 450 error code that Postfix sends as a response to the MAIL FROM command):

```
$ telnet mail.example.com 25
220 mail.example.com ESMTP Postfix
HELO client.example.com
250 mail.example.com
MAIL FROM: <sender@domain.invalid>
250 Ok
RCPT TO: <recipient@example.com>
450 <sender@domain.invalid>: Sender address rejected: Domain not found
```

Restricting the Envelope Recipient

As a final step in forcing incoming connections to adhere to the RFCs, you can reject any message that has a nonexistent domain or user in the envelope recipient.

A mail server shouldn't accept any message for a domain that does not exist, because there is no way to deliver such a message. If the mail server accepts a message and bounces it back later, the user might think something is wrong with the mail server because it initially accepted the message.

Configuring your mailer to reject messages to nonexistent domains passes the problem back to the client or the user, where it originated. To set this up in Postfix, use the reject_unknown_recipient_domain option inside your smtpd_recipient_restrictions set, like this:

```
smtpd_recipient_restrictions =
  reject_unknown_recipient_domain
  permit_mynetworks
  reject_unauth_destination
  reject_non_fqdn_hostname
  reject_invalid_hostname
  permit
```

As usual, you can test it by sending a nonexistent recipient domain in a manual connection to the server. Here's an example where Postfix rejects a message because invalid.domain is not a valid domain:

```
$ telnet mail.example.com 25
220 mail.example.com ESMTP Postfix
HELO client.example.com
250 mail.example.com
MAIL FROM: <sender@example.com>
250 Ok
RCPT TO: <recipient@domain.invalid>
450 <recipient@domain.invalid>: Recipient address rejected: Domain not found
```

Mail to Unknown Recipients

You can configure Postfix to deliver messages for an unknown user in your domain to the postmaster. At first glance, this might seem like a good idea because the postmaster can examine and manually deliver these messages whenever possible.

Although this would theoretically constitute excellent customer service, setting up a default delivery target would probably result in a denial-of-service (DoS) attack on your mail server as soon as it became the target of a spammer's or worm's *dictionary attack*. In such an attack, the attacker attempts to deliver a message to existing recipients by sending messages to addresses using all possible combinations of letters. For example, the attacker could start with aa@yourdomain.com, then try ab@yourdomain.com, and go on through all two-letter combinations until reaching zz@yourdomain.com.

Not only is it difficult to winnow out the valid messages from the mess created by this kind of attack, but the server is also exposed to the risk of consuming too much bandwidth, CPU time, memory, and disk space, until your server finally caves in and stops servicing message transmission requests. For example, the Sobig.F virus overloaded many mail servers in August 2003.

Keep in mind that Postfix tries to provide the most reliable service possible. Reliability implies consistency, and that's why it rejects mail addressed to unknown users by default, without any manual intervention. This is great for a stand-alone Postfix installation, but it's also useful for a Postfix server running on a smart host that protects other mail servers.

Postfix determines the validity of recipients by consulting maps. There are two configuration parameters that tell Postfix where to find this information: local_recipient_maps and relay_recipient_maps. Both parameters expect one or more maps that contain valid recipients. The local_recipient_maps parameter defines valid local recipients, as shown in this example, which defines recipients in the Unix password file and alias maps:

```
# postconf -d local_recipient_maps
local_recipient_maps = proxy:unix:passwd.byname $alias_maps
```

On the other hand, relay_recipient_maps defines recipients for when Postfix is relaying messages to a final destination (such as a mailbox server):

```
# postconf -d relay_recipient_maps
relay_recipient_maps = hash:/etc/postfix/relay_recipients
```

When using relay_recipient_maps, take special care that Postfix knows all valid recipients for its relay target(s). If the destination happens to be a Microsoft Exchange server, consult Chapter 13 on how to extract the user map.

CAUTION *The use of* luser_relay *disables the* local_recipient_maps *parameter because it makes all local recipients valid. Likewise, a catchall wildcard entry in your* virtual_alias_maps *entries disables rejection of mail to nonexistent recipients because the wildcard renders all recipients valid. For example, the following map entry makes all recipients in* example.com *valid:*

```
@example.com    catchall@localhost
```

Mail to Unqualified Recipient Names

An address that is not fully qualified, such as recipient, contains the localpart of the email address. It's okay to accept these addresses for local recipients on a machine that receives mail for a single domain, but it is a big problem as soon as your mail server receives messages for another domain.

This is because the localpart leaves too much room for interpretation when standing on its own.

Let's say that you're an ISP for both example.com and example.net, two competing businesses. If you get a message for sales, where does that go to? Should it go to sales@example.com or to sales@example.net if email services for both are hosted on the same machine?

This is why you should reject addresses that aren't fully qualified. Don't assume responsibility for something you shouldn't have anything to do with. It's the sender's job to prepare the message for proper transmission, and this means specifying a unique recipient.

NOTE *There's just one exception: You must accept mail for postmaster in non-FQDN form.*

Postfix rejects messages to non-FQDN recipients as soon as you add the reject_non_fqdn_recipient option to the smtpd_recipient_restrictions parameter, as in this example:

```
smtpd_recipient_restrictions =
    reject_non_fqdn_recipient
    reject_unknown_recipient_domain
    permit_mynetworks
    reject_unauth_destination
    reject_non_fqdn_hostname
    reject_invalid_hostname
    permit
```

Test it by connecting to your mail server from a remote host and providing an incomplete envelope recipient. A session such as the following should be sufficient to verify that the restriction works:

```
$ telnet mail.example.com 25
220 mail.example.com ESMTP Postfix
HELO client.example.com
250 mail.example.com
MAIL FROM: <sender@example.com>
250 Ok
RCPT To: <recipient>
504 <recipient>: Recipient address rejected: need fully-qualified address
```

Maintaining RFC Conformance

You have probably noticed in this chapter that restrictions can become fairly complex. The dark side of restrictions is that the more complex they become, the higher the chance that you will specify one that makes your mail system malfunction (if not rendering it completely useless) by rejecting content that you must accept under all circumstances. The following sections show you how to avoid inadvertently locking some or all senders out. This is important, because you can accidentally exclude the senders that might be able to tell you that something is wrong with your configuration.

Empty Envelope Sender

First, never block the empty envelope sender (<>). This address belongs to MAILER-DAEMON, and the mail server uses it when sending bounces and status notifications. If you block it, remote servers can't tell your users if something goes wrong with messages they send.

CAUTION *Blacklists, such as dsn.rfc-ignorant.org, list mail servers that categorically block empty envelope senders, so mail servers that use these blacklists won't accept mail from such servers. (This is discussed later in the "Rejecting Blacklisted Sender Domains" section).*

All you need to do is treat the empty envelope sender as any other valid recipient and build good (antispam) restrictions to protect your recipients. Let the restrictions do the work, and if a message with an empty envelope sender comes in, accept it. After all, any sender address could be fake. . . .

Special Role Accounts

There are two addresses for which you must always accept messages on a mail server; they are required to run an RFC-compliant mail server:

postmaster

Always accept mail for postmaster; it's the clearinghouse for mail-related problems. Users must be able to contact the postmaster if they need help with mail (see RFC 2821 at http://www.rfc-editor.org/rfc/rfc2821.txt).

abuse

Accepting mail for abuse ensures that users can tell you of potential mail abuse originating from your mail server (see RFC 2142 at http://www.rfc-editor.org/rfc/rfc2142.txt).

Optionally, you should accept messages for the following addresses if you run certain servers (see RFC 2142; http://www.rfc-editor.org/rfc/rfc2142.txt):

webmaster

Accept mail for webmaster if you run a web server.

hostmaster

Accept mail for hostmaster if you run a nameserver.

You can accept messages for these recipients by using the check_recipient_access parameter in combination with a map, such as /etc/postfix/roleaccount_exceptions, that lists the recipients that are to accept messages. The map might look like this (the OK value for each map key tells Postfix that it's fine to accept messages for this recipient regardless of recipient restrictions):

```
# addresses that you must always accept
postmaster@    OK
abuse@         OK
```

```
# addresses that you should accept if you run DNS and WWW servers
hostmaster@    OK
webmaster@     OK
```

After setting up this file, convert it to a map with the **postmap hash:/etc/postfix/roleaccount_exceptions** command. Then, specify the map as a parameter to the check_recipient_access setting in your list of restrictions in main.cf. Here's an example setting:

```
smtpd_recipient_restrictions =
    reject_non_fqdn_recipient
    reject_non_fqdn_sender
    reject_unknown_sender_domain
    reject_unknown_recipient_domain
    check_recipient_access hash:/etc/postfix/roleaccount_exceptions
    permit_mynetworks
    reject_unauth_destination
    permit
```

After reloading Postfix, you're safe to proceed building more complex rules. The map with the exceptions is being queried after Postfix has checked for unauthorized relaying; thus it's safe to specify postmaster@.

Processing Order for RFC Restrictions

You might have noticed by now that the options added to smtpd_recipient_restrictions in the preceding sections weren't specified in the same order as the sections themselves. This is because the restriction options can interfere with each other if they aren't in the proper order. Have a look at the following listing:

```
smtpd_recipient_restrictions =
  reject_non_fqdn_recipient
  reject_non_fqdn_sender
  reject_unknown_sender_domain
  reject_unknown_recipient_domain
  permit_mynetworks
  reject_unauth_destination
  check_recipient_access hash:/etc/postfix/roleaccount_exceptions
  reject_multi_recipient_bounce
  reject_non_fqdn_hostname
  reject_invalid_hostname
  permit
```

The permit_mynetworks option denotes an important boundary between clients on your internal network and clients outside. Options that appear up to and including this point apply to both internal and external clients, but those below permit_mynetworks apply to external clients only.

The options that precede `permit_mynetworks` require basic RFC conformance from all clients, whether they are inside or outside your network.

The `reject_unauth_destination` option prevents your server from becoming an open relay. It's best not to specify any options that will allow messages to go through before you specify `permit_mynetworks`. After that it is good to follow up with `reject_unauth_destination` as soon as possible to make sure that there is no way an unauthorized host can use your server as an open relay.

Checks for SMTP AUTH should go between `reject_unauth_destination` and `permit_mynetworks`. Then, before specifying any more rejection options, use `check_recipient_access` to enable unconditional delivery to the special role mailboxes on your system.

Finally, after rejecting possible multiple-recipient spam bounce attempts and bogus envelope-recipient hostnames, you can accept messages with the `permit` option.

Antispam Measures

Spammers need to disguise their messages' origin unless they want to be taken to court. Usually they will fake the envelope sender or try to lull the receiving server to sleep by telling it their client is to be trusted—that it belongs to the local network. Restrictions can check and reject such messages. Furthermore, they can query blacklists, where spammers and other parties you don't want to receive messages from are listed. The following section shows you how to put such restrictions into effect.

Preventing Obvious Forgeries

Some spam software tries to disguise message origin by using your mail server's hostname as its own in the `HELO/EHLO` greeting. To Postfix, this seems like a paradox, because the only host that is allowed to use the server hostname is the host itself. However, Postfix would never connect to its `smtpd` daemon to send mail to itself unless it were configured incorrectly and a mail loop was created.

Adding these restrictions behind `permit_mynetworks` will make them apply only to external clients and not to proxy filters or local clients with incomplete SMTP implementations.

Therefore, you can safely decline SMTP communication with any client that greets your mail server with the mail server's hostname. To do this, first create a map file called /etc/postfix/helo_checks that contains variations on your hostname. Here are some examples that cover the hostname, the host's IP address, and the bracketed IP address that clients outside of the mail server should not use:

```
/^mail\.example\.com$/         550 Don't use my hostname
/^192\.0\.34\.166$/            550 Don't use my IP address
/^\[192\.0\.34\.166\]$/        550 Don't use my IP address
```

According to RFC 2821, an IP address all by itself is not a valid argument to the HELO handshake request. An IP address is allowed, as long as it is specified as [ipv4address] (enclosed in angular brackets) or as an IPv6 address, [ipv6:ipv6address], also enclosed in angular brackets. To be strict and refuse service to any client that sends an unbracketed IP address, add this line:

```
/^[0-9.]+$/                        550 Your client is not RFC 2821 compliant
```

To put the map in action, specify it (and its type) as an argument to the check_helo_access option in your smtpd_recipient_restrictions parameter. Here's how it might look:

```
smtpd_recipient_restrictions =
  reject_non_fqdn_recipient
  reject_non_fqdn_sender
  reject_unknown_sender_domain
  reject_unknown_recipient_domain
  permit_mynetworks
  reject_unauth_destination
  check_recipient_access hash:/etc/postfix/roleaccount_exceptions
  reject_non_fqdn_hostname
  reject_invalid_hostname
  check_helo_access pcre:/etc/postfix/helo_checks
  permit
```

To test this, connect to your mail server and issue your own name in the HELO greeting. You should get a rejection, as shown in this example session:

```
$ telnet mail.example.com 25
220 mail.example.com ESMTP Postfix
HELO mail.example.com
250 mail.example.com
MAIL FROM: <sender@example.com>
250 Ok
RCPT TO: <recipient@example.com>
550 <mail.example.com>: Helo command rejected: Don't use my hostname
QUIT
221 Bye
```

Bogus Nameserver Records

Postfix can reject messages if there is evidence that the nameserver records for the HELO domain, sender domain and recipient domain are forged or do not allow correct message transport. Here are some questionable things you might see in DNS records:

Bogus networks

Some mail servers claim to be from networks that Postfix cannot reach, including those of private IP networks that you're not using (see RFC 1918, ftp://ftp.rfc-editor.org/in-notes/rfc1918.txt), the loopback network, broadcast addresses, and multicast networks.

Spam havens

Spam havens are networks known to be owned by spammers or those that provide services to spammers. It's possible to reject all messages from such domains. You can look up spam havens or spam operations on ROKSO (the Register of Known Spam Operations, `http://www.spam-haus.org/rokso/index.lasso`).

Wildcard MTAs

Wildcard MTAs claim to be responsible for any domain, even for those that do not exist. Normally, this wouldn't be a problem, because you can refuse access involving unknown sender and recipient domains. Unfortunately, some domain registries got the bright idea that they could redirect unknown domain names to their own domain. This provides a valid A record to unknown domains, and therefore renders the restriction options `reject_unknown_sender_domain` and `reject_unknown_recipient_domain` useless.

NOTE   *The first domain registry to redirect unknown domains was VeriSign (`http://www.verisign.com`) in 2003. VeriSign abused its power over the .net and .com namespaces and redirected all nonexistent .com and .net domains to its own site (sitefinder.verisign.com). In addition, VeriSign set up its own mail service for unknown domains, which made it impossible to reject messages from unknown domains. This is an open invitation to spammers, and you can reject messages from wildcard MTAs blocking the MX host in wildcard domains.*

All of the preceding setups either provide bogus nameserver records or support spammers. To reject mail from such domains and networks, you can create a map file called `/etc/postfix/bogus_mx` that holds the IP addresses in nameserver records along with the type of response that you want to give to them (see Appendix C for a full list of responses). Here's an example map file:

```
# bogus networks
0.0.0.0/8            550 Mail server in broadcast network
10.0.0.0/8           550 No route to your RFC 1918 network
127.0.0.0/8          550 Mail server in loopback network
255.0.0.0/4          550 Mail server in class D multicast network
192.168.0.0/16       550 No route to your RFC 1918 network
# spam havens
69.6.0.0/18          550 REJECT Listed on Register Of Known Spam Operations ❶
# wild-card MTA
64.94.110.11/32      550 REJECT VeriSign Domain wildcard ❷
```

❶ This network was listed on spamhaus.org (`http://www.spamhaus.org/sbl/sbl.lasso?query=SBL6636`) as a network known to originate spam when we wrote the book.

❷ This host was known to act as a wildcard MTA at the time of this writing.

Since we're editing a CIDR type map, which is a sequential map type (see Chapter 5), you need not and cannot convert it using postmap. Postfix will use the file as is. Simply add the check_sender_mx_access option with the map as an argument to our smtpd_recipient_restrictions parameter. It might look like this:

```
smtpd_recipient_restrictions =
  reject_non_fqdn_recipient
  reject_non_fqdn_sender
  reject_unknown_sender_domain
  reject_unknown_recipient_domain
  permit_mynetworks
  reject_unauth_destination
  check_recipient_access hash:/etc/postfix/roleaccount_exceptions
  reject_non_fqdn_hostname
  reject_invalid_hostname
  check_helo_access pcre:/etc/postfix/helo_checks
  check_sender_mx_access cidr:/etc/postfix/bogus_mx
  permit
```

The restriction takes effect after reloading Postfix. You can see the restriction's effect in the mail log:

```
Sep 17 12:19:23 mail postfix/smtpd[3323]: A003D15C021: reject: RCPT from
  unknown[61.238.134.162]:
  554 <recipient@example.com>: Sender address rejected: VeriSign Domain
  wildcard;
  from=<alli.k_lacey_mq@joymail.com> to=<recipient@example.com> proto=ESMTP
  helo=<example.com>
```

You can check on the IP address with the host command:

```
# host -t mx joymail.com
# host -t a joymail.com
joymail.com has address 64.94.110.11
```

NOTE *This domain actually exists now; it looks like it was registered in October of 2003.*

Bounces to Multiple Recipients

In the "Empty Envelope Sender" section, you learned that you should not block empty envelope senders. There is one exception to this rule—you should block mail with an empty envelope sender sent to multiple recipients, because there is currently no known legitimate use of multi-recipient status notifications, so any such messages are likely to be illegitimate.

To reject messages from an empty envelope sender to multiple recipients, add the reject_multi_recipient_bounce option to your smtpd_recipient_restrictions list. It can appear just about anywhere in the restriction list, but the following is an example where it appears after the permit_mynetworks option.

```
smtpd_data_restrictions =
  reject_multi_recipient_bounce
```

As stated in the documentation, reject_multi_recipient_bounce can be used reliably only in smtpd_data_restrictions, when all the recipients are known.

You can test this with a manual connection, just as you did for earlier restriction options. Submitting an empty envelope sender and multiple recipients should result in a refusal of service, as shown in the following session:

```
$ telnet localhost 25
220 mail.example.com ESMTP Postfix
EHLO client.example.com
250-mail.example.com
250-PIPELINING
250-SIZE 10240000
250-VRFY
250-ETRN
250 8BITMIME
MAIL FROM:<>
250 Ok
RCPT TO: <recipient1@example.com>
RCPT TO: <recipient2@example.com>
550 : Recipient address rejected: Multi-recipient bounce
QUIT
221 Bye
```

Using DNS Blacklists

A blacklist DNS server is a server that tells you about resources (such as IP addresses, envelope senders, and domains) that are probably untrustworthy. Blacklists can be very useful for blocking mail sent from clients to your server if you choose the right blacklist. However, picking the wrong blacklist might result in your server refusing mail that you may consider legitimate. Be sure to check a blacklist's policy before using it. Any site running a blacklist should list the criteria that it applies when blacklisting a resource, and it should publish and provide a straightforward procedure for removing resources that no longer need to be blacklisted.

If you're looking for a blacklist, one place to start is dmoz.org (http://dmoz.org/Computers/Internet/Abuse/Spam/Blacklists).

CAUTION *All blacklists are based on the domain name service, meaning that Postfix must perform DNS lookups. Uncached DNS lookups can take up to a second, and if they time out, the rate at which the server can accept messages will drop considerably. Therefore, blacklist checks are relatively expensive in terms of latency. You should always use them as a last resort in your list of restriction options.*

Rejecting Blacklisted Clients

You can reject blacklisted clients using DNSBL (DNS-based Blackhole List) blacklists. Postfix has a `reject_rbl_client` restriction option that takes the FQDN hostname of the blacklist server as an argument. Here's an example of the option in use:

```
smtpd_recipient_restrictions =
reject_non_fqdn_recipient
  reject_non_fqdn_sender
  reject_unknown_sender_domain
  reject_unknown_recipient_domain
  permit_mynetworks
  reject_unauth_destination
  check_recipient_access hash:/etc/postfix/roleaccount_exceptions
  reject_non_fqdn_hostname
  reject_invalid_hostname
  check_helo_access pcre:/etc/postfix/helo_checks
  reject_rbl_client relays.ordb.org
  permit
```

After reloading Postfix, the new option takes effect.

NOTE *To see if a client is listed in a DNSBL list, invert the order of the four octets of the client's IP address (that is, change* `a.b.c.d` *to* `d.c.b.a`*), append* `rbl.domain` *(such as* `relays.ordb.org`*), and look up the result. If the host is blacklisted, you will get a response pointing to the original IP address, as in this example:*

```
$ host 2.0.0.127.relays.ordb.org
2.0.0.127.relays.ordb.org A 127.0.0.2
```

Multivalue Results

Postfix can handle this additional information (a host isn't just listed, but the IP address returned makes it possible to distinguish why it is listed). For example, the following configuration rejects messages from any host that maps to an A record of `127.0.0.2` in our imaginary `domain.tld` blacklist:

```
reject_rbl_client domain.tld=127.0.0.2
```

Rejecting Blacklisted Sender Domains

In addition to restricting mail from IP addresses, you can block mail from blacklisted sender domains. This kind of blacklist is called a right-hand-side blacklist (RHSBL). Configuring Postfix for an RHSBL involves the same procedure. The example in this section uses a special blacklist at `dsn.rfc-ignorant.org`:

> **`www.rfc-ignorant.org` mission statement:**
>
> We maintain a number of lists (at present `dsn`, `abuse`, `postmaster`, `bogusmx` and `whois`) which contain domains whose administrators choose not to obey the RFCs, the building block "rules" of the net.
>
> It is important to note that NOTHING requires ANYONE to comply with an RFC (pedantically a "Request for Comments"), however, the "cooperative interoperability" the net has enjoyed is based upon everyone having the same "rule book" and following it. A listing here simply implies that a site has chosen not to implement the conditions described in a particular RFC. It is, of course, up to other sites to decide for themselves whether or not they wish to communicate with sites that have not chosen to implement, say, RFC2142, and have a working `<abuse@domain>` address.
>
> —dredd, `www.rfc-ignorant.org`

There are many MTAs that do not accept mail in the ways that the RFCs mandate (for example, they might refuse an empty envelope sender), for a number of erroneous reasons, including these:

- bogus mail from anonymous senders not allowed
- empty sender disallowed (to combat the spam problem)

Comment to these error messages of non–RFC-compliant mail servers: Anybody can forge anybody's email address. You could be sending out email as `president@whitehouse.gov`, and it would be just as anonymous as an empty envelope sender.

Spam can be sent with arbitrary senders, but bounces can *only* be sent with the empty envelope sender.

Any mail server that blocks empty envelope senders prohibits its users from knowing that their mail may have been rejected by another mail server, because their server blocks the bounce sent by the other RFC-compliant server, which uses an empty envelope sender, just as described in the RFC:

RFC 2821 explicitly states that an MTA *must* accept mail with an empty return path (envelope sender), because "the use of the empty sender when sending a bounce prevents an undeliverable bounce from looping between two systems."

Postfix has a reject_rhsbl_sender restriction option that strips the local-part from any email address and uses the domain to query a blacklist (such as dsn.rfc-ignorant.org). If the client's envelope sender domain is in the blacklist, Postfix rejects the incoming message. Like other blacklist options, you should place this option at the end of the list, as in this example:

```
smtpd_recipient_restrictions =
  reject_non_fqdn_recipient
  reject_non_fqdn_sender
  reject_unknown_sender_domain
  reject_unknown_recipient_domain
  permit_mynetworks
  reject_unauth_destination
  reject_multi_recipient_bounce
  reject_rbl_client relays.ordb.org
  check_recipient_access hash:/etc/postfix/roleaccount_exceptions
  reject_non_fqdn_hostname
  reject_invalid_hostname
  check_helo_access pcre:/etc/postfix/helo_checks
  reject_rhsbl_sender dsn.rfc-ignorant.org
  permit
```

A reload puts the change in effect, and you can test this by connecting to your server and using an envelope sender from a domain listed at dsn.rfc-ignorant.org, as in this example (sender@example.com is the official test address):

```
$ telnet localhost 25
220 mail.example.com ESMTP Postfix
EHLO client.example.com
250-mail.example.com
250-PIPELINING
250-SIZE 10240000
250-VRFY
250-ETRN
250 8BITMIME
MAIL FROM:<sender@example.com>
250 Ok
RCPT TO: <recipient@example.com>
554 Service unavailable; Sender address [sender@example.com] blocked \
    using dsn.rfc-ignorant.org; Not supporting null originator (DSN)
QUIT
221 Bye
```

Manual Blacklist Check

Checking a domain in an RHSBL is similar to the procedure for checking an IP address, except that you don't have to reverse the order of any elements. Simply append the blacklist server name to the domain that you want to check, and do a DNS lookup.

The following is a check for a domain that's not in the blacklist:

```
$ host postfix-book.com.dsn.rfc-ignorant.org
Host postfix-book.com.dsn.rfc-ignorant.org not found: 3(NXDOMAIN)
```

A blacklisted domain will look like this:

```
$ host example.com.dsn.rfc-ignorant.org
example.com.dsn.rfc-ignorant.org has address 127.0.0.2
```

Exceptions for Blacklisted Sender Domains

If you want to reject mail from mail servers that do not follow the rules, but you need to maintain communication with a particular domain that would otherwise be rejected by your restrictions, you can create a list of exceptions. Use the check_sender_access option with a map to implement the exception.

First, create a file such as /etc/postfix/rhsbl_sender_exceptions containing users and domains you want to accept messages from. For example, the following file permits mail from all users from example.com and for the single user sender@example.org:

```
example.com              OK
sender@example.org       OK
```

With this file in place, use postmap hash:/etc/postfix/rhsbl_sender_exceptions to build the map. Then add the check_sender_access option immediately before the reject_rhsbl_sender option, as in this example:

```
smtpd_recipient_restrictions =
  reject_non_fqdn_recipient
  reject_non_fqdn_sender
  reject_unknown_sender_domain
  reject_unknown_recipient_domain
  permit_mynetworks
  reject_unauth_destination
  reject_multi_recipient_bounce
  reject_rbl_client relays.ordb.org
  check_recipient_access hash:/etc/postfix/roleaccount_exceptions
  reject_non_fqdn_hostname
  reject_invalid_hostname
  check_helo_access pcre:/etc/postfix/helo_checks
  check_sender_access hash:/etc/postfix/rhsbl_sender_exceptions
  reject_rhsbl_sender dsn.rfc-ignorant.org
  permit
```

This example used check_sender_access, *but here is the full list of exception options:*

- check_sender_access
- check_client_access
- check_helo_access
- check_recipient_access

You already saw check_helo_access *in the section "Preventing Obvious Forgeries." The Postfix documentation explains the remaining two.*

Verifying the Sender

The crown jewel of the Postfix antispam tools is sender address verification, which verifies that the envelope sender exists in the sender's domain: if the sender does not exist, Postfix does not accept the message.

Unfortunately, this feature is expensive because the verification process takes time and consumes additional system resources. These are the steps involved:

1. A client submits an envelope sender.
2. Postfix generates and queues a probe message to the envelope sender.
3. Postfix looks up the MX or A record of the envelope sender's domain.
4. Postfix tries to connect to the sender's mail server. If it cannot connect to the remote server, smtpd defers the decision of whether to accept the message by returning a temporary error code of 450 to the client. Meanwhile, Postfix keeps trying to verify the address.
5. Postfix initiates an SMTP session with the remote server.
6. Postfix submits the earlier envelope sender as the envelope recipient to the remote mail server.
7. Based on the remote server's response, Postfix can do one of two things:
   - If the remote mail server accepts the recipient (the original envelope sender), Postfix disconnects, destroys the probe message, and accepts the message from the original client.
   - If the remote mail server rejects the recipient (the original envelope sender), Postfix disconnects, destroys the probe message, and rejects the message from the client.

With address verification active, normal mail will suffer a short delay of up to nine seconds while Postfix checks the address for the *first* time. However, Postfix caches the status of an address, so subsequent messages have no delay.

If the verification process takes longer than nine seconds, smtpd rejects the mail from the client (sending machine) with a 450 reply. Normal mail clients will connect again after some delay, but hijacked proxies won't, because they're just relaying SMTP commands, and the person who's controlling the proxy won't want to waste any more time with the address.

Sender-Address Verification Configuration

To enable sender-address verification, add the `reject_unverified_sender` option to your `smtpd_recipient_restrictions` parameter, as shown in this example:

```
smtpd_recipient_restrictions =
  reject_non_fqdn_recipient
  reject_non_fqdn_sender
  reject_unknown_sender_domain
  reject_unknown_recipient_domain
  permit_mynetworks
  reject_unauth_destination
  reject_multi_recipient_bounce
  reject_rbl_client relays.ordb.org
  check_recipient_access hash:/etc/postfix/roleaccount_exceptions
  reject_non_fqdn_hostname
  reject_invalid_hostname
  check_helo_access pcre:/etc/postfix/helo_checks
  check_sender_access hash:/etc/postfix/rhsbl_sender_exceptions
  reject_rhsbl_sender dsn.rfc-ignorant.org
  reject_unverified_sender
  permit
```

There are several options other than `reject_unverified_sender` that you can add to your restrictions. However, the parameters come with reasonable defaults, and they serve to tune sender-address verification rather than configure it. The following subsections describe the most common changes to sender-address verification behavior. You can find additional tuning parameters in the `ADDRESS_VERIFICATION_README` file that comes with your Postfix installation.

The Probe's Envelope Sender

When Postfix generates the probe message to verify the sender in question, it must introduce itself to the remote server with an envelope sender of its own. You can configure this address with the `address_verify_sender` parameter. The default is `postmaster@$myorigin`.

If you'd like to set a different probe-envelope sender, add the `address_verify_sender` parameter to `main.cf`, as in this example:

```
address_verify_sender = sender@example.com
```

Of course, this sender must exist, because other servers might use the same sender-address verification against you.

NOTE   *The recipient address specified as a parameter for the `address_verify_sender` is exempt from any restrictions.*

Caching

By default, Postfix keeps verified senders in memory. If you reload or restart Postfix, you will lose them, unless you specify an optional database to permanently store the addresses. To use a database, set the `address_verify_map` parameter to a database path (make sure that you pick a filesystem that has *plenty* of space). Here's an example:

```
address_verify_map = btree:/var/spool/postfix/verified_senders
```

After a reload, Postfix creates the database and proceeds to add both positive and negative verifications. If you want to disable collecting the negative verifications, set the `address_verify_negative_cache` parameter in `main.cf` as follows:

```
address_verify_negative_cache = no
```

Selective Sender-Address Verification

As the load on your mail server increases, sender-address verification is more likely to become a bottleneck. At this point, you should switch to selective sender-address verification.

Selective sender-address verification works by creating a map of common envelope sender domains that spammers typically use. If an incoming envelope sender domain is in the map, Postfix verifies the sender, but otherwise it does not bother. Create a map file such as `/etc/postfix/common_spam_senderdomains`, and set the `reject_unverified_sender` parameter as the action to be taken if the envelope sender matches the domain. Here's an example of how such a file looks:

```
hotmail.com  reject_unverified_sender
web.de       reject_unverified_sender
msn.com      reject_unverified_sender
mail.ru      reject_unverified_sender
```

The access(5) manual page explains that the right side of this map is the name of a valid restriction or `smtpd_restriction_class`. In this example, Postfix does one of two things when a client initiates message transmission:

- If the sender's domain matches an entry in `common_spam_senderdomains`, the map lookup returns `reject_unverified_sender`, so Postfix verifies the envelope sender. If it's valid, `reject_unverified_sender` returns DUNNO, and Postfix evaluates the next restriction. If the address is invalid, Postfix rejects the message.
- If the sender domain does not match anything in `common_spam_senderdomains`, the map lookup fails, the selective evaluator returns DUNNO, and Postfix evaluates the next restriction without verifying the sender address.

After creating the map, convert it to a database using the `postmap hash:/etc/postfix/common_spam_senderdomains` command. Finally, replace the existing `reject_unverified_sender` option with the `check_sender_access` option and map argument. Here's an example that uses the `hash:/etc/postfix/common_spam_senderdomains` map:

```
smtpd_recipient_restrictions =
  reject_non_fqdn_recipient
  reject_non_fqdn_sender
  reject_unknown_sender_domain
  reject_unknown_recipient_domain
  permit_mynetworks
  reject_unauth_destination
  reject_multi_recipient_bounce
  check_recipient_access hash:/etc/postfix/roleaccount_exceptions
  reject_non_fqdn_hostname
  reject_invalid_hostname
  check_helo_access pcre:/etc/postfix/helo_checks
  check_sender_access hash:/etc/postfix/rhsbl_sender_exceptions
  reject_rhsbl_sender dsn.rfc-ignorant.org
  check_sender_access hash:/etc/postfix/common_spam_senderdomains
  permit
```

You can take this one step further and introduce criteria other than the envelope sender, such as content. Create another map named `common_spam_senderdomain_keywords` that includes domain name keywords to trigger sender-address verification, such as this example:

```
/sex/    reject_unverified_sender
/girl/   reject_unverified_sender
/sell/   reject_unverified_sender
/sale/   reject_unverified_sender
/offer/  reject_unverified_sender
/power/  reject_unverified_sender
```

Then add another `check_sender_access` option pointing to the map:

```
smtpd_recipient_restrictions =
  reject_non_fqdn_recipient
  reject_non_fqdn_sender
  reject_unknown_sender_domain
  reject_unknown_recipient_domain
  permit_mynetworks
  reject_unauth_destination
  reject_multi_recipient_bounce
  check_recipient_access hash:/etc/postfix/roleaccount_exceptions
  reject_non_fqdn_hostname
  reject_invalid_hostname
  check_helo_access pcre:/etc/postfix/helo_checks
```

```
check_sender_access hash:/etc/postfix/rhsbl_sender_exceptions
reject_rhsbl_sender dsn.rfc-ignorant.org
check_sender_access hash:/etc/postfix/common_spam_senderdomains
check_sender_access regexp:/etc/postfix/common_spam_senderdomain_keywords
permit
```

Restriction Process Order

Antispam protection is expensive from a system resource point of view. The following restriction listing shows how to order antispam options.

```
smtpd_recipient_restrictions =
  reject_non_fqdn_recipient
  reject_non_fqdn_sender
  reject_unknown_sender_domain
  reject_unknown_recipient_domain
  permit_mynetworks ❶
  (permit_sasl_authenticated)
  (pop-before-smtp)
  reject_unauth_destination
  check_recipient_access hash:/etc/postfix/roleaccount_exceptions
  reject_multi_recipient_bounce
  check_helo_access pcre:/etc/postfix/helo_checks ❷
  reject_non_fqdn_hostname
  reject_invalid_hostname
  check_sender_mx_access /etc/postfix/verisign_mx_access ❸
  check_sender_access hash:/etc/postfix/rhsbl_sender_exceptions ❹
  reject_rhsbl_sender dsn.rfc-ignorant.org ❺
  check_sender_access hash:/etc/postfix/common_spam_senderdomains ❻
check_sender_access regexp:/etc/postfix/common_spam_senderdomain_keywords
  permit
```

General rules to order "cheap" before "expensive" restrictions:

❶ Place all antispam options *after* permit_mynetworks so that they apply to external clients (clients not listed in mynetworks) only.

❷ You can reject any client that uses your server's hostname without any further investigation. It doesn't matter if they use a non-FQDN hostname or an invalid hostname.

❸ This option marks the beginning of expensive restrictions. check_sender_mx_access requires one or two DNS lookups. If you're running a caching nameserver, you can resolve DNS queries locally.

❹ This map goes in front of the blacklist option because it contains exceptions for users and domains that might otherwise be rejected.

❺ This option is expensive, requiring a query to a remote system (the DNS server for dsn.rfc-ignorant.org) that might be under a heavy load or temporarily out of order. That's why it comes close to the end of the restriction option list.

❺ The two most expensive actions come last. If triggered, Postfix must create a dummy message, attempt to deliver it, and register the result. Very expensive. Therefore, it is a last resort.

Uses for Restriction Classes

The example to follow in this section restricts envelope senders in two ways. First, it requires that mail from the outside *not* have a sender address inside your domain; and second, it states that mail from inside clients *must* contain a sender address inside your domain.

The idea is to let Postfix first check to see if an incoming client connection is from your network:

1. If the client is on your network, Postfix sends the client to a restriction class. This class contains a check for the envelope sender address.

    -   If the envelope sender matches your domain wildcard, the check returns OK. Postfix stops evaluating restrictions and allows the client to proceed.

    -   If the envelope sender does not match the domain wildcard, the next restriction option is *reject*, so Postfix refuses service to the client.

2. If the client does not belong to your network, Postfix does not use the restriction class. Instead, it moves along to the next restriction option, which checks the envelope sender address.

    -   If the client uses your domain as part of the envelope sender, Postfix refuses service.

    -   If the client does not use your domain as part of the envelope sender, it passes the test and moves along to the next restriction.

To implement what we just wrote about, create a map file containing a list of IP addresses and networks inside your network. You can name the file /etc/postfix/internal_networks; it should look like this:

```
192.0.34       has_our_domain_as_sender
192.168        has_our_domain_as_sender
192.168.1      has_our_domain_as_sender
```

Then, create another map file named /etc/postfix/our_domain_as_sender containing your domain wildcard and the empty envelope sender (remember that your server should accept this without question); this is the list of envelope sender domains that internal clients may use. The map file will look like this:

```
example.com    OK
<>             OK
```

Now, create a map file that contains the domains that external clients may not use in their envelope sender. For this example, we'll use the filename /etc/postfix/not_our_domain_as_sender, containing just one line:

```
example.com        554 Do not use my domain in your envelope sender
```

After creating maps for these two map files with the postmap command, set the restriction class and the required restriction options in your main.cf file:

```
smtpd_restriction_classes =
  has_our_domain_as_sender
has_our_domain_as_sender =
  check_sender_access hash:/etc/postfix/our_domain_as_sender
  reject
smtpd_recipient_restrictions =
  check_client_access hash:/etc/postfix/internal_networks
  check_sender_access hash:/etc/postfix/not_our_domain_as_sender
  reject_unauth_destination
  ...
  permit
```

As usual, you will need to reload the Postfix configuration to put the changes into effect.

9

HOW BUILT-IN CONTENT FILTERS WORK

Checks examine the content of a message and execute a predefined action based on the content. This chapter shows you the checks that are available and what actions Postfix provides for enforcing content control.

Checks complement restrictions. Whereas *restrictions* supervise the SMTP dialog, *checks* control the content of a message. At first, though, you might see checks as being very different from restrictions. Checks are easy to enable, but the syntax used to create search patterns can become rather complicated because checks use regular expressions to define search patterns.

Because Postfix focuses on being an MTA, the built-in checks are not designed to replace a full-featured content scanner; rather, they provide the means for simple tasks. Here are some of the things you can do with checks:

- Block messages generated by certain programs, such as your SAP mail gateway.
- Block messages with specific subject lines.

- Weed out messages containing potentially harmful attachments.
- Remove pieces of information from message headers.

NOTE   *If you have never worked with regular expressions before, you may need to spend some time learning the basics.* Mastering Regular Expressions, 2nd Edition *by Jeffrey E.F. Friedl is an excellent book on the subject.*

How Do Checks Work?

Checks scan messages for a set of search patterns. If a pattern matches any content in a message, an action is taken. Postfix can apply separate filters to distinct sections of a message; the sections currently supported by Postfix are as follows:

- Message headers
- MIME headers
- Message body parts, including attachments
- Message headers of attached messages

To create a set of checks, you define separate search patterns using separate maps, and then assign these maps to the different check parameters that apply to different sections. Postfix uses the maps with a built-in MIME parser to examine the content of a message. The parser works like the `egrep` command; it can only recognize plaintext words one line at a time. Here's how the process works:

1. The parser steps through a message line by line.
2. The parser decides which message section the current line belongs to.
3. If a check exists for the section, Postfix uses the assigned map to search the message for matching patterns.
4. If the search pattern matches, Postfix triggers an action, and the execution of other checks is discontinued. Therefore, the first match "wins."

As you might have guessed by now, checks are CPU-intensive, and you can also see that the order of search patterns in a map can become crucial, because an earlier match causes the check process to use less CPU time.

Applying Checks to Separate Message Sections

Postfix uses a separate configuration parameter for each message section it knows. The check parameters are as follows (note that they are not enabled in the `main.cf` file by default).

header_checks

These apply to the message header—that is, to everything from the first line of the message to the first blank line. This also includes headers that span multiple physical lines.

body_checks

These apply to the message body; the parser considers the body to be everything between headers.

CAUTION *Extensive body_checks commands can be very CPU-intensive, slowing down your machine noticeably, because a body check scans every line of a body segment and compares the line to every regular expression that you define in the body_checks map.*

To prevent excessive CPU overload, Postfix checks only the first 51,200 bytes of the current body segment by default. You can increase this limit with the body_checks_ size_limit parameter. You can also handle an increased load by delegating the content inspection to a different application on a separate machine by using the content_filter feature described in Chapter 11.

mime_header_checks

These apply to MIME headers in the top-level message headers, MIME entity headers, and to MIME headers in nested message RFC 822 message headers (see Figure 6-3).

nested_header_checks

These apply to headers of attached email messages except MIME headers. These checks work only on the headers of nested message/rfc822 messages, except for the MIME headers listed for mime_header_checks above.

What's So Special about These Parameters?

Postfix 2.*x* handles the body of a message as *n* body segments, and each section is marked with a MIME header. This MIME processing is enabled by default, but you can disable it using disable_mime_input_processing = yes in your main.cf file.

The MIME parser makes a decision for each line it reads: Does the line belong to a header or to a body segment? Postfix applies checks based on this decision. If a message segment has mail headers (that is, if it is an attached message of type message/rfc822), those headers are evaluated by nested_header_checks.

Anything within a segment after these nested headers is evaluated by body_checks, up to the limit specified by the body_checks_size_limit parameter. For example, if you have a message with five 100KB MIME segments (or attachments), Postfix checks the first body_checks_size_limit of *each* segment.

Postfix uses mime_header_checks to evaluate each MIME header (the start of every new segment). If there are mail headers after any MIME header, they are evaluated by nested_header_checks on every segment.

Figure 9-1 shows which checks are applied to each line of a message.

Figure 9-1: Postfix decides on every line of the message which check to apply

When Does Postfix Apply Checks?

A client transports a message after successfully completing the initial SMTP dialog. Thus, Postfix processes *_checks after the smtpd_*_restrictions have been processed. Figure 9-2 shows when the Postfix cleanup daemon takes care of checks.

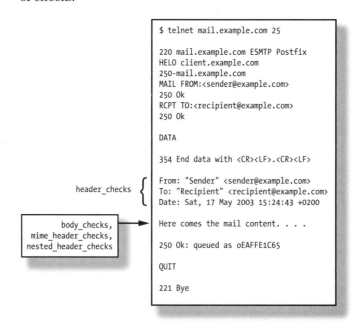

Figure 9-2: Checks are applied after restrictions and only to the content of the message

What Actions Can Checks Invoke?

You can define only one action per search pattern. Postfix currently supports these actions:

REJECT *[optional text...]*

Declines acceptance of the message. The optional text will be sent back to the client trying to deliver the message. Postfix will also record the text in the mail log.

IGNORE

Removes the line in the message that matches the search pattern in the check.

WARN *[optional text...]*

Causes Postfix to write a notice to the mail log. If there is optional text, Postfix logs it as well. Postfix will deliver the message without any modification.

HOLD *[optional text...]*

Places the message in the hold queue until the postmaster picks it up and decides what to do with it. Postfix logs the matched header/body line with the optional text.

DISCARD *[optional text...]*

Tells the mail client that the message has been successfully delivered, but silently deletes the message instead of transporting it to the final destination. If there is optional text, Postfix logs it together with the matched text in the mail log.

FILTER transport:nexthop

Sends the message to a filter (a service defined in master.cf that transports the message to another processing system, such as a virus scanner). You will learn more about defining filters in Chapter 11.

REDIRECT user@domain

Reroutes the message to the address specified instead of to the original recipient(s), and it overrides any FILTER action.

10

USING BUILT-IN CONTENT FILTERS

Postfix can examine the content of a message with tables of patterns and actions, as described in Chapter 9. This chapter shows you how to implement these patterns and actions. Keep in mind that checks are for simple content filtering. For more complicated tasks, refer to Chapter 11.

Checks look for characters in a message and can also modify a message. The names of the configuration parameters that enable checks end with _checks, and whether you use header_checks, body_checks, mime_header_checks, or nested_header_checks, all follow the same scheme:

1. Postfix examines a message line by line against a map of patterns made out of regular expressions (regexps) or Perl regular expressions (PCREs).

2. If a line matches the regular expression, Postfix takes the action defined for the expression *and* examines the next line of input.

This chapter's examples make heavy use of the line continuation syntax that Postfix offers to improve readability on paper. Namely, a line starting with whitespace characters continues *the preceding line.*

Checking Postfix for Checks Support

Postfix supports header or body filtering by default, but because it may use regexp and/or PCRE maps, you should find out whether Postfix supports both types or only regexps. To check which maps your Postfix supports, run **postconf -m** to report all the map types your system supports. The Postfix package in the following example supports both regexp and PCRE, among several other maps:

```
$ postconf -m

btree
cidr
environ
hash
nis
pcre
proxy
regexp
static
tcp
unix
```

All systems should support regexp tables by default. If your system has performance problems when it uses regexp-style maps (or even worse, if your system uses a buggy regexp implementation), you can install the PCRE libraries and headers and rebuild Postfix with PCRE support.

Building Postfix with PCRE Map Support

To build Postfix with PCRE support, you need the PCRE libraries and header files. You can get them in a development package from your distribution, or you can download the PCRE source code at http://www.pcre.org and install it by hand.

Configure Postfix with PCRE support by adding -DHAS_PCRE and a -I preprocessor flag for the PCRE include directory to CCARGS, and the PCRE library and path flags to AUXLIBS. For example, let's say that pcre.h is in /usr/local/include, and pcre.a is in /usr/local/lib:

```
$ CCARGS="-DHAS_PCRE -I/usr/local/include" \
  AUXLIBS="-L/usr/local/lib -lpcre" \
  make makefiles
$ make
```

NOTE   *Solaris needs* -R/usr/local/lib *as well.*

Safely Implementing Header or Body Filtering

Regular expressions can get to be quite complicated, and you might end up with a pattern that doesn't work, that matches more than you intended, or that you just don't understand anymore.

To help you debug patterns, Postfix offers the WARN action. If you use this action on the right side of your pattern, Postfix delivers the message if the expression matches, and it also writes a note to the mail log. After you're sure that your pattern works, you can safely change WARN to the desired action.

The safe procedure for adding checks is as follows:

1. Add your pattern to the map with WARN as the action.
2. Create a file that contains an expression that matches your filter pattern.
3. Verify that the pattern in the map matches the test pattern.
4. Set the check in the main Postfix configuration file.
5. Test it with real mail.

Adding a Regular Expression and Setting a WARN Action

The first step is to add the pattern you want to check to a map, and to define a WARN action for when the content of a message matches the test pattern. The example we'll use in this section tests for a filter pattern in a Subject header, but you can use the procedure described here for other headers and other *_checks parameters.

Add the filter pattern to the /etc/postfix/header_checks file. This file holds the map for header_checks. Here's an example:

```
/^Subject: FWD: Look at pack from Microsoft/
  WARN Unhelpful virus warning
```

Creating a Test Pattern

All you need to do to create a test pattern is put a matching message in a file such as /tmp/testpattern. The following will do for this example:

```
From: dingdong@example.com
Subject: FWD: Look at pack from Microsoft
blah blah
```

Does the Regular Expression Match the Test Pattern?

Test your filter pattern by feeding the checks map and the test pattern to postmap. For example, run this command:

```
$ postmap -q - regexp:/etc/postfix/header_checks < /tmp/testpattern
```

If it works, the command should print the matching line in the test pattern, like this:

```
Subject: FWD: Look at pack from Microsoft          WARN Unhelpful virus warning
```

If the pattern doesn't match, the `postmap` command doesn't print anything.

Setting the Check in the Main Configuration

If everything looks good so far, you can edit your `main.cf` file to use the file containing the `header_checks` you just created and tested:

```
header_checks = regexp:/etc/postfix/header_checks
```

Reload Postfix and send a test message containing the same test pattern.

Testing with Real Mail

To test the filter with real mail, feed your earlier test pattern to Postfix. This command will do it:

```
$ /usr/sbin/sendmail recipient@example.com < /tmp/testpattern
```

Now, examine your mail log to verify that Postfix logged the warning for the test pattern. The second line in the following log excerpt is the warning message:

```
Mar 30 17:17:52 mail postfix/pickup[2455]: 53CAB633B3: uid=7945 from=<sender@example.com>
Mar 30 17:17:52 mail postfix/cleanup[2461]: 53CAB633B3: warning: header Subject: FWD: Look at
   pack from Microsoft from local; from=<sender@example.com> to=<recipient@example.com>:
   Unhelpful virus warning
Mar 30 17:17:52 mail postfix/cleanup[2461]: 53CAB633B3:
   message-id=<20040330151752.53CAB633B3@mail.example.com>
Mar 30 17:17:52 mail postfix/qmgr[2456]: 53CAB633B3: from=<sender@example.com>, size=346,
   nrcpt=1 (queue active)
```

After you're confident that your filter pattern works, you can safely change the action from `WARN` to an action that actually does something, such as `REJECT` or `DISCARD`.

Checking Headers

Postfix can perform a variety of actions with `header_checks`, such as rejecting or holding messages, removing headers, or discarding, redirecting, or filtering messages. This section discusses how to implement those actions.

Rejecting Messages

Postfix can reject messages using the REJECT action. You can use this action to block messages that match a pattern, such as those that contain a particular Subject header.

The rejection prevents the messages from entering your system, and therefore keeps them away from a computationally expensive virus checker, spam detector, or (possibly worse) your users. We'll look at a few examples.

This pattern rejects useless virus warnings generated by ScanMail (which always warns the sender, even if the virus fakes the sender address):

```
/^Subject: ScanMail Message: To Sender, sensitive content found and action/
    REJECT Unhelpful virus warning
```

If you'd like to block messages with an incorrect Undisclosed-recipients header, you can use the following pattern. This matches the situation where To: <Undisclosed Recipients> occurs in the headers (with or without the brackets, with or without the final "s" at the end). (A correct Undisclosed-recipients header would be To: undisclosed-recipients:;.)

```
/^To:.*<?Undisclosed Recipients?>?$/
    REJECT Wrong undisclosed recipients header
```

This pattern is best described by its comment and accompanying message:

```
#
# Spam that contains Subject: something     565876
#
/^Subject:.*[[:space:].]{5,}\(?#?[[:digit:]]{2,}\)?$/
    REJECT More than 5 whitespaces and a number follow the Subject:
```

We've never seen To:...<> in headers of a valid message:

```
/^To:.*<>/
    REJECT To: <> in headers
```

Finally, some subject lines are just dead ringers for fraud spam. You should get the idea from these four patterns. (Using different numbers for each warning message makes it easier to debug false positives.)

```
#
# Certain Subject lines are indicative of fraud spam.
#
/^Subject:.*is NOT being SEEN/          REJECT fraud spam #1
/^Subject:.*URGENT BUSINESS RELATIONSHIP/ REJECT fraud spam #2
/^Subject:.*Confidential Proposal/       REJECT fraud spam #3
/^Subject: SEX-FLATRATE/                 REJECT fraud spam #4
```

Holding Delivery

Postfix can hold the delivery of messages with the HOLD action. You can use this to put suspicious messages "on hold" for further inspection. To look at the messages, use postcat, and to let a message through, use postsuper -H. If you'd like to delete a message from the Postfix queue, use postsuper -d.

Here's a pattern that matches any message containing a Subject header starting with Subject: [listname]. One use of this to hold mail to all users from internal mailing lists until the after-business hours, when the system is not in full use:

```
/^Subject: \[listname\]/
    HOLD
```

Here's a pattern that holds messages using a lone carriage return in MIME headers. Most of these messages are viruses and spam, with the few exceptions being from broken Windows installations of SquirrelMail:

```
/\r/
    HOLD Lone CR in headers indicates virus or spam!
```

Removing Headers

If you'd like to remove lines from headers, use the IGNORE action. You can use this to hide information written to headers, such as the kind of MUA you use, or to prune the Received headers that your internal mail servers, firewalls, or virus scanners might add. Here's one that removes the Received headers added by a program Postfix had delegated the email to do something with it by means of the content_filter directive (for example, from amavisd-new):

```
/^Received: from localhost/
    IGNORE
```

Here's another that removes the Sender header—some versions of Outlook behave strangely when replying to a message that contains this header:

```
/^Sender:/
    IGNORE
```

Discarding Messages

Postfix can silently discard messages using the DISCARD action. For example, you might want messages with a certain subject line to be removed without anybody taking notice. Here's a silly example.

```
/^Subject:.*deadbeef/
    DISCARD No dead meat!
```

When Postfix discards a message, it logs the action as usual. For example, you might see this in your mail log:

```
Apr  9 23:14:28 mail postfix/cleanup[11580]: BB92B15C009: discard: header Subject: deadbeef
    from client.example.com[10.0.0.1]; from=<sender@example.com> to=<recipient@example.com>
    proto=ESMTP helo=<client.example.com>: No dead meat!
```

Redirecting Messages

Postfix can reroute messages to another recipient using the REDIRECT action if a pattern in the headers and the body matches. Here's an example that gets the point across (though we really don't recommend it):

```
/Subject:.*deadbeef/
    REDIRECT bigbrotheriswatchingyou@example.com
```

In the mail log, a redirected message will look like this:

```
Apr  9 23:20:38 mail postfix/smtpd[11873]: 9305215C009: client=client.example.com[10.0.0.1]
Apr  9 23:20:38 mail postfix/cleanup[11865]: 9305215C009: redirect: header Subject: deadbeef
    from client.example.com[10.0.0.1]; from=<sender@example.com> to=<recipient@example.com>
    proto=ESMTP helo=<client.example.com>: bigbrotheriswatchingyou@example.com
Apr  9 23:20:38 mail postfix/cleanup[11865]: 9305215C009:
    message-id=<20040409212038.GK3406@example.com>
Apr  9 23:20:38 mail postfix/qmgr[11857]: 9305215C009: from=<sender@example.com>, size=1111,
    nrcpt=1 (queue active)
Apr  9 23:21:08 mail postfix/smtp[11874]: 9305215C009:
    to=<bigbrotheriswatchingyou@example.com>,
    orig_to=<recipient@example.com>, relay=none, delay=30, status=deferred (connect to example.com
    [192.0.34.166]: Connection timed out)
```

Filtering Messages

Postfix can route messages to a content_filter (see Chapter 11) using the FILTER action. For example, you can redirect certain classes of mail to different kinds of transports based upon their headers.

This action overrides content_filter settings in your main.cf file and requires you to configure different cleanup servers as well—one before the filter, and one after the filter. Header_checks and body_checks must be turned off in the second cleanup server, or you will create a loop! See Chapter 12 for more information on dealing with this problem (look for no_header_body_checks and receive_override_options). The first of the following patterns doesn't send a message to a filter, and the second one does.

```
/^To:.*@example\.org/    FILTER nofilter:dummy
/^To:.*@example\.com/    FILTER virusfilter:dummy
```

NOTE   *Keep in mind that this is just an example. You should not use it on a production*
server! One message destined to recipients in both domains would match the first regu-
lar expression and would thus never be filtered (the first match wins); the second action
would never be taken.

Filtered messages produce these sorts of messages in the mail log:

```
Apr  9 23:34:12 mail postfix/cleanup[12543]: 2B97315C00D: filter: header To:
   nofilter@example.com from client.example.com[10.0.0.1]; from=<sender@example.com>
   to=<nofilter@example.com> proto=ESMTP helo=<client.example.com>: nofilter:dummy
Apr  9 23:38:00 mail postfix/cleanup[12543]: 2299815C00E: filter: header To:
   virusfilter@example.com from client.example.com[10.0.0.1]; from=<sender@example.com>
   to=<virusfilter@example.com> proto=ESMTP helo=<client.example.com>: virusfilter:dummy
```

Checking MIME Headers

MIME headers apply to files attached to a message. By default, the
header_checks map is used for scanning MIME headers for patterns, unless
you define a separate map and tell Postfix to use it with the mime_header_checks
parameter.

NOTE   *It makes sense to define separate maps when you want to keep your mime_header_checks*
map small as possible, only using the MIME header patterns if Postfix detects that
there's an attachment within the message.

First you need to create a map file to hold your MIME header patterns.
Let's say you pick /etc/postfix/mime_header_checks, and it contains the
following checks:

```
# Files blocked by their suffix
/name=\"(.*)\.(386|bat|bin|chm|cmd|com|do|exe|hta|jse|lnk|msi|ole)\"$/
   REJECT Unwanted type of attachment $1.$2
/name=\"(.*)\.(pif|reg|rm|scr|shb|shm|shs|sys|vbe|vbs|vxd|xl|xsl)\"$/
   REJECT Unwanted type of attachment $1.$2
```

In this example, Postfix looks for MIME headers that contain name="
followed by an arbitrary number of characters, followed by a literal dot (.).
A large submatch enclosed in parentheses follows, which contains several
prohibited extensions separated by a vertical bar (|). The regular expression
ends with the literal quote (\"), which also must be at the end of the line ($).

The action on the right side makes use of the optional text behind the
REJECT. In this example, the two submatches are being referenced with $1 (for
the first submatch—(.*)) and $2 (for the file extension).

So, if somebody sends an attachment named `image.pif`, then the mime header line in the mail looks somewhat like this:

```
filename="image.pif"
```

and the error message constructed from this will be

```
Unwanted type of attachment image.pif
```

because $1 equals image, and $2 equals `pif`.

Now add the `mime_header_checks` parameter to `main.cf` file, giving it the path to your map:

```
mime_header_checks = pcre:/etc/postfix/mime_header_checks
```

After reloading Postfix, the `mime_header_checks` parameter becomes effective.

Checking Headers in Attached Messages

Postfix can apply separate actions to headers that appear in messages that are attached to a message. By default, any `header_checks` parameter will take care of these, but if you want to create a separate map (to save CPU cycles or to create exceptions), you can use the `nested_header_checks` parameter to define a separate map.

Like the other kinds of checks, you should create a separate map file, such as `/etc/postfix/nested_header_checks`, to hold your checks. Here's a sample that logs a message ID in a nested header:

```
/^Message-Id:/   WARN Nested Message-Id:
```

Now, add the `nested_header_checks` parameter to your `main.cf` file:

```
nested_header_checks = pcre:/etc/postfix/nested_header_checks
```

After reloading Postfix, you should be able to find log entries like this one:

```
Apr 14 13:17:55 mail postfix/cleanup[32397]: 59C3115C02A: warning: header Message-ID:
    <DIDL27HL1L4H87CA@example.com> from mgate22.so-net.ne.jp[210.139.254.169];
    from=<> to=<recipient@example.com> proto=ESMTP helo=<mgate22.so-net.ne.jp>: Nested Message-Id:
```

NOTE *The example in this section isn't really useful, because neither we nor the mailing list could come up with a real-world scenario. If you need `nested_header_checks`, you'll probably know it.*

Checking the Body

Scanning body parts is useful when you need to detect a pattern inside a body part in order to raise an action. Like the other checks, you examine the content for a given pattern using the body_checks parameter in combination with a map that holds patterns and appropriate actions.

CAUTION *Body checks apply to all messages, both incoming and outgoing, and to all senders and recipients. Therefore, they also apply to mail sent to abuse and postmaster.*

If you implement a check for spam, people complaining about spam that was supposedly sent from your networks cannot reach abuse and postmaster if their complaints contain the original spam that they received. You cannot override checks for certain users in the current version of Postfix.

Start out with the usual map file, such as /etc/postfix/body_checks. Here are some patterns and actions:

```
# Skip over base 64 encoded blocks. This saves lots of CPU cycles.
# Expressions by Liviu Daia, amended by Victor Duchovni.
~^[[:alnum:]+/]{60,}\s*$~        OK
```

The preceding pattern matches base64-encoded blocks. Note that a tilde (~) instead of the usual slash (/) is being used to delimit the regular expression, making it unnecessary to escape the slash within the regular expression.

Here are some patterns that contain known and unique patterns of spam messages; Postfix will reject them:

```
# SPAM
/(AS SEEN ON NATIONAL TV|READ THIS E-MAIL TO THE END)/
    REJECT Spam #1
/We are shanghai longsun electrical alloy/
    REJECT Chinese spammer from hell
/Do you want EVERYONE to know your business/
    REJECT Spam #2
/(Zainab|San?ni) Abacha/
    REJECT Nigeria spam
/MILITARY HEAD OF STATE IN NIGERIA/
    REJECT Nigeria fraud spam
/antivirus\.5xx\.net/
    REJECT Virus hoax (0190-dialer)
/MOSE CHUKWU/
    REJECT Business fraud spam #1
/Ahmed Kabbah/
    REJECT Business fraud spam #2
/Godwin Igbunu/
    REJECT Business fraud spam #3
/I PRESUME THIS EMAIL WILL NOT BE A SURPRISE TO YOU/
    REJECT Business fraud spam #4
```

```
/http:\/\/www\.a1-opportunity4u\.com\/euro2/
    REJECT Business fraud spam #5
/http:\/\/66.151.240.30\//
    REJECT Spam of the worst kind
/http:\/\/members.tripod.com.br\/lev3irkd/
    REJECT Spam of the worst kind II
```

Messages containing the following patterns will be rejected; the envelope sender will receive a bounce message pointing toward a hoax database.

```
# Hoaxes
/jdbgmgr\.exe/
    REJECT Virus hoax!
/ready to dictate a war/
    REJECT Hoax: http://www.tu-berlin.de/www/software/hoax/unicwash.shtml
/inquiries@un\.org/
    REJECT Hoax: http://www.tu-berlin.de/www/software/hoax/unicwash.shtml
/UNO is ready to receive signatures/
    REJECT Hoax: http://www.tu-berlin.de/www/software/hoax/unicwash.shtml
/Third World War/
    REJECT Hoax: http://www.tu-berlin.de/www/software/hoax/unicwash.shtml
```

Sometimes you might want to use body_checks as an immediate measure to reject malicious messages if your mail virus scanner does not recognize the virus yet. Remember to remove the pattern as soon as your scanner can deal with the virus:

```
## Virus
# Win32.Netsky.V
/The processing of this message can take a few minutes\.\.\.\./
    REJECT Win32.Netsky.V
/Converting message. Please wait\.\.\.\./
    REJECT Win32.Netsky.V
/Please wait while loading failed message\.\.\.\./
    REJECT Win32.Netsky.V
/Please wait while converting the message\.\.\.\./
    REJECT Win32.Netsky.V
```

After you have your map file in place, add the body_checks parameter to your main.cf file:

```
body_checks = regexp:/etc/postfix/body_checks
```

As before, you need to reload Postfix to activate the body checks.

11

HOW EXTERNAL CONTENT FILTERS WORK

Be liberal in what you accept, and conservative in what you send.
—Jon Postel, Internet pioneer (1943–1998)

The built-in filters described in the previous chapters are meant to solve simple problems; more sophisticated filtering has to be delegated to external software.

You can make Postfix run content-inspection applications before or after it queues messages. When mail is filtered before it is queued, Postfix can leave the responsibility for notifying the sender with the client. When mail is filtered after it is queued, responsibility is with Postfix.

This chapter outlines the process of delegation. You'll see how to configure the Postfix daemon architecture to send messages to external filtering mechanisms and how to let them reenter the Postfix system for final delivery once they've been successfully filtered.

External content filters pick up where built-in header and body filters leave off; not only do they allow external applications to inspect and reject messages, but they also allow the applications to modify message content. These are some typical tasks for filters:

- Adding disclaimers
- Scanning for viruses and worms
- Detecting spam
- Archiving mail

Postfix has two filter mechanisms named content_filter and smtpd_proxy_filter that are similar in spirit, but differ in their capabilities and the way they process content. Table 11-1 lists the differences between the two filter types.

Table 11-1: Filter Differences

Filter Name	Transports	Rejection Behavior
content_filter	smtp, lmtp, pipe	Rejects after queuing
smtpd_proxy_filter	smtp	Rejects before queuing

This chapter explains these differences in detail and will help you decide which filter type best fits your situation.

When Is the Best Moment to Filter Content?

The RFC Internet standards say that a mail server *must* decide whether to accept or reject a message no later than the DATA stage of the SMTP dialog. Unfortunately, this leaves little time for a mail server to inspect the content of a message, because mail clients implement a relatively short timeout to protect against getting stuck communicating with a malfunctioning mail server. For example, the Postfix SMTP client timeout is defined by the smtp_data_done_timeout parameter, which is very tolerant and defaults to 600s.

If the mail server finishes looking at the content *before* the client runs into the timeout, everything works fine, because the server can notify the client of its decision about accepting the message. However, if the server is too slow, the client goes away and tries again later, and chances are that the next attempt will be just as unsuccessful.

The Postfix content_filter implementation avoids hiccups by processing content inspection differently:

1. The mail client sends the content during the DATA stage.
2. The Postfix server accepts and queues the message. The client presumes that transmission was successful.

3. The queue manager inspects the mail and schedules delivery according to the content_filter entry.

4. Postfix hands the message to an external application.

5. The external application takes responsibility for delivering the message. The external application could do any of the following with the message:

   - Accept the message and hand it back to Postfix for delivery.

   - Accept the message and hand it to another application or server.

   - Drop or bounce the message.

The second filter (smtpd_proxy_filter) handles mail differently:

1. The mail client sends the content during the DATA stage.

2. The Postfix smtpd daemon proxies the SMTP commands and the content to an external application.

3. The external application sends SMTP responses back to the Postfix smtpd daemon, and smtpd then passes them on to the mail client.

This filter may have problems with mail client timeouts and does not scale to many concurrent mail client connections. This is because the smtpd_proxy_filter has no queue mechanism to schedule content filtering. Without a queue mechanism, the external application needs to start work immediately on each message that Postfix receives. As a result, you can have a severe slowdown if the external application cannot get its work done as quickly as messages come in. This is likely to be a problem with spam detection or virus scanning applications, which often require time-consuming unpacking and decoding of attachments.

Both approaches have disadvantages:

- content_filter generates extra traffic because Postfix initially accepts messages before processing. This could result in a bounce later on, if the filter application decides to reject the message.

- smtpd_proxy_filter rejects unwanted content early on, but it does not scale well and may not be fast enough to get the job done.

Filters and Address Rewriting

When rewriting addresses in the mail header, you need to think about where to apply filters. In particular, you need to decide whether to make Postfix rewrite addresses (e.g., due to virtual_alias_maps) before or after filtering.

If you choose to rewrite addresses before filtering, you run the risk of using internal addresses for bounces and warnings. For example, a warning caused by a message to moe_helden@example.com might be bounced with an address such as mh123@mailbox.example.com.

Therefore, it is our view that you should make Postfix rewrite addresses (by means of virtual_alias_maps or canonical_maps) *after* reinjecting mail back into the Postfix queue for final delivery. This allows an external application (such as a virus scanner) to see the original recipients and generate appropriate warnings before Postfix rewrites the addresses.

There are two ways to disable address mapping (virtual alias expansion, canonical mapping, address masquerading, and so on) before filtering. One way is to set the following option in main.cf:

```
receive_override_options = no_address_mappings
```

You can also turn off address rewriting in master.cf just for the daemon that accepts the mail from the network (which is usually smtpd):

```
smtp     inet n     -     n     -     -     smtpd
  -o content_filter=foo:[127.0.0.1]:54321
  -o receive_override_options=no_address_mappings
  ...
```

After the filter processes the message, the message is usually reinjected into the Postfix queue. This is the right time to perform address manipulation, and to do this, you will need an additional smtpd that accepts filtered mail. Instead of using the receive_override_options=no_address_mappings setting, this extra smtpd will use receive_override_options=no_unknown_recipient_checks. You'll see more details about content_filter and smtpd_proxy_filter in the following sections.

content_filter: Queuing First, Filtering Later

To configure a mailer with the content_filter mechanism, you normally need two smtpd instances (see Figure 11-1). The first smtpd accepts unfiltered messages and uses content_filter to delegate messages to the external filtering application. The second smtpd instance listens for connections from the external application so that messages can reenter the Postfix queue system for further treatment.

CAUTION *Do not configure the second instance to run the content_filter application that the first instance runs. This would create an infinite loop, where Postfix would send the message to the filtering application, and the message would come back into the Postfix queue at the same place as before.*

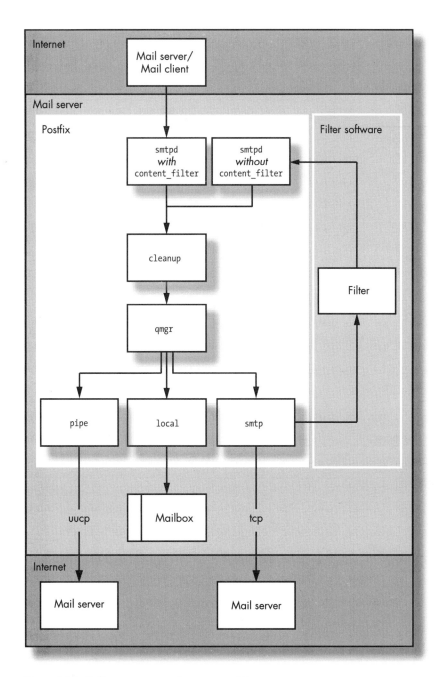

Figure 11-1: Delivery process using content_filter

Here's how it works:

1. The smtpd configured with content_filter hands a message to the queue manager.
2. The queue manager gives the message either to smtp, lmtp, or a pipe in order to deliver it to the external filter application.

NOTE *Figure 11-1 shows one of the possible three scenarios where* qmgr *hands mail over to* smtp.

3. The external filter application takes control of the message and processes it.
4. If the filter program reinjects the message back into Postfix, it connects to a Postfix smtpd configured to not use content_filter.
5. The second smtpd hands the message to the queue manager.
6. Postfix delivers the message locally or transports it to another mail server.

In addition to the message, Postfix can send extra information to the external filter application to assist it. The exact information depends on the daemon (lmtp, smtp, or pipe) that Postfix invokes to send the message to the application.

Filter-Delegation Daemons

When using content_filter, you have three basic daemons at your disposal for delegating mail to an external filter application. The daemons differ in what they can do and transmit. Here is an overview:

pipe

The pipe daemon sends messages to scripts and other executable programs. They can trigger nearly any imaginable action, from archiving messages to performing other kinds of automated work on the message content, such as virus detection.

The open-ended range of tasks that these programs perform makes it necessary to pass several arguments and flags to a filter program along with the message. You can read about these arguments in the pipe(8) manual page.

smtp

You can use the Postfix smtp daemon to transmit a message to a filter application with SMTP or ESMTP (for example, to another MTA). The information that you can send along with the message is limited by the protocol; the smtp(8) manual page has more details.

lmtp

The Postfix lmtp daemon is also available to send messages to filter programs via the LMTP protocol. As with the SMTP client, the LMTP protocol limits the amount of extra information that you can transmit along with the message, and you can read about it in the lmtp(8) manual page.

Unlike the Postfix SMTP client, which currently does not implement Delivery Status Notification (DSN) to generate separate notifications, the LMTP protocol allows a server to send per-recipient status reports for a message (that is, reports on whether the message has been rejected or accepted for each recipient). This makes it possible to avoid confusing status notifications for multiple recipients when the message goes through for some recipients, but not for others.

The Basics of Configuring content_filter

To send messages to an external filter program using content_filter, you need to modify the behavior of all of the daemons that handle incoming mail. In particular, you need to do the following:

1. Define a transport as content_filter in your main.cf file.
2. Configure the transport in your master.cf file.
3. Configure an additional reinjection path in master.cf if you want to send the message back to the Postfix queue after filtering.

Defining the Transport

To tell Postfix that it must hand over messages to an external application, use the content_filter in your main.cf file. You must tell Postfix to transport all messages to a (to-be-created) Postfix service that waits to hand over messages to a filter application. For example, the following line tells Postfix to send messages to a transport named foo, via port 54321 on localhost (127.0.0.1). Remember that the square brackets prevent Postfix from looking up an MX record for 127.0.0.1:

```
content_filter = foo:[127.0.0.1]:54321
```

Configuring the Transport

Next you need to configure the transport service that you just created in main.cf. The transport service configuration file is master.cf, because it's the master daemon that needs to know about all of the services available. For a new transport service, you need to give the master daemon the following information:

1. The name of the service.
2. The name of the Postfix daemon program that will carry out the transport.
3. Options and other information that the program needs to do its job.

Here's an example that builds on the foo transport:

```
#====================================================================
# service type      private unpriv chroot wakeup maxproc command
#                   (yes)   (yes)   (yes)  (never) (100)
```

```
# ================================================================
...
foo       unix       -       -       n       -       2       smtp
  -o smtp_data_done_timeout=1200s
  -o disable_dns_lookups=yes
...
```

The line that begins with foo is the essential transport configuration, containing eight columns. The first column must match the transport name that you defined in main.cf. The command column contains the command that will send the message to the filter application (here, it's the Postfix SMTP client). The subsequent two lines are options to the command.

CAUTION *Command Option Syntax: When listing additional command parameters, add whitespace to the beginning of every new line that contains the parameters, because a line that starts with whitespace continues a logical line. However, you should trim whitespace between parameters and values (such as between* smtp_data_done_timeout *and* 1200s *); otherwise the* master *daemon will not recognize your additions.*

So far, so good—you can transmit messages to external applications. However, if the application is to give the message back to Postfix, you need to configure a reinjection path.

Configuring an Additional Reinjection Path

A reinjection path is simply a local Postfix injection method (such as SMTP, LMTP, or local submission via sendmail) that doesn't use content_filter. It's usually another instance of the smtpd daemon that runs with special options to override global parameters set in the main.cf file. For example, if you wanted an additional smtpd reinjection path daemon to listen on port 10025, you could put the following in your master.cf file:

```
#=================================================================
# service type          private unpriv chroot wakeup maxproc command
#                       (yes)   (yes)  (yes)  (never) (100)
# ================================================================
...
127.0.0.1:10025  inet n        -      n      -       -       smtpd
  -o content_filter=
  -o receive_override_options=no_unknown_recipient_checks
  -o smtpd_recipient_restrictions=permit_mynetworks,reject
  -o mynetworks=127.0.0.0/8
  ...
```

Notice that the transport type is inet this time, for an Internet transport (the preceding example was a Unix domain socket transport type).

You can specify Internet services as host:port without defining the transport in the main.cf file first (the host can be a hostname or an IP address defined in /etc/hosts, whereas the port can be a number or the name of a services defined in the /etc/services file).

You can omit host:, but this makes the service available on all network interfaces as defined in inet_interfaces. In order to minimize your risk of creating an open relay with your reinjection path, you should restrict the listening network interfaces to just the ones you need, and in this case you need only localhost/127.0.0.1.

There are additional command options:

- The explicitly empty content_filter setting disables the filter transport in the main.cf file, so that you don't run into an infinite loop of filtering.

- The receive_override_options setting disables recipient checking for local_recipient_maps and relay_recipient_maps—because these checks have already been performed by the smtpd daemon that accepted the mail from the Internet, there's no need to perform them a second time.

- The final two parameters work together, first allowing mail only from the mynetworks parameter, and then explicitly setting the mynetworks parameter to 127.0.0.0/8. This is an additional safeguard against external hosts trying to access your reinjection path as an open relay.

smtpd_proxy_filter: Filtering First, Queuing Later

To use the smtpd_proxy_filter mechanism, you need to modify the existing smtpd daemon (the before-filter smtpd) to proxy connections from mail clients to the external filter program (see Figure 11-2).

NOTE *The Postfix smtpd protects the external application by weeding out potentially nasty stuff such as pipelining, long arguments, and odd characters that may come in from the connection.*

Depending on the filter application you use and its purpose, you may also have to create a second smtpd instance (an after-filter smtpd) that listens for messages sent back by the external filter application.

Here's how it works:

1. The before-filter smtpd daemon connects to the external application.

2. The smtpd daemon proxies the incoming SMTP commands and data to the external application.

3. The external filter application keeps the connection open as it processes the message content.

4. If the filter application accepts the message, it can inject it into an after-filter smtpd daemon or send it to another application.

5. After deciding whether to accept or reject the message, the external filter application sends SMTP responses (such as 250 OK or 554 Reject) to the before-filter smtpd.

6. The before-filter smtpd daemon proxies these responses to the originating mail client.

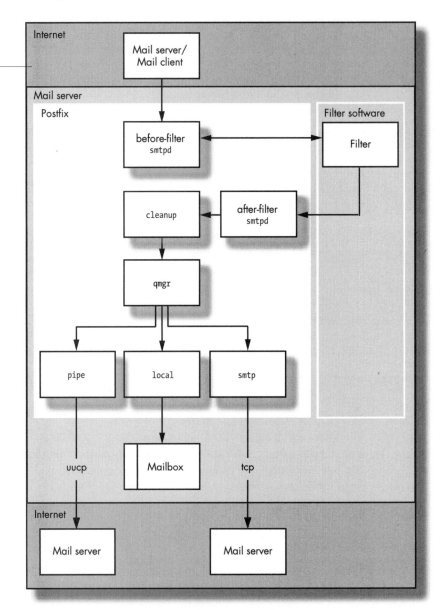

Figure 11-2: Delivery process with a pass-through proxy

Considerations for Proxy Filters

When working with smtpd_proxy_filter, keep the following points in mind:

ESMTP communication

When sending a message into the filter, Postfix speaks ESMTP, but it does not use command pipelining. The Postfix smtpd generates its own EHLO, XFORWARD (for logging the remote client IP address instead of localhost[127.0.0.1]), DATA, and QUIT commands. Otherwise, Postfix just forwards unmodified copies of the MAIL FROM and RCPT TO commands that the before-filter smtpd got from the remote mail client.

External application requirements

The filter (which *must* speak SMTP) should accept the same MAIL FROM and RCPT TO command syntax as the Postfix smtpd.

Content reinjection

The filter application is expected to pass unmodified SMTP commands from the before-filter smtpd to an after-filter Postfix smtpd (which usually listens on a nonstandard port for reinjection on a path that is not subject to the same filter; this is similar to the case of the content_filter mechanism discussed earlier in this chapter).

Rejecting content

If the filter rejects content, it should send a negative SMTP response (5xx code) back to the before-filter Postfix smtpd and then abort the connection with the after-filter Postfix smtpd without completing the SMTP conversation with the after-filter Postfix smtpd. Otherwise, the after-filter smtpd may accidentally deliver a message.

The Basics of Configuring smtpd_proxy_filter

To send messages to an external filter using smtpd_proxy_filter, you need to modify the behavior of the smtpd daemon. The following two steps are necessary:

1. Modify the existing smtpd. At this point, we'll refer to this daemon as the before-filter smtpd.

2. Configure an additional smtpd instance to reinject mail back into the Postfix queue; this is the after-filter smtpd.

Modifying the Existing smtpd (Before-Filter smtpd)

To make the existing smtpd proxy connections to a filter application, append an smtpd_proxy_filter parameter to the smtpd service in your master.cf file. You must provide the IP address or FQDN and the port of the proxy.

Here's an example that uses port 10024 on localhost:

```
#===================================================================
# service type         private unpriv chroot wakeup maxproc command
#                      (yes)   (yes)  (yes)  (never) (100)
# ==================================================================
...
smtp       inet          n       -      n       -      20      smtpd
    -o smtpd_proxy_filter=localhost:10024
```

Configuring an Additional smtpd Reinjection Instance (After-Filter smtpd)

To create another instance of smtpd that accepts filtered messages on
localhost, you need to add another line to your master.cf file. This will be
similar to the default smtpd, but it will listen on a different port and should
not have the same proxy filter option as the before-filter smtpd. Here's an
example for an after-filter smtpd that listens on port 10025:

```
#===================================================================
# service type         private unpriv chroot wakeup maxproc command
#                      (yes)   (yes)  (yes)  (never) (100)
# ==================================================================
...
127.0.0.1:10025    inet n       -      n       -      -       smtpd
    -o smtpd_authorized_xforward_hosts=127.0.0.0/8
    -o smtpd_client_restrictions=
    -o smtpd_helo_restrictions=
    -o smtpd_sender_restrictions=
    -o smtpd_recipient_restrictions=permit_mynetworks,reject
    -o mynetworks=127.0.0.0/8
    -o receive_override_options=no_unknown_recipient_checks
    -o content_filter=
```

12

USING EXTERNAL CONTENT FILTERS

I know where to get it, if you want it.
—*Jailer #1 in* Monty Python's Life of Brian

Each tool has its purpose. Imagine you try to develop a hammer that can also be used for polishing. Most likely, you end up with a bad hammer *and* a bad polisher. That's the reason Postfix does not do spam filtering, mail archiving, or sanitizing mail. Instead it gives you the opportunity to plug the best external filter that is available into the best MTA that is available. In the previous chapters, you saw that Postfix offers slightly different approaches for filtering mail that differ in when they process incoming messages. This chapter addresses the practice of these approaches.

In particular, you will see how to append disclaimers to messages by piping messages to a script and how to scan messages for viruses using either content_filter or smtpd_proxy_filter to send them off to amavisd-new.

Appending Disclaimers to Messages with a Script

Among the countless things that you can do with a `content_filter` script is add a disclaimer to all outgoing messages. The following example uses alterMIME, a small program that is used to alter mime-encoded mail, in a script to add a disclaimer to every message that is sent from internal clients. Figure 12-1 shows you how alterMIME will be integrated into the message transport process.

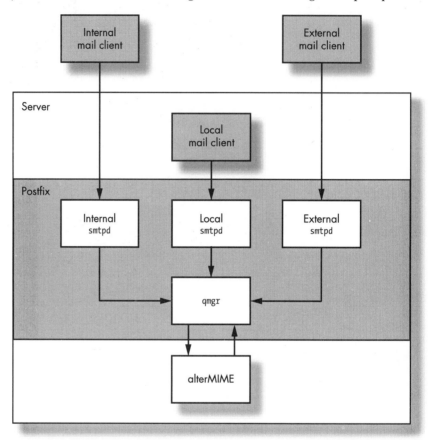

Figure 12-1: AlterMIME integration into Postfix

To add disclaimers to outbound messages without touching inbound and local messages, you need to separate the traffic for each direction. Let's say that your mail server has separate network interfaces for your internal and external networks. This means you need to create three separate instances of smtpd and bind them to the localhost, internal, and external network interfaces. The following example shows you how a message transport from your internal network to a remote destination would be processed if you created separate instances of smtpd for separate network interfaces.

1. When a message leaves your network, a mail client connects to the `smtpd` instance listening on the internal interface.

2. This internal `smtpd` accepts the message and sends it to `qmgr`.

3. `qmgr` sends the message to the `content_filter` service.

4. The `content_filter` service uses the `pipe` daemon to feed the message to the script.

5. The script adds a disclaimer.

6. The script reinjects the message to the `smtpd` instance listening on the local network interface.

7. The local `smtpd` sends the reinjected message to `qmgr`.

8. `qmgr` sends the message to `smtp` and out to the Internet.

Before you configure the transport, however, you must create the script that will invoke alterMIME from Postfix.

Installing alterMIME and Creating the Filter Script

The script will run alterMIME (`http://www.pldaniels.com/altermime`) to modify the outgoing message. If you don't have alterMIME (and you don't have a binary package for your operating system), download it, unpack it, change into your source directory, and run **make** and **make install**. This should leave you with an alterMIME executable in `/usr/local/bin/altermime`.

Creating the alterMIME Environment

You should run alterMIME as an unprivileged system user. For example, if you would like to use the `filter` username on your machine, you could run these commands to create the user:

```
# groupadd filter
# useradd -d /var/spool/altermime -G filter altermime
```

Creating a Script Directory

It's not a very good idea to clutter up your `/etc/postfix` directory with a bunch of scripts. Create a separate subdirectory as the superuser to store your scripts, and make the subdirectory accessible to `filter` and `root` only.

For example, the following command sequence creates a directory with the correct permissions and ownership:

```
# mkdir /etc/postfix/filter
# chown root /etc/postfix/filter
# chgrp filter /etc/postfix/filter
# chmod 770 /etc/postfix/filter
```

Creating the Script

The following script, named /etc/postfix/filter/add_disclaimer.sh, invokes alterMIME on an incoming message from Postfix (sent from the pipe daemon). The alterMIME program adds a disclaimer to the message and reinjects it back into the Postfix queue. AlterMIME requires a location to write a temporary file; it cannot operate on stdin.

```
#!/bin/sh
# System dependent settings
ALTERMIME=/usr/local/bin/altermime
ALTERMIME_DIR=/var/spool/altermime
SENDMAIL=/usr/sbin/sendmail
# Exit codes of commands invoked by Postfix are expected
# to follow the conventions defined in <sysexits.h>.
TEMPFAIL=75
UNAVAILABLE=69
# Change in to alterMIME's working directory and
# notify Postfix if 'cd' fails.
cd $ALTERMIME_DIR || { echo $ALTERMIME_DIR does not exist; exit $TEMPFAIL; }
# Clean up when done or when aborting.
trap "rm -f in.$$" 0 1 2 3 15
# Write mail to a temporary file
# Notify Postfix if this fails
cat >in.$$ || { echo Cannot write to $ALTERMIME_DIR; exit $TEMPFAIL; }
# Call alterMIME, hand over the message and
# tell alterMIME what to do with it
$ALTERMIME  --input=in.$$ \
            --disclaimer=/etc/postfix/disclaimer.txt \
            --disclaimer-html=/etc/postfix/disclaimer.txt \
            --xheader="X-Copyrighted-Material: Please visit http:// \
            www.example.com/message_disclaimer.html" || \
            { echo Message content rejected; exit $UNAVAILABLE; }
# Call sendmail to reinject the message into Postfix
$SENDMAIL "$@" <in.$$
# Use sendmail's EXIT STATUS to tell Postfix
# how things went.
exit $?
```

After creating the script, give write access only to root, but give execute permission to the filter user:

```
# chown root add_disclaimer.sh
# chgrp filter add_disclaimer.sh
# chmod 750 add_disclaimer.sh
```

Of course, now you need to create the disclaimer referenced in the script.

Creating the Disclaimer

If you already have a disclaimer, put the text in `/etc/postfix/filter/disclaimer.txt`. If you're still looking for the right disclaimer, you may want to visit emaildisclaimers.com (`http://www.emaildisclaimers.com`), a site dedicated to disclaimers and related email law. This example just uses the following dummy text (from `http://www.lipsum.com`):

```
Lorem ipsum dolor sit amet, consectetuer adipiscing elit. Nam commodo
lobortis magna. Quisque neque. Etiam aliquam. Nulla tempor vestibulum.
```

With the text in place, permit only the `filter` group to read your disclaimer:

```
# chgrp filter disclaimer.txt
# chmod 640 disclaimer.txt
```

This wraps up the filter script. Now you have to configure Postfix to use the script.

Configuring Postfix for the Disclaimer Script

Configuring Postfix to invoke the script is a two-step process:

1. Define a `content_filter` parameter for the proper `smtpd` in the `master.cf` file.
2. Define the transport in the `master.cf` file.

Defining the content_filter Parameter

As explained in Chapter 11, you would now add the `content_filter` parameter to `main.cf` and specify a transport name. However, this would globally specify a `content_filter`, and the filter would apply to all processes that handle incoming mail. You don't want that to happen in this particular example, though, because you want to apply the filter only to messages that come from the internal network interface.

To assign the filter to messages coming from the internal network interface only, you will add the `content_filter` only to the single `smtpd` instance in the `master.cf` file. The address of the internal interface in the following example of `master.cf` is `172.16.0.1`:

```
127.0.0.1:smtp      inet     n     -     n     -     -     smtpd ❶
172.16.0.1:smtp     inet     n     -     n     -     -     smtpd ❷
    -o content_filter=disclaimer:
192.0.34.166:smtp   inet     n     -     n     -     -     smtpd ❸
```

❶ This is the local `smtpd` instance.

❷ This is the `smtpd` instance that listens on the internal network interface.

❸ This is the `smtpd` instance that listens to the external network.

Notice that the name of the filter transport is `disclaimer`; this is not the script name. You'll define this transport in the next section.

Defining the Transport

You now need to define the `disclaimer` transport in the `master.cf` file. Create an instance of the `pipe` transport that runs the `add_disclaimer.sh` script. Here's how you would do it with the script shown earlier in this chapter:

```
disclaimer  unix  -       n       n       -       -       pipe
    flags=Rq user=filter argv=/etc/postfix/filter/add_disclaimer.sh -f ${sender} -- ${recipient}
```

This definition runs the `pipe` daemon as the `filter` user, calling `add_disclaimer.sh` when fed a message. It also passes the envelope sender and envelope recipient to the script. The `R` flag prepends a `Return-Path` message header with the envelope sender address, and the `q` flag quotes whitespace and other special characters in the command-line `$sender` and `$recipient` arguments.

NOTE *The pipe(8) manual page contains a full list of flags and options.*

Testing the Filter

To test the filter, you will need to perform the following steps, which are discussed in the following sections:

1. Send mail to a remote user through the internal network interface.
2. Check the mail log for filter actions.
3. Check the sent message for a disclaimer.

Sending Mail to a Remote User

To generate a message for Postfix to send to the filter, use telnet to connect to the internal network interface (where the `smtpd` instance should use the filter). Here's an example session:

```
$ telnet 172.16.0.1 25
Trying 172.16.0.1...
Connected to 172.16.0.1.
Escape character is '^]'.
220 mail.example.com ESMTP Postfix
HELO client.example.com
250 mail.example.com
MAIL FROM: <sender@example.com>
250 Ok
RCPT TO: <recipient@remote-example.com>
250 Ok
DATA
354 End data with <CR><LF>.<CR><LF>
FROM: Sender <sender@example.com>
TO: Recipient <recipient@remote-example.com>
```

```
Subject: Testing disclaimer
This is a test. There should be text at the bottom of this message
added by a disclaimer script.
.
250 Ok: queued as 3C4D043F2F
QUIT
221 Bye
```

Checking the Mail Log

The mail log should contain evidence of filter action, as in this example:

```
Mar 12 01:59:53 mail postfix/smtpd[30206]: connect from client.example.com[172.16.0.2]
Mar 12 02:00:21 mail postfix/smtpd[30206]: 3C4D043F2F: client=client.example.com[172.16.0.2]
Mar 12 02:01:53 mail postfix/cleanup[30209]: 3C4D043F2F:
  message-id=<20040312010021.3C4D043F2F@mail.example.com>
Mar 12 02:01:53 mail postfix/nqmgr[30193]: 3C4D043F2F: from=<sender@example.com>, size=444,
  nrcpt=1 (queue active)
Mar 12 02:01:53 mail postfix/pipe[30213]: 3C4D043F2F: to=<recipient@remote-example.com>,
  relay=disclaimer, delay=92, status=sent (mail.example.com) ❶
Mar 12 02:01:53 mail postfix/pickup[30192]: 8421143F2F: uid=100 from=<sender@example.com> ❷
Mar 12 02:01:53 mail postfix/cleanup[30209]: 8421143F2F:
  message-id=<20040312010021.3C4D043F2F@mail.example.com>
Mar 12 02:01:53 mail postfix/nqmgr[30193]: 8421143F2F: from=<sender@example.com>, size=977,
  nrcpt=1 (queue active)
Mar 12 02:01:55 mail postfix/smtpd[30206]: disconnect from client.example.com[172.16.0.2]
Mar 12 02:02:03 mail postfix/smtp[30220]: 8421143F2F: to=<recipient@remote-example.com>,
  relay=mail.remote-example.com[212.14.92.89], delay=10, status=sent (250 Ok: queued as
  56851E1C65) ❸
```

❶ The pipe daemon uses the disclaimer transport to send the message to the script.

❷ The script reinjects the message with the original envelope sender.

❸ The smtp daemon successfully delivers the message to the envelope recipient.

Checking the Message for a Disclaimer

As a final (and somewhat obvious) test, retrieve the message and see if it contains the X-header and the disclaimer that alterMIME is supposed to add on outgoing messages. You can see both in the following example:

```
Return-Path: <sender@example.com>
X-Original-To: recipient@remote-example.com
Delivered-To: recipient@remote-example.com
Received: from mail.example.com (mail.example.com [192.0.34.166])
  by mail.remote-example.com (Postfix) with ESMTP id 56851E1C65
  for <recipient@remote-example.com>; Fri, 12 Mar 2004 02:01:25 +0100 (CET)
```

```
Received: by mail.example.com (Postfix, from userid 100)
    id 8421143F2F; Fri, 12 Mar 2004 02:01:53 +0100 (CET)
Received: from client.example.com (client.example.com [172.16.0.2])by
    mail.example.com+(Postfix) with SMTP id 3C4D043F2Ffor
    <recipient@remote-example.com>; Fri, 12 Mar 2004+02:00:21 +0100 (CET)
From: Sender <sender@example.com>
To: Recipient <recipient@remote-example.com>
Subject: Testing disclaimer
Message-Id: <20040312010021.3C4D043F2F@mail.example.com>
Date: Fri, 12 Mar 2004 02:00:21 +0100 (CET)
X-Copyrighted-Material: Please visit http://www.example.com/
message_disclaimer.html

This is a test. There should be text at the bottom of this message
added by a disclaimer script.
Lorem ipsum dolor sit amet, consectetuer adipiscing elit. Nam commodo
lobortis magna. Quisque neque. Etiam aliquam. Nulla tempor vestibulum.
```

Scanning for Viruses with content_filter and amavisd-new

This section describes an advanced use of content_filter described in
Chapter 11—how to integrate the popular program amavisd-new into
Postfix. amavisd-new links an MTA and one or more virus scanners or spam-
detection programs, such as SpamAssassin. It is actively developed and is
recommended by many postmasters on the Postfix mailing list.

NOTE *To get virus-scanning functionality, you need to have at least one supported virus
scanner installed in addition to amavisd-new; check the documentation for a survey of
the supported products.*

Figure 12-2 illustrates how Postfix and amavisd-new work together with
other applications such as spam detectors and virus scanners. Here's the
message flow:

1. A mail client sends a message to Postfix.

2. smtpd accepts the message.

3. smtpd sends the message to qmgr.

4. qmgr sends the message to amavisd-new.

5. amavisd-new sends the message to other applications (virus scanners in
    this example).

6. amavisd-new reinjects the message into the local smtpd.

7. The local smtpd sends the message to qmgr.

8. qmgr either bounces or delivers the message.

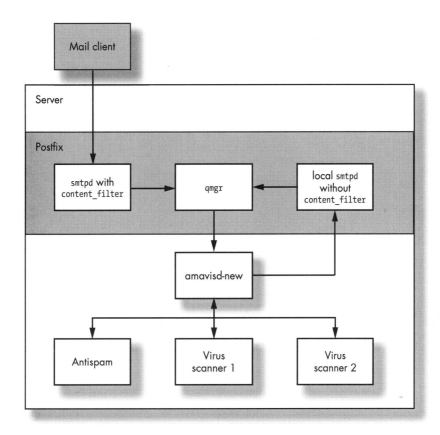

Figure 12-2: amavisd-new integration with Postfix using `content_filter`

Installing amavisd-new

To get amavisd-new, download it from one of the mirrors mentioned on the amavisd-new website (`http://www.ijs.si/software/amavisd`). After unpacking the archive, follow the steps in the `INSTALL` file to install amavisd-new for Postfix.

You should also read the `README.postfix` (`http://www.ijs.si/software/ amavisd/README.postfix`) file for up-to-date instructions and notes specific to Postfix.

TIP *You need to build only the daemon version of amavisd-new. The helper applications, such as `amavis(.c)` and `amavisd-milter(.c)`, are not necessary for use with Postfix.*

Installing Perl Modules for amavisd-new from CPAN

amavisd-new needs a number of Perl modules to work correctly, and the `INSTALL` document in amavisd-new's `SOURCE` directory contains a full list of these modules. When installing the modules, you usually have the choice between choosing a package provided by the makers of your distribution or directly downloading the modules from CPAN (the Comprehensive Perl Archive Network, at `http://www.cpan.org`).

CPAN is generally the best source for the most recent modules, but you may want to choose your operating system's packages for consistency instead.

To install modules such as `Compress::Zlib` from CPAN, you need to run Perl with the CPAN module as follows:

```
# perl -MCPAN -e shell;
cpan shell -- CPAN exploration and modules installation (v1.76)
ReadLine support enabled
cpan> install Compress::Zlib
Running install for module Compress::Zlib
Running make for P/PM/PMQS/Compress-Zlib-1.33.tar.gz
Fetching with LWP:
  ftp://ftp-stud.fht-esslingen.de/pub/Mirrors/CPAN/authors/id/P/PM/PMQS/
Compress-Zlib-1.33.tar.gz
CPAN: Digest::MD5 loaded ok
Fetching with LWP:
  ftp://ftp-stud.fht-esslingen.de/pub/Mirrors/CPAN/authors/id/P/PM/PMQS/
CHECKSUMS
Checksum for /root/.cpan/sources/authors/id/P/PM/PMQS/Compress-Zlib-
1.33.tar.gz ok
Scanning cache /root/.cpan/build for sizes
Compress-Zlib-1.33/
... lots of building output ...
All tests successful, 1 test skipped.
Files=6, Tests=287,  2 wallclock secs ( 0.73 cusr +  0.11 csys =  0.84 CPU)
  /usr/bin/make test -- OK
Running make install
Installing /usr/lib/perl5/site_perl/5.6.0/i386-linux/auto/Compress/Zlib/
Zlib.so
Files found in blib/arch: installing files in blib/lib into architecture
dependent library tree
Installing /usr/lib/perl5/site_perl/5.6.0/i386-linux/Compress/Zlib.pm
Installing /usr/man/man3/Compress::Zlib.3pm
Writing /usr/lib/perl5/site_perl/5.6.0/i386-linux/auto/Compress/Zlib/.packlist
Appending installation info to /usr/lib/perl5/site_perl/5.6.0/i386-linux/
perllocal.pod
  /usr/bin/make install  -- OK
```

After getting the modules in place and installing amavisd-new, you should test it.

Testing amavisd-new

To test amavisd-new in isolation, before attempting to get it interoperating with Postfix, perform the following steps:

1. Start amavisd-new in debug mode to see if it starts up properly.

2. Perform a network test to see if it listens on a network port.

Running amavisd-new in Debug Mode

Invoking amavisd-new in debug mode gives you the answers to the following questions at once:

- Does it run? All mandatory Perl modules need to be installed for amavisd-new to start up. If a module is missing, you will get an error message that indicates the missing module.

- Can you run it as an unprivileged user? amavisd-new requires a new group (vscan by default) and a user account in this group (also vscan by default).

- Does it find optional Perl modules that implement additional functionality, such as SpamAssassin, LDAP, and SQL?

- Does it use the proper installation of Perl? If you have more than one version of Perl installed, you may not have all of the modules installed for the particular version of Perl that you're trying to use.

- Does it find auxiliary programs, such as virus scanners?

- Which configuration file is it using? Normally, it's /etc/amavisd.conf, but you can override this if you know exactly what you're doing.

- Can it bind to the ports specified in the configuration file?

For your first attempt, it's best to start amavisd-new interactively, keeping it attached to the terminal. To do this, switch to the user vscan and run amavisd-new with the debug option. This example session shows the output that you're looking for:

```
# su - vscan
$ /usr/local/sbin/amavisd debug
Jan 28 11:10:43 mail amavisd[29188]: starting.  amavisd at mail amavisd-new-20030616-p6
Jan 28 11:10:43 mail amavisd[29188]: Perl version            5.006 ❶
Jan 28 11:10:43 mail amavisd[29188]: Module Amavis::Conf     1.15
Jan 28 11:10:43 mail amavisd[29188]: Module Archive::Tar     1.08
Jan 28 11:10:43 mail amavisd[29188]: Module Archive::Zip     1.09
Jan 28 11:10:43 mail amavisd[29188]: Module Compress::Zlib   1.33
Jan 28 11:10:43 mail amavisd[29188]: Module Convert::TNEF    0.17
Jan 28 11:10:43 mail amavisd[29188]: Module Convert::UUlib   1.0
Jan 28 11:10:43 mail amavisd[29188]: Module MIME::Entity     5.404
Jan 28 11:10:43 mail amavisd[29188]: Module MIME::Parser     5.406
Jan 28 11:10:43 mail amavisd[29188]: Module MIME::Tools      5.411
Jan 28 11:10:43 mail amavisd[29188]: Module Mail::Header     1.60
Jan 28 11:10:43 mail amavisd[29188]: Module Mail::Internet   1.60
Jan 28 11:10:43 mail amavisd[29188]: Module Mail::SpamAssassin 2.63
Jan 28 11:10:43 mail amavisd[29188]: Module Net::Cmd         2.24
Jan 28 11:10:43 mail amavisd[29188]: Module Net::DNS         0.40
Jan 28 11:10:43 mail amavisd[29188]: Module Net::SMTP        2.26
Jan 28 11:10:43 mail amavisd[29188]: Module Net::Server      0.86
Jan 28 11:10:43 mail amavisd[29188]: Module Time::HiRes      1.55
Jan 28 11:10:43 mail amavisd[29188]: Module Unix::Syslog     0.99
```

```
Jan 28 11:10:43 mail amavisd[29188]: Found myself: /usr/sbin/amavisd -c /etc/amavisd.conf
Jan 28 11:10:43 mail amavisd[29188]: Lookup::SQL code        NOT loaded ❷
Jan 28 11:10:43 mail amavisd[29188]: Lookup::LDAP code       NOT loaded
Jan 28 11:10:43 mail amavisd[29188]: AMCL-in protocol code   loaded
Jan 28 11:10:43 mail amavisd[29188]: SMTP-in protocol code   loaded
Jan 28 11:10:43 mail amavisd[29188]: ANTI-VIRUS code         loaded
Jan 28 11:10:43 mail amavisd[29188]: ANTI-SPAM  code         loaded ❸
Jan 28 11:10:43 mail amavisd[29188]: Net::Server: 2004/01/28-11:10:43 Amavis (type \
  Net::Server::PreForkSimple) starting! pid(29188)
Jan 28 11:10:43 mail amavisd[29188]: Net::Server: Binding to UNIX socket file \
  /var/amavis/amavisd.sock using SOCK_STREAM
Jan 28 11:10:43 mail amavisd[29188]: Net::Server: Binding to TCP port 10024 on host 127.0.0.1
Jan 28 11:10:43 mail amavisd[29188]: Net::Server: Setting gid to "54322 54322"
Jan 28 11:10:43 mail amavisd[29188]: Net::Server: Setting uid to "7509"
Jan 28 11:10:43 mail amavisd[29188]: Net::Server: Setting up serialization via flock
Jan 28 11:10:43 mail amavisd[29188]: Found $file      at /usr/bin/file
Jan 28 11:10:43 mail amavisd[29188]: Found $arc       at /usr/bin/arc
Jan 28 11:10:43 mail amavisd[29188]: Found $gzip      at /usr/bin/gzip
Jan 28 11:10:43 mail amavisd[29188]: Found $bzip2     at /usr/bin/bzip2
Jan 28 11:10:43 mail amavisd[29188]: Found $lzop      at /usr/local/bin/lzop
Jan 28 11:10:43 mail amavisd[29188]: Found $lha       at /usr/bin/lha
Jan 28 11:10:43 mail amavisd[29188]: Found $unarj     at /usr/bin/unarj
Jan 28 11:10:43 mail amavisd[29188]: Found $uncompress at /usr/bin/uncompress
Jan 28 11:10:43 mail amavisd[29188]: Found $unfreeze  at /usr/local/bin/unfreeze
Jan 28 11:10:43 mail amavisd[29188]: Found $unrar     at /usr/bin/rar
Jan 28 11:10:43 mail amavisd[29188]: Found $zoo       at /usr/bin/zoo
Jan 28 11:10:43 mail amavisd[29188]: Found $cpio      at /bin/cpio ❹
Jan 28 11:10:43 mail amavisd[29188]: No primary av scanner: KasperskyLab AntiViral Toolkit \
  Pro (AVP)
Jan 28 11:10:43 mail amavisd[29188]: No primary av scanner: KasperskyLab AVPDaemonClient
Jan 28 11:10:43 mail amavisd[29188]: No primary av scanner: H+BEDV AntiVir or \
  CentralCommand Vexira Antivirus
Jan 28 11:10:43 mail amavisd[29188]: No primary av scanner: Command AntiVirus for Linux
Jan 28 11:10:43 mail amavisd[29188]: No primary av scanner: Symantec CarrierScan via \
  Symantec CommandLineScanner
Jan 28 11:10:43 mail amavisd[29188]: No primary av scanner: Symantec AntiVirus Scan Engine
Jan 28 11:10:43 mail amavisd[29188]: No primary av scanner: Dr.Web Antivirus for \
  Linux/FreeBSD/Solaris
Jan 28 11:10:43 mail amavisd[29188]: No primary av scanner: F-Secure Antivirus
Jan 28 11:10:43 mail amavisd[29188]: No primary av scanner: CAI InoculateIT
Jan 28 11:10:43 mail amavisd[29188]: No primary av scanner: MkS_Vir for Linux (beta)
Jan 28 11:10:43 mail amavisd[29188]: No primary av scanner: MkS_Vir daemon
Jan 28 11:10:43 mail amavisd[29188]: No primary av scanner: ESET Software NOD32
Jan 28 11:10:43 mail amavisd[29188]: No primary av scanner: ESET Software NOD32 - \
  Client/Server Version
Jan 28 11:10:43 mail amavisd[29188]: No primary av scanner: Norman Virus Control v5 / Linux
Jan 28 11:10:43 mail amavisd[29188]: No primary av scanner: Panda Antivirus for Linux
```

```
Jan 28 11:10:43 mail amavisd[29188]: Found primary av scanner NAI McAfee AntiVirus (uvscan) \
    at /usr/local/bin/uvscan ❺
Jan 28 11:10:43 mail amavisd[29188]: No primary av scanner: VirusBuster
Jan 28 11:10:43 mail amavisd[29188]: No primary av scanner: CyberSoft VFind
Jan 28 11:10:43 mail amavisd[29188]: No primary av scanner: Ikarus AntiVirus for Linux
Jan 28 11:10:43 mail amavisd[29188]: No primary av scanner: BitDefender
Jan 28 11:10:43 mail amavisd[29188]: No secondary av scanner: Clam Antivirus - clamscan
Jan 28 11:10:43 mail amavisd[29188]: No secondary av scanner: FRISK F-Prot Antivirus
Jan 28 11:10:43 mail amavisd[29188]: No secondary av scanner: Trend Micro FileScanner
Jan 28 11:10:43 mail amavisd[29188]: SpamControl: initializing Mail::SpamAssassin ❻
```

❶ This line indicates the Perl version.

❷ This line and the following one indicate that no SQL or LDAP code is present.

❸ This line indicates that the antispam code was loaded; this only succeeds when SpamAssassin or dspam are present.

❹ This line and the preceding lines indicate that various external unpackers have been found—thus enabling amavisd-new to unpack attachments compressed with these packers.

❺ This line indicates that McAfee AntiVirus is present.

❻ At this point, amavisd-new is ready.

Testing Network Connectivity

With the stand-alone amavisd-new still running, you should now see if it accepts connections. Use telnet sessions to test both of the ESMTP and LMTP alternatives.

Testing ESMTP Availability

Open a telnet connection to the local port 10024 (the default for amavisd-new). You should check that it is listening on the port and responds to ESMTP commands. amavisd-new should respond to an EHLO command with a set of available commands, as in the following sample session:

```
# telnet localhost 10024
220 [127.0.0.1] ESMTP amavisd-new service ready
EHLO mail.example.com
250-[127.0.0.1]
250-PIPELINING
250-SIZE
250-8BITMIME
250 ENHANCEDSTATUSCODES
QUIT
221 2.0.0 [127.0.0.1] (amavisd) closing transmission channel
```

Testing LMTP Availability

Next you need to check that amavisd-new is listening on local port 10024 (the amavisd-new default for LMTP) and responds to LMTP commands. You should be able to run an **LHLO** command, as in this session:

```
# telnet localhost 10024
220 [127.0.0.1] ESMTP amavisd-new service ready
LHLO mail.example.com
250-[127.0.0.1]
250-PIPELINING
250-SIZE
250-8BITMIME
250 ENHANCEDSTATUSCODES
QUIT
221 2.0.0 [127.0.0.1] (amavisd) closing transmission channel
```

Optimizing amavisd-new Performance

If you get a lot of mail, you might want to tweak the performance of amavisd-new. Because it makes heavy use of the filesystem to prepare messages for further inspection, amavisd-new's performance can be bound to the speed and latency of disk I/O. You can significantly optimize the read-write operation speed by moving this preparation to a RAM disk style of filesystem. The procedure described in the following sections uses the Linux temporary filesystem type (tmpfs).

Is This Safe?

You can rest assured that you won't lose any email during the filtering process due to the way that you integrate amavisd-new into Postfix. Take a look at what happens during filtering:

1. Upon receiving a new message, the Postfix queue manager sends a mail delivery request to a Postfix SMTP or LMTP client; the client transports the message to amavisd-new.

2. amavisd-new starts working on the message (doing scanning, spam checking, and so on), but it does not immediately acknowledge that it received the message.

3. While waiting for amavisd-new, Postfix keeps the message in its queue, waiting for amavisd-new to tell it that it received the message properly.

4. After amavisd-new finishes its work, it reinjects the message back into the Postfix queue.

5. The Postfix smtpd that handles the reinjection accepts the message from amavisd-new.

6. Upon getting the acknowledgement from the reinjecting smtpd, amavisd-new acknowledges successful transport back to the originating Postfix lmtp or smtp client, which in turn reports back to the queue manager that the message is delivered.

As you can see, amavisd-new only tells the prefilter Postfix component that it got the message after the post-filter smtpd accepts the processed message. This way, you can never lose mail in amavisd-new.

Sizing tmpfs

To calculate the correct size for tmpfs, consider this: If you run n amavisd-new instances, and each one accepts messages of at most message_size_limit, you need this much space:

```
n * (1 + maximum_expected_expansionfactor) * message_size_limit * 7/8
```

The expansionfactor is tricky, but a factor of 2 is quite okay (a compressed message—think *.zip or *.rar files here—may grow to twice the original size). For example, if you have five amavisd-new instances and a 10MB message limit, you would get the following result for the size of tmpfs:

```
5 * (1 + 2) * 10MB * 7/8 = 131.25MB
```

NOTE *Make sure that you have enough physical memory to hold the tmpfs; otherwise, your machine will start swapping memory out to disk, and you will end up with performance that's worse than a regular filesystem.*

Configuring the Optimization

There are a few steps involved in setting up amavisd-new to use tmpfs:

1. Find amavisd-new's $TEMPBASE parameter.
2. Create a tmpfs filesystem.
3. Stop amavisd-new.
4. Mount the tmpfs filesystem.
5. Start amavisd-new.
6. Make sure that amavisd-new still works.

First, you need to find out where the amavisd-new $TEMPBASE is defined. This is the mount point for the tmpfs that you will create. The default $TEMPBASE is $MYHOME, which is /var/amavis by default. To find out for sure, use grep on your configuration file. This example shows that it is set to $MYHOME:

```
# grep TEMPBASE /etc/amavisd.conf
$TEMPBASE = $MYHOME;            # (must be set if other config vars use is)
$ENV{TMPDIR} = $TEMPBASE;       # wise, but usually not necessary
    "-f=$TEMPBASE {}", [0,8], [3,4,5,6], qr/infected: ([^\r\n]+)/ ],
```

```
# adjusting /var/amavis above to match your $TEMPBASE.
#    directory $TEMPBASE specifies) in the 'Names=' section.
```

Run another **grep** to find out what $MYHOME is. In the following example, you can see that the definition of $MYHOME is commented out, so it uses the default value:

```
# grep MYHOME /etc/amavisd.conf
# $MYHOME serves as a quick default for some other configuration settings.
# $MYHOME is not used directly by the program. No trailing slash!
#$MYHOME = '/var/lib/amavis';   # (default is '/var/amavis')
$TEMPBASE = $MYHOME;            # (must be set if other config vars use is)
#$TEMPBASE = "$MYHOME/tmp";     # prefer to keep home dir /var/amavis clean?
#$helpers_home = $MYHOME;       # (defaults to $MYHOME)
#$daemon_chroot_dir = $MYHOME;  # (default is undef, meaning: do not chroot)
#$pid_file  = "$MYHOME/amavisd.pid";  # (default is "$MYHOME/amavisd.pid")
#$lock_file = "$MYHOME/amavisd.lock"; # (default is "$MYHOME/amavisd.lock")
#$forward_method = "bsmtp:$MYHOME/out-%i-%n.bsmtp";
$unix_socketname = "$MYHOME/amavisd.sock"; # amavis helper protocol socket
                                # (usual setting is $MYHOME/amavisd.sock)
$LOGFILE = "$MYHOME/amavis.log";  # (defaults to empty, no log)
    "{} -ss -i '*' -log=$MYHOME/vbuster.log", [0], [1],
```

Now you need to create a tmpfs entry in your /etc/fstab file, using the filesystem size calculated in the previous section ("Sizing tmpfs"). The following example uses a 150MB size and limits access to a particular user and group. In this case the user ID is 7509 and the GID is 54322, which match the user and group vscan in the /etc/passwd and /etc/group files; keep in mind that your system almost certainly has different numbers, and you will need to look them up by yourself:

```
/dev/shm   /var/amavis   tmpfs defaults,size=150m,mode=700,uid=7509,gid=54322 0 0
```

Before you mount /var/amavis, make sure to stop amavisd-new with a command such as this:

```
# /etc/init.d/amavisd-new stop
```

Next, mount /var/amavis (remember that this is the tmpfs filesystem that you just defined in /etc/fstab):

```
# mount /var/amavis
```

Now start amavisd-new again:

```
# /etc/init.d/amavisd-new start
```

Check whether all is well by looking at the logs and examining `df -h` output. In the following example, /var/amavis is 100MB, and only 76KB are currently in use:

```
# df -h /var/amavis
Filesystem          Size  Used Avail Use% Mounted on
/dev/shm            100M   76k   99M   1% /var/amavis
```

NOTE *Sometimes amavisd-new leaves stale files in its $TEMPBASE directory. To prevent $TEMPBASE from getting filled with these files, you can stop amavisd-new daily, remove the stale files, and restart. A daily cron job script such as the following will get the job done:*

```
#!/bin/bash
/etc/init.d/amavisd stop
rm -Rf /var/amavis/amavis-200*
/etc/init.d/amavisd start
```

Configuring Postfix to Use amavisd-new

At this point, Postfix and amavisd-new should each run independently of the other. Therefore, you need to configure Postfix to send messages to amavisd-new and create another `smtpd` instance for message reinjection. The following steps (discussed in the following sections) will integrate amavisd-new into Postfix:

1. Create a transport.
2. Configure the transport.
3. Configure a reinjection path.

NOTE *Because the filtered mail needs a way of getting back into the Postfix queue system without being scanned again, you need a dedicated smtpd that doesn't use* content_filter. *This allows amavisd-new to reinject the mail into the system without generating loops. Port 25 is already taken, so you can make a copy of smtpd listen to a nonstandard port. This example uses port 10025 on* localhost.

amavisd-new also needs a port to listen on. The default of port 10024 on localhost *is fine.*

Creating a Transport Using content_filter in main.cf

The first step in delegating the content processing to an external program is to define the transport that sends messages to the filtering program. Postfix uses the content_filter parameter in the main.cf file. The parameter expects a notation of *transportname:nexthop:port.*

In the example we're working on, amavisd-new is running on the same machine as Postfix, so you can access it at port 10024 on localhost (127.0.0.1). You need to define the following content_filter parameter in the main.cf file to make Postfix connect to amavisd-new:

```
content_filter = amavisd-new:[127.0.0.1]:10024
```

Running amavisd-new on a Different Host

If you feel that the filtering load is too much for a single machine, you can run amavisd-new on one or more machines. The nexthop part of *transportname*:*nexthop*:*port* allows you to easily specify a different host for the filter. Consider vscanners.example.com in the following example:

```
content_filter = amavisd-new:vscanners.example.com:10024
```

The name vscanners.example.com could be any one of the following:

- One machine (through one A record)
- Multiple machines (through multiple round-robin A records)
- Multiple machines (one or more machines with different priority MX records)

Defining the Transport in master.cf

Next you need to define the daemon that will connect to amavisd-new and specify the environment for the daemon. Remember that the daemon can be smtp, lmtp, or pipe. You saw an example of pipe earlier in this chapter; it's time to look at the other two.

Defining an ESMTP Transport

If you want to use the ESMTP protocol to send messages to amavisd-new, add the following entries to your master.cf file:

```
#==========================================================================
# service type       private unpriv chroot  wakeup  maxproc command
#                    (yes)   (yes)  (yes)   (never) (100)
# ==========================================================================
...
amavisd-new    unix    -       -      n       -       2       smtp
  -o smtp_data_done_timeout=1200s
  -o disable_dns_lookups=yes
```

There are a few things to note in the preceding entries:

- The special transport amavisd-new is a copy of the normal smtp transport. Its name must match the transport name that you gave to the content_filter parameter that you defined in main.cf.

- amavisd-new is quite resource-hungry. Unless you have a fast machine, you might want to leave the maximum number of simultaneous instances at 2.

- The smtp_data_done_timeout parameter is the first of two additional settings that modify this daemon's behavior. amavisd-new can take a significant amount of time to process an incoming message, and increasing the timeout after smtp sends the message protects Postfix from giving up before amavisd-new is done.

- Because you are probably dealing only with local machine names at this point, the disable_dns_lookups parameter disables unnecessary DNS lookups for the smtp client.

NOTE *You don't necessarily need a dedicated SMTP transport, because the default smtp does the job well. However, for performance reasons (and because of the relatively long amavisd-new timeout), it can make sense to customize a transport just for amavisd-new.*

Defining an LMTP Transport

If you decide to use the LMTP protocol (instead of SMTP) to transport messages to amavisd-new, add the following entry to your master.cf file:

```
#==========================================================================
# service type             private unpriv chroot   wakeup    maxproc  command
#                          (yes)   (yes)  (yes)    (never)   (100)
#==========================================================================
...
amavisd-new    unix    -        -       n        -         2        lmtp
  -o lmtp_data_done_timeout=1200s
  -o disable_dns_lookups=yes
```

Configuring a Reinjection Path

Finally, you need to create a reinjection path that allows amavisd-new to feed messages back into the Postfix queue. It's important that this reinjection path bypass the amavisd-new transport. Otherwise the message will get caught in a loop, where Postfix sends the message to amavisd-new, the mail is reinjected into the Postfix queue, and it is sent back to amavisd-new again.

A reinjection path that bypasses any previously defined content_filter parameter looks like this in your master.cf file:

```
#==========================================================================
# service type             private unpriv chroot   wakeup    maxproc  command
#                          (yes)   (yes)  (yes)    (never)   (100)
```

```
# ===========================================================================
...
127.0.0.1:10025  inet   n         -        n        -        -          smtpd
  -o content_filter=
  -o local_recipient_maps=
  -o relay_recipient_maps=
  -o smtpd_restriction_classes=
  -o smtpd_client_restrictions=
  -o smtpd_helo_restrictions=
  -o smtpd_sender_restrictions=
  -o smtpd_recipient_restrictions=permit_mynetworks,reject
  -o mynetworks=127.0.0.0/8
  -o strict_rfc821_envelopes=yes
```

Of all the options in the preceding entry, the one that is *absolutely* essential is the empty content_filter parameter. This overrides the content_filter parameter in the main.cf file. The remaining options override other main.cf parameters, including options to turn off restrictions that make no sense for a transport listening only on the localhost network interface.

After putting all of the settings in place, you're ready to test the filter. Remember that changes in master.cf require you to reload Postfix.

Testing the Postfix amavisd-new Filter

To test that Postfix and amavisd-new work well together, you must verify that Postfix can send mail to amavisd-new, and that amavisd-new can reinject messages. Testing involves the following steps:

1. See if Postfix listens on the reinjection path.
2. Send a message to Postfix, checking that it sends the message to amavisd-new, and that the message comes back into the Postfix queue.
3. See if a virus scanner detects a test pattern.

Checking the Reinjection Path

Once you've changed the master.cf file, run the **postfix reload** operation to make Postfix read the revised file and then examine the log file for any complaints. Then, check whether the smtpd reinjection daemon is listening on localhost, port 10025, as in the following session:

```
$ telnet 127.0.0.1 10025
220 mail.example.com ESMTP Postfix
EHLO 127.0.0.1
250-mail.example.com
250-PIPELINING
250-SIZE 10240000
```

```
250-VRFY
250-ETRN
250-STARTTLS
250-AUTH LOGIN PLAIN DIGEST-MD5 CRAM-MD5
250-XVERP
250 8BITMIME
QUIT
221 Bye
```

Sending a Test Message to Postfix

Postfix should be able to let an uninfected message pass through the system.
Send a message from the command line, and track it with the log file
messages from Postfix and amavisd-new. For example, you could use the
following command to mail your `main.cf` file to recipient@example.com:

```
# sendmail -f sender@example.com recipient@example.com < /etc/postfix/main.cf
```

Then take a look at the log file. The bottom of the file should have a
session that starts like the following, where Postfix assigns a message ID to
the message that you can use to track the message:

```
Jan 31 10:45:08 mail postfix/pickup[10096]: 2788029AB29: uid=0 from=<sender@example.com>
Jan 31 10:45:08 mail postfix/cleanup[10652]: 2788029AB29:
 message-id=<20040131094508.2788029AB29@mail.example.com>
```

The next set of messages should show Postfix handing the message to
localhost for processing by amavisd-new (unfortunately, Postfix does not log
the port number or the name of the transport):

```
Jan 31 10:45:08 mail postfix/qmgr[10097]: 2788029AB29: from=<sender@example.com>, size=1271,
 nrcpt=1 (queue active)
Jan 31 10:45:08 mail postfix/smtp[10660]: 2788029AB29: to=<recipient@example.com>,
 relay=localhost[127.0.0.1], delay=0, status=sent (250 2.6.0 Ok, id=25809-04, from MTA: 250
 Ok: queued as 377D829AB2A)
```

Now amavisd-new scans the message and logs that the message passed:

```
Jan 31 10:45:08 mail amavis[25809]: (25809-04) Passed, <sender@example.com> ->
 <recipient@example.com>, Message-ID: <20040131094508.2788029AB29@mail.example.com>, Hits: -
```

Next, the message comes back into Postfix from amavisd-new for
reinjection into the queue. Notice that the second smtpd also logs the
message ID:

```
Jan 31 10:45:08 mail postfix/smtpd[10658]: connect from localhost[127.0.0.1]
Jan 31 10:45:08 mail postfix/smtpd[10658]: 377D829AB2A: client=localhost[127.0.0.1]
```

```
Jan 31 10:45:08 mail postfix/cleanup[10652]: 377D829AB2A:
  message-id=<20040131094508.2788029AB29@mail.example.com>
Jan 31 10:45:08 mail postfix/qmgr[10097]: 377D829AB2A: from=<sender@example.com>, size=1723,
  nrcpt=1 (queue active)
Jan 31 10:45:08 mail postfix/smtpd[10658]: disconnect from localhost[127.0.0.1]
```

Finally, Postfix relays the message to another host for delivery (it could also deliver locally, if this server happened to be the final destination):

```
Jan 31 10:45:08 mail postfix/smtp[10655]: 377D829AB2A: to=<recipient@example.com>,
  relay=relayhost[10.0.0.1], delay=0, status=sent (250 OK id=1AmrgY-00073g-00)
```

Checking a Test Virus Pattern

Your last test is to simulate a message infected by a virus. You can do this by getting the EICAR test virus pattern (http://www.eicar.org) and sending it to Postfix. Any virus scanners that don't have this pattern specifically disabled should be able to recognize it. For example, the following command should send a virus to recipient@example.com:

```
# sendmail -f sender@example.com recipient@example.com < eicar.com
```

The log messages look like they did before, up to the point where amavisd-new scans the message:

```
Feb  6 15:48:54 mail postfix/pickup[30051]: 13B9E29AB29: uid=0 from=<sender@example.com>
Feb  6 15:48:54 mail postfix/cleanup[30741]: 13B9E29AB29:
  message-id=<20040206144854.13B9E29AB29@mail.example.com>
Feb  6 15:48:54 mail postfix/qmgr[19295]: 13B9E29AB29: from=<sender@example.com>, size=347,
  nrcpt=1 (queue active)
Feb  6 15:48:54 mail postfix/smtp[30744]: 13B9E29AB29: to=<recipient@example.com>,
  relay=localhost[127.0.0.1], delay=0, status=sent (250 2.5.0 Ok, id=10217-07, BOUNCE)
...
Feb  6 15:48:54 mail amavis[10217]: (10217-07) INFECTED (Eicar-Test-Signature),
  <sender@example.com> -> <recipient@example.com>, quarantine virus-20040206-154854-10217-07,
  Message-ID: <20040206144854.13B9E29AB29@mail.example.com>, Hits: -
```

Seeing that the message contains a virus, amavisd-new alerts virusalert@example.com and bounces the message back to the sender:

```
Feb  6 15:48:54 mail postfix/smtpd[30747]: connect from localhost[127.0.0.1]
Feb  6 15:48:54 mail postfix/smtpd[30747]: 639A729AB2A: client=localhost[127.0.0.1]
Feb  6 15:48:54 mail postfix/cleanup[30741]: 639A729AB2A: message-id=<VA10217-07@mail>
Feb  6 15:48:54 mail postfix/qmgr[19295]: 639A729AB2A: from=<>, size=1463, nrcpt=1
  (queue active)
Feb  6 15:48:54 mail postfix/local[30749]: 639A729AB2A: to=<virusalert@example.com>,
  relay=local, delay=0, status=sent (forwarded as 8484829AB2C)
```

```
Feb  6 15:48:54 mail postfix/smtpd[30747]: disconnect from localhost[127.0.0.1]
...
Feb  6 15:48:54 mail postfix/smtpd[30747]: connect from localhost[127.0.0.1]
Feb  6 15:48:54 mail postfix/smtpd[30747]: 7A2FD29AB2B: client=localhost[127.0.0.1]
Feb  6 15:48:54 mail postfix/cleanup[30741]: 7A2FD29AB2B: message-id=<VS10217-07@mail>
Feb  6 15:48:54 mail postfix/qmgr[19295]: 7A2FD29AB2B: from=<>, size=2554, nrcpt=1
  (queue active)
Feb  6 15:48:55 mail postfix/smtp[30744]: 7A2FD29AB2B: to=<sender@example.com>,
  relay=relayhost[10.0.0.1], delay=1, status=sent (250 OK id=1Ap7Ho-00014I-00)
```

Bouncing the message to the sender isn't a particularly good idea, because the sender is nearly always forged in current email viruses, but this is unfortunately the default for amavisd-new.

Scanning for Viruses with smtpd_proxy_filter and amavisd-new

A different and newer approach to content filtering in Postfix is to inspect incoming messages before queuing them. This type of filter is called smtpd_proxy_filter. You can use it with amavisd-new, as shown in Figure 12-3.

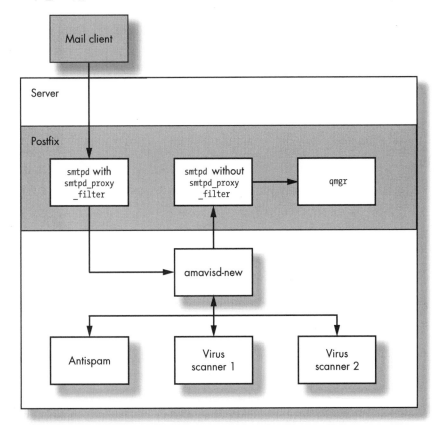

Figure 12-3: amavisd-new integration with Postfix using smtpd_proxy_filter

This is how the message would flow if you use `smtpd_proxy_filter`:

1. A mail client sends a message to a Postfix `smtpd`.

2. The `smtpd` (with `smtpd_proxy_filter` enabled) hands the message to amavisd-new. Notice that this is different from the case with `content_filter`, where the queue manager requests the Postfix `lmtp` or `smtp` client to send the message to amavisd-new.

3. amavisd-new sends the message to other applications (in this example, to two virus scanners).

4. amavisd-new tells `smtpd` whether it accepted or rejected the message. If it accepts the message, it reinjects it back into a second `smtpd` instance, but if it rejects the message, it acts according to your configuration.

5. The original `smtpd` listens to the amavisd-new replay, accepting or rejecting the message from the client.

NOTE *`smtpd_proxy_filter` is the `smtpd` daemon being broken in two parts:*

- *One part sanitizes the incoming mail with the filter.*
- *The other part does the queuing.*

This section explains how to configure amavisd-new with `smtpd_proxy_filter` using the general steps described in Chapter 11. You need to perform the following steps to integrate amavisd-new with the `smtpd_proxy_filter` parameter:

1. Install amavisd-new (described earlier in the chapter in the "Installing amavisd-new" section).

2. Test amavisd-new (described in the earlier "Testing amavisd-new" section).

3. Configure Postfix to use amavisd-new.

4. Test the configuration.

Configuring Postfix to Use amavisd-new with smtpd_proxy_filter

The first step is to define the transports the emails should take into the filtering program. You'll do these three things:

1. Modify the existing `smtpd` transport to proxy for amavisd-new.

2. Create an additional `smtpd` instance to have the mail reinjected into Postfix, circumventing any global `smtpd_proxy_filter` parameter.

3. Test the configuration as described in the previous section.

Modifying the Existing smtpd to Proxy

To make `smtpd` proxy messages to amavisd-new, append the `smtpd_proxy_filter` parameter to the existing smtp service in the `master.cf` file. For example, the following entry makes `smtpd` send messages to port 10024 on localhost (remember that these are the default settings for amavisd-new):

```
#==============================================================================
# service type       private  unpriv  chroot  wakeup  maxproc  command
#                    (yes)   (yes)   (yes)   (never)  (100)
# ==============================================================================
...
smtp     inet        n        -       n       -        20       smtpd
    -o smtpd_proxy_filter=localhost:10024
    -o smtpd_client_connection_count_limit=10
```

Notice that `-o smtpd_client_connection_count_limit=10` prevents one SMTP client from using up all 20 SMTP server processes defined in the `maxproc` column. This limit is not necessary if you receive all mail from a trusted relay host.

Also, unlike the process used earlier for the `content_filter` mechanism, you're not defining a global parameter in the `main.cf` file, so it will not be necessary to explicitly override it in the reinjection transport.

Creating an Additional smtpd Instance for Message Reinjection

To let the messages reenter the Postfix queue on a non-proxying `smtpd` instance, you need to add a special instance of `smtpd` in your `master.cf` file. This example creates another instance on port 10025 of localhost:

```
#==============================================================================
# service type       private  unpriv  chroot  wakeup  maxproc  command
#                    (yes)   (yes)   (yes)   (never)  (100)
# ==============================================================================
...
127.0.0.1:10025 inet  n        -       n       -        -        smtpd
    -o smtpd_authorized_xforward_hosts=127.0.0.0/8
    -o smtpd_client_restrictions=
    -o smtpd_helo_restrictions=
    -o smtpd_sender_restrictions=
    -o smtpd_recipient_restrictions=permit_mynetworks,reject
    -o mynetworks=127.0.0.0/8
    -o receive_override_options=no_unknown_recipient_checks
```

The `-o smtpd_authorized_xforward_hosts=127.0.0.0/8` parameter allows the after-filter `smtpd` to receive remote SMTP client information from the before-filter `smtpd`. Specifically, the after-filter `smtpd` will accept any XFORWARD commands sent by a host listed in `smtpd_authorized_xforward_hosts`. This is very useful for debugging, because the `smtpd` will use the original client IP address instead of `localhost[127.0.0.1]`.

The remaining parameters lighten the load on the after-filter `smtpd`, because the before-filter `smtpd` already did this work.

PART III

ADVANCED CONFIGURATIONS

In this part of the book, you will see common situations where Postfix interacts with other third-party applications, such as SQL servers, Cyrus SASL, OpenSSL, and OpenLDAP. Here is an overview of the chapters in this section:

Mail Gateways

Mail relays transport messages on behalf of other mail servers or clients. In most cases, mail relays are exposed to the Internet, while the other servers sit safely behind a firewall. In Chapter 13, you'll see how to make a "smart" host out of a simple mail relay.

A Mail Server for Multiple Domains

Chapter 14 describes the two ways that Postfix can handle mail for multiple domains. In addition, you will see how to configure Postfix to query an SQL Server instead of looking at static maps.

Understanding SMTP Authentication

SMTP authentication is a system for authenticating mail clients before they relay messages. Because SMTP authentication in Postfix relies on the Cyrus SASL software, Chapter 15 shows you how to configure Cyrus SASL before you can use it with Postfix.

SMTP Authentication

Continuing the discussion of SMTP authentication, Chapter 16 shows you how to configure Postfix for server- or client-side authentication or both.

Understanding Transport Layer Security

Transport Layer Security (TLS) encrypts the communication layer between Postfix and other hosts. The Postfix implementation of TLS requires OpenSSL, so Chapter 17 shows you not only how TLS works, but also how to prepare the required certificates.

Using Transport Layer Security

Chapter 18 shows you how to set up the Postfix server to offer encryption to other hosts and how to make the Postfix client use it when other servers offer TLS. You will also see how certificate-based relaying works.

A Company Mail Server

Chapter 19 explains how to configure Postfix to query an LDAP server. In doing so, you will delegate the job of local delivery to an MDA (message delivery agent) and configure a basic Courier IMAP server. In the end, you will have a complete mail system that gets user data from an OpenLDAP server.

Running Postfix in a chroot Environment

Chapter 20 shows you how to configure Postfix to run chrooted. It explains why some daemons must not run chrooted and gives you an example of how to run Postfix chrooted in combination with SASL.

13

MAIL GATEWAYS

A *mail gateway* (also called a "smarthost") is a server that connects between networks that are logically separate. Usually, the mail gateway shows up as the final destination in DNS records for other mail servers on the Internet, and those servers have no idea that other mail servers lie beyond the mail gateway. This chapter shows you how to set up a mail gateway, and it discusses the characteristics of a *real* smarthost.

Companies and ISPs use mail gateways to control SMTP traffic traveling to and from their network. Usually the network setup permits traffic on port 25 to only reach the mail gateway, and forces clients within the network to use this machine for outgoing mail. The firewall has the job of blocking the ports, and Postfix performs the mail gatewaying.

Figure 13-1 shows a groupware server that relays all messages to the mail gateway and vice versa. The mail gateway protects the groupware server from outside attacks—clients and servers from outside cannot connect directly to the groupware server.

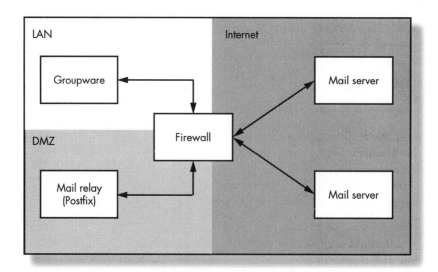

Figure 13-1: Postfix as mail relay for a groupware server

TIP *You can extend the functionality of a mail gateway by integrating features such as a virus scanner and a centralized spam filter. In doing so, you protect the groupware not only from malicious connections, but also from malicious content.*

  If you provide a relay service to customers, this chapter can help you set up a basic mail gateway. You can extend its services by adding support for SMTP authentication (see Chapter 16) and Transport Layer Security (see Chapter 18).

Basic Setup

A basic mail gateway setup allows Postfix to run on an external mail server and relay mail destined for certain domains to another (internal) mail server. To create such a mail gateway, you need to perform the following steps on the relay:

1. Allow the internal server to use the gateway as relay.
2. Set the domains that mail will be relayed to the inside (`relay_domains`).
3. Set the host that mail will be relayed to (`relayhost`).
4. Define the recipients mail will be relayed to the inside (`relay_recipient_maps`).

Setting Gateway Relay Permissions

Your first step is to permit relaying on the mail gateway for your "hidden" mail server. Add the internal mail server's IP address to the list of servers in the mynetworks parameter. For example, if the internal server's address is 172.16.1.1, you might put this line in the mail gateway's main.cf file:

```
mynetworks = 127.0.0.0/8 172.16.1.1/32
```

Limit relay access to your mail gateway's localhost address (127.0.0.1) and the internal mail server (which is 172.16.1.1 in this example), so that other hosts inside your network can't use the gateway as a relay.

Setting a Relay Domain on the Gateway

The next step is to tell Postfix to accept mail from the outer network for a host on the inner network. Postfix uses the relay_domains parameter to define a list of domains that it relays for, even if it is not the final destination for those domains. For example, if you want to relay mail for example.com, use this setting:

```
relay_domains = example.com
```

Setting the Internal Mail Host on the Gateway

Now that the gateway knows that it should accept mail for a certain domain, you must tell it where to relay incoming messages that are bound for that domain. You do this by creating a transport map, which is a file such as /etc/postfix/transport. For example, if you want to relay messages for example.com to mail.office.example.com, the file might look like this:

```
example.com    smtp:[mail.office.example.com]
```

In this line, smtp means that Postfix should use the smtp transport type defined in the master.cf file. The square brackets are important, because they disable MX lookups for mail.office.example.com. Without the brackets, Postfix would look for the MX record for mail.office.example.com. Because this record likely belongs to the server host itself, it would try to deliver the mail to itself, and incoming messages would loop.

Now you need to create the indexed file with this command:

```
# postmap hash:/etc/postfix/transport
```

Finally, set the transport_maps parameter in your main.cf file as follows (and then reload Postfix):

```
transport_maps = hash:/etc/postfix/transport
```

Defining Relay Recipients

What makes a gateway "smart"? A regular gateway accepts *any* message for *any* recipient for a relay domain, including invalid recipients that do not exist on the internal mail server that ultimately delivers the messages.

Considering the sheer amount of spam and malware flying around the Internet today, and because there may be recipients that are not allowed to receive messages from the outside (such as shared folders, internal mailing lists, and perhaps even some real people), a regular gateway can cause problems because it accepts everything. In particular, it will relay mail, spam, and viruses to nonexistent and unauthorized accounts.

Also, by accepting mail for a non-existent address, the gateway takes the responsibility to inform the sender when mail could not be delivered. This pollutes the mail queue with MAILER-DAEMON messages, and this causes backscatter mail to people all over the Internet for mail that they did not send.

When Postfix does not accept the mail, that responsibility stays with the client. When that client is a back-doored Windows PC, then no backscatter mail will be sent at all.

A smart host knows to separate the wheat from the chaff because it has a list of valid recipients on the internal servers. Use the `relay_recipient_maps` parameter to define and activate a list of valid users. For example, if your map name is `/etc/postfix/relay_recipients`, you would use this line in your `main.cf` file:

```
relay_recipient_maps = hash:/etc/postfix/relay_recipients
```

CAUTION   *If you define this parameter, the map* must *provide a list of valid relay recipients. Otherwise, your gateway won't have any consistency. If you can't provide a list, then disable the map with a setting of* `relay_recipient_maps =`.

Of course, when you tell Postfix where to find a map, you need to actually provide the list. If you configured your map as in the preceding example, create a plaintext file named `/etc/postfix/relay_recipients` containing valid recipients. For example, the following file enables relaying for `john@example.com` and `linda@example.com`:

```
john@example.com        OK
linda@example.com       OK
```

If you want to explicitly deny relay access to a certain recipient, use an error code and message such as `554 Delivery not permitted` instead of `OK`.

As with any map, you need to convert the map to the indexed database type that you defined in the `relay_recipient_maps` parameter. For example, run **postmap hash:/etc/postfix/relay_recipients** to do so.

NOTE   *It's simple to set up a list of valid users by hand if you have just a few users on the remote mail server that change once in a while. More likely than not, though, you'll have many users that continuously change, and you may not even know the list of users. See the "Exporting Valid Recipients from Active Directory" section, later in the chapter, for a discussion on how to automate the process. In particular, that section describes how to get a list of valid recipients from a Microsoft Exchange 2003 server.*

Advanced Gateway Setup

An advanced gateway not only forwards mail to other servers, but also protects against local mail attacks and automates the process of updating the list of valid recipients in the relay domain. The following sections show several techniques for improving the general mail service provided by your gateway.

Improving Security on the Mail Gateway

So far, your Postfix installation relays all messages with an example.com address to the inner mail server, mail.office.example.com. If that's the only task that your smarthost must perform (that is, if your smarthost does not receive mail for users local to the smarthost), you should disable local delivery so that the smarthost won't be vulnerable to malicious messages sent to local users on the smarthost.

Perform the following steps to disable local delivery:

1. Empty the local destination. The first step is to tell Postfix that it is not a final destination by setting the mydestination parameter with no destination, like this:

```
mydestination =
```

2. Disable local recipients. Set the local_recipient_maps parameter to nothing so that Postfix will be unable to look up any local recipient:

```
local_recipient_maps =
```

3. Forward required local recipients. When you set the empty local_recipient_maps parameter, messages to all local recipients are disabled. However, you still need to keep the gateway RFC compliant, so you must set forwarding addresses for postmaster and abuse that go to your inner mail server.

   Create a map to use as a target for the virtual_alias_maps parameter (/etc/postfix/virtual will do fine), and add forwarding addresses for these two recipients on the inner mail server. For example, your map file might look like this:

```
postmaster          postmaster@example.com
abuse               abuse@example.com
```

   Now, build an indexed map from the file with **postmap hash:/etc/postfix/virtual** and refer to it in your main.cf file, like this:

```
virtual_alias_maps = hash:/etc/postfix/virtual
```

4. Create a local delivery error message. When you disable local delivery, you should also tell any client that tries to send a message to the smarthost that you disabled delivery to local recipients. To do this, define a special local transport with the local_transport parameter that transmits an error message. For example, the following line sends all local messages to the error daemon, which will provide an appropriate error message:

```
local_transport = error:local mail delivery is disabled
```

5. Redirect replies to local services. If you've followed the steps in the previous sections, Postfix now will not accept mail for local users other than postmaster and abuse. However, local services, such as cron, that use Postfix to send status reports to administrators and users still send out mail using sender addresses associated with the hostname of the machine. This can be confusing, because you cannot reply to these messages.

   To prevent users from sending a reply to these applications, change the value of the myorigin parameter that Postfix appends as the domain part of email addresses. Set myorigin to a domain that actually has a mail server and that has mailboxes or aliases for these senders. For example, if the internal mail server that is the ultimate destination for example.com can provide this service, you might use this setting:

```
myorigin = example.com
```

6. Disabling the local delivery agent. Finally, you can prevent the master daemon from starting the local delivery agent—this effectively turns off the local delivery agent because there are no recipients on this machine. Edit your master.cf file, and comment out the line containing the local service by placing a hash (#) in front of the line, like this:

```
# ==========================================================================
# service type  private unpriv  chroot  wakeup  maxproc command + args
#               (yes)   (yes)   (yes)   (never) (100)
# ==========================================================================
smtp      inet  n       -       n       -       -       smtpd
# local   unix  -       n       n       -       -       local
virtual   unix  -       n       n       -       -       virtual
lmtp      unix  -       -       n       -       -       lmtp
anvil     unix  -       -       n       -       1       anvil
```

   After you reload Postfix, it will no longer accept messages for local recipients.

Using Postfix with Microsoft Exchange Server

Microsoft Exchange Server is, without a doubt, a powerful groupware server, but its security record and stability when under attack is not so hot. Therefore, many postmasters augment its groupware functionality with a Postfix gateway. This section discusses how you can provide a Postfix gateway host with a list of valid recipients and how to automate the procedure.

   The easiest and most common solution to making Postfix and Exchange Server work together is to have the Postfix relay host query the Exchange Server using LDAP (Lightweight Directory Access Protocol). The relay host will query the Exchange Server every time a message arrives in order to determine whether the recipient is valid. However, this approach involves risks and limitations. The alternative is to have the Exchange Server push the list of recipients to the Postfix server, which is better in the following respects:

Security

No matter what package you run on your inner mail server, you want to keep it as far as possible from security threats. That's why you put it behind a firewall in the first place. One of the basic rules of security is to permit *only* what should be permitted and to deny *everything* else.

The first impulse of many systems administrators is to have Postfix use LDAP queries to ask the remote Exchange Server for valid recipients. To do this, you must open port 389 (TCP/UDP) on the Exchange Server to permit connections from Postfix. This is relatively easy, but it opens a port to your internal LAN.

Switching directions is safer, with Exchange providing Postfix with a list of valid recipients only when the recipient list changes. With the administrator of the Exchange Server pushing this list to the smarthost with scp or rsync, you don't need to open a port from the DMZ to the LAN.

Performance

LDAP queries are slow compared to the indexed maps that Postfix uses. If you provide Postfix with a static list of valid recipients, the smarthost can process messages very quickly.

Stability

A smarthost exists to protect the inner mail server, and it's counterproductive when a smarthost under attack brings down the inner server. This can happen because spammers use dictionary attacks to send messages to a large number of recipients at once, and this would cause a mail relay using LDAP to send a large number of queries to the server that it is supposed to protect, asking about valid recipients. This would slow down (if not disable) the Active Directory and thus Exchange Server, turning a dictionary attack into a denial-of-service attack. If a mail server is to go down, you want it to be the smarthost on the outside, not the inner mail server.

In this section you will send valid recipients from an Exchange 2003 Server to a Postfix mail relay by following these steps:

1. Export a list of all valid recipients.
2. Copy the list to the mail relay.
3. Extract the valid recipients from the list.
4. Create a map of relay recipients.
5. Index the map of relay recipients.
6. Automate the procedure.

Exporting Valid Recipients from Active Directory

Microsoft uses the `proxyAddresses` attribute in its Active Directory to store the valid recipient addresses for Exchange. An easy way to export `proxyAddresses` from Microsoft's Active Directory is to use `csvde`, a command-line tool available on every Exchange Server—it will not require you to use a self-written script. For example, to export the values for `proxyAddresses` to a file named C:\export\example_com_recipients.txt, you can simply use this command from a Command Prompt window:

```
C:\> csvde -m -n -g -f "C:\export\example_com_recipients.txt" \
    -r "(|(&(objectClass=user)(objectCategory=person)) \
    (objectClass=groupOfNames) (objectClass=msExchDynamicDistributionList))" \
    -l proxyAddresses
```

TIP   *There are thousands of ways to organize and structure an Active Directory, so it can be difficult to find the object names that you need to export from your Active Directory.*
    The Exchange installation gives you the option to install several support tools, including the ADSI Edit module. Add it to your MMC (Microsoft Management Console). With this in place, running `mmc.exe` *from the command line gives you full access to the object names in the Active Directory.*

The output from the preceding command contains much more information than Postfix needs. For example, you might get this in the output file:

```
DN,proxyAddresses
"CN=Administrator,CN=Users,DC=example,DC=com",smtp:abuse@example.com;SMTP:\
  Administrator@example.com; X400:c=DE\;a= \;p=Example Corporat\;o=Exchange\;s=Administrator\
  ;;smtp:postmaster@example.com
"CN=Gast,CN=Users,DC=example,DC=com",
"CN=SUPPORT_388945a0,CN=Users,DC=example,DC=com",
"CN=krbtgt,CN=Users,DC=example,DC=com",
"CN=IUSR_MAIL,CN=Users,DC=example,DC=com",
"CN=IWAM_MAIL,CN=Users,DC=example,DC=com",
"CN=Wilma Pebble,OU=purchasing,DC=example,DC=com",smtp:wilmapebble@example.com;smtp:\
  wilma@example.com;smtp:wilma.pebble@example.com;SMTP:w.pebble@example.com;smtp:\
  pebble@example.com; X400:c=DE\;a= \;p=Example Corporat\;o=Exchange\;s=Pebble\;g=Wilma\;
"CN=Betty McBricker,OU=purchasing,DC=example,DC=com",smtp:mcbricker@example.com;smtp:\
  bettymcbricker@example.com;smtp:betty@example.com;smtp:betty.mcbricker@example.com;\
  SMTP:b.mcbricker@example.com;X400:c=DE\;a= \;p=Example Corporat\;o=Exchange\;\
  s=McBricker\;g=Betty\;
"CN=Fred Flintstone,OU=sales,DC=example,DC=com",smtp:fredflintstone@example.com;\
  SMTP:fred.flintstone@example.com;smtp:f.flintstone@example.com;smtp:fred@example.com;\
  smtp:flintstone@example.com;X400:c=DE\;a= \;p=Example Corporat\;o=Exchange\;\
  s=Flintstone\;g=Fred\;
```

```
"CN=Barney Rubble,OU=sales,DC=example,DC=com",SMTP:barney.rubble@example.com;\
  smtp:barneyrubble@example.com; smtp:rubble@example.com;smtp:barney@example.com;smtp:\
  b.rubble@example.com;X400:c=DE\;a= \;p=Example Corporat\;o=Exchange\;s=Rubble\;g=Barney\;
"CN=Bamm Bamm,OU=it,DC=example,DC=com",smtp:bammbamm@example.com;smtp:\
  bamm@example.com;smtp:bamm.bamm@example.com;SMTP:b.bamm@example.com;\
  X400:c=DE\;a= \;p=Example Corporat\;o=Exchange\;s=Bamm\;g=Bamm\;
"CN=SystemMailbox{C5C3EAFC-A32F-4925-85A5-3C08709DE617},CN=Microsoft Exchange System\
  Objects,DC=example,DC=com", SMTP:SystemMailbox{C5C3EAFC-A32F-4925-85A5-3C08709DE617}\
  @example.com;X400:c=DE\;a= \;p=Example Corporat\;o=Exchange\;s=SystemMailbox?\
  C5C3EAFC-A32F-4925-85A5-3C\;
"CN=it-department,OU=it,DC=example,DC=com",SMTP:it-department@example.com;\
  X400:c=DE\;a= \;p=Example Corporat\;o=Exchange\;s=it-department\;
"CN=purchasing-department,OU=purchasing,DC=example,DC=com",SMTP:purchasing-department@example.com;\
  X400:c=DE\;a= \;p=Example Corporat\;o=Exchange\;s=purchasing-department\;
"CN=sales-department,OU=sales,DC=example,DC=com",SMTP:sales-department@example.com;\
  X400:c=DE\;a= \;p=Example Corporat\;o=Exchange\;s=sales-department\;
```

The valid recipients are the values marked with smtp (aliases) and SMTP (primary addresses). You need to extract the values associated with smtp and SMTP to create a list that the Postfix smarthost can use. You'll eventually do this with a script on the smarthost, but for now you simply need to get the list to the smarthost.

Sending the Recipient List to the Mail Relay

There are many ways to copy a file from your Exchange Server to your smarthost, but among the best is secure copy (scp), an encrypting, automatable utility supported by both Windows and Unix.

The following steps are involved in automating the file transfer to the smarthost:

1. Get a secure copy (scp) client for Windows; for example, PuTTY.
2. Create a copy user on the smarthost.
3. Create authentication keys.
4. Add the public key to the authorized keys.
5. Copy the private key to the Windows host.
6. Convert the SSH key into PuTTY's key format.
7. Copy the export file to the smarthost.

Getting a Secure Copy Client for Windows

Among the many clients that allow you to use scp to copy files from a Windows host is PuTTY, a free Telnet and SSH client. You can download it from http://www.chiark.greenend.org.uk/~sgtatham/putty.

You need to download pscp.exe and puttygen.exe from this package to perform the operations required in this example. Copy the executables to a path that Windows searches, such as C:\Windows.

Creating a Copy User on the Smarthost

To accommodate the file transfer, create a user on your smarthost. This account will serve only to receive the exported list of recipients. For example, you could create a user named e3k with this command:

```
# useradd e3k
```

After creating a user, set its password using the passwd command. You'll use the password during the setup process, but you can disable it when everything is running smoothly.

Creating Authentication Keys

The next step is to create a set of authentication keys so that you don't need a password to transfer the files from the Windows server to the smarthost. As root on the smarthost, run **su - e3k** to switch to the e3k user and run **ssh-keygen** to create the keys: For example, you can run the following command as e3k:

```
$ ssh-keygen -t rsa
Generating public/private rsa key pair.
Enter file in which to save the key (/home/e3k/.ssh/id_rsa):
Created directory '/home/e3k/.ssh'.
Enter passphrase (empty for no passphrase): ❶
Enter same passphrase again:
Your identification has been saved in /home/e3k/.ssh/id_rsa.
Your public key has been saved in /home/e3k/.ssh/id_rsa.pub.
The key fingerprint is:
17:7e:78:9e:39:0e:04:b7:ee:6d:39:28:c6:21:e4:84 e3k@mail.example.com
```

❶ Do not provide a passphrase if you want the copy process to run unattended. If you enter a passphrase, you will need to use it whenever copying the export file to the smarthost.

The preceding command creates two files: .ssh/id_rsa and .ssh/id_rsa.pub. The former is the private key; don't let it out of your sight (no host should have it other than your Windows machine).

Adding the Public Key to the Authorized Key List

Now that you have the keys, you need to tell your SSH server about the public key that you just created. To append a public key from the file id_rsa.pub to the list in the $HOME/.ssh/authorized_keys file for your copy user (e3k), run the following command.

```
$ cd .ssh
$ cat id_rsa.pub >> authorized_keys
```

After creating the authorized_keys file, make sure that it has the correct permissions, or else the SSH server will refuse to use the file for authentication:

```
$ chmod 644 authorized_keys
$ ls -l authorized_keys
-rw-r--r--    1 e3k      e3k           230 May 13 10:38 authorized_keys
```

Copying the Private Key to Windows

Next you need to copy the private key from the smarthost to your Windows host. The easiest way to do this is to use the pscp.exe command on the Windows machine. If the IP address of your smarthost were 172.16.1.1, you would run this command at the command prompt:

```
> C:\export> pscp e3k@172.16.1.1:/home/e3k/.ssh/id_rsa .
e3k@172.16.1.1's password:
id_rsa                    |            0 kB |   0.9 kB/s | ETA: 00:00:00 | 100%
```

Use the password you created for the user in the "Creating a Copy User on the Smarthost" section.

Converting the SSH Key to the PuTTY Key Format

PuTTY uses a format different than most Unix SSH packages do to store public and private keys, so you will need to convert the private key into PuTTY's own format to use it. The puttygen utility can convert the key; run it from the command line as follows:

```
C:\export> puttygen id_rsa
```

This command starts a GUI client that loads the private key. You should now see the dialog box in Figure 13-2.

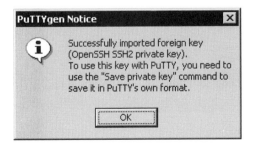

Figure 13-2: Successful key import with PuTTYgen

Click **OK** to confirm the message. The PuTTY Key Generator dialog box shown in Figure 13-3 will be displayed. Give the converted key a name (such as example_com.ppk), and click the **Save private key** button.

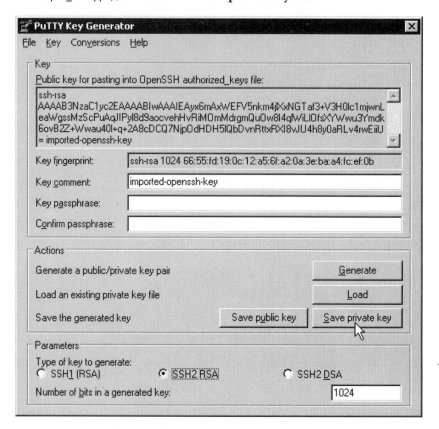

Figure 13-3: Saving the private key in PuTTYgen

As shown in Figure 13-4, the Key Generator will warn you about the empty passphrase in the key. Click **Yes** to save the key without a passphrase and to store the private key. Now your Windows host is ready to use scp to transfer files to the smarthost using an authentication key.

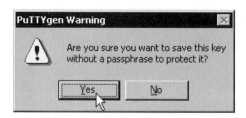

Figure 13-4: PuTTY warning about the empty passphrase in the key

Copying the List of Recipients to the Smarthost

Keep your Command Prompt window open to copy a file from your Windows host to the smarthost using the pscp.exe utility (the scp belonging to PuTTY). When you run pscp, you must identify the private key, the file to be copied, and the user that will do the copying. In our example, the private key is in the example_com.ppk file, example_com_recipients.txt is the file to be copied, and the user is e3k. To put the file in /home/e3k, you would use this command:

```
C:\export> pscp -i example_com.ppk example_com_recipients.txt e3k@172.16.1.1:/home/e3k/
Authenticating with public key "rsa-key-20040512"
example_com_recients.txt  |        2 kB |   2.4 kB/s | ETA: 00:00:00 | 100%
```

After successfully copying the file to the smarthost, you can store the csvde export command from the earlier "Exporting Valid Recipients from Active Directory" section and the preceding pscp command in a batch file named export_valid_recipients.bat. Then you can run it with a mouse click whenever you create, change, or delete a recipient. The file would look something like this:

```
csvde -m -n -g -f "C:\export\example_com_recipients.txt" \
    -r "(|(&(objectClass=user)(objectCategory=person)) \
    (objectClass=groupOfNames) (objectClass=msExchDynamicDistributionList))" \
    -l proxyAddresses
pscp -i example_com.ppk example_com_recients.txt e3k@172.16.1.1:/home/e3k/
```

After verifying that this batch file works, you can disable the copy user password on the smarthost using a command such as **usermod -L e3k** so that remote access to the e3k account is only possible with an authentication key.

Building the Recipient Map

You now have the Active Directory export file on your smarthost, so you can extract recipients from the file with a script. There are two things to remember when doing so:

- Microsoft uses both SMTP and smtp to denote recipient addresses, so the script must catch both variants.

- Your script must be able to exempt a few recipients that should not receive mail from the outside. An example is the SystemMailbox mailbox used by Exchange for internal communication.

The following script, called extract_valid_recipients, extracts all valid recipients and places them in a file, but it does not include the recipients listed in the file blacklist.

```
#!/bin/sh
# Extract all addresses that start with SMTP or smtp from
# an Active Directory export, but omit those that are listed in blacklist
cat $1 | tr -d \" | tr , \\n | tr \; \\n | awk -F\: '/(SMTP|smtp):/ {printf("%s\tOK\n",$2)}' | \
  grep -v -f blacklist > $2
```

The blacklist file looks like this:

```
Administrator
SystemMailbox
```

Run the command **extract_valid_recipients** to run the script, and it will produce a list of valid recipients in the relay_recipients file.

extract_valid_recipients /home/e3k/example_com_recipients.txt relay_recipients

The output should look like this:

```
abuse@example.com                    OK
postmaster@example.com                   OK
wilmapebble@example.com                 OK
wilma@example.com                    OK
wilma.pebble@example.com                OK
w.pebble@example.com               OK
pebble@example.com               OK
mcbricker@example.com               OK
bettymcbricker@example.com               OK
betty@example.com               OK
betty.mcbricker@example.com                OK
b.mcbricker@example.com               OK
fredflintstone@example.com                OK
fred.flintstone@example.com                OK
f.flintstone@example.com               OK
fred@example.com               OK
flintstone@example.com               OK
barney.rubble@example.com                OK
barneyrubble@example.com                OK
rubble@example.com               OK
barney@example.com               OK
b.rubble@example.com                OK
bammbamm@example.com                OK
bamm@example.com               OK
bamm.bamm@example.com                OK
b.bamm@example.com               OK
it-department@example.com                OK
purchasing-department@example.com                  OK
sales-department@example.com                 OK
```

If this output looks correct, convert it using `postmap` (for example, with a command like this: **`postmap hash:relay_recipients`**), and move it to the path that your relay_recipient_maps parameter points to (this was discussed in the earlier "Defining Relay Recipients" section). For example, you can use a command like the following:

```
# mv relay_recipients.db /etc/postfix/relay_recipients.db
```

CAUTION   *Do not point `relay_recipient_maps` directly to your newly created `relay_recipients` map (for example, hash:/home/e3k/relay_recipients)! Postfix would quit services if the map conversion failed. The safe way is to convert the map first, and only if this succeeds move it to the location where `relay_recipient_maps` points.*

Building the Sender Access Map

As an added bonus, your Active Directory export file can also give Postfix a list of senders that are permitted to send mail to the outside world. To do this, you can write a script just like the one in the "Building the Recipient Map" section, but with one small change: Microsoft uses SMTP to denote valid sender addresses, so the address extraction script should process only elements with this mark.

NOTE   *This is useful for preventing viruses from using the Outlook Contacts folder to build false sender addresses and then sending mail out of your network.*

You can call the script extract_valid_senders, and it should look like this:

```
#!/bin/bash
# Extract all addresses that start with SMTP from an Active Directory
# export, but omit those that are listed in blacklist
cat $1 | tr -d \" | tr , \\n| tr \; \\n | awk -F\: '/SMTP:/ {printf("%s\tOK\n",$2)}' | \
grep -v -f blacklist > $2
```

This time, when you run the following command, you should get a shorter list than before because there are no aliases:

```
# ./extract_valid_senders /home/e3k/example_com_recipients.txt example_com_senders
```

The output should look something like the following, which is based on the earlier example:

```
w.pebble@example.com            OK
b.mcbricker@example.com            OK
fred.flintstone@example.com            OK
barney.rubble@example.com            OK
b.bamm@example.com            OK
it-department@example.com            OK
purchasing-department@example.com            OK
sales-department@example.com            OK
```

In the preceding command-line example you redirected the output to a file named example_com_senders. Now create an indexed database from it with the **postmap hash:example_com_senders** command. Then create a restriction (see Chapter 8) that checks envelope senders with these constraints:

- If the mail comes from the internal server, it must carry one of the valid envelope sender addresses.

- If the mail does not come from the internal server, the restriction does not apply.

To configure Postfix to apply this conditional restriction, define a restriction class that triggers the envelope sender restriction when the mail comes from the internal mail server. For example, your main.cf file might contain the following:

```
smtpd_restriction_classes =
    must_be_valid_sender ❶
must_be_valid_sender = ❷
    check_sender_access hash:/etc/postfix/example_com_senders
    reject
smtpd_recipient_restrictions =
    check_client_access hash:/etc/postfix/example_com_ip ❸
    reject_unauth_destination
    ...
```

❶ must_be_valid_sender is the name of a restriction that contains the subset of restrictions that are applied when mail stems from the internal mail server; this line simply lists the restriction classes.

❷ The definition of this restriction contains the procedure for messages coming from the internal server: first check the list of valid envelope senders, and reject any other envelope sender.

❸ check_client_access triggers the execution of the must_be_valid_sender restriction class.

Finally, you need to add the IP address of your internal mail server to the/etc/postfix/example_com_ip file, along with the restriction action to be taken. For example, the following line specifies that if a message comes from 172.16.1.1, Postfix should apply the must_be_valid_sender restriction:

```
172.16.1.1    must_be_valid_sender
```

After adding these configuration options, you must reload Postfix to make the changes take effect.

Automating the Map-Building Process

You can automate the map-building process on the smarthost. The following example uses a Makefile that you can download from the *Book of Postfix* website (http://www.postfix-book.com).

```
## Makefile to automate map build process
## configuration settings
# Location of the file we extract the data from
ADS_DUMP=/home/e3k/example_com_recipients.txt
# Location of the .proto files
PROTO_PATH=relay_recipients
PROTO_PATH2=valid_senders
# destination of successfully built maps
MAP_PATH=/etc/postfix/relay_recipients
MAP_PATH2=/etc/postfix/valid_senders
# type and suffix of the maps to build
DB_TYPE=hash
DB_SUFFIX=db
## Makefile options
#
# build all maps
all:                    $(MAP_PATH).$(DB_SUFFIX) $(MAP_PATH2).$(DB_SUFFIX) blacklist
# extract valid recipients from $(ADS_DUMP) to $(PROTO_PATH).proto
$(PROTO_PATH).proto:    $(ADS_DUMP)
                        ./extract_valid_recipients $(ADS_DUMP) $(PROTO_PATH).proto
# extract valid senders from $(ADS_DUMP) to $(PROTO_PATH2).proto
$(PROTO_PATH2).proto:   $(ADS_DUMP)
                        ./extract_valid_senders $(ADS_DUMP) $(PROTO_PATH2).proto
# build map of valid recipients from $(PROTO_PATH).proto
$(MAP_PATH).$(DB_SUFFIX):   $(PROTO_PATH).proto
                        /usr/sbin/postmap -w $(DB_TYPE):$(PROTO_PATH).proto && \
                        mv $(PROTO_PATH).proto.$(DB_SUFFIX) $(MAP_PATH).$(DB_SUFFIX)
# build map of valid senders from $(PROTO_PATH2).proto
$(MAP_PATH2).$(DB_SUFFIX):  $(PROTO_PATH2).proto
                        /usr/sbin/postmap -w $(DB_TYPE):$(PROTO_PATH2).proto && \
                        mv $(PROTO_PATH2).proto.$(DB_SUFFIX) $(MAP_PATH2).$(DB_SUFFIX)
# remove all proto maps
clean:
                        rm -f $(PROTO_PATH).* $(PROTO_PATH2).* *~
```

Once you've successfully run make to verify that the conversion works, you can create a cron job to run it automatically. For example, the following job in your crontab would run every 15 minutes:

```
0,15,30,45 * * * * cd /root/relay_recipients && /usr/bin/make
```

Configuring Exchange and Postfix Communication

This section explains how to configure Microsoft Exchange to relay all mail through your Postfix gateway, and also how to configure Exchange so that it does not accidentally swamp your Postfix server.

By default, Exchange does not relay outbound messages to a gateway. To initiate the configuration for a relay, perform the following steps.

1. Start the Exchange System Manager from the Programs menu.
2. Select Server from the tree menu on the left.
3. Select your mail host from the subtree.
4. Select Protocols from the Hosts menu.
5. Select SMTP from the Protocols menu.
6. Right-click the SMTP menu, and select Properties from the Default SMTP Virtual Server menu entry.
7. Select the Delivery tab in the Default SMTP Virtual Server properties window.

You're now ready to finish the configuration. The steps are described in the following sections.

Setting the Postfix Server as the Smarthost

The first thing to do is configure Exchange to send all outbound messages to your Postfix gateway. Select Advanced Delivery from the Delivery tab, and enter the fully qualified domain name (FQDN) of your Postfix smarthost (such as postfix.example.com), as shown in Figure 13-5.

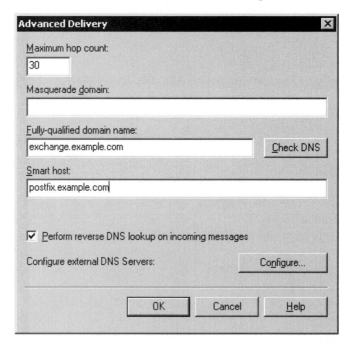

Figure 13-5: Configuring the location of the smarthosts in Exchange 2003

NOTE   *Exchange does not accept an IP address as a value for the Smart host field. Either add the smarthost to the (internal) DNS queried by the Exchange Server, or set it statically with the hosts file on your Exchange Server.*

After setting the FQDN of the smarthost, you need to stop and start the Default SMTP Virtual Server of your Exchange Server to make the changes effective.

Limiting Outbound Connections

So far, you've put a lot of effort into protecting the internal mail server from rude behavior from the smarthost. The next step serves to protect Postfix from being overloaded by messages from your Exchange Server. All you need to do is limit the number of simultaneous outgoing connections.

NOTE *The default setting in Exchange is 1,000 simultaneous connections. If the outgoing mail queue carries that many messages (which is likely to happen on a larger network after a restart of Exchange's SMTP services), it will displace its large load to the smarthost within a matter of minutes, and this can bind too many resources on the smarthost, especially if it does not offer services for a single internal mail server.*

In this case, it's better to have the Exchange Server process its outgoing mail queue at a slower pace. If you don't have access to the server, you can also use the Postfix rate-limiting mechanisms described in Chapter 21 to force a limited number of connections from the host.

Select Outbound Connections from the Delivery tab of the Default SMTP Virtual Server window, and set the limit to 50 simultaneous connections, as shown in Figure 13-6. This has proved to be a good setting under regular circumstances.

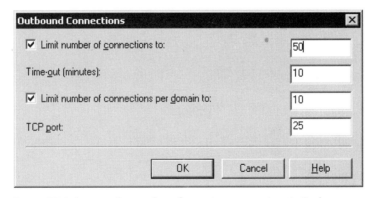

Figure 13-6: Limiting the number of outgoing connections in Exchange

NAT Setup

A Postfix mail server behind a NAT gateway runs into problems because the NAT gateway modifies the IP packets (replacing the destination address) before it transmits them to Postfix. This means that smtpd will listen only to the gateway's private IP address, while the NAT gateway accepts connections to the "official" IP address.

This is only an issue because the email RFCs require the mail server to accept mail sent to postmaster@[*address*] where *address* is an IP address. Some blacklists send delisting information only to that address.

You can configure Postfix to accept mail to postmaster@[*address*] by using the proxy_interfaces parameter. Even if Postfix only listens to an internal IP address, it will accept mail addressed to user@[*address*]. If your NAT gateway has the address 192.0.34.166, you would use this setting:

```
proxy_interfaces = 192.0.34.166
```

14

A MAIL SERVER FOR MULTIPLE DOMAINS

Postfix can send, receive, and store messages for more than one domain by using either of two distinct methods. The first method uses *virtual alias domains,* which simply expands the number of domains for which the server is the final destination. The second method involves *virtual mailbox domains* and goes further, because virtual mailbox domains do not need local accounts. This chapter shows you how to implement both approaches for offering SMTP services to more than one domain.

Virtual Alias Domains

Normally, Postfix recognizes itself as the final destination only for domain names specified with the mydestination parameter.[1] The domains listed in mydestination are called the canonical domains, because they normally list all the names of the local machine (and perhaps its parent domain name).

---

[1] Postfix also recognizes itself as the final destination for addresses of the form user@[ipaddress] that list one of Postfix's IP addresses.

In this chapter we describe a number of methods to make Postfix the final destination for additional domains. These additional domains are called virtual because they have nothing to do with the machine's own name.

To configure basic services for a virtual alias domain, you must perform the following steps:

1. Set the virtual alias domain name.
2. Create a map of recipient addresses.
3. Configure Postfix to receive mail for virtual alias domains.
4. Test the new configuration.
5. Create advanced mappings.

These steps are described in the following sections.

Setting the Virtual Alias Domain Name

Your first step is to tell Postfix that it is the final destination for a domain in addition to the system default. Postfix uses the virtual_alias_domains parameter to define a map of virtual domains. To use this parameter, create a map file, such as /etc/postfix/virtual_alias_domains, containing the virtual domains in a format like this:

```
# virtual alias domains
postfix-book.com        20021125
```

In the preceding example, the number on the right hand side is the domain's creation date, but you can set it to whatever you like. Postfix does not use the right-hand side when looking at a map for the virtual_alias_domains parameter, but Postfix maps always require both a right-hand side and a left-hand side.

After creating the file, convert it to an indexed map with this command:

```
# postmap hash:/etc/postfix/virtual_alias_domains
```

NOTE   *If you list a domain as being virtual, don't use it as the value for your mydestination parameter, because unexpected things may happen. Postfix would not know if it should deliver the mail locally or send it off to virtual rewriting. That's why Postfix will complain loudly about such a configuration in the log.*

Creating a Recipient Address Map

The next step in configuring a virtual alias domain is to create an /etc/postfix/virtual_alias_maps file to map the virtual alias domain recipient addresses to local recipient addresses. The following example includes single and multiple recipients.

```
# postfix-book.com
postmaster@postfix-book.com    ralf@example.com
abuse@postfix-book.com         abuse@example.com, patrick@example.com
ralf@postfix-book.com          ralf@example.com
patrick@postfix-book.com       patrick@example.com
```

Make sure that you include targets for postmaster and abuse, because the RFCs require that all domains have recipients for these addresses.

CAUTION *Always use fully qualified domain names in your recipient addresses on the right side of your virtual_alias_maps file. Otherwise you leave too much room for interpretation. If you specify just the localpart (for example, ralf) the Postfix trivial-rewrite daemon will add the domain part specified by myorigin. The local user ralf@$myorigin may not be correct, depending on the values of myorigin and mydestination.*

With this file in place, create an indexed map with this command:

```
# postmap hash:/etc/postfix/virtual_alias_maps
```

Configuring Postfix to Receive Mail for Virtual Alias Domains

Now that you have both maps in place, you must configure Postfix to receive mail for your virtual alias domain according to the rules in the recipient map. The parameters you need to set in main.cf are virtual_alias_domains and virtual_alias_maps. Using the file names from previous sections, the parameters should read as follows:

```
virtual_alias_domains = hash:/etc/postfix/virtual_alias_domains
virtual_alias_maps = hash:/etc/postfix/virtual_alias_maps
```

Reload Postfix and test the virtual alias domains as described in the next section.

Testing Virtual Alias Domain Settings

You can test your virtual alias domain settings by sending a message to existing and unknown recipients in both domains.

Sending to a Valid Address in a Virtual Alias Domain

This is how you might send a message to a valid recipient (postmaster):

```
$ echo test | /usr/sbin/sendmail postmaster@postfix-book.com
```

Verify that the message went through by looking at the log file. You should see log messages like the following.

```
Apr 19 11:20:50 mail postfix/pickup[17850]: B8C4629AB38: uid=0 from=<root>
Apr 19 11:20:50 mail postfix/cleanup[17863]: B8C4629AB38:
  message-id=<20040419092050.B8C4629AB38@mail.example.com>
Apr 19 11:20:50 mail postfix/qmgr[17851]: B8C4629AB38:
  from=<root@mail.example.com>, size=282, nrcpt=1 (queue active)
Apr 19 11:20:50 mail postfix/local[17866]: B8C4629AB38: to=<ralf@example.com>,
  orig_to=<postmaster@postfix-book.com>, relay=local, delay=0, status=sent
  (mailbox)
```

The test message first went to postmaster@postfix-book.com; due to the
entries in virtual_alias_maps, mail to postmaster@postfix-book.com goes to
ralf@example.com. It was then delivered locally to the user ralf, because
example.com is the "real" domain.

Sending to an Invalid Address in a Virtual Alias Domain

This is how you might send a message to an invalid recipient (nouser):

```
$ echo test | /usr/sbin/sendmail nouser@postfix-book.com
$ tail -f /var/log/mail.log
Apr 19 11:21:23 mail postfix/pickup[17850]: 9B61F29AB38: uid=0 from=<root>
Apr 19 11:21:23 mail postfix/cleanup[17863]: 9B61F29AB38:
  message-id=<20040419092123.9B61F29AB38@mail.example.com>
Apr 19 11:21:23 mail postfix/qmgr[17851]: 9B61F29AB38:
  from=<root@mail.example.com>, size=282, nrcpt=1 (queue active)
Apr 19 11:21:23 mail postfix/error[17887]: 9B61F29AB38:
  to=<nouser@postfix-book.com>, relay=none, delay=0, status=bounced
  (user unknown in virtual alias table)
```

This mail was addressed to nouser@postfix-book.com. Because there was no
entry in virtual_alias_maps, mail to nouser@postfix-book.com bounces with the
error message "user unknown in virtual alias table."

Advanced Mappings

The more virtual alias domains you add, the likelier it is that you will have
to add the same map entries over and over again. That's when catchalls—
regular expression entries and implicit mappings—come in handy. They are
described in the following subsections.

Catchall Entries

In some situations, you may want mail to an unknown user in a virtual
alias domain to go to a catchall address. The virtual(5) manual page lists
a number of ways that you can do this in a virtual_alias_maps map entry.
The one that has the least precedence is as follows:

```
@postfix-book.com    catchall@example.com
```

For the preceding entry, if your Postfix server cannot find a match for *unknownuser*@postfix-book.com in the virtual alias domain alias map for postfix-book.com, Postfix maps this address to catchall@example.com.

Regular Expression Entries

You can use regular expressions in virtual_alias_maps to map mail to a set of unknown users in a virtual alias domain to a catchall account. In addition, you can substitute the match on the LHS into the target address on the RHS—this is shown in the example below. This can be handy if you send matched addresses to a program that you specify in an alias_maps entry.

To get an idea of how this works, consider the following virtual_alias_maps entry:

```
/^(.*)@postfix-book\.com$/    catchall+$1@example.com
```

When a message arrives for an unknown user, the following happens:

1. Mail to **unknownuser**@postfix-book.com is mapped to catchall+**unknown-user**@example.com.

2. Postfix delivers the message to the local, existing recipient catchall@example.com, but during delivery to a program, it sets the $EXTENSION environment variable to *unknownuser*—as described in the local(8) manual page. (The recipient_delimiter parameter sets the extension delimiter; by default, it is +.)

3. If a program handles mail for the catchall address, it can use the $EXTENSION environment variable to find the intended recipient and construct an informational message to send back to the original sender. You can find an example of such a program, named fuzzy, at http://www.stahl.bau.tu-bs.de/~hildeb/postfix.

There are plenty of other ways that you can use regular expressions in your virtual_alias_maps map. One particularly useful practice is to map addresses that match a certain pattern to a single recipient. Let's say that you have several admin-*name*@example.com addresses that should go to a single mailbox. You could try an entry like this:

```
/^admin-.*@postfix-book\.com$/    mailbox@example.com
```

This is much nicer than specifying each mapping by hand, like this:

```
admin-firewall@postfix-book.com   mailbox@example.com
admin-mail@postfix-book.com       mailbox@example.com
admin-web@postfix-book.com        mailbox@example.com
...
```

Implicit Mappings for Multiple Domains

At times, it can be useful to create a generic mapping that applies to multiple domains. For example, your goal could be to create a generic postmaster recipient that always matches, no matter how many virtual alias domains you host. You can do this by adding the following entry to your virtual alias map:

```
postmaster    postmaster@example.com
```

With this in place, all messages addressed to a recipient with a localpart of postmaster go to postmaster@example.com. Because of the preceding entry, Postfix will accept mail for these addresses and deliver them to postmaster@example.com:

- postmaster@$myorigin
- postmaster@[$inet_interfaces]
- postmaster@$mydestination

Notice that not all of these are virtual alias domains and that these three domains may not necessarily cover all of your virtual alias domains. Take a look at the virtual(5) man page, which describes the search order in detail. If you want all of your virtual alias domains to have the same postmaster address, write a script to add them to the virtual_alias_maps.

CAUTION *You can't use configuration variables (such as $myorigin) in a map. Postfix won't expand the variables. Our notation only serves as an illustration.*

Virtual Mailbox Domains

Virtual mailbox domains are domains for users that don't have a local account (that is, for users that aren't in /etc/passwd). Originally introduced as a patch that included a separate delivery agent daemon, the virtual mailbox domain feature is now a standard Postfix component.

The virtual delivery agent in Postfix is based on the local delivery agent. Unlike the local agent, the virtual delivery agent cannot access your system's local user information (for example in /etc/passwd) to look up recipient names. Instead, the virtual delivery agent relies entirely on map types that have nothing to do with your system.

There are two reasons for preventing the virtual delivery agent from knowing anything about system accounts:

Scalability

On Linux, using local accounts defined in /etc/passwd restricts mail servers to roughly 65,536 recipients. Solaris and *BSD are not bound to this limitation. They have much longer UIDs. The virtual delivery agent is not bound to these limits.

Security

There is a much lower probability of a system compromise if usernames and passwords aren't required in order for local accounts to simply send and receive mail. Also, the virtual delivery agent does not execute user-specified shell commands or append mail to user-specified local files.

Because the virtual delivery agent knows nothing about your system, it cannot process files such as $HOME/.forward or make use of applications such as procmail and vacation. The virtual delivery agent has been reduced to delivering mail to mailboxes only.

Checking Postfix for Virtual Delivery Agent Support

To use virtual mailbox domains, the master daemon must be able to run the virtual daemon. Check your master.cf file; the default is for the daemon to be enabled, as in the following example:

```
# ============================================================================
# service type  private unpriv  chroot  wakeup   maxproc command + args
#               (yes)   (yes)   (yes)   (never)  (100)
# ============================================================================
smtp      inet  n       -       n       -        -       smtpd
...
local     unix  -       n       n       -        -       local
virtual   unix  -       n       n       -        -       virtual
...
```

NOTE   *Make sure that the virtual daemon is not running chrooted (see the fifth column in the preceding example).*

Basic Configuration

To configure a basic virtual mailbox domain, you must make the virtual delivery agent store all messages using the same UID and GID in a flat hierarchy. You will need to perform the following steps:

1. Set the name of the virtual mailbox domain.
2. Set the file ownership for the virtual delivery agent.
3. Set the base directory for the domain's mailboxes.
4. Create the recipient map.
5. Create an alias map.

Setting the Virtual Mailbox Domain Name

First, you will need to tell Postfix that it is the final destination for one or more virtual mailbox domains by setting the virtual_mailbox_domains parameter in your main.cf file to a list of domains. For example, if you wanted to create a virtual mailbox domain mailbox for example.com, you would use this setting:

```
virtual_mailbox_domains = example.com
```

Setting File Ownership

Although virtual mailbox domains do not require that each mailbox have a unique user, you still need at least one user ID (UID) and group ID (GID) to give the virtual delivery agent access to the mailboxes. To do so, you must define ownership maps with the virtual_uid_maps and virtual_gid_maps parameters.

Setting the User

To set the mailbox owner, you need to create a local user for the mailboxes, if you have not already done so. To create a mailbox user named vbox with a user ID of 1000, run this command:

```
# useradd vuser -u 1000
```

CAUTION   *By default, the mailbox owner may not have a UID lower than 100. This is a security measure set by the* virtual_minimum_uid *parameter, which prevents* virtual *from over-writing sensitive files owned by system accounts. You can set a different boundary by setting the* virtual_minimum_uid *in your main.cf file.*

With the mailbox owner user in place, you must tell virtual to use this UID when it writes messages to the filesystem. Set the UID with the virtual_uid_maps parameter in your main.cf file, as in this example for a UID of 1000:

```
virtual_uid_maps = static:1000
```

NOTE   *Use the* static *option for the UID to make the* virtual *daemon use this UID exclusively. You can also apply UIDs dynamically, as explained shortly in the "Advanced Configuration" section.*

Setting the Group

You need a local group in addition to the user that you just set. For a basic setup, create a GID with the same number as the UID in the previous section. Your useradd command may have already done this for you (check your /etc/group file), but if not, use a command such as this one:

```
# groupadd vuser -g 1000
```

Now set the `virtual_gid_maps` parameter in your `main.cf` just as you did for the virtual mailbox user:

```
virtual_gid_maps = static:1000
```

Setting the Virtual Mailbox Domain Base Directory

The virtual delivery agent needs to know where to find the mailboxes for its recipients. Normally, it's up to the operating system to provide environment variables and configuration files that tell applications about default system settings. Because the virtual delivery agent does not recognize environment variables you have to state explicitly where to put the messages it should deliver to the users.

Set the `virtual_mailbox_base` parameter in your `main.cf` file to specify where to store incoming messages. Here's an example:

```
virtual_mailbox_base = /var/spool/virtual_mailboxes
```

NOTE   *The full path of an individual virtual mailbox consists of the `virtual_mailbox_base` value and a value in the lookup map (described in the next section). In other words, it is `$virtual_mailbox_base/$mailboxname`.*

After setting the `virtual_mailbox_base` parameter, it's a good idea to actually create the directory and make it accessible to the user that you defined in the previous sections:

```
# mkdir /var/spool/virtual_mailboxes
# chown vuser:vuser /var/spool/virtual_mailboxes
# chmod 700 /var/spool/virtual_mailboxes
```

Creating the Recipient Map

You must define virtual mailbox domain recipients in a map. For example, you could create a file named `/etc/postfix/virtual_mailbox_recipients` with the fully qualified recipients on the left side and the mailbox names on the right side. Here's an example of how it might look:

```
wilma.pebble@example.com        wilmapebble
betty.mcbricker@example.com     bettymcbricker
fred.flintstone@example.com     fredflintstone
barney.rubble@example.com       barneyrubble
bamm.bamm@example.com           bammbamm/
```

The virtual daemon prepends the value of the `virtual_mailbox_base` parameter to the mailbox name to form the full mailbox file pathname. The default format for mailboxes is mbox format, but you can specify Maildir format by appending a slash (/) to the mailbox name, as in the preceding entry for `bamm.bamm@example.com`.

Once you're happy with this file, you have to build an indexed version by entering this command:

```
# postmap hash:/etc/postfix/virtual_mailbox_recipients
```

Then you can tell Postfix where to find the map by setting the virtual_mailbox_maps parameter in main.cf, as follows:

```
virtual_mailbox_maps = hash:/etc/postfix/virtual_mailbox_recipients
```

Recipient Map Limitations

For security reasons, there are a few limitations on recipient maps:

- Virtual mailbox domain recipients cannot use an address extension, such as user+extension@domain.tld.
- The virtual daemon cannot invoke external programs as local can.
- Regular expression maps are allowed, but you can't use expression substitution (this means you can't put $1 in the RHS).
- You can't perform table lookups with the proxymap daemon.

Creating the Alias Map

You can have aliases for a virtual mailbox domain, but you have to put them in a separate map, such as /etc/postfix/virtual_mailbox_aliases. The format calls for the fully qualified alias name on the left side and the fully qualified target on the right side, as in this example:

```
wilma@example.com          wilma.pebble@example.com
pebble@example.com         wilma.pebble@example.com
...
postmaster@example.com     bamm.bamm@example.com
abuse@example.com          bamm.bamm@example.com
```

As with other maps, you must create an indexed version with this command:

```
# postmap hash:/etc/postfix/virtual_mailbox_aliases
```

Finally, tell Postfix to use the map for aliases by setting the virtual_alias_maps parameter in your main.cf file, like this:

```
virtual_alias_maps = hash:/etc/postfix/virtual_mailbox_aliases
```

After reloading Postfix, your mail server will accept messages for your virtual mailbox domain recipients.

Advanced Configuration

If you need to provide mail services for many virtual mailbox domains, the chances are that storing all messages in a single directory hierarchy will cause trouble, because there may be two users with the same name. Furthermore, backing up data separately becomes very complicated. To solve these problems, you can configure virtual mailbox domains to store messages for different domains in different directories. You also have the option of using different user IDs (UIDs) and group IDs (GIDs).

To set up this kind of advanced configuration, you must do the following.

1. Set the names of the virtual mailbox domains.
2. Set file ownership for the virtual delivery agent.
3. Set the base directory for the mailboxes.
4. Create the recipient map.
5. Create an alias map.
6. Set the storage and access permissions.

Setting the Virtual Domain Names

As described in the earlier "Setting the Virtual Mailbox Domain Name" section, you set the virtual mailbox domain names with the `virtual_mailbox_domains` parameter. Here's an example with two domains:

```
virtual_mailbox_domains = example.com, postfix-book.com
```

Setting File Ownership

For an advanced configuration, you need to create a UID and GID set for each virtual recipient domain. Let's say you want to use the user and group name `example` for `example.com` and `pfxbook` for `postfix-book.com`. Refer back to the "Setting File Ownership" section for details; to create the users, you might use these commands:

```
# useradd example -u 1001
# useradd pfxbook -u 1002
# groupadd example -g 1001
# groupadd pfxbook -g 1002
```

Take note of these UIDS and GIDS; you'll use them again soon when you create lookup maps in the "Setting Storage and Access Permissions" section.

Setting the Base Directory for Virtual Mailbox Domains

You need to set the `virtual_mailbox_base` parameter to tell `virtual` where it should store messages, just as in the earlier "Setting the Virtual Mailbox Domain Base Directory" section.

Let's use the same setting as in that section:

```
virtual_mailbox_base = /var/spool/virtual_mailboxes
```

However, the difference between what we're doing here and the basic configuration we set up earlier is that you must change the directory permissions for `virtual_mailbox_base`. Otherwise the virtual daemon—using different UIDs and GIDs for each user and domain when it stores a message—will not be allowed to write to the subdirectories:

```
# mkdir /var/spool/virtual_mailboxes
# chown vuser:vuser /var/spool/virtual_mailboxes
# chmod 775 /var/spool/virtual_mailboxes
```

Now you will have to create the subdirectories (for example, `example.com` and `postfix-book.com`) because virtual will create only the mbox or Maildir of the recipient, not the parent directory of its domain.

```
# mkdir example.com
# chown example example.com/
# chgrp example example.com/
# chmod 700 example.com/
```

CAUTION   *Postfix 2.0 and earlier will not create Maildir-style mailboxes in world-writable parent directories; you will need to create Maildirs in advance.*

If mail delivery fails due to some permissions problem, you will see messages like the following in the mail log:

```
May 26 12:04:33 mail postfix/virtual[14196]: warning: maildir access problem
  for UID/GID=1002/1002: create /var/spool/mailboxes/postfix-book.com/
  patrick/tmp/1085565873.P14196.mail.example.com: Permission denied
May 26 12:04:33 mail postfix/virtual[14196]: warning: perhaps you need to
  create the maildirs in advance
```

Creating Recipient Maps

Now you need to create a map for valid recipients in your virtual mailbox domains. The process is the same as in the earlier "Creating the Recipient Map" section, except that you need to prepend directories to the mailbox names. This way, messages for separate domains go in different directories, so that you don't need to worry about name conflicts.

For example, you can create an `/etc/postfix/virtual_mailbox_recipients` file like this:

```
wilma.pebble@example.com          example.com/wilmapebble/
betty.mcbricker@example.com       example.com/bettymcbricker/
```

```
fred.flintstone@example.com          example.com/fredflintstone/
barney.rubble@example.com            example.com/barneyrubble/
bamm.bamm@example.com                example.com/bammbamm/
ralf@postfix-book.com                postfix-book.com/ralf/
patrick@postfix-book.com             postfix-book.com/patrick/
```

Remember that after creating the map, you need to build an indexed version with this command:

```
# postmap hash:/etc/postfix/virtual_mailbox_recipients
```

As before, set the `virtual_mailbox_maps` parameter to the map in your `main.cf` file.

```
virtual_mailbox_maps = hash:/etc/postfix/virtual_mailbox_recipients
```

This takes care of all recipients except for the alias maps, which you create in the same way as described in the earlier "Creating the Alias Map" section.

Setting Storage and Access Permissions

You *cannot* define separate storage and access permissions for different virtual mailbox domains, as was described in the earlier "Setting File Ownership" section. Instead, you must create maps that associate mailboxes to user IDs and group IDs.

Now you will need the UIDs and GIDs you created in the "Setting File Ownership" section. You must assign a UID to each mailbox in a map specified with the `virtual_uid_maps` parameter. For example, you could set the map name to `hash:/etc/postfix/virtual_uid_map` with this line in your `main.cf` file:

```
virtual_uid_maps = hash:/etc/postfix/virtual_uid_map
```

Now, put the recipients in the map by entering the full recipient address on the left side and the UID on the right side, as in this example:

```
wilma.pebble@example.com             1001
betty.mcbricker@example.com          1001
fred.flintstone@example.com          1001
barney.rubble@example.com            1001
bamm.bamm@example.com                1001
ralf@postfix-book.com                1002
patrick@postfix-book.com             1002
```

NOTE *Don't forget to create the indexed version of the map with the* `postmap` *command. An even shorter version would be:*

```
@example.com 1001
@postfix-book.com 1002
```

The GID mapping works just like the UID mapping. Here's a sample map that you can use for this example in a /etc/postfix/virtual_gid_map file:

```
wilma.pebble@example.com          1001
betty.mcbricker@example.com       1001
fred.flintstone@example.com       1001
barney.rubble@example.com         1001
bamm.bamm@example.com             1001
ralf@postfix-book.com             1002
patrick@postfix-book.com          1002
```

Specify this file in your virtual_gid_maps parameter as follows:

```
virtual_gid_maps = hash:/etc/postfix/virtual_gid_map
```

TIP   *Because the entries for* virtual_gid_maps *in this example are exactly the same as the ones for* virtual_uid_maps, *you can skip the work of making the GID map file and just refer to the UID map in your* main.cf *as follows:*

```
virtual_gid_maps = $virtual_uid_maps
```

After setting up the maps and configuration file, reload Postfix to have the virtual daemon deliver messages to subdirectories named after recipient domains.

Generating Maps with Scripts

As you may have noticed, virtual needs at least three maps to look up recipients, mailboxes, and owner and group permissions. You can make your life a lot easier by having a script build all of the maps from a single source file, such as /etc/postfix/virtual_build_map_source, that contains all of the required information. For example, let's say that the source file contains the following lines:

```
wilma.pebble@example.com        example.com/wilmapebble/      1001    1001
betty.mcbricker@example.com     example.com/bettymcbricker/   1001    1001
fred.flintstone@example.com     example.com/fredflintstone/   1001    1001
barney.rubble@example.com       example.com/barneyrubble/     1001    1001
bamm.bamm@example.com           example.com/bammbamm/         1001    1001
ralf@postfix-book.com           postfix-book.com/ralf/        1002    1002
patrick@postfix-book.com        postfix-book.com/patrick/     1002    1002
```

The following script (let's call it /etc/postfix/build_virtual_maps) reads the data from the map source and creates the three target maps:

```
# !/bin/bash
#
# Build all virtual mailbox maps from one source
```

```
# section: paths
SOURCE=/etc/postfix/virtual_build_map_source
VMAP=/etc/postfix/virtual_mailbox_recipients
VUID=/etc/postfix/virtual_uid_map
VGID=/etc/postfix/virtual_gid_map
AWK=/usr/bin/awk
POSTMAP=/usr/sbin/postmap
# section: build
# build $virtual_mailbox_maps
$AWK '{printf("%s %s\n",$1,$2)}' $SOURCE > $VMAP
$POSTMAP hash:$VMAP
# build $virtual_uid_maps
$AWK '{printf("%s %s\n",$1,$3)}' $SOURCE > $VUID
$POSTMAP hash:$VUID
# build $virtual_gid_maps
$AWK '{printf("%s %s\n",$1,$4)}' $SOURCE > $VGID
$POSTMAP hash:$VGID
```

NOTE *You can download this script from the* Book of Postfix *website at http://www. postfix-book.com. (You may need to change the paths at the beginning, of course.)*

After running the script, all of the maps, except the source file and the virtual alias map, should have the same date and time:

```
-rw-r--r--  1 root    root    532 May 26 12:12 virtual_build_map_source
-rw-r--r--  1 root    root    251 May 26 13:21 virtual_gid_map
-rw-r--r--  1 root    root    12288 May 26 13:21 virtual_gid_map.db
-rw-r--r--  1 root    root    394 May 26 13:21 virtual_mailbox_recipients
-rw-r--r--  1 root    root    12288 May 26 13:21 virtual_mailbox_recipients.db
-rw-r--r--  1 root    root    251 May 26 13:21 virtual_uid_map
-rw-r--r--  1 root    root    12288 May 26 13:21 virtual_uid_map.db
```

Database-Driven Virtual Mailbox Domains

If you're interested in an enterprise or an ISP MTA, you can have Postfix access a database to get virtual mailbox domain information. This arrangement is especially flexible, because you can delegate the user administration to other people without giving them root access on the server. If you provide a powerful web interface, your customers can manage their own data (add aliases, change their SMTP AUTH, POP3, and IMAP passwords, and so on). Furthermore, changes to data in the database show up immediately, so you don't need to reload Postfix every time you change data.

On the other hand, indexed maps are faster to access, and map lookups don't consume as many system resources as SQL queries, because you don't need to run a database server. Furthermore, a database-driven solution may be more complex.

If you run into performance problems with database lookups, you can set up a dedicated database server that can be available to many Postfix servers (and other services) on your network. Combined with load-balancing mechanisms such as round robin and special hardware, you can build high-performance mail services with a database.

This section shows you how to implement database-driven virtual mailbox domains using MySQL as the database. Here's what you need to do:

1. Check Postfix for MySQL map support.
2. Build Postfix to support MySQL maps.
3. Configure the database.
4. Test database-driven virtual mailbox domains.

NOTE *Database-driven maps aren't limited to being used in virtual mailbox domains. You can use them in many other scenarios. Postfix also supports PostgreSQL and LDAP queries (the PostgreSQL configuration is nearly identical to that of MySQL; LDAP is discussed in Chapter 19).*

Checking Postfix for MySQL Map Support

Before you configure Postfix to query MySQL, you should probably verify that your installation actually supports this type of map. Use the `postconf -m` command to print the supported map types. If you have MySQL support, you should see `mysql` in the output, as in this example:

```
# postconf -m
btree
cidr
environ
hash
ldap
mysql
nis
pcre
proxy
regexp
sdbm
static
unix
```

If you don't have MySQL support in your installation, you can either install a Postfix package from your operating system distribution that supports MySQL, or you can build it yourself manually and then install your new version (as described in the next section).

Building Postfix to Support MySQL Maps

To build Postfix with MySQL table support, first locate the header files and libraries that the Postfix build needs. To find the header file directory, use this command:

```
# find /usr -name 'mysql.h'
/usr/include/mysql/mysql.h
```

The preceding output shows that the header files on this particular system are in /usr/include/mysql. To find the MySQL client libraries, run this command:

```
# find /usr -name 'libmysqlclient.*'
/usr/lib/mysql/libmysqlclient.so.10
/usr/lib/mysql/libmysqlclient.so.10.0.0
/usr/lib/mysql/libmysqlclient.so
/usr/lib/mysql/libmysqlclient.a
```

The output here shows that the libraries are in /usr/lib/mysql.

Now that you know the correct paths, you can set the variables for the Postfix Makefile build configuration process. For the paths in this example, you would use the following command to configure and build Postfix:

```
$  make tidy
$  make makefiles CCARGS='-DHAS_MYSQL -I/usr/include/mysql'
   AUXLIBS='-L/usr/lib/mysql -lmysqlclient -lz -lm'
$  make
```

After the build completes and you install Postfix, verify that you have MySQL support as described in the previous section.

Configuring the Database

When you're ready to set up the MySQL database to hold your virtual domain information, connect to MySQL as root and create a database. The following command creates a database named mail:

```
mysql> CREATE DATABASE `mail`;
```

TIP *You can download the complete set of SQL statements for this section from* The Book of Postfix *website at* http://www.postfix-book.com. *If you need to learn something about SQL statements first, A Gentle Introduction to SQL can be found at* http://sqlzoo.net.

Creating a Recipient Domain Table

Create a table with a name such as `virtual_mailbox_domains` to hold the domains for which Postfix will consider itself the final destination. You can use this command:

```
mysql> CREATE TABLE `virtual_mailbox_domains` (
mysql>    `Id` int(10) unsigned NOT NULL auto_increment,
mysql>    `domain` varchar(255) default NULL,
mysql>    PRIMARY KEY (`Id`),
mysql>    FULLTEXT KEY `domains` (`domain`)
mysql> ) TYPE=MyISAM COMMENT='Postfix virtual aliases';
```

If this command is successful, you can add your virtual domains to the table. For example, to add example.com to the table, type this SQL command to insert a row:

```
mysql> INSERT INTO virtual_mailbox_domains VALUES (1,'example.com');
```

Adding Users

Now it's time to create a table where each row contains a recipient, mailbox name, UID, and GID. You can name it `virtual_users`; the structure is very similar to the columns of the /etc/postfix/virtual_build_map_source file that we used in the earlier "Generating Maps with Scripts" section.

NOTE   *The following table builds upon the MySQL SMTP AUTH table described in Chapter 18. It contains passwords and other information, so you can use it as an authentication backend source for both SMTP authentication and for virtual mailbox domains.*

Run the following command to create the virtual_users table:

```
mysql> CREATE TABLE `virtual_users` (
mysql>    `id` int(11) unsigned NOT NULL auto_increment,
mysql>    `username` varchar(255) NOT NULL default '0',
mysql>    `userrealm` varchar(255) NOT NULL default 'mail.example.com',
mysql>    `userpassword` varchar(255) NOT NULL default '1stP@ss',
mysql>    `auth` tinyint(1) default '1',
mysql>    `active` tinyint(1) default '1',
mysql>    `email` varchar(255) NOT NULL default '',
mysql>    `virtual_uid` smallint(5) default '1000',
mysql>    `virtual_gid` smallint(5) default '1000',
mysql>    `virtual_mailbox` varchar(255) default NULL,
mysql>    PRIMARY KEY (`id`),
mysql>    UNIQUE KEY `id` (`id`),
mysql>    FULLTEXT KEY `recipient` (`email`)
mysql> ) TYPE=MyISAM COMMENT='SMTP AUTH and virtual users';
```

The active field is optional; you can use it to enable or disable a recipient's mailbox (which might be useful if a customer hasn't paid, and you need to disable the service, but you don't want to lose the account configuration).

With the table in place, you need to add data for testing. Here is a command that adds a sample row:

```
mysql> INSERT INTO virtual_users VALUES (5,'bamm.bamm','mail.example.com','1stP@ss',1,1,
mysql> 'bamm.bamm@example.com',1001,1001,'example.com/bammbamm/');
```

Creating a Table for Virtual Aliases

The last table that you must create is for virtual aliases. As with other alias maps, the table rows contain the alias name and the real recipient address. Create a table (with a name such as virtual_aliases) as follows:

```
mysql> CREATE TABLE `virtual_aliases` (
mysql>     `Id` int(10) unsigned NOT NULL auto_increment,
mysql>     `alias` varchar(255) default NULL,
mysql>     `virtual_user_email` text,
mysql>     PRIMARY KEY  (`Id`),
mysql>     FULLTEXT KEY `aliases` (`alias`,`virtual_user_email`)
mysql> ) TYPE=MyISAM COMMENT='Postfix virtual recipients';
```

As with the other tables, you should fill it with some data. Start with the aliases that the RFCs require:

```
mysql> INSERT INTO virtual_aliases VALUES (1,'postmaster@example.com','bamm.bamm@example.com');
mysql> INSERT INTO virtual_aliases VALUES (2,'abuse@example.com','bamm.bamm@example.com');
```

Creating a MySQL User for Postfix

Your last task in configuring the database is to create a MySQL user to query the tables. You should limit the user's permissions so that Postfix cannot modify the data. The following command adds a new user named postfix that can connect from localhost:

```
mysql> CONNECT mysql;
mysql> INSERT INTO user VALUES
     ('localhost','postfix','','Y','Y','Y','Y','Y','Y','Y','Y','Y','Y','Y','Y','Y','Y');
mysql> UPDATE mysql.user SET password=PASSWORD("Yanggt!") WHERE user='postfix' AND
     host='localhost';
mysql> FLUSH PRIVILEGES;
```

You need to restrict the account to read-only (SELECT) access. Postfix shouldn't be able to alter or create tables. Use the GRANT command to do this:

```
mysql> GRANT USAGE ON *.* TO 'postfix'@'localhost' IDENTIFIED BY PASSWORD '2fc879714f7d3e72';
mysql> GRANT SELECT ON mail.virtual_aliases TO 'postfix'@'localhost';
mysql> GRANT SELECT ON mail.virtual_users TO 'postfix'@'localhost';
mysql> GRANT SELECT ON mail.virtual_mailbox_domains TO 'postfix'@'localhost';
```

Configuring Postfix to Use the Database

When configuring a SQL query system for Postfix, you must set the following parameters in a special file. Postfix substitutes these parameters into a series of SQL statements that culminates with a SELECT statement:

user

> The username that connects to the database.

password

> The password of the database user. It must be in plaintext form.

hosts

> A list of one or more FQDN hostnames or IP addresses of SQL servers. If Postfix fails when trying to contact the first host in the list, it will try the other hosts in random order. If no server is available, Postfix defers the job until a server is online.
>
> When you use localhost as a server, Postfix automatically uses a Unix domain socket instead of a TCP/UDP connection.

dbname

> The database to connect to.

table

> The name of the table that contains the virtual domain data.

select_field

> The field that contains a result from the query (for example, a user's email address).

where_field

> The field to match when querying the database (for example, an email alias).

additional_conditions

> Additional conditions on the query; for example, you may want to query only user accounts that are currently active. This parameter is optional.

Table 14-1 illustrates how the fields of indexed maps correspond to database parameters. You can use it when creating a SELECT statement if you're not sure of the table fields you need to specify.

Table 14-1: How Fields of Indexed Maps Correspond to Database Parameters

Map Type	LHS	RHS	Conditions
indexed map	left column	right column	-
SQL database table	where_field	select_field	additional_conditions

Protecting the Postfix SQL Configuration

Postfix currently supports two ways of configuring MySQL (and PostgreSQL) SELECT statements.

The first requires that you write Postfix's SQL server username and password in your main.cf file. Because this is not very safe, it will not be covered in this book (main.cf is normally world-readable, so every user on your system would be able to get these credentials). If you insist on using this method, see MYSQL_README in the Postfix readme directory for more information, but be aware that future versions of Postfix will not support this style.

The second method is preferable because it handles security far better. The SELECT statements (including the username and password) go in separate files outside of main.cf. Furthermore, you will put them into a subdirectory accessible only to Postfix and root (you'll specify the location of the files in main.cf).

To set up the file structure, first create a directory, such as /etc/postfix/sql, and set appropriate permissions:

```
# mkdir /etc/postfix/sql
# chown postfix /etc/postfix/sql
# chgrp root /etc/postfix/sql
# chmod 500 /etc/postfix/sql
```

Now you're ready to add files here, where they are safe from (most) prying eyes.

Constructing the Recipient Domains Query

The first file you need to add will define the parameters for a query that retrieves the domains for which Postfix considers itself a final destination. Add the following configuration to a file such as /etc/postfix/sql/virtual_mailbox_domains.cf:

```
user = postfix
password = Yanggt!
dbname = mail
table = virtual_mailbox_domains
select_field = domain
where_field = domain
hosts = localhost
```

As mentioned earlier, these parameters correspond to values in a SQL SELECT statement. The statement for the preceding file would be as follows, with *domainpart* being the domain part of the incoming recipient email address:

```
mysql> SELECT domain FROM virtual_mailbox_domains WHERE domain = 'domainpart'
```

It may seem a little strange to read the domain from the table when you already know it, but the point of this query is to see whether there are actually any rows in the database that match the domain part. If there are none, the query fails, and Postfix knows that it is not the final destination for the domain.

NOTE *You do not need to enter any of these SELECT statements (Postfix constructs them automatically when accessing the database), but it helps to know them when tracking down database problems at the MySQL prompt.*

Now you need to tell Postfix (in main.cf) to use MySQL and where to find the parameters for virtual_mailbox_domains. The specification looks much like a regular indexed map, but with the hash keyword replaced with mysql:

```
virtual_mailbox_domains = mysql:/etc/postfix/sql/virtual_mailbox_domains.cf
```

Creating the User ID and Group ID Queries

Next you need to add the parameters for the UID and GID queries (remember that these define the virtual mailbox file owner). Add the following lines to a file named /etc/postfix/sql/virtual_uid_maps.cf:

```
user = postfix
password = Yanggt!
dbname = mail
table = virtual_users
select_field = virtual_uid
where_field = email
hosts = localhost
```

The SELECT statement that corresponds to this file looks like the following (where *recipient* is the recipient address of an incoming message):

```
mysql> SELECT virtual_uid FROM virtual_users WHERE email = 'recipient'
```

Use the virtual_uid_maps parameter in main.cf to tell Postfix where it can find the SQL query to lookup the UID:

```
virtual_uid_maps = mysql:/etc/postfix/sql/virtual_uid_maps.cf
```

Creating a SQL lookup for the GID is similar to the UID procedure. Use a filename such as /etc/postfix/sql/virtual_gid_maps.cf to create the SQL SELECT statement:

```
user = postfix
password = Yanggt!
dbname = mail
```

```
table = virtual_users
select_field = virtual_gid
where_field = email
hosts = localhost
```

The corresponding SQL SELECT statement for this file is as follows:

```
mysql> SELECT virtual_gid FROM virtual_users WHERE email = 'recipient'
```

Then tell Postfix where to lookup the GID. Point the virtual_gid_maps parameter in main.cf to the SQL query file:

```
virtual_gid_maps = mysql:/etc/postfix/sql/virtual_gid_maps.cf
```

Creating the Recipient Query

Perhaps the most important query is the one that retrieves the recipient mailbox name when given a recipient address. Add the following query parameters to the /etc/postfix/sql/virtual_mailbox_recipients.cf file:

```
user = postfix
password = Yanggt!
dbname = mail
table = virtual_users
select_field = virtual_mailbox
where_field = email
additional_conditions = and active = '1'
hosts = localhost
```

Notice the additional_conditions parameter here. The parameters in this file correspond to the following SELECT statement:

```
mysql> SELECT virtual_mailbox FROM virtual_users WHERE email = 'recipient' AND active = '1'
```

The virtual_mailbox_maps parameter tells Postfix where to look for virtual mailbox recipients and their mailboxes. In main.cf, add this line:

```
virtual_mailbox_maps = mysql:/etc/postfix/sql/virtual_mailbox_recipients.cf
```

Creating the Aliases Query

Finally, it's time to specify the parameters for the virtual aliases query. Put the following lines in a file such as /etc/postfix/sql/virtual_alias_maps.cf:

```
user = postfix
password = Yanggt!
dbname = mail
```

```
table = virtual_aliases
select_field = virtual_user_email
where_field = alias
hosts = localhost
```

This is the SELECT statement that corresponds to the preceding file:

```
mysql> SELECT virtual_user_email FROM virtual_aliases WHERE alias = 'recipient'
```

To wrap it up, tell Postfix where to find the aliases query configuration file with the virtual_alias_maps parameter in main.cf:

```
virtual_alias_maps = mysql:/etc/postfix/sql/virtual_alias_maps.cf
```

Reload Postfix to put all the changes in main.cf into effect, and start testing.

Testing Database-Driven Virtual Mailbox Domains

Tracking down a problem can become quite tedious if you can't tell whether the problem lies with Postfix or MySQL. That's why you should test MySQL and Postfix separately. If the MySQL tests succeed, then you know the problem lies with the Postfix configuration.

Testing MySQL

The very first thing you should test is whether the username and password that you supplied in the query configuration files are allowed to access MySQL and make queries.

Then try to connect to the database that holds your virtual mailbox domain data. Both tests will be shown in the following example:

```
# mysql -u postfix -p -h localhost -A
```

Upon successful login, you will see this output:

```
Welcome to the MySQL monitor.  Commands end with ; or \g.
Your MySQL connection id is 144 to server version: 3.23.58
Type 'help;' or '\h' for help. Type '\c' to clear the buffer.
mysql>
```

Use the CONNECT statement to access the mail database, and you should get a confirmation that looks like this:

```
mysql> CONNECT mail;
Connection id:    145
Current database: mail
mysql>
```

If you can't connect to the server, check the username and password that you specified to MySQL in the earlier "Creating a MySQL User for Postfix" section. On the other hand, if you're having trouble connecting to the mail database, check the GRANT statements (in the same section).

Querying Recipient Domains

Now it's time to run a SELECT statement that will verify that your Postfix MySQL user can look up virtual mailbox domains in the virtual_mailbox_domains table. Enter a command such as this:

```
mysql> SELECT domain FROM virtual_mailbox_domains WHERE domain = 'example.com';
```

If this is successful, you should see one row of output that contains the query input (recall from the "Constructing the Recipient Domains Query" section that this is the correct behavior):

```
+-------------+
| domain      |
+-------------+
| example.com |
+-------------+
1 row in set (0.00 sec)
```

If you don't get a match, check whether the domain exists in your table. One easy way to check this is to retrieve all rows from the table by omitting the WHERE clause:

```
mysql> SELECT domain FROM virtual_mailbox_domains;
```

Querying Virtual Mailbox UIDs and GIDs

Next you verify that your MySQL user is able to retrieve a known recipient address. Try to the retrieve the virtual_uid field from a known recipient address in your virtual_users table, as in this successful example, which shows the mapping from bamm.bamm@example.com to the virtual mailbox UID 1001:

```
mysql> SELECT virtual_uid FROM virtual_users WHERE email =
  'bamm.bamm@example.com';
+-------------+
| virtual_uid |
+-------------+
|        1001 |
+-------------+
1 row in set (0.00 sec)
```

Do the same for the GID:

```
mysql> SELECT virtual_gid FROM virtual_users WHERE email =
  'bamm.bamm@example.com';
```

```
+-------------+
| virtual_gid |
+-------------+
|        1001 |
+-------------+
1 row in set (0.00 sec)
```

Querying Recipient Mailboxes

Test whether the Postfix MySQL user can look up a mailbox for a given recipient. Recall that this is the virtual_mailbox in the virtual_users table. Here's an example that maps bamm.bamm@example.com to the Maildir-style mailbox example.com/bammbamm/:

```
mysql> SELECT virtual_mailbox FROM virtual_users WHERE email =
  'bamm.bamm@example.com';
+-----------------------+
| virtual_mailbox       |
+-----------------------+
| example.com/bammbamm/ |
+-----------------------+
1 row in set (0.00 sec)
```

Querying Aliases

Your final database check is for aliases. For a known alias, retrieve the recipient address (the virtual_user_email field in the virtual_aliases table). Here's an example:

```
mysql> SELECT virtual_user_email FROM virtual_aliases WHERE alias =
  'postmaster@example.com';
+-----------------------+
| virtual_user_email    |
+-----------------------+
| bamm.bamm@example.com |
+-----------------------+
1 row in set (0.00 sec)
```

Testing Postfix

You can test Postfix MySQL lookups without sending any test email messages. The postmap command can perform any kind of query, including those in a MySQL table. Here's the general format of a postmap command that does a MySQL query:

```
# postmap -q "value" mysql:path-to-parameter-file
```

For example, here's how to tell Postfix to query MySQL for a known virtual mailbox domain:

```
# postmap -q "example.com" mysql:/etc/postfix/sql/virtual_mailbox_domains.cf
```

If this is successful, the data matching the query should be displayed on the command line:

```
example.com
```

If no result is being returned, check whether that virtual domain name exists in your table (see the earlier "Querying Recipient Domains" section). If that test was successful, verify the username and password information in your virtual_mailbox_domains.cf file.

Querying UIDs and GIDs

To proceed with testing, tell Postfix to query MySQL for the UID and GID of a known virtual mailbox recipient:

```
# postmap -q "bamm.bamm@example.com" mysql:/etc/postfix/sql/virtual_uid_maps.cf
1001
# postmap -q "bamm.bamm@example.com" mysql:/etc/postfix/sql/virtual_gid_maps.cf
1001
```

Querying Recipients

Next, verify Postfix can query for known recipients. The postmap command that corresponds to the SELECT statement in the earlier "Querying Recipient Mailboxes" section is as follows:

```
# postmap -q "bamm.bamm@example.com" mysql:/etc/postfix/sql/virtual_mailbox_recipients.cf
example.com/bammbamm/
```

Querying Aliases

Your final test is to tell Postfix to query MySQL for the virtual user email address of a known alias. A successful query looks like this:

```
# postmap -q "postmaster@example.com" mysql:/etc/postfix/sql/virtual_alias_maps.cf
bamm.bamm@example.com
```

15

UNDERSTANDING SMTP AUTHENTICATION

SMTP authentication is a way of identifying mail clients independent of their IP addresses, which makes it possible for a server to relay messages for mail clients with IP addresses that the server does not trust. This chapter is a primer on SMTP authentication (SMTP AUTH). Not only will you learn about SMTP authentication and its advantages over other approaches, but you will also see how to install and configure Cyrus SASL, a package required for SMTP authentication support in Postfix.

The Architecture and Configuration of Cyrus SASL

In the early days, SMTP servers would forward mail from any client to any destination. When spam became a problem, MTAs had to be extended with the ability to only accept mail forwarding requests from specific clients. MTA implementors decided to identify these specific clients by their IP address, and then administrators had to configure their systems to reject untrusted clients (see Figure 15-1).

Today mail-relay abuse attempts are still a daily nuisance, and administrators spent lots of time fortifying their servers using further restrictions (see Chapter 8). Still, basing relay access on an IP address is difficult in the case of the extremely large and distributed networks in use today, and it is completely unworkable for mobile users.

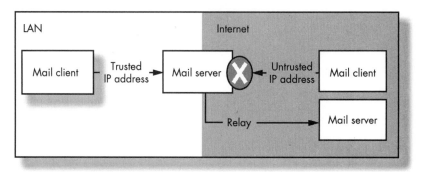

Figure 15-1: Modern mail servers reject relaying from untrusted IP addresses

Mobile users (which are defined in RFC 2977) need to access their own domain's resources regardless of their current location on the Internet. Unfortunately, mobile users almost never use the same IP address, and furthermore, the mobile user and postmaster will never know their IP addresses in advance, rendering rules based on static IP addresses useless.

There are several ways of allowing relay access to mobile users:

- SMTP-after-POP and SMTP-after-IMAP
- SMTP authentication
- Certificate-based relaying
- Virtual private networks (VPNs)

The SMTP-after-POP or SMTP-after-IMAP method (see Figure 15-2) delegates the problem of identification to a POP or IMAP server.

These are the basic steps in the SMTP-after-POP or SMTP-after-IMAP method:

1. The mail client authenticates to a POP or IMAP server.

2. After successful authentication, the POP or IMAP server writes the mail client's IP address into a database shared with the mail server. The IP address stays in the database for a limited amount of time.

3. The mail client attempts to relay a message through the SMTP server.
4. The SMTP server looks up the mail client's IP address in the database. If the IP address is in the database, the server allows relaying.

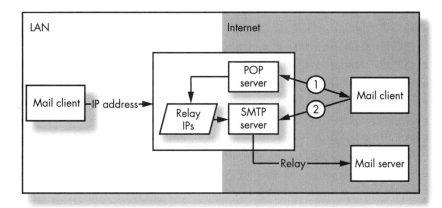

Figure 15-2: SMTP-after-POP as authentication for relaying

SMTP authentication solves the problem at its root (see Figure 15-3). These are the basic steps in the SMTP AUTH method:

1. The SMTP server offers SMTP AUTH to a mail client.
2. The client passes its credentials to the server.
3. The server verifies the credentials and permits relaying if they are valid.

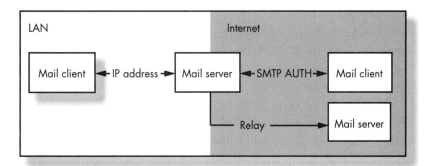

Figure 15-3: SMTP AUTH as authentication for relaying

Certificate-based relaying, covered in Chapter 18, is based upon the exchange and validation of TLS client certificates (see Figure 15-4). These are the basic steps in certificate-based relaying:

1. The SMTP server offers a TLS connection to the mail client.
2. The client sends its certificate to the server.
3. The server verifies the certificate and permits the client to relay if the certificate is among those that the server recognizes.

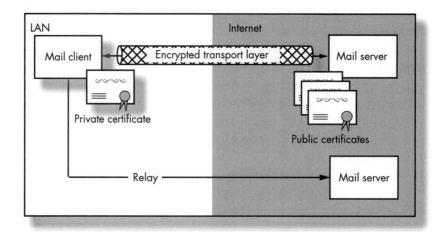

Figure 15-4: Client certificate as authentication for relaying

Virtual private networks (VPNs) give clients access to a mail server by setting up a secure virtual network running on top of the regular Internet. In a VPN, administrators have control over IP addresses, so you can use relaying based on IP address. Because the VPN configuration has nothing to do with the SMTP server configuration, it is not covered in this book. These are the basic steps in using a VPN:

1. The mail client's computer connects to a VPN.
2. The SMTP server allows the client to relay based on the client's IP address in the virtual network.

Which Approach Is Best?

Certificate-based relaying with TLS is great, because it provides a high level of security, but many mail clients do not yet support it. In addition, the overhead of managing certificates on the clients and server is not trivial. These two factors constitute a substantial effort for a company-wide or ISP-wide rollout. If you can't yet use certificates to relay, your choices boil down to SMTP-after-POP, SMTP AUTH, and VPNs.

From a system architect's point of view, SMTP-after-POP is far less than ideal, because the solution is not even within the server and protocol where the problem lies. Instead, another server (a POP or IMAP server), which is at least as complex as an SMTP server, provides a stopgap solution. This complicates matters, because the two servers must communicate, and because the servers were almost certainly developed by different people there is a high risk of incompatibility, especially as new releases appear.

The design of SMTP-after-POP isn't its only drawback. It actually doesn't provide very good security because of its IP address–based decision mechanism. It's not difficult to spoof an IP address—an attacker can discover the IP address of a mail client that has just been granted permission to relay for a certain time slot and spoof that IP address until the time has passed. This kind of abuse is not possible when the client has to authenticate for every new message that it wants to send.

A VPN-based system is very easy to set up if you already have a VPN, but setting up a VPN just for a mail server is a tremendous amount of effort. In addition, a VPN requires ongoing maintenance because each new mobile user needs VPN software.

If you want something simple, independent, and secure, SMTP AUTH is probably for you.

SASL: The Simple Authentication and Security Layer

Postfix implements SMTP authentication with the help of SASL (Simple Authentication and Security Layer). SASL is an authentication framework described in RFC 2222, and understanding how it works is critical to understanding SMTP authentication as a whole. There are several SASL implementations, and Postfix uses the Cyrus-SASL libraries derived from the original SASL implementation in Project Cyrus.

NOTE *Project Cyrus is the name of Carnegie Mellon University's project to build a new campus mail system. See* `http://asg.web.cmu.edu/cyrus` *for more information.*

SASL consists of three layers that you must configure. Figure 15-5 shows the three layers: the authentication interface, the mechanism, and the method.

In an application that uses the Cyrus SASL framework, the authentication process requires the following steps:

1. An application supporting SASL (such as the Postfix `smtpd` daemon) listens for network connections.
2. A client connects and initiates authentication in these four substeps:
   a. The client chooses an SMTP AUTH mechanism.
   b. The client prepares to transmit its credentials according to the requirements of the mechanism.
   c. The client tells the server which mechanism it has chosen.
   d. The client transmits the credentials.
3. The application stores the information about the chosen mechanism and the credentials.
4. The application hands the information over to a mechanism driver, which passes it along to the password-verification service.
5. The password-verification service accesses an authentication backend, such as `/etc/shadow`. The backend tries to match the client's credentials with one of its entries.

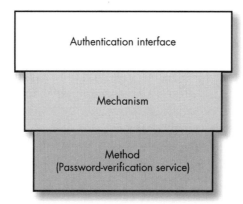

Figure 15-5: The SASL layers

6. The password-verification service hands the result from the backend to smtpd.

7. smtpd takes action based on the result. For example, it can let authenticated users relay mail.

The following sections explain Cyrus SASL in more detail. You will learn all about the SASL authentication interface, methods, mechanisms, and authentication backends, and about how to prepare Cyrus SASL and Postfix to offer server-side SMTP AUTH.

Authentication Interface

The purpose of an authentication interface is to tell a client that authentication is available and which authentication mechanisms may be used. Many services, to name only LDAP or SMTP, may require authentication, but they differ in their client-server protocol. That's why SASL has no authentication interface of its own. Instead, it leaves it to the specific service and its protocol to integrate how the capability of authentication is brought to the attention of the client.

For email, the place where client and server meet, is the SMTP dialog. The ESMTP protocol integrates authentication into the dialog by adding it to the list of the mail server's capabilities. You can see if a mail server offers SMTP AUTH functionality by connecting to the server and using the EHLO greeting, like this:

```
$ telnet mail.example.com 25
220 mail.example.com ESMTP Postfix
EHLO client.example.com
250-mail.example.com
250-PIPELINING
250-SIZE 20480000
250-VRFY
250-ETRN
```

```
250-AUTH PLAIN LOGIN
250-AUTH=PLAIN LOGIN
250-XVERP
250 8BITMIME
QUIT
221 Bye
```

The boldface-italic lines in the preceding output indicate SMTP authentication support with the PLAIN and LOGIN authentication mechanisms. The second line (with the equal sign) is present for broken mail clients that do not follow the final SASL specification.

CAUTION *The application interface is configured within the application that offers SMTP AUTH. In Postfix, that's the smtpd daemon; you'll see how to configure the interface in Chapter 16.*

SMTP AUTH Mechanisms

SMTP AUTH mechanisms, such as PLAIN and LOGIN, define the verification strategy used during authentication. The mechanisms that the server offers show up in the application interface; in this case, that's the SMTP dialog. When initiating authentication, the client chooses a mechanism, transmits its choice to the server, and then transmits its credentials.

Cyrus SASL offers a wide variety of SASL mechanisms that differ in the way they transmit credentials and in the level of security they provide. A few of them are nonstandard and are designed for specific clients. You don't have to use all of the mechanisms available to you; you can configure Postfix to offer only a limited range of Cyrus SASL mechanisms.

TIP *In practice, it is best to use PLAIN, LOGIN, and CRAM-MD5 in an environment where you need to support Windows, Mac OS, and Unix clients.*

Here are the mechanisms:

ANONYMOUS

The ANONYMOUS mechanism (defined in RFC 2245) was created to permit anonymous access to mail services. To use this mechanism, all a mail client needs to do is send any string to the server, and the server will then allow the client to relay.

CAUTION *Do not use the ANONYMOUS mechanism with Postfix unless you want your mail server to become an open relay. Spammers know how to abuse this mechanism.*

CRAM-MD5, DIGEST-MD5

The Cyrus SASL library supports two "shared secret" mechanisms: CRAM-MD5 and its successor, DIGEST-MD5. These methods rely on the client and the server sharing a secret, usually a password. The server generates a challenge based on the secret, and the client responds, proving that it knows the shared secret. This is much more secure than simply sending an unencrypted password over a network, but the server still needs to store the secret.

EXTERNAL

The EXTERNAL mechanism allows you to bind TLS/SSL credentials to SASL. In particular, the EXTERNAL mechanism allows you to extract some form of username from the certificate used during TLS/SSL negotiation.

GSSAPI, KERBEROS_V4

The Cyrus SASL library comes with two mechanisms that make use of the Kerberos authentication system: KERBEROS_V4, which should be able to use any Kerberos v4 implementation, and GSSAPI (tested against MIT Kerberos v5 and Heimdal Kerberos v5). Because these mechanisms make use of the Kerberos infrastructure, they have no password database.

NOTE   *Unfortunately, KERBEROS_V4 has some security problems. Use GSSAPI instead.*

NTLM

The NTLM mechanism is a nonstandard, undocumented mechanism developed by Microsoft. The SASL distribution includes it for sites that need to interoperate with Microsoft clients (such as Outlook) and servers (such as Exchange).

OTP

The one-time pad (OTP) mechanism is similar to CRAM-MD5 and DIGEST-MD5 in that it uses a shared secret and a challenge/response exchange. However, OTP is considered to be more secure than the other shared secret mechanisms because the secret is used to generate and store a sequence of one-time (single-use) passwords that prevent replay attacks, so you don't need to store secrets on the server.

PLAIN, LOGIN

Credentials that are sent using PLAIN as the mechanism are transmitted as base64-encoded plaintext. This mechanism is simple, and most mail clients implement it, but base64-encoded strings can be decoded easily. LOGIN is the same as PLAIN, but it is used for mail clients (such as Outlook Express) that do not follow the RFC.

CAUTION   *The fact that credentials are sent in plaintext across the network creates a security risk. Anyone running a sniffer, such as snort or tcpdump, can read the secrets. You can overcome this problem by using TLS in combination with plaintext SMTP authentication. In particular, you can tell Postfix to offer plaintext mechanisms only after a TLS session has been established (see Chapter 18).*

SRP

SRP combines the safety of shared secret authentication with the single-use feature of OTP. It is based on public key cryptography and relies on passwords (not certificates) during authentication.

Authentication Methods (Password-Verification Services)

Authentication methods (also known as password-verification services) handle the mechanisms, taking care of the communication between the application that offers SMTP authentication and the backend that stores the credentials.

Cyrus SASL offers two password verification services: saslauthd and auxprop. The two services differ in the mechanisms they can offer and in the backends they can connect to. The application that offers authentication through its interface must choose which password-verification service to use. (You'll see the configuration later in the "Installing and Configuring Cyrus SASL" section.) Here is an overview of the services:

saslauthd

> saslauthd is a stand-alone daemon that may be run with superuser privileges. It may connect to many kinds of authentication backends, but especially those that require superuser privileges, such as /etc/shadow. saslauthd is limited to the plaintext mechanisms (PLAIN and LOGIN).

auxprop

> auxprop is a catchall password-verification service for a number of auxiliary plug-ins. Each plug-in is specialized for one distinct type of authentication backend, such as sasldb2 and SQL servers.

CAUTION   *The auxprop plug-ins connect to the authentication backend with the privileges of the application that provides the authentication. In Postfix, the application is* smtpd, *which runs with the fewest privileges required.*

> *Versions of Cyrus SASL prior to 2.x allowed access to* /etc/shadow *using auxprop. This required increasing the privileges of the daemon offering SMTP AUTH and defeated the Postfix security architecture. You are strongly discouraged from using a backend that forces you to increase the application privileges.*

Authentication Backends

As a final step, Cyrus SASL requires one or more authentication backends to verify the credentials provided by the client. The password-verification service checks whether the credentials match what is stored in the authentication backend. The official list of authentication backends supported by Cyrus SASL includes the following:

imap

> An IMAP server can verify the credentials.

kerberos

> Cyrus SASL can check Kerberos tickets.

ldap

> Cyrus SASL can read credentials from an OpenLDAP server.

pam

> Cyrus SASL can read from any modules that you make available through PAM (Pluggable Authentication Modules).

passwd/shadow

Cyrus SASL can read from the system user databases (/etc/passwd and possibly /etc/shadow).

sasldb2

Cyrus SASL has its own user database named sasldb2. This database is required for the Cyrus IMAP server, but you don't need an IMAP server to use it with SMTP authentication.

sql

Cyrus SASL can access user data on SQL servers. The currently supported servers are MySQL and PostgreSQL.

Planning Server-Side SMTP Authentication

If you want to support SMTP authentication on your mail server, you need only perform two steps:

1. Determine the clients that will use SMTP AUTH and the mechanisms these clients support.
2. Define the authentication backend that you wish to use, and derive the appropriate password-verification service.

Finding Clients and Their Supported Mechanisms

One tenet of computer security is that you cannot attack a service that does not exist. Therefore, you should consider configuring Postfix for only the mechanisms that your users need. On a small network where you have good control over the mail clients in use, you can very effectively limit mechanisms. Table 15-1 is a simplified version of the SASL client reference (http://www.melnikov.ca/mel/devel/SASL_ClientRef.html) by Alexey Melnikov, and it lists the mechanisms supported by various mail clients. It provides a fairly comprehensive overview of the POP, IMAP, ACAP, and LDAP AUTH capabilities of mail clients.

However, if you need to support as many clients as possible, offer at least the PLAIN, LOGIN, and CRAM-MD5 mechanisms. Most mail clients support these.

NOTE *You will probably notice that there are fewer mechanisms listed in Table 15-1 than in the SASL client reference. There are so many mechanisms that it was necessary to abridge the SASL client reference, but those listed in Table 15-1 will give you the most mileage in heterogeneous IT environments.*

After determining the mechanisms that you need to support the mail clients, you need to choose the appropriate authentication backend.

Table 15-1: Mechanisms of SMTP AUTH–Capable Clients

Client	ANONYMOUS	CRAM-MD5	DIGEST-MD5	EXTERNAL	GSSAPI	Kerberos 4	LOGIN	NTLM	PLAIN	SCRAM-MD5	SKEY
AKmail	no	yes	no	no	no	no	no	no	no	no	no
Bat! (SecureBat!)	no	yes	yes	no	no	no	yes	no	yes	no	no
Control Data's IMAPSP	no	yes	no	no	no	no	no	no	yes	no	yes
Eudora Pro 4.3 and later	no	yes	no	no	no	no	yes	no	yes	no	no
fetchmail 5.0.3	no	no	no	no	no	no	no	no	no	no	no
Forte Agent	no	no	no	no	no	no	no	no	no	no	no
Gnus	no	yes	no	no	no	no	yes	no	no	no	no
JavaMail	no	no	no	no	no	no	yes	no	yes	no	no
MH UCI 6.8.3	?	no	no	no	no	no	no	no	no	no	no
Mozilla 1.0	no	yes	no	yes	no	no	no	no	yes	no	no
Mulberry v3	no	yes	yes	no	yes	no	yes	yes	yes	no	no
mutt 1.2.5i	n/a[1]	n/a	n/a	n/a	n/a	n/a	n/a	n/a	n/a	n/a	n/a
Nestcape Messenger 4.51+	no	no	no	yes	no	no	no	no	yes	no	no
nmh 1.0.4	—[2]	no	no	no	no	no	no	no	no	no	no
Novell Evolution	no	yes	yes	no	no	yes	no	yes	yes	no	no
Orangsoft Winbiff > 2.30	no	yes	no	no	no	no	yes	no	yes	no	no
Outlook Express > 4.0[3]	no	no	no	no	no	no	yes	yes	no	no	no
Outlook > 98[3]	no	no	no	no	no	no	yes	yes	no	no	no
Paladin	no	yes	no	no	no	no	no	no	no	no	no
PalmOS Eudora	no	yes	no	no	no	no	no	no	no	no	no
Pegasus Mail 3.12	no	yes	no	no	no	no	yes	no	no	no	no
Pine 4.33 and later	no	yes	no	no	yes	yes	yes	no	yes	no	no
PMMail	no	no	no	no	no	no	no	no	no	no	no
Sylpheed	no	yes	yes	no	no	no	yes	no	no	no	no
Wanderlust	yes	yes	yes	no	no	yes	yes	no	no	yes	no

[1] Does not support SMTP directly; relies on a local MTA.

[2] See the CMU SASL library.

[3] Supports draft 10 of SMTP AUTH spec (i.e., "AUTH=" but not "AUTH ").

Defining the Authentication Backend and Password-Verification Service

An easy but not terribly secure place to get user credentials is your system's local user database, /etc/passwd. This authentication backend already exists, and unless you are an ISP, you probably have created accounts for all mail users.

Unfortunately, too many administrators create user accounts that permit shell access. Anyone who gains access to the usernames and passwords used in an SMTP AUTH session could easily gain shell access to your server (and as a result, would likely also gain superuser access, because it is much easier to do this when you already have a shell account). This alone could be reason enough to choose an authentication backend that has nothing to do with your system users.

Theoretically, the ideal authentication backend has no relation to system users, especially if you use a plaintext mechanism, because the consequences of compromising credentials used only for mail relaying are not very serious compared to a system break-in. You can use a self-contained database, such as sasldb, an SQL server, or even an LDAP server. Tables 15-2 and 15-3 identify the mechanisms you can use for each type of authentication backend. Notice that your choice of backend also determines which password-verification service you must use.

Table 15-2: Authentication Backends and Mechanisms Compatible with the saslauthd Password-Verification Service

Authentication Backend	PLAIN	LOGIN	CRAM-MD5	DIGEST-MD5	OTP	NTLM
getpwent (regular system users)	yes	yes	no	no	no	no
kerberos	yes	yes	no	no	no	no
pam	yes	yes	no	no	no	no
rimap (remote IMAP server)	yes	yes	no	no	no	no
shadow	yes	yes	no	no	no	no
ldap	yes	yes	no	no	no	no

Table 15-3: Authentication Backends and Mechanisms Compatible with the auxprop Password-Verification Service

Authentication Backend	PLAIN	LOGIN	CRAM-MD5	DIGEST-MD5	OTP	NTLM
sasldb2	yes	yes	yes	yes	yes	yes
sql	yes	yes	yes	yes	yes	yes

After deciding on an authentication backend, you're ready to configure Cyrus SASL for smtpd.

Installing and Configuring Cyrus SASL

Postfix requires Cyrus SASL to provide SMTP AUTH functionality to mail clients or to use it by itself when a remote mail server offers SMTP AUTH.

If you just need to configure the Postfix `smtp` client to authenticate with a remote server, all you need to do is install Cyrus SASL and proceed to Chapter 16.

However, if you want Postfix, acting as an MTA, to offer SMTP AUTH to remote mail clients, you need to install and configure Cyrus SASL. In addition, Postfix needs to be told how to interact with Cyrus SASL when you want to use server-side SMTP AUTH. In all, you need to do the following:

1. Install Cyrus SASL.
2. Create the Postfix application configuration file.
3. Configure logging and the log level.
4. Set the password-verification service.
5. Select SMTP AUTH mechanisms.
6. Configure saslauthd or auxprop.
7. Test authentication.

Installing Cyrus SASL

If your system doesn't come with Cyrus SASL preinstalled or as a package, you need to download the Cyrus SASL library from the Download Cyrus Software web page, `http://asg.web.cmu.edu/cyrus/download`.

CAUTION *The following sections assume that you're using at least Cyrus SASL 2.1.17, but it's only natural that a later version will be available when you read this. If you want to get version 2.1.17, you can get it from the CVS repository, `http://asg.web.cmu.edu/cyrus/download/anoncvs.html`.*

After unpacking the software, change into the Cyrus SASL SOURCE directory. If you're using a version of SASL that you got from CVS, you need to run `sh ./SMakefile` to build the `configure` script.

Run the following command to configure Cyrus SASL for all of the backends described in the rest of this chapter:

```
# ./configure \
    --with-plugindir=/usr/lib/sasl2 \
    --disable-java \
    --disable-krb4 \
    --with-dblib=berkeley \
    --with-saslauthd=/var/state/saslauthd \
    --without-pwcheck \
    --with-devrandom=/dev/urandom \
    --enable-cram \
    --enable-digest \
    --enable-plain \
```

```
--enable-login \
--disable-otp \
--enable-sql \
--with-ldap=/usr \
--with-mysql=/usr \
--with-pgsql=/usr/lib/pgsql
```

NOTE   *Cyrus SASL has many more configuration options. Run ./configure --help in the source directory to find out what Cyrus SASL supports. However, if you don't think you need all of the backends, you can change the options.*

After the configuration script creates the Makefile, you can run **make** to build Cyrus SASL, then **make install** (as root) to install it.

Next you will have to create a symbolic link. The installation process puts the SASL libraries in /usr/local/lib/sasl2 by default, but the configuration parameters set in the configure script cause Cyrus SASL to search for the libraries in /usr/lib/sasl2. Create the link like this:

```
# ln -s /usr/local/lib/sasl2 /usr/lib/sasl2
```

Finally, see if the syslogd daemon is set up to log Cyrus SASL messages. Cyrus SASL logs to the syslog auth facility, so if you don't have anything that catches this facility already, you should add the following line to your syslog.conf file and restart your syslogd:

```
auth.*                          /var/log/auth
```

Creating the Postfix Application Configuration File

Every application that offers SASL services must be told how to use the SASL libraries. Cyrus SASL has one configuration file for each application, rather than one large global configuration file. This makes it possible to define different configurations for different applications. The application configuration file for Postfix is named smtpd.conf, because by default the Postfix application that offers SASL services is the smtpd daemon. The file is located in /usr/lib/sasl2 by default.

NOTE   *Debian users must put smtpd.conf in /etc/postfix/sasl to make SMTP AUTH work.*

Some operating systems come with a smtpd.conf containing a few default settings; check for the file beforehand. If the file does not exist, create it as root with the following commands:

```
# touch /usr/lib/sasl2/smtpd.conf
# chmod 644 /usr/lib/sasl2/smtpd.conf
```

The preceding commands won't harm a preexisting configuration file. Once you have created the configuration file, you are ready to configure how Postfix will use the SASL libraries.

CAUTION *The Cyrus configuration file syntax is different from that of Postfix. A parameter and its value must be on a single line. In Cyrus, every parameter ends with a colon, and a space separates the parameter from its value.*

Configuring Logging and the Log Level

The first parameter in the `/usr/lib/sasl2/smtpd.conf` file that you should configure is the `log_level` parameter. The possible values are listed in Table 15-4.

Table 15-4: Log Level Values for Cyrus SASL

`log_level` **Value**	**Description**
0	No logging
1	Log unusual errors; this is the default
2	Log all authentication failures
3	Log nonfatal warnings
4	More verbose than 3
5	More verbose than 4
6	Log traces of internal protocols
7	Log traces of internal protocols, including passwords

While you configure and test Cyrus SASL, you should set the log level at least to 3. Here's how to set it in the `smtpd.conf` file:

```
# Global parameters
log_level: 3
```

This file will grow as you proceed through the following sections.

Setting the Password-Verification Service

The next step is to tell Postfix which password-verification service to use for authenticating users. At this point, you should make a clear decision between saslauthd and auxprop, because the subsequent steps differ significantly depending on the password-verification service.

Cyrus SASL determines the password-verification service from the `pwcheck_method` parameter. If you plan to use saslauthd, configure your `smtpd.conf` as follows:

```
# Global parameters
log_level: 3
pwcheck_method: saslauthd
```

If you plan to use an auxiliary plug-in instead, use this in your smtpd.conf:

```
# Global parameters
log_level: 3
pwcheck_method: auxprop
```

Selecting SMTP AUTH Mechanisms

Cyrus SASL leaves it to the client to pick the mechanisms to use for authentication. This can lead to authentication failures under the following conditions:

- If you offer mechanisms that require configuration that you haven't done. For example, if you don't use Kerberos, but your server offers KERBEROS and the client picks it, the authentication will fail.
- If you chose saslauthd as the password-verification service, but you did not limit the mechanisms to plaintext mechanisms. In this case, authentication would fail if a non-plaintext mechanism were selected because saslauthd cannot handle mechanisms other than PLAIN and LOGIN.

You can ensure that your server offers a specific list of mechanisms with the mech_list parameter. For example, if you're using saslauthd, your smtpd.conf file *must* look like this:

```
# Global parameters
log_level: 3
pwcheck_method: saslauthd
mech_list: PLAIN LOGIN
```

With auxiliary plug-ins, you can choose a different list, such as this:

```
# Global parameters
log_level: 3
pwcheck_method: auxprop
mech_list: PLAIN LOGIN CRAM-MD5 DIGEST-MD5
```

With the mechanism choice in place, you now have to configure either saslauthd or an auxiliary plug-in. Proceed with the next section if you want to configure saslauthd, or skip ahead to the "Configuring Auxiliary Plug-ins (auxprop)" section to configure auxprop.

Configuring saslauthd

saslauthd is a stand-alone daemon that communicates with authentication backends. You configure saslauthd with command-line options. Before starting the daemon, do the following.

1. Check the authentication backends that your saslauthd supports.
2. Prepare the saslauthd environment.
3. Configure an authentication backend for saslauthd.

Checking for Supported Authentication Backends

You won't get very far if saslauthd does not support the authentication backend that you want to use. Run **saslauthd -v** to get a list of authentication backends that your saslauthd binary supports. Here's an example:

```
# saslauthd -v
saslauthd 2.1.17
authentication mechanisms: getpwent pam rimap shadow ldap
```

Notice that saslauthd labels its backends as "authentication mechanisms." Don't confuse this with SMTP AUTH mechanisms such as PLAIN and CRAM-MD5.

If the mechanism you need is not in the list, you need to rebuild Cyrus SASL. Running ./configure --help in the Cyrus SASL source directory yields a set of options for enabling various backends.

Preparing the saslauthd Environment

saslauthd requires a state directory to store a socket and PID file. The Cyrus SASL installation scripts do not create the state directory for you, but if you install Cyrus SASL from a binary package, such as an RPM, the package installer might create the directory. The default state directory is /var/state/saslauthd, but /var/run/saslauthd is also common.

You can set the state directory location at build time with the --with-saslauthd=DIR option to the configure script. You can check the state directory by starting saslauthd in debug mode:

```
# saslauthd -a shadow -d
saslauthd[31076] :main       : num_procs  : 5
saslauthd[31076] :main       : mech_option: NULL
saslauthd[31076] :main       : run_path   : /var/run/saslauthd
saslauthd[31076] :main       : auth_mech  : shadow
saslauthd[31076] :main       : could not chdir to: /var/run/saslauthd
saslauthd[31076] :main       : chdir: No such file or directory
saslauthd[31076] :main       : Check to make sure the directory exists and is
saslauthd[31076] :main       : writable by the user this process runs as.
```

In the preceding output, run_path indicates the state directory where saslauthd will create the socket. Notice that the saslauthd debugging output shows that this directory does not exist.

If the directory does not exist, create it and make it accessible only to root and members of root. The following example shows how you might do that.

```
# mkdir /var/state/saslauthd
# chown root:root /var/state/saslauthd
# chmod 750 /var/state/saslauthd
```

Using a Different State Directory

If you would like to use a state directory other than the default (for example,
if you found a state directory for saslauthd on your system), you can use the
-m dir command-line option to override the default setting. For example, if
you'd like to use the /var/run/saslauthd directory, you can run the daemon as
follows:

```
# saslauthd -m /var/run/saslauthd -a shadow
```

Here, the path is the directory name, and it does not include the name
of the socket (mux). The -a option is for the authentication backend; you'll
see this in the next section.

However, you also have to tell Postfix about the new state directory by
setting the saslauthd_path parameter in your smtpd.conf file. This time, you
must include the filename of the socket, as noted in boldface-italic in the
following example:

```
# Global parameters
log_level: 3
pwcheck_method: saslauthd
# saslauthd parameters
saslauthd_path: /var/run/saslauthd/mux
```

After you have the state directory in place, you're ready to connect
saslauthd to an authentication backend.

Configuring an Authentication Backend for saslauthd

saslauthd uses the option -a *backend_name* to select an authentication backend.
The name should be one of the backends listed when you run saslauthd -v, as
mentioned in Table 15-2. The following example uses the shadow backend to
read from the shadow password file:

```
# saslauthd -a shadow
```

The following sections list the most common authentication backends
used with saslauthd. Have a look at the saslauthd(8) manual page for a
complete list of authentication backends for saslauthd.

Authenticating from Local User Accounts

saslauthd can access the local password file, which should work on most Unix
systems, and it can access the local shadow password file on systems that
support shadow passwords. To read from the regular password file (/etc/
passwd), use the -a getpwent parameter.

```
# saslauthd -a getpwent
```

On systems that use shadow passwords, you can start saslauthd with the option -a shadow to make it access /etc/shadow; you must run **saslauthd** as root to access /etc/shadow:

```
# saslauthd -a shadow
```

Authenticating from PAM

saslauthd supports PAM (Pluggable Authentication Modules) for authenticating SMTP users. To gain access to the backends that PAM supports, create /etc/pam.d/smtp and add configuration parameters specific to your needs and your system, or add the appropriate settings to /etc/pam.conf.

Here's an example of what you might put in /etc/pam.d/smtp on a Red Hat Fedora Core 1 system:

```
#%PAM-1.0
auth        required      /lib/security/pam_stack.so service=system-auth
account     required      /lib/security/pam_stack.so service=system-auth
```

NOTE *The configuration filename must be smtp, because RFC 2554 says that the service name for SASL over SMTP is smtp. Postfix passes the value smtp as the service name to the sasl_server_new() function. This service name is then passed to saslauthd and ultimately to PAM, which in turn looks in smtp for authentication instructions.*

After configuring PAM, you can start saslauthd as follows:

```
# saslauthd -a pam
```

Authenticating with an IMAP Server

saslauthd supports an unusual authentication backend that connects to an IMAP server. This one is different because it is the IMAP server checking the username and password, but not the SASL libraries.

You configure IMAP as an authentication backend for saslauthd with two parameters. The first is the usual -a to select a backend, and then use -O to specify an IMAP server, as in this example:

```
# saslauthd -a rimap -O imap.example.com
```

Authenticating from LDAP

saslauthd can read credentials from an OpenLDAP server. LDAP queries and other parameters for connecting to an LDAP server can be very complicated, so you don't pass these parameters to saslauthd through the command line. Instead, it reads the configuration from a separate file. The default filename is /usr/local/etc/saslauthd.conf, but you can specify a different file with the -O file parameter.

Here's an example saslauthd.conf file:

```
ldap_servers: ldap://127.0.0.1/ ldap://172.16.10.7/
ldap_bind_dn: cn=saslauthd,dc=example,dc=com
ldap_bind_pw: Yanggt!
ldap_timeout: 10
ldap_time_limit: 10
ldap_scope: sub ·
ldap_search_base: dc=people,dc=example,dc=com
ldap_auth_method: bind
ldap_filter: (|(&(cn=%u)(&(uid=%u@%r)(smtpAuth=Y)))
ldap_debug: 0
ldap_verbose: off
ldap_ssl: no
ldap_start_tls: no
ldap_referrals: yes
```

Obviously, the query (defined here with the ldap_search_base and ldap_filter parameters) depends on your own LDAP configuration.

NOTE *There are many more LDAP parameters than are listed here. See the auth_ldap module for saslauthd for the complete list.*

Let's say that you put your configuration in /etc/saslauthd.conf. You would start saslauthd as follows:

```
# saslauthd -a ldap -O /etc/saslauthd.conf
```

Configuring Auxiliary Plug-ins (auxprop)

Unlike saslauthd-based backends, applications that use auxiliary plug-ins with the auxprop system run the plug-ins directly, reading the configuration from the application's own SASL configuration file. As mentioned earlier, the application configuration file for Postfix is smtpd.conf. The following sections show you how to configure the auxiliary plug-ins that come with the SASL source.

NOTE *There are more auxiliary plug-ins for SASL than are listed in this section, such as ldapdb, which you can find in the /contrib section of the OpenLDAP source files. The ldapdb plug-in is excellent, but it is difficult to install because it doesn't come with a Makefile or other build tool. The discussion in this chapter focuses on configurations for intermediate users.*

Using the sasldb2 Plug-In

Cyrus SASL comes with a standard plug-in named sasldb2 that is used mostly in Cyrus IMAP, but can be used separately. The sasldb2 plug-in comes with two utilities: saslpasswd2 for user management, and sasldblistusers2 for listing all users in sasldb2.

CAUTION *The database and tool names end with a "2" because they belong to Cyrus SASL 2.x. They had to be renamed to avoid conflicts with Cyrus SASL 1.x, because the Cyrus SASL API changed between the two versions. If you find tools without a number at the end, they are probably for Cyrus SASL 1.x and will not work with version 2.*

To configure Cyrus SASL with sasldb2, you need to do two things:

1. Create the sasldb2 database.
2. Configure SASL to read from the database.

Creating the sasldb2 Database

You can create the sasldb2 database by running the `saslpasswd2` command as root. The option `-c` creates a sasldb2 database in the `/etc/sasldb2` file. Here's an example that creates the database, adds a user, and a realm of the Postfix `myhostname` (you cannot create the database unless you add a user):

```
# saslpasswd2 -c -u `postconf -h myhostname` test
Password:
Again (for verification):
```

CAUTION *The sasldb2 plug-in requires a realm in addition to the credentials. Postfix uses the value of the smtpd_sasl_local_domain parameter as the realm (it is empty by default). Postfix can have only one realm per smtpd instance, effectively limiting authentication to a single realm.*

After creating the database, limit access to the `root` user and the `postfix` group:

```
# chmod 640 /etc/sasldb2
# chgrp postfix /etc/sasldb2
# ls -l /etc/sasldb2
-rw-r-----   1 root    postfix    12288 Feb  4 16:23 /etc/sasldb2
```

If you offer the OTP mechanism, you must also make the database file writable by Postfix, so that it can mark expired passwords. You may need to modify the ownership and permissions if another group needs to access the database file.

Configuring SASL to Read from the sasldb2 Database

To tell Postfix about the sasldb2 database, edit the `smtpd.conf` file and specify `auxprop` as the password-verification service and `sasldb` as the auxprop plug-in type:

```
# Global parameters
log_level: 3
pwcheck_method: auxprop
```

```
mech_list: PLAIN LOGIN CRAM-MD5 DIGEST-MD5
# auxiliary Plugin parameters
auxprop_plugin: sasldb
```

Using the sql Plug-In

Cyrus SASL 2 offers access to two popular relational databases: MySQL and PostgreSQL. Both are available through the sql auxiliary plug-in, and they use these same configuration parameters:

sql_engine

> The sql_engine parameter specifies the database type. As of Cyrus SASL 2.1.17, you can pick mysql or pgsql.

sql_hostnames

> The sql_hostnames parameter specifies the database server name. You can specify one or more FQDNs or IP addresses separated by commas. If you pick localhost, the SQL engine tries to communicate over a socket.

sql_database

> The sql_database parameter defines the name of the database to connect to.

sql_user

> The sql_user parameter defines the database username.

sql_passwd

> The sql_passwd parameter defines the password (in plaintext) for the database user.

sql_select

> The sql_select parameter defines the SELECT statement used to find the password for a given username and realm.

sql_insert

> The sql_insert parameter defines an INSERT statement for allowing the SASL library to create users in the SQL database (making it accessible to programs such as saslpasswd2).

sql_update

> The sql_update parameter defines the UPDATE statement that allows the SASL library or a plug-in to update a user in the SQL database for a mechanism such as OTP. The sql_update parameter must be used in combination with sql_insert.

sql_usessl

> The sql_usessl parameter allows you to use an encrypted connection to the database. By default, it is off (sql_usessl: no); use a setting of yes, 1, on, or true to enable SSL.

Cyrus SASL provides the following macros that you can use in your parameter settings to build database queries:

%u   This macro is replaced with the username provided during authentication.

%p   This is a placeholder for the password; this is the default column name for plaintext passwords.

%r   This macro is replaced with the realm provided during authentication.

%v   This specifies the submitted value that should replace an existing value during an SQL UPDATE or INSERT operation.

CAUTION   *Macros must be quoted separately with single quotation marks (') when you define a query in* smtpd.conf.

Configuring MySQL for SASL

The first thing to do when configuring MySQL for SASL in Postfix is to create a database and table. This example SQL statement creates a table with the default fields that Cyrus SASL expects, plus an extra field that lets you disable relay access for a particular user:

```
mysql> CREATE TABLE `users` (
        `id` int(11) unsigned NOT NULL auto_increment,
        `username` varchar(255) NOT NULL default '0',
        `userrealm` varchar(255) NOT NULL default 'mail.example.com',
        `userpassword` varchar(255) NOT NULL default '1stP@ss',
        `auth` tinyint(1) default '1',
        PRIMARY KEY  (`id`),
        UNIQUE KEY `id` (`id`)
        ) TYPE=MyISAM COMMENT='SMTP AUTH relay users';
```

As you can see, all of the fields (id, username, userrealm, userpassword, and auth) have default values. It's particularly important that there be a default password so that an attacker can't try a null password.

Next you need to create a MySQL user that can read and write to the SASL authorization database. For example, this sequence of commands creates a user named postfix:

```
mysql> CONNECT mysql;
mysql> INSERT INTO user VALUES
        ('localhost','postfix','','Y','Y','Y','Y','Y','Y','Y','Y','Y','Y','Y','
        Y','Y','Y');
mysql> UPDATE mysql.user SET password=PASSWORD("Yanggt!") WHERE user='postfix'
        AND host='localhost';
mysql> GRANT SELECT, UPDATE ON mail.users TO 'postfix'@'localhost';
mysql> FLUSH PRIVILEGES;
```

Add a test entry to the users table with a command like this:

```
mysql> INSERT INTO `users` VALUES (1,'test','mail.example.com','testpass',0);
```

Finally, after setting up the MySQL database, configure the auxiliary plug-in authentication backend in your smtpd.conf file with settings such as these:

```
# Global parameters
log_level: 3
pwcheck_method: auxprop
mech_list: PLAIN LOGIN CRAM-MD5 DIGEST-MD5
# auxiliary Plugin parameters
auxprop_plugin: sql
sql_engine: mysql
sql_hostnames: localhost
sql_database: mail
sql_user: postfix
sql_passwd: Yanggt!
sql_select: SELECT %p FROM users WHERE username = '%u' AND userrealm = '%r' AND auth = '1'
sql_usessl: no
```

Notice the auxprop password-verification service and the sql plug-in. Refer back to the "Using the sql Plug-In" section for the meanings of the other parameters and the macros.

NOTE   *Read options.html in the Cyrus SASL doc directory for more detailed information on notation and parameters.*

Configuring PostgreSQL for SASL

The process for using PostgreSQL with SASL is very similar to that for using MySQL. Here's how to create a mail database in PostgreSQL:

```
# createdb mail
CREATE DATABASE
```

Now, connect to the database and create a table for the SASL users as follows:

```
# psql -d mail
Welcome to psql 7.3.4, the PostgreSQL interactive terminal.
Type:  \copyright for distribution terms
       \h for help with SQL commands
       \? for help on internal slash commands
       \g or terminate with semicolon to execute query
       \q to quit
mail=# CREATE TABLE public.users
```

```
mail-# (
mail(#    id int4 NOT NULL,
mail(#    "username" varchar(255),
mail(#    "userrealm" varchar(255),
mail(#    "userpassword" varchar(255),
mail(#    auth int2 DEFAULT 0,
mail(#    CONSTRAINT id PRIMARY KEY (id)
mail(# ) WITHOUT OIDS;
NOTICE:  CREATE TABLE / PRIMARY KEY will create implicit index 'id' for table 'users'
CREATE TABLE
mail=# COMMENT ON TABLE public.users IS 'mail users';
COMMENT
mail=#
```

Next, make a user that can read from and write to the database:

```
mail=# CREATE USER postfix PASSWORD 'Yanggt!' NOCREATEDB NOCREATEUSER;
CREATE USER
```

Give this user SELECT and UPDATE access to the table:

```
mail=# GRANT UPDATE,SELECT ON users TO postfix;
GRANT
```

The next step is to create a test account entry in the mail table:

```
mail=# INSERT INTO users VALUES ('1','test','mail.example.com','testpass','1');
```

Finally, with the PostgreSQL database in place, you can configure the auxiliary plug-in like this in smtpd.conf:

```
# Global parameters
log_level: 3
pwcheck_method: auxprop
mech_list: PLAIN LOGIN CRAM-MD5 DIGEST-MD5
# auxiliary Plugin parameters
auxprop_plugin: sql
sql_engine: pgsql
sql_hostnames: localhost
sql_database: mail
sql_user: postfix
sql_passwd: Yanggt!
sql_select: SELECT %p FROM users WHERE username = '%u' AND realm = '%r' AND auth = '1'
sql_usessl: no
```

After configuring your authentication backend, you are ready to test authentication.

Testing the Authentication

After configuring Cyrus SASL with either saslauthd or an auxiliary plug-in and one backend, you should test it *before* you configure SMTP AUTH in Postfix as described in Chapter 16. Experience has shown that most problems with SMTP AUTH arise from problematic Cyrus SASL installations, not from Postfix itself.

The first step in testing is to find the testing tools. Unless you installed Cyrus SASL from source code, this might not be an easy task (by default, the tools are in the sample/ subdirectory of the source distribution). If you use a Cyrus SASL installation that came with an operating system distribution, you will have to look closely for programs named client and server.

NOTE *The names of the binaries are far from consistent among operating system packages, and some packages don't even install all of the binaries. Check for cyrus-*-devel packages, and look at the names of the programs in these packages. They're not necessarily named client and server.*

For example, Red Hat Linux ships a mixture of Cyrus SASL 1.x and 2.x, renaming the binaries to sasl-sample-client and sasl-sample-server for Cyrus SASL 1.x and sasl2-sample-client and sasl2-sample-server for 2.x.

Once you have found the client and server programs, follow these steps to test authentication:

1. Start saslauthd if you use a backend that requires saslauthd as a password-verification service.

2. Create the server configuration file.

3. Start the server program.

4. Test authentication with the client program.

Starting saslauthd

If you chose a backend that uses saslauthd as the password-verification service (that is, it does not use an auxiliary plug-in such as sasldb or a SQL database), you should start saslauthd with debugging parameters from command line. Don't use an init script; you want to be able to use the -d option, which tells the main saslauthd not to go into daemon mode, but rather to remain attached to the current terminal and print debugging output.

Here's an example of starting up saslauthd for shadow password authentication:

```
# saslauthd -m /var/state/saslauthd -a shadow -d
saslauthd[4401] :main            : num_procs : 5
saslauthd[4401] :main            : mech_option: NULL
saslauthd[4401] :main            : run_path  : /var/run/saslauthd
saslauthd[4401] :main            : auth_mech : shadow
```

```
saslauthd[4401] :ipc_init        : using accept lock file: /var/run/saslauthd/mux.accept
saslauthd[4401] :detach_tty       : master pid is: 0
saslauthd[4401] :ipc_init        : listening on socket: /var/run/saslauthd/mux
saslauthd[4401] :main            : using process model
saslauthd[4402] :get_accept_lock : acquired accept lock
saslauthd[4401] :have_baby        : forked child: 4402
saslauthd[4401] :have_baby        : forked child: 4403
saslauthd[4401] :have_baby        : forked child: 4404
saslauthd[4401] :have_baby        : forked child: 4405
```

Creating the Server Configuration File

Now you need to create the configuration file for the server program. Recall that each SASL application requires its own configuration file; the test program server will need a sample.conf file. However, the test configuration should be the same as the configuration you used for Postfix. The easiest way to do this is to create a symbolic link to your smtpd.conf file, as follows:

```
# cd /usr/lib/sasl2/
# ln -s smtpd.conf sample.conf
```

Starting the Server Program

Open a new shell and run the server program with the -s and -p options to specify the service and port for the server:

```
# server -s rcmd -p 8000
trying 10, 1, 6
socket: Address family not supported by protocol
trying 2, 1, 6
```

Make sure you use a port that your machine isn't already using.

NOTE   *The meaning of rcmd is not well documented.*

Testing with the Client Program

Finally, start the client program, and let it connect to the server. Once connected, the client program asks you to enter an authentication ID, an authorization ID, and a password. Use the -m command-line option to choose a mechanism. The following example uses test as the authentication and authorization IDs and testpass as the password on localhost (127.0.0.1):

```
# client -s rcmd -p 8000 -m PLAIN 127.0.0.1
receiving capability list... recv: {11}
PLAIN LOGIN
PLAIN LOGIN
please enter an authentication id: test
please enter an authorization id: test
```

```
Password:
send: {5}
PLAIN
send: {1}
Y
send: {18}
test[0]test[0]testpass
successful authentication
closing connection
```

You're looking for the successful authentication message. You can also monitor the communication on the server program's side. The following example shows the connection initiation and the credentials coming in and being verified:

```
# server -s rcmd -p 8000
trying 10, 1, 6
socket: Address family not supported by protocol
trying 2, 1, 6
accepted new connection
send: {11}
PLAIN LOGIN
recv: {5}
PLAIN
recv: {1}
Y
recv: {18}
test[0]test[0]testpass
successful authentication 'test'
closing connection
```

Finally, if you're using a backend that requires saslauthd, you can see what's happening as saslauthd verifies the credentials. It should look something like this:

```
# saslauthd -m /var/run/saslauthd -a shadow -d
saslauthd[4547] :main           : num_procs  : 5
saslauthd[4547] :main           : mech_option: NULL
saslauthd[4547] :main           : run_path   : /var/run/saslauthd
saslauthd[4547] :main           : auth_mech  : shadow
saslauthd[4547] :ipc_init       : using accept lock file: /var/run/saslauthd/mux.accept
saslauthd[4547] :detach_tty     : master pid is: 0
saslauthd[4547] :ipc_init       : listening on socket: /var/run/saslauthd/mux
saslauthd[4547] :main           : using process model
saslauthd[4548] :get_accept_lock : acquired accept lock
saslauthd[4547] :have_baby      : forked child: 4548
saslauthd[4547] :have_baby      : forked child: 4549
saslauthd[4547] :have_baby      : forked child: 4550
```

```
saslauthd[4547] :have_baby       : forked child: 4551
saslauthd[4548] :rel_accept_lock : released accept lock
saslauthd[4548] :do_auth         : auth success: [user=test] [service=rcmd] [realm=]
   [mech=shadow]
saslauthd[4548] :do_request      : response: OK
saslauthd[4548] :get_accept_lock : acquired accept lock
```

If something goes wrong, you should be able to zero in on the problem by going through the following steps:

1. If you're using saslauthd as a password-verification service, look for [reason=...] in the debugging output.

2. Verify that the user and password are correct in your authentication backend.

3. Make sure that saslauthd has permission to access your authentication backend.

4. Verify that you submitted the correct strings for username and password.

Once you have successfully authenticated, proceed to Chapter 16 and configure the Postfix smtpd daemon to offer SMTP AUTH to mail clients.

The Future of SMTP AUTH

The current SMTP AUTH implementation is far from final. Future versions of Postfix will see a big change in SASL. Currently the SASL libraries that access authentication backends are linked and are used from within the smtpd daemon (the same daemon that handles communication with mail clients). Figure 15-6 shows what the connection chain looks like.

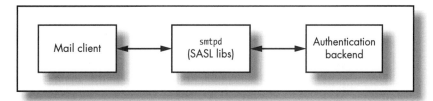

Figure 15-6: Current SASL integration into Postfix

Accessing the authentication backends usually requires a privileged user, so anyone who could hijack the daemon responsible for SMTP AUTH would be very close to the user database in a system.

Postfix tries to avoid privileged processes wherever possible, especially when the authentication daemon is exposed directly to the (always hostile) network. In addition, complexity is an enemy of security, and Cyrus SASL definitely qualifies as complex.

Sometime in the future, Postfix will have a new daemon (perhaps named sasld) whose only job is to connect Postfix and the Cyrus SASL libraries. The communication between Postfix and the new daemon should be as simple as possible. Figure 15-7 shows how the new connection chain might look.

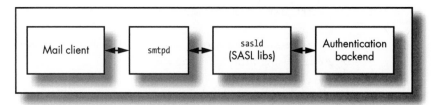

Figure 15-7: Future SASL integration into Postfix

The new design will make the daemon that needs to be exposed to the network less vulnerable to exploits, and this will take Postfix a step closer to one of its main goals—secure services.

16

SMTP AUTHENTICATION

SMTP authentication (SMTP AUTH) allows authorized mail clients with dynamic IP addresses to relay messages through your server without creating an open relay. This chapter shows you how to enable SMTP AUTH in your server and client-side SMTP AUTH in Postfix.

Checking Postfix for SMTP AUTH Support

Although the Postfix source code includes support for SMTP authentication, it is not enabled by default because Postfix does not come with the SMTP AUTH library that handles the actual work. When you build Postfix, you need to tell the build process about this library.

The Postfix packages provided with many distributions come with SMTP AUTH support. You can easily verify whether your version of Postfix already has support for SMTP AUTH enabled. Run `ldd `postconf -h daemon_directory`/smtpd` as root and search for `libsasl2.so` in the output.

```
# ldd `postconf -h daemon_directory`/smtpd
        libldap.so.2 => /usr/lib/libldap.so.2 (0x00117000)
        liblber.so.2 => /usr/lib/liblber.so.2 (0x008a9000)
        libpcre.so.0 => /lib/libpcre.so.0 (0x00b86000)
        libsasl2.so.2 => /usr/lib/libsasl2.so.2 (0x00101000) ❶
        libssl.so.4 => /lib/libssl.so.4 (0x00b11000)
        libcrypto.so.4 => /lib/libcrypto.so.4 (0x00977000)
        libgssapi_krb5.so.2 => /usr/lib/libgssapi_krb5.so.2 (0x00afc000)
        libkrb5.so.3 => /usr/lib/libkrb5.so.3 (0x00a6f000)
        libcom_err.so.2 => /lib/libcom_err.so.2 (0x00a6a000)
        libk5crypto.so.3 => /usr/lib/libk5crypto.so.3 (0x00ad8000)
        libresolv.so.2 => /lib/libresolv.so.2 (0x00965000)
        libdl.so.2 => /lib/libdl.so.2 (0x008b8000)
        libz.so.1 => /usr/lib/libz.so.1 (0x008bd000)
        libdb-4.1.so => /lib/libdb-4.1.so (0x00c18000)
        libnsl.so.1 => /lib/libnsl.so.1 (0x008fe000)
        libc.so.6 => /lib/libc.so.6 (0x0076e000)
        libcrypt.so.1 => /lib/libcrypt.so.1 (0x008d0000)
        /lib/ld-linux.so.2 => /lib/ld-linux.so.2 (0x00759000)
        libpthread.so.0 => /lib/libpthread.so.0 (0x00912000)
```

❶ The output of libsasl.so.2, which is the current major Cyrus SASL version, indicates that SASL support has been compiled into Postfix and you are ready to configure SMTP authentication.

NOTE *Postfix also supports the older Cyrus SASL version, 1.5. If you find libsasl.so.7 in the output of the ldd command, your version of Postfix was built with Cyrus SASL 1.5. If you find only libsasl.so.7, consider upgrading to Cyrus SASL 2; the authentication backend support in this release is a substantial improvement over that of version 1.5.*

Adding SMTP AUTH Support to Postfix

If you don't have SASL support in your Postfix installation and want to use SMTP AUTH, you need to rebuild Postfix. The first thing you need to do is locate the Cyrus SASL libraries and header files on your system. Search for the libraries with a find command like this:

```
# find /usr -name 'libsasl*.*'
/usr/lib/sasl2/libsasldb.la
/usr/lib/sasl2/libsasldb.a
/usr/lib/sasl2/libsasldb.so.2.0.15
/usr/lib/sasl2/libsasldb.so
/usr/lib/sasl2/libsasldb.so.2
/usr/lib/libsasl2.so.2.0.15
/usr/lib/libsasl2.so.2
```

```
/usr/lib/libsasl2.la
/usr/lib/libsasl2.a
/usr/lib/libsasl2.so
```

In the preceding example, you can see that the Cyrus SASL 2 library is in /usr/lib. Make a note of this location, and then search for the corresponding include files with this command:

```
# find /usr -name '*sasl*.h'
/usr/include/sasl/sasl.h
/usr/include/sasl/saslplug.h
/usr/include/sasl/saslutil.h
```

NOTE *Linux distributions put header files and libraries in separate packages in a misguided effort to save disk space. If you can't find the include files for Cyrus SASL on your system, but the libraries are there, locate and install the SASL packages that end in -dev or -devel.*

If you don't have the Cyrus SASL library on your system, read Chapter 15 to configure and install it. Once you know where the header and include file directories are, you can build Postfix with SASL support like this:

1. Unpack the Postfix source as a regular user.

2. Change into the Postfix source directory.

3. Set the build options and run **make makefiles** and **make**, like this:

```
$ CCARGS="-DUSE_SASL_AUTH -I/usr/include/sasl AUXLIBS="-L/usr/lib -lsasl2"
  make makefiles
$ make
```

Keep in mind that these are the options for SASL only; you may wish to add more options as described in the *_README files in the README_FILES directory of the Postfix source tree.

4. Become the superuser (root).

5. If this is your first Postfix installation, run **make install**. However, if you're upgrading or replacing an existing installation, run **make upgrade**.

6. Verify that you have SASL support as described at the beginning of this chapter.

Server-Side SMTP Authentication

This section of the chapter explains how to configure the Postfix smtpd server to offer SMTP AUTH to mail clients. Once authenticated, the clients can relay messages through the Postfix server even if their IP address is not within the range of IP addresses defined by the mynetworks configuration parameter.

CAUTION *To properly configure SMTP AUTH on your server, you not only need to configure and link the Postfix library with the Cyrus SASL library, but you must also configure Cyrus SASL to communicate with an authentication backend. See Chapter 15 for the details.*

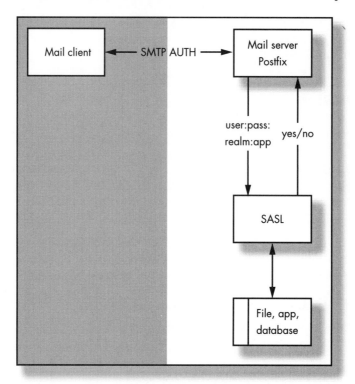

Figure 16-1: Server-side SMTP AUTH architecture

Figure 16-1 shows a mail client that authenticates itself with a mail server before sending a message to be relayed to a remote destination. The server compares the credentials from the mail client against the credentials stored in an authentication backend. The server relays messages for the client only if the credentials that were sent match the ones that are stored.

Enabling and Configuring the Server

After configuring an authentication backend in SASL, as described in Chapter 15, you must configure the server as follows:

1. Enable server-side SMTP AUTH.
2. Configure the SASL mechanisms that will be offered to clients.
3. Configure SMTP AUTH support for nonstandard mail clients.
4. Configure the realm Postfix will pass to the SASL library.
5. Configure relay permissions in Postfix.

Running Postfix chrooted and offering SMTP AUTH is not complicated. Follow the instructions in this chapter to set up server-side authentication. Once you have proven that non-chrooted SMTP authentication works, proceed to Chapter 20; running SMTP AUTH with a chrooted Postfix is used as an example to describe chroot setups.

Enabling Server-Side SMTP AUTH

The first thing you need to do is enable server-side SMTP authentication for the Postfix smtpd server, because this feature is disabled by default. Set the smtpd_sasl_auth_enable parameter in main.cf to turn it on:

```
smtpd_sasl_auth_enable = yes
```

Configuring SASL Mechanisms

Now you must define the authentication mechanisms that Postfix should offer to mail clients. Cyrus SASL provides several mechanisms that range from anonymous "authentication" to very strong systems such as Kerberos.

You can control the offered mechanisms with the smtpd_sasl_security_options parameter. Set it to a comma-separated list of one or more of the following options:

noanonymous

This setting ensures that the server actually verifies the client's credentials. This is the default setting, and you should definitely keep this, because some spammers know about anonymous SMTP authentication. Make sure that your smtpd_sasl_security_options parameter always lists noanonymous; otherwise, your mail server will almost certainly be abused as an open relay.

noplaintext

Adding noplaintext to the list of SASL security options excludes all plaintext authentication mechanisms, such as PLAIN and LOGIN. This is recommended because plaintext credentials are trivial to sniff from a network.

noactive

This setting excludes SASL mechanisms that are susceptible to active (non-dictionary) attacks. For example, mutual authentication is not susceptible to active attacks.

nodictionary

This keyword excludes all mechanisms that can be broken by means of a dictionary attack. A dictionary attacker attempts to break a password by brute force, trying many different passwords until one works.

mutual_auth

Using mutual_auth allows only mechanisms that provide mutual authentication. This form of authentication requires the server to authenticate itself to the client as well as the other way around.

When testing the configuration, you do not need to change this parameter; the default of smtpd_sasl_security_options = noanonymous keeps you safe from spammers but still allows plaintext mechanisms so that debugging is slightly easier. Later, when you have verified that SMTP AUTH works, you *should* disable plaintext authentication by expanding your smtpd_sasl_security_options parameter in main.cf to at least this:

```
smtpd_sasl_security_options = noanonymous, noplaintext
```

CAUTION *A mail client using plaintext mechanisms sends the username and password as a base64-encoded string. It is trivial to decode this, so anyone listening to an SMTP dialog can use this data to abuse your mail server. Unfortunately, this is the only mechanism that Outlook Express supports. If you want to offer plaintext mechanisms, offer them only over an encrypted communication layer, as described in Chapter 18.*

Configuring SMTP AUTH Support for Nonstandard Mail Clients

The next thing you should probably do is tell Postfix to offer an alternative notation in the SMTP dialog so that broken mail clients still can use SMTP AUTH.

Broken mail clients do not recognize SMTP AUTH when it is offered as described in RFC 2222; instead, they recognize a notation that had been used in a draft of the standards document, where an equal sign (=) instead of a blank space appeared between the AUTH statement and the mechanisms.

Clients known to be "broken" are old versions of Microsoft Outlook, Microsoft Outlook Express, and Netscape Mail.

To support broken mail clients, set broken_sasl_auth_clients in main.cf as follows:

```
broken_sasl_auth_clients = yes
```

After reloading Postfix, you will notice another AUTH line in the SMTP dialog that includes the equal sign. Here's an example:

```
# telnet mail.example.com 25
220 mail.example.com ESMTP Postfix
EHLO client.example.com
250-mail.example.com
250-PIPELINING
250-SIZE 51200000
250-VRFY
250-ETRN
250-AUTH LOGIN PLAIN
250-AUTH=LOGIN PLAIN
250 8BITMIME
QUIT
```

Configuring the SASL Realm

You may need to set a `realm` within in `main.cf` to be sent to the Cyrus SASL password-verification service that you use, depending on the version of Cyrus SASL and the specific service. When a client wants to authenticate, Postfix sends the `realm` to Cyrus SASL along with the client's credentials. You can define the `realm` in Postfix with the `smtpd_sasl_local_domain` parameter in `main.cf`; this parameter is empty by default and should be left empty unless you use an auxiliary plug-in that actually requires a `realm`:

```
smtpd_sasl_local_domain =
```

You should change this to match the password-verification service that you use:

auxprop

The services that use auxiliary properties expect a realm. Set `smtpd_sasl_local_domain` to the realm your SMTP AUTH users have in the authentication backend. For example, if your SMTP AUTH users in `/etc/sasldb2` have the realm `example.com`, use the following:

```
smtpd_sasl_local_domain = example.com
```

saslauthd prior to Cyrus SASL 2.1.17

saslauthd prior to Cyrus SASL 2.1.17 cannot deal with realms; you should not use one. Remove the value for `smtpd_sasl_local_domain` as follows:

```
smtpd_sasl_local_domain =
```

saslauthd for Cyrus SASL 2.1.17

saslauthd for Cyrus SASL 2.1.17 does not know what to do with a realm, so it ignores this information. It doesn't matter what realm you send, so you don't have to touch the `smtpd_sasl_local_domain` parameter.

saslauthd Cyrus SASL 2.1.19

saslauthd Cyrus SASL 2.1.19 and later versions made sending the realm configurable. Use the option `-r` when you start saslauthd to have the realm passed to your password-verification backend.

Configuring Relay Permissions

The final step is to tell Postfix to permit relaying for SASL-authenticated clients. To do this, add `permit_sasl_authenticated` to the list of `smtpd_recipient_restrictions` in your configuration. Here's an example:

```
smtpd_recipient_restrictions =
    [...]
    permit_sasl_authenticated,
```

```
permit_mynetworks,
reject_unauth_destination
[...]
```

Make sure you put the `permit_sasl_authenticated` keyword early enough in the parameter so that an authenticating client doesn't accidentally get kicked out by another rule first (most importantly `reject_unauth_destination`).

You're now finished with the basic server SMTP AUTH setup. Reload your configuration and start testing.

Testing Server-Side SMTP AUTH

Testing server-side SMTP authentication involves these steps:

1. Check the mail log to find errors that Postfix can detect on its own.
2. Check the SMTP dialog to make sure that `smtpd` offers SMTP AUTH.
3. Authenticate a user to ensure that Postfix can communicate with Cyrus SASL.
4. Send a test message to a remote user to verify that authenticated users can relay messages to nonlocal destinations through your server.

Checking the Mail Log

Check the log file by printing out all lines in `/var/log/maillog` that contain the words reject, error, warning, fatal, or panic followed by a colon (`:`) with this command:

```
# egrep '(reject|error|warning|fatal|panic):' /var/log/maillog
```

You shouldn't see any errors related to SMTP AUTH, but if there are any, check your configuration for typographical errors or Cyrus SASL–related problems.

Now, enable verbose logging for the `smtpd` daemon, and keep the logging level set this way for as long as you test SMTP AUTH. Make this change by adding a `-v` to the `smtpd` command in `master.cf`:

```
# ==========================================================================
# service type  private unpriv  chroot  wakeup  maxproc command + args
#               (yes)   (yes)   (yes)   (never) (100)
# ==========================================================================
smtp    inet  n       -       n       -       -       smtpd -v
#smtps  inet  n       -       n       -       -       smtpd
```

Once you reload Postfix, the changes will take effect.

Checking the SMTP Dialog

The next test is to make sure that Postfix offers SMTP AUTH to mail clients, so that clients know when they can initiate SMTP authentication. Connect to your server, and send an EHLO introduction to the server (SMTP AUTH only works in extended SMTP communication). Here's an example:

```
$ telnet mail.example.com 25
220 mail.example.com ESMTP Postfix
EHLO client.example.com
250-mail.example.com
250-PIPELINING
250-SIZE 10240000
250-VRFY
250-ETRN
250-STARTTLS
250-AUTH NTLM LOGIN PLAIN DIGEST-MD5 CRAM-MD5
250-AUTH=NTLM LOGIN PLAIN DIGEST-MD5 CRAM-MD5
250-XVERP
250 8BITMIME
QUIT
221 Bye
```

You can easily see that the AUTH parameter not only tells you that SMTP AUTH is enabled, but also supplies a list of possible authentication mechanisms. Furthermore, a near-identical line follows for broken clients.

If the server doesn't offer the AUTH parameter, check that you did the following:

- Compiled Postfix with Cyrus SASL support
- Configured the basic parameters correctly, and that you don't have any typos in main.cf; use **postconf -n** to verify the parameters
- Connected to the correct servers and that you use EHLO, not HELO

Authenticating a User

To authenticate a user, you need a base64-encoded string that contains a valid username and password from your authentication backend. For example, if your username is test and your password is testpass, use this command:

```
$ perl -MMIME::Base64 -e 'print encode_base64("test\0test\0testpass");'
```

The output will look like this:

```
dGVzdAB0ZXN0AHR1c3RwYXNz
```

Now, connect to your server and start an extended SMTP communication using `EHLO`, and then use `AUTH PLAIN` to tell Postfix that you want to authenticate using the plaintext mechanism with the base64-encoded string. Here's an example of a successful test:

```
$ telnet mail.example.com 25
220 mail.example.com ESMTP Postfix
EHLO client.example.com
250-mail.example.com
250-PIPELINING
250-SIZE 10240000
250-VRFY
250-ETRN
250-STARTTLS
250-AUTH NTLM LOGIN PLAIN DIGEST-MD5 CRAM-MD5
250-AUTH=NTLM LOGIN PLAIN DIGEST-MD5 CRAM-MD5
250-XVERP
250 8BITMIME
AUTH PLAIN dGVzdAB0ZXN0AHR1c3RwYXNz
235 Authentication successful
QUIT
221 Bye
```

You can easily see the `235 Authentication successful` confirmation. If you experience problems and the server responds with `535 Error: authentication failed`, try the following:

- Check your log file for errors.
- Verify the username and password in your authentication backend.
- Check over your Cyrus SASL configuration in /usr/lib/sasl2/smtpd.conf, as described in Chapter 15.
- Reload Postfix if you changed /usr/lib/sasl2/smtpd.conf.
- Decode your base64 string, and compare the output against your original input. (If you want to test the null bytes, redirect the output to a file and run a text editor on the file.) Here's an example:

```
$ perl -MMIME::Base64 -e 'print decode_base64("dGVzdAB0ZXN0AHR1c3RwYXNz");'
testtesttestpass
```

CAUTION   *If you post your logs to a mailing list, you probably should alter them to remove the username and password information that comes with the verbose logging level. As an alternative, you could create a test user that you will delete as soon as you finish.*

Relaying a Test Message

You're finally ready to see if the Postfix server permits an authenticated user to relay a message. First, though, you need to make sure that other relay permissions don't interfere with your new authentication-based rules. To ensure this, connect from a host or network that is *not* permitted to relay *without* SMTP authentication. It pays to double-check, so first try to send a message without using SMTP AUTH.

If you don't have access to a client outside the network range defined in mynetworks, disable the mynetworks parameter, and set mynetworks_style = host while you test. This restricts relay permission to the server only, so you can use any host on your local area network to test the server.

Connect to the server as described in the previous section, but *do not* QUIT after you have authenticated successfully. Instead, proceed with a regular SMTP communication session that sends mail to a nonlocal user. Here's an example that sends a message from john.doe@example.com to echo@postfix-book.com:

```
$ telnet mail.example.com 25
220 mail.example.com ESMTP Postfix
EHLO client.example.com
250-mail.example.com
250-PIPELINING
250-SIZE 10240000
250-VRFY
250-ETRN
250-AUTH DIGEST-MD5 CRAM-MD5 GSSAPI PLAIN LOGIN
250-AUTH=DIGEST-MD5 CRAM-MD5 GSSAPI PLAIN LOGIN
250-XVERP
250 8BITMIME
AUTH PLAIN dGVzdAB0ZXN0AHRlc3RwYXNz
235 Authentication successful
MAIL FROM: <john.doe@example.com>
250 Ok
RCPT TO: <echo@postfix-book.com>
250 Ok
DATA
354 End data with <CR><LF>.<CR><LF>
This is a server side SMTP AUTH test. If the mail is
accepted, relaying works.
.
250 Ok: queued as 3FF15E1C65
QUIT
221 Bye
Connection closed by foreign host.
```

Notice the 250 0k message that the server sends as a response to the RCPT TO: command; this is usually a good sign, but you still want to confirm that a message goes through. If this test doesn't work, try the following:

- Check your log file for errors.
- Ensure that you set permit_sasl_authenticated correctly, as explained in the earlier "Configuring Relay Permissions" section.
- Double-check your base64 string.
- Check your SMTP dialog for typographical errors.

Advanced Server Settings

Since the arrival of SMTP AUTH capability in Postfix, some parameters have been added to give you better control over how SMTP AUTH should be handled. The following subsections will tell you what Postfix can do today.

Offering SMTP AUTH Selectively

You can exclude networks so that Postfix will not offer SMTP AUTH to them. This is extremely useful when you have Netscape mail clients (Netscape 4.x) that insist on using SMTP AUTH as soon as it is offered; no matter whether you configured them to use it or not.

Set the smtpd_sasl_exceptions_networks parameter in main.cf, and either use the variables Postfix knows from its own configuration, such as mynetworks, or define a list in IP address/CIDR notation (for example, 172.16.0.117/32):

```
smtpd_sasl_exceptions_networks = $mynetworks, 172.16.0.117/32
```

Enforcing an SMTP AUTH User to Match a Specific Envelope Sender

As soon as a mail client is authenticated, it is allowed to send with any envelope sender it chooses. You can limit the mail clients, however, to using a specific envelope sender address with the smtpd_sender_login_maps parameter; it defines the path to a map that matches envelope sender addresses with SASL login names. The map, such as /etc/postfix/smtpd_sender_login_map, would look like this:

```
flintstone@example.com    flintstone
rubble@example.com        rubble
sales@example.com         flintstone, rubble
```

The left-hand side of the map contains the envelope sender, and the right-hand side contains either a single login name or a list of comma-separated login names. Convert the map with postmap, for example postmap hash:/etc/postfix/smtpd_sender_login_map, and tell Postfix to read the map in main.cf.

```
smtpd_sender_login_maps = hash:/etc/postfix/smtpd_sender_login_map
```

You might also use NIS, LDAP, or SQL queries, instead of a `hash` map type.

Once Postfix knows about the map, you must choose one of two restrictions to specify what should be done with clients whose envelope sender doesn't match their login name.

reject_sender_login_mismatch

This will restrict all clients, whether they are SMTP-authenticated or not.

reject_unauthenticated_sender_login_mismatch

This will restrict only clients that haven't SMTP-authenticated themselves.

Either one or the other parameter goes into the list of `smtpd_recipient_restrictions` in `main.cf`:

```
smtpd_recipient_restrictions =
    ...
    reject_unauthenticated_sender_login_mismatch
    ...
```

Client-Side SMTP Authentication

In client-side SMTP authentication, the `smtp` and `lmtp` Postfix daemons use Cyrus SASL to authenticate themselves with a remote server. In a client configuration, you need to configure Postfix, but you *don't* need to worry about configuring Cyrus SASL. Both daemons, `smtp` and `lmtp`, can use any mechanism that the Cyrus SASL library supports.

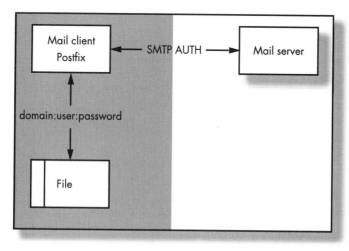

Figure 16-2: Client-side SMTP AUTH architecture

Figure 16-2 shows the Postfix `smtp` daemon engaged in an SMTP AUTH session with a remote mail server. The client (`smtp`) sends credentials stored in an SASL password file to acquire relay permission from the remote server.

AUTH for the Postfix SMTP Client

Configuring SMTP authentication for the Postfix client is *much* easier than configuring it for the server. Although you still need the Cyrus SASL library, you don't need to configure SASL.

Here's what you need to do:

1. Ask the remote server for the mechanisms that it offers.
2. Enable client-side SMTP AUTH.
3. Provide a file that holds your SMTP AUTH credentials.
4. Configure Postfix to use the credential file.
5. Disable unsafe authentication mechanisms.

Checking for Valid Authentication Mechanisms

Your first step is to find out what mechanisms the remote server offers and make sure that your Cyrus SASL installation provides you with libraries to support those mechanisms. Connect to your mail server, and send an `EHLO` greeting to list the mechanisms. Here's an example:

```
$ telnet mail.remote-example.com 25
220 mail.remote-example.com ESMTP
EHLO mail.example.com
250-mail.remote-example.com
250-PIPELINING
250-SIZE 10240000
250-VRFY
250-ETRN
250-STARTTLS
250-AUTH LOGIN PLAIN DIGEST-MD5 CRAM-MD5
250-AUTH=LOGIN PLAIN DIGEST-MD5 CRAM-MD5
250-XVERP
250 8BITMIME
QUIT
221 Bye
```

You can see that the server not only supports the LOGIN, PLAIN, DIGEST-MD5, and CRAM-MD5 mechanisms, but also will talk to the broken clients described earlier in the "Configuring SMTP AUTH Support for Nonstandard Mail Clients" section.

Now, list the libraries in your Cyrus SASL library directory. For example, if your Cyrus installation prefix is `/usr/local`, you would run the following.

```
# ls -1 /usr/local/lib/sasl2/lib*.so
```

The output should look something like this:

```
/usr/local/lib/sasl2/libanonymous.so
/usr/local/lib/sasl2/libcrammd5.so
/usr/local/lib/sasl2/libdigestmd5.so
/usr/local/lib/sasl2/liblogin.so
/usr/local/lib/sasl2/libplain.so
/usr/local/lib/sasl2/libsasldb.so
```

It's easy to see that this installation supports the ANONYMOUS, CRAM-MD5, DIGEST-MD5, LOGIN, and PLAIN mechanisms. (Note that libsasldb.so is not an authentication mechanism library.)

Once you have all this information, compare the mechanisms the remote server offers to the listing of your own server's Cyrus SASL libraries, and you will know which mechanisms your Postfix client will be able to use to connect to that server.

Enabling Client-Side SMTP AUTH

By default, client-side SMTP authentication is disabled. To turn it on, set the smtp_sasl_auth_enable parameter in main.cf to yes:

```
smtp_sasl_auth_enable = yes
```

This enables client-side SMTP AUTH; you still have to tell Postfix where to find the secrets needed to authenticate and which of the mechanisms (from those the remote server offers) Postfix may use.

Storing SMTP AUTH Credentials

Your next step is to prepare the data that the Postfix client will use when it wants to authenticate with one or more remote servers. As root, create the /etc/postfix/sasl_passwd map file if it does not already exist:

```
# touch /etc/postfix/sasl_passwd
```

TIP *Postfix always open maps before chrooting, so this table can safely be kept outside the jail.*

Edit this file, putting the fully qualified domain name of a mail server that requires authentication on the left-hand side, and a colon-separated username and password pair on the right. Here's an example that sets usernames and passwords for mail.example.com and relay.another.example.com:

```
mail.example.com          test:testpass
relay.another.example.com username:password
```

After editing sasl_passwd, change the permissions so that only root can read it; remember that it holds confidential information that local users should not be able to read. Do this with the chown and chmod commands:

```
# chown root:root /etc/postfix/sasl_passwd && chmod 600 /etc/postfix/sasl_passwd
```

NOTE *Don't worry about the permissions for Postfix; it reads sasl_passwd before it switches to a user with fewer privileges and before entering a chroot jail.*

With the proper permissions in place, convert the map file into an indexed map that Postfix can access quickly (you need to do this every time you change sasl_passwd):

```
# postmap hash:/etc/postfix/sasl_passwd
```

Configuring Postfix to Use the SMTP AUTH Credentials

Next, you need to tell the Postfix client where to find the authentication credential map that you just set up. Set the smtp_sasl_password_maps parameter in main.cf to the full path of your sasl_passwd file, but specify that the map values are stored in a hash file with the hash: qualifier. Here's an example:

```
smtp_sasl_password_maps = hash:/etc/postfix/sasl_passwd
```

Restricting Authentication Mechanisms

As a final client configuration step, you should disable the use of unsafe mechanisms. Set the smtp_sasl_security_options parameter to a comma-separated list of mechanism types that the client may not use (see the earlier "Configuring SASL Mechanisms" section for a list of valid types). By default, smtp_sasl_security_options is set to noanonymous, but you should disable plaintext mechanisms if you can (that is, if your server supports an encrypted mechanism, such as DIGEST-MD5 or CRAM-MD5). To do this, add the following line to main.cf:

```
smtp_sasl_security_options = noanonymous, noplaintext
```

TIP *If the remote server offers only plaintext mechanisms, but you don't want to use them over an unencrypted communication layer, you can see if the server offers STARTTLS. If it does, you can force Postfix to use TLS, as described in Chapter 18, so that the client sends plaintext credentials only after establishing an encrypted communication layer.*

Testing Client-Side SMTP AUTH

Testing your client's authentication involves both local and remote testing:

1. Verify the credentials with the remote server to make sure that the credentials you have are valid and are known to the remote server.
2. Check the log file.
3. Use Postfix to send a test message to a remote user, showing that you can relay messages through the server.

Verifying Credentials with the Remote Server

Your first step is to verify that the username and password you have actually work. Connect to the remote server, as described in the earlier "Authenticating a User" section, and authenticate with the given username and password.

NOTE *If the remote server does not offer plaintext mechanisms over an unencrypted communication layer, you can try to use OpenSSL's* s_client *to establish a TLS session, see if it offers plaintext mechanisms, and try to* AUTH *then. See Chapter 18 for the details on how to do this.*

You can also try configuring the credentials into a GUI mail client that supports various authentication mechanisms. Send a message with the client to see if the server accepts the credentials.

After you're sure that the server accepts your username and password, you can focus on your Postfix configuration.

Checking the Log File

The next step is to look for obvious errors in the Postfix log file with the now-familiar egrep command:

```
# egrep '(reject|error|warning|fatal|panic):' /var/log/maillog
```

Using the Postfix Client to Send a Test Message to a Remote User

The final test is to send a message to a remote destination using your Postfix mail client daemon (smtp). Perform the following steps:

1. Increase the log level for the smtp daemon.
2. Send a message to a remote destination.
3. Check the log file for confirmation of successful authentication.

Increasing the Log Level for the smtp Daemon

To increase the amount of log output for the `smtp` client daemon, edit your `master.cf` file and give the `smtp` program a `-v` argument as follows (make sure not to confuse the `smtpd` line with `smtp`):

```
# ========================================================================
# service type  private unpriv  chroot  wakeup  maxproc command + args
#               (yes)   (yes)   (yes)   (never) (100)
# ========================================================================
smtp      inet  n       -       n       -       -       smtpd
#smtps    inet  n       -       n       -       -       smtpd
...
smtp      unix  -       -       n       -       -       smtp -v
...
```

After you reload the Postfix configuration, the `smtp` daemon will log the SMTP AUTH communication *and* the calculation of credential information, such as encoding or decoding the base64 string.

CAUTION *You probably want to be careful about sending your Postfix log to a mailing list, because* smtp *logs your credentials in plaintext. Take care to replace your username and password (with XXX, for example) before posting your log.*

Sending a Test Message to a Remote Destination

You can check whether client-side authentication works by using a GUI mail client to transport the message to your Postfix client daemon. Or you can use the following command line to send a message to echo@postfix-book.com, which sends a message back to the envelope sender that includes the complete header and body of the original message:

```
$ mail -s 'Testing client side authentication' echo@postfix-book.com
Testing...
.
Cc:
$
```

Checking the Log File for Successful Authentication

Finally, check the Postfix log file for successful authentication with the grep command:

```
# grep '235 Authentication successful' /var/log/maillog
```

If everything went well, you should see one or more lines like the following that says that the authentication with `relay.example.com` worked:

```
Jan 20 12:40:39 mail postfix/smtp[21740]: < relay.example.com[172.16.0.100]:
  235 Authentication successful
```

NOTE *You should also have a new message in the destination mailbox; check the headers of this message.*

The lmtp Client

Configuring the Postfix lmtp client to use SMTP AUTH is very similar to configuring the smtp client (see the earlier "AUTH for the Postfix SMTP Client" section). These are the steps you need to perform:

1. Enable client-side SMTP AUTH by setting lmtp_sasl_auth_enable = yes in your main.cf file.

2. Create a file that holds the SMTP AUTH credentials. To do this, refer to the earlier "Storing SMTP AUTH Credentials" section, but use lmtp_passwd as a filename instead of smtp_passwd (of course, you could also share the credential file with the smtp client).

3. Configure Postfix to use the file with the SASL credentials; set lmtp_sasl_password_maps = /etc/postfix/lmtp_passwd in your main.cf file.

4. Restrict the client to safe authentication mechanisms (as described in the next section).

Restricting lmtp to Groups of Mechanisms

The process for banning unsafe mechanisms for the lmtp client daemon is very similar to the process for the smtp client daemon, described in the section, "Restricting Authentication Mechanisms." For example, if you want to make sure that the client does not use plaintext mechanisms, set the lmtp_sasl_security_options parameter as follows:

```
lmtp_sasl_security_options = noplaintext, noanonymous
```

However, there's one slight difference from the smtp daemon settings: If your lmtp client daemon happens to be on the same machine as your Postfix server, and if they communicate via sockets, you might as well loosen the settings a little and allow plaintext mechanisms:

```
lmtp_sasl_security_options = noanonymous
```

Testing SMTP AUTH for the lmtp Client

To test the lmtp client, perform the same steps as described earlier in the "Testing Client-Side SMTP AUTH" section. In addition, you may want to use imtest, a utility in the Cyrus IMAP package. This is particularly useful when your goal is to make the Postfix lmtp client deliver mail to the LMTP server that comes with the Cyrus IMAP server.

17

UNDERSTANDING TRANSPORT LAYER SECURITY

So far, you have seen that Postfix is rather secure from the system point of view—that is, Postfix tries hard to eliminate common security holes that might lead to a break-in. As noble as these efforts are, however, there's still something missing. The problem is that SMTP, as designed, does not protect you from intruders that may be snooping on your network packets. This may sound like a bleak situation, and although you may think there is a bit of exaggeration in descriptions of the dangers, there are some real instances where it really does make sense to protect the SMTP conversation from eavesdroppers.

For example, a company that exchanges content over the Internet through mail servers may want to consider encrypting this content, and anyone running an SMTP server that supports SMTP AUTH allowing plaintext authentication has a reason to be worried. Sensitive message content and passwords will be transferred in plaintext TCP packets, and anyone who might have access to the path of that data stream could dump the TCP packets to their own computer and reconstruct the data stream.

You can fix this problem with Transport Layer Security (TLS), a system that encrypts communication between two hosts *before* any sensitive data goes out over the wire. In Postfix, you can even use TLS to permit relaying, based on a certificate system. This chapter explains the theory of TLS in Postfix, whether it is acting as a mail client, a mail server, or a mail server that permits relaying based on client certificates. When you are finished with this chapter, you will also know when it makes sense to use TLS and its prerequisites.

TLS Basics

The default SMTP client-server communication is not encrypted. The client simply establishes a TCP connection and starts transmitting data (see Figure 17-1). Unless the content itself was encrypted by another system, it is transported in plaintext, readable by anyone capable of listening to the data stream. An unwanted listener could easily see the content, and if they had control of a router, could possibly alter it.

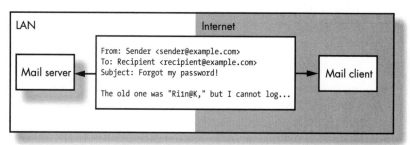

Figure 17-1: Unencrypted communication—readable by everyone

These attacks are impossible when the client and server use TLS (see Figure 17-2), because this system provides three things:

Privacy

The communication between the client and server is encapsulated inside an encrypted session. A third party without access to the client and server cannot decipher the data that is exchanged.

Integrity

Even though a man-in-the-middle attack is possible, both sides can immediately detect any alteration in the content.

Proof of authenticity

The client and server can exchange certificates that are validated by a trusted certification authority (CA) and that prove the authenticity of the hosts involved. A certificate contains information such as the FQDN of the host. DNS spoofing, to name just one possible attack, would be detected before data was sent.

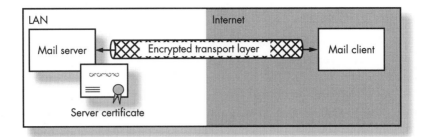

Figure 17-2: Encrypted communication—readable by the sender and recipient only

There are three common misconceptions about TLS:

- TLS does not protect the content after it goes from the client to the server. As soon as the server receives and stores the message, it is once again in clear text.

- TLS only guarantees encryption from the mail client to the mail server. Remember that the mail server may need to pass the message along to another server. Other mail servers on message's path to the final destination might not support TLS. Therefore, although you can enforce encryption on your own mail hubs, it is likely that you do not have control over the transport as soon as the message leaves your organization. As soon as one of the servers along the way does not support TLS, it goes back to clear text.

- TLS does not necessarily protect mail that is accepted and later returned as undeliverable. There is no guarantee that the return mail will follow the same path.

If any of these is a concern, you must encrypt the message content before sending it. Popular email encryption tools include S/MIME, PGP, and GnuPG.

How TLS Works

Transport Layer Security encrypts the communication between exactly two hosts. A TLS-enabled session proceeds as follows:

1. A client connects to a server.
2. The hosts initiate the SMTP communication.
3. The server offers TLS with the STARTTLS keyword within the SMTP communication.
4. If the client is capable of using TLS, it responds by sending STARTTLS to the server.
5. The public server certificate is signed with the private key and sent to the client.
6. The client verifies the server's certificate by checking its CA signature against the public CA signature in the client's own root store.

7. The client verifies the server's certificate by comparing the certificate's Common Name string with the server's DNS hostname.

8. The client and server switch to encrypted communication.

9. The hosts exchange data.

10. The session ends.

As you can see from this procedure, certificates play an important role in TLS.

Understanding Certificates

Encryption technology does not depend on certificates, but they are necessary to ensure that only the hosts intended to talk to each other can actually do so. If each host can verify the other's certificate, they agree to encrypt their session. Otherwise, they abort the whole process of encryption and issue warnings, because the basis for trust (authenticity) is absent.

How to Establish Trust

When you create a certificate, your system writes two files to the disk; one contains the public key and the other one the private key. The sending host encrypts some data with its private key, and the receiving host uses the public key to decrypt and verify the authenticity of the sender. It's possible to verify a public key that has been signed by a CA—the CA acts as guarantor for the validity of the sending host.

The receiving host does not query the CA directly every time it wants to verify a certificate. This would not only cause a lot of traffic, but also leave too much room for external manipulation when the verification data goes over the network. Instead, the receiver locally compares the signature of the CA's public key against a checksum of the certificate in question. The CA calculates and adds this checksum to the sender's certificate during the signing process. Any changes to the signed certificate would alter the checksum and render it useless, because the TLS mechanism would immediately detect the tampering.

To establish trust between a client and a server they must meet different requirements:

Client
A mail client that verifies the authenticity of a server certificate must have access to the CA's public key. Someone must import this key into the client's operating system certification store, where the mail client and other applications can read it.

Server
A mail server that issues a certificate must have valid private and public keys. The public keys must be signed by a CA.

Which Certification Authority Suits Your Needs?

There are several certification authorities out there who will be happy to sign your certificate. The question of which CA suits your needs best depends on the CA's services and prices, and your reason for using certificates:

Private use

> If you can only envision using your certificate for private purposes, where you or a limited number of users need a signed certificate (for example, coworkers at your company or servers in a larger network at various locations all under your control), then you can consider being your own certificate authority. Sign the server certificate yourself, and then provide both your CA root certificate and your server certificate to your clients and servers. This involves less effort and money, but mail clients and servers outside your organization won't trust your certificate.

Official use

> If you need official contact with outside users and mail servers that you have no control over, you should employ the services of an official CA. You can start your search for a CA that suits your specific needs at the PKI page (http://www.pki-page.org), where you will find a comprehensive list of CAs around the world.

Creating Certificates

Whether you plan to roll your own CA or have your certificate signed by an official certification authority, you will always have to create a certificate request to have it signed.

It's easy to create a new certificate—all you need to do is run a script and a few commands that do most of the work for you. All you need is some information at hand when you run the script.

Required Information

Most of the following parameters speak for themselves; you shouldn't have any trouble figuring them out. However, there is one entry where you must be a little careful: Common Name. The value you provide in server certificates must match the DNS name of your host. If there is a mismatch, TLS suspects a man-in-the-middle attack (in which someone stole the certificate), and it aborts verification. With client certificates, it's common to specify a personal name instead.

Here is the information you need to have at hand:

- Country
- State or province
- City or other municipal area
- Organization

- Organization unit
- Common name
- Email address

Creating the CA Certificate

If you decide that you want to sign your own certificates, you need to create your own CA certificate first. (If you're using an official CA, skip ahead to the "Distributing and Installing the CA Certificate" section.) Run `misc/CA.pl -newca` in your OpenSSL distribution:

```
# ./CA.pl -newca
CA certificate filename (or enter to create)
Making CA certificate ...
Generating a 1024 bit RSA private key
......++++++
....++++++
writing new private key to './demoCA/private/cakey.pem'
Enter PEM pass phrase: ❶
Verifying - Enter PEM pass phrase:
-----
You are about to be asked to enter information that will be incorporated
into your certificate request.
What you are about to enter is what is called a Distinguished Name or a DN.
There are quite a few fields but you can leave some blank
For some fields there will be a default value,
If you enter '.', the field will be left blank.
-----
Country Name (2 letter code) [AU]:EX
State or Province Name (full name) [Some-State]:Examplia
Locality Name (eg, city) []:Exampleton
Organization Name (eg, company) [Internet Widgits Pty Ltd]:Example Inc.
Organizational Unit Name (eg, section) []:Certification Authority
Common Name (eg, YOUR name) []:mail.example.com
Email Address []:postmaster@example.com
```

❶ When generating your CA certificate, you need to enter a passphrase. This will be required any time you work as a CA to sign and revoke certificates.

The `misc/CA.pl` program creates subdirectories where it puts files and directories needed to run a CA. After you have run the program, you should have a new `misc/demoCA` subdirectory, which should look like this:

```
# tree demoCA/
demoCA/
|-- cacert.pem ❶
|-- certs
|-- crl
|-- index.txt
|-- newcerts
```

```
|-- private
|    `-- cakey.pem ❷
`-- serial
```

❶ `cacert.pem` is the CA's public key. Your hosts will need it in their certificate root store to verify the signature in the Postfix public certificate.

❷ `cakey.pem` is the CA's private key. It must be protected and only the user who runs the CA should have read/write permission.

Distributing and Installing the CA Certificate

The next step is to distribute the CA certificate to all clients that will use TLS. If you run your own CA you will find the CA certificate located in `misc/demoCA`. By default openssl will save it as `cacert.pem`. If you've chosen an official certification authority you will have to find and download their CA certificate.

How you distribute the CA certificate mainly depends on the applications that will use the certificate and the environment they run in. GUI applications usually have a certificate root store provided by the operating system, which offers centralized management of all certificates.

On servers that provide a command-line interface only and use Open-SSL, there is no such thing as a *single*, centralized root store. Command-line applications can use their own store, and the location of the store must be configured within each application. Since Postfix is a command-line application, you will need to configure either the `smtp` daemon or the `smtpd` daemon or both to gain access to a store containing CA certificates. This part of the configuration will be explained in Chapter 18.

NOTE *Separate stores add flexibility for designing specialized solutions, but they also add complexity to keeping certificates in various certificate stores up-to-date.*

Windows Installation

Windows wants the certificate in a different format—OpenSSL can convert the CA certificate for you. You don't have to use `CA.pl`; you can run `openssl` directly. In the following example, the SSL installation directory is `/usr/local/ssl`:

```
# cd /usr/local/ssl/misc/demoCA
# openssl x509 -in cacert.pem -out cacert.der -outform DER
```

After you've done this, you will find a new file named `cacert.der` in `/usr/local/ssl/misc/demoCA`.

Installing a CA certificate on Windows is fairly easy:

1. Copy `cacert.der` to your Windows machine.

2. Double-click `cacert.der` to start the installation process (see Figure 17-3).

3. Click **Install Certificate**, and follow the Certificate Import Wizard.

Figure 17-3: A successfully installed CA certificate on a Windows host

4. Click **Yes** when asked to add the certificate to the root store.

5. After the installation is done, double-click `cacert.der` again to verify that you successfully added it.

Linux (KDE-3.1.x) Installation

Installing a CA certificate on Linux/KDE is just as easy as on Windows:

1. Copy `cacert.der` to your Linux machine.

2. Double-click `cacert.der` in Konqueror to start the installation process.

3. KDE starts KDE Secure Certificate Import.

4. Choose Import.

5. A dialog box will appear, confirming that the import was successful.

6. Start KDE Control Center, and choose Security & Privacy from the left pane.

7. Choose Crypto from the left pane.

8. Click the SSL Signers tab in the right pane.

9. Verify that the new certificate is there (see Figure 17-4).

Mac OS X Installation

Installing a certificate on Max OS X depends on the version you run. Here's a mixture of command-line and GUI steps that should work on all versions (OS X prior to 10.3 and later).

Figure 17-4: A successfully installed CA certificate on a Linux host

To install a certificate manually, follow these steps:

1. Copy the cacert.pem to your home directory.
2. Open a Terminal window.
3. Import cacert.pem into the keychain:

```
$ sudo certtool i cacert.pem k=/System/Library/Keychains/X509Anchors
...certificate successfully imported
```

To verify that the certificate was successfully imported, follow these steps:

1. In the GUI open keychain in /Applications/Utilities/. You will only see your local keychain.
2. Choose Add Keychain from the File menu, and add /System/Library/ Keychains/X509Anchors to your keychain.
3. Search for your CA certificate by scrolling in the X509Anchors keychain. The Name column should refer to it by the Common Name you used (see Figure 17-5).

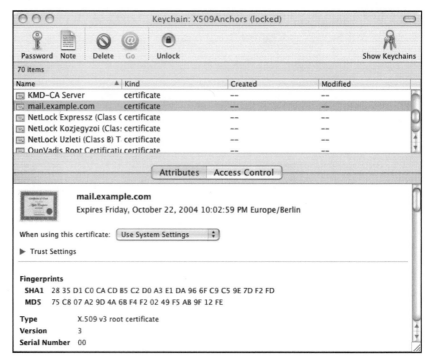

Figure 17-5: A successfully installed CA certificate on a Mac OS X host

Creating Your Server's Certificate

Once you've installed the CA certificate, it's time to create the Postfix server certificate. On the command line in /usr/local/ssl/misc, run the following command. It generates the certificate request that you'll have the CA sign in the following "Signing Your Server's Certificate" section:

```
# openssl req -new -nodes -keyout postfix_private_key.pem -out
  postfix_private_key.pem -days 365
Generating a 1024 bit RSA private key
.....................++++++
..........++++++
writing new private key to 'postfix_private_key.pem'
-----
You are about to be asked to enter information that will be incorporated
into your certificate request.
What you are about to enter is what is called a Distinguished Name or a DN.
There are quite a few fields but you can leave some blank
For some fields there will be a default value,
If you enter '.', the field will be left blank.
-----
Country Name (2 letter code) [AU]:EX
State or Province Name (full name) [Some-State]:Examplia
Locality Name (eg, city) []:Exampleton
Organization Name (eg, company) [Internet Widgits Pty Ltd]:Example Inc.
```

```
Organizational Unit Name (eg, section) []:MX Services
Common Name (eg, YOUR name) []:mail.example.com
Email Address []:postmaster@example.com
Please enter the following 'extra' attributes
to be sent with your certificate request
A challenge password []:
An optional company name []:
#
```

CAUTION *Don't use misc/CA.pl to create the private key file, unless you edit it so that it does not ask for a private passphrase to be included in the key. Adding a passphrase would mean that whenever Postfix wanted to use the certificate, someone would have to enter the passphrase! Postfix loads the certificate upon any start or restart of its smtp and smtpd daemons, and if there's a password, a user has to enter it. Needless to say, it would be absurdly impractical for a server like Postfix not to be able to restart on its own.*

Signing Your Server's Certificate

The final step in building the server certificate is to get it signed by a CA. If you are using an official CA, follow their instructions. Otherwise, run **openssl** from the command line to create postfix_public_cert.pem from postfix_private_key.pem.

```
# openssl ca -policy policy_anything -out postfix_public_cert.pem -infiles
    postfix_private_key.pem
Using configuration from /usr/local/ssl/openssl.cnf
Enter pass phrase for ./demoCA/private/cakey.pem:
Check that the request matches the signature
Signature ok
Certificate Details:
        Serial Number: 1 (0x1)
        Validity
            Not Before: Nov  9 21:25:13 2003 GMT
            Not After : Nov  8 21:25:13 2004 GMT
        Subject:
            countryName               = EX
            stateOrProvinceName       = Examplia
            localityName              = Exampleton
            organizationName          = Example Inc.
            organizationalUnitName    = MX Services
            commonName                = mail.example.com
            emailAddress              = postmaster@example.com
        X509v3 extensions:
            X509v3 Basic Constraints:
            CA:FALSE
            Netscape Comment:
            OpenSSL Generated Certificate
            X509v3 Subject Key Identifier:
            9E:36:9D:9B:ED:4E:32:73:0E:86:55:2A:FF:1B:49:F9:1C:47:17:75
```

```
        X509v3 Authority Key Identifier:
        keyid:00:52:AD:B7:FA:C2:EF:01:1A:9E:7B:0F:57:DB:DC:E4:82:59:8D:0B
        DirName:/C=EX/ST=Examplia/L=Exampleton/O=Certification Authority
Example Inc./CN=mail.example.com/emailAddress=postmaster@example.com
        serial:00
Certificate is to be certified until Nov  8 21:25:13 2004 GMT (365 days)
Sign the certificate? [y/n]:y
1 out of 1 certificate requests certified, commit? [y/n]y
Write out database with 1 new entries
Data Base Updated
```

postfix_public_cert.pem is the certificate that will be sent to clients during the initial TLS negotiation. Along with this certificate, Postfix will also send the signature from postfix_private_key.pem. To verify postfix_public_cert.pem the receiving host will then do some calculation based on Postfix's private key signature and the CA certificate signature. The result must match the signature of postfix_public_cert.pem. Otherwise the public key will be considered forged, and the communication will be ended immediately.

Preparing Certificates for Use in Postfix

Regardless of whether you plan to use the certificates for smtp (mail client) or smtpd (mail server), you should copy all of the certificates to /etc/postfix/certs:

```
# mkdir /etc/postfix/certs
# cp cacert.pem /etc/postfix/certs
# cp ../*.pem /etc/postfix/certs
```

Then you must protect the server's private key, postfix_private_key.pem, from access by other users on your machine:

```
# cd /etc/postfix/certs
# chmod 600 postfix_private_key.pem
```

When you're finished, the permissions should look like this:

```
# ls -all certs/
total 20
drwxr-xr-x  2 root   root   4096 Nov  9 23:03 .
drwxr-xr-x  3 root   root   4096 Oct 28 00:13 ..
-rw-r--r--  1 root   root   1379 Nov  9 23:02 cacert.pem
-rw-------  1 root   root   1620 Nov  9 23:02 postfix_private_key.pem
-rw-r--r--  1 root   root   3806 Nov  9 23:02 postfix_public_cert.pem
```

You are now ready to use the Postfix TLS features described in the next chapter.

18

USING TRANSPORT LAYER SECURITY

Transport Layer Security (TLS) for Postfix comes in two forms: client-side and server-side TLS. In addition to basic TLS, both forms provide functionality for performance tuning and fine-grained TLS enforcement, as well as enabling wrappers for secure plaintext SMTP AUTH and having the capability to permit relaying based on client certificates.

This chapter shows you how to configure Postfix for client- and server-side TLS. You will see different approaches for deploying TLS and the TLS daemons that supplement the default set of Postfix daemons.

Checking Postfix for TLS Support

Before you can set up the Postfix configuration files for TLS (described in RFC 2487), you must check whether your version of Postfix supports it. This is important, because the stock Postfix source code does not come with TLS capability at all—you must patch the Postfix source code to get TLS and STARTTLS support. If you use a prepackaged binary, though, you may already have TLS, because many Linux distributions include it in their Postfix packages. Postfix 2.2 includes TLS as a compile time option.

NOTE   *The TLS patch for Postfix was developed by Dr. Lutz Jänicke, a member of the OpenSSL development team who develops encryption technology professionally. As noted on the OpenSSL website, "The OpenSSL Project is a collaborative effort to develop a robust, commercial-grade, full-featured, and Open Source toolkit implementing the Secure Sockets Layer (SSL v2/v3) and Transport Layer Security (TLS v1) protocols as well as a full-strength general purpose cryptography library." For more information on the OpenSSL Project, visit http://www.openssl.org.*

Although TLS support comes as a patch, you may already have TLS support in your Postfix, because many distributions include it in their Postfix packages.

To check whether your Postfix installation supports TLS, check the output of postconf -d for tls. A pipeline to a grep command should return TLS parameters and their default values. Here is an example:

```
# postconf -d | grep tls
smtp_enforce_tls = no
smtp_starttls_timeout = 300s
smtp_tls_CAfile =
smtp_tls_CApath =
smtp_tls_cert_file =
smtp_tls_cipherlist =
smtp_tls_dcert_file =
smtp_tls_dkey_file = $smtp_tls_dcert_file
smtp_tls_enforce_peername = yes
smtp_tls_key_file = $smtp_tls_cert_file
smtp_tls_loglevel = 0
smtp_tls_note_starttls_offer = no
smtp_tls_per_site =
smtp_tls_session_cache_database =
smtp_tls_session_cache_timeout = 3600s
smtp_use_tls = no
smtpd_enforce_tls = no
smtpd_tls_CAfile =
smtpd_tls_CApath =
smtpd_tls_ask_ccert = no
smtpd_tls_auth_only = no
smtpd_tls_ccert_verifydepth = 5
smtpd_tls_cert_file =
smtpd_tls_cipherlist =
smtpd_tls_dcert_file =
smtpd_tls_dh1024_param_file =
```

```
smtpd_tls_dh512_param_file =
smtpd_tls_dkey_file = $smtpd_tls_dcert_file
smtpd_tls_key_file = $smtpd_tls_cert_file
smtpd_tls_loglevel = 0
smtpd_tls_received_header = no
smtpd_tls_req_ccert = no
smtpd_tls_session_cache_database =
smtpd_tls_session_cache_timeout = 3600s
smtpd_tls_wrappermode = no
smtpd_use_tls = no
tls_daemon_random_bytes = 32
tls_daemon_random_source =
tls_random_bytes = 32
tls_random_exchange_name = ${config_directory}/prng_exch
tls_random_prng_update_period = 60s
tls_random_reseed_period = 3600s
tls_random_source =
```

The existence of all these TLS-related parameters indicates that TLS is supported.

Building Postfix with TLS Support

If your binary does not have TLS support, you must build a new Postfix installation. First, check your system for the OpenSSL libraries and header files (the .h include files). Use find to search for the SSL libraries and includes as follows:

```
# find /usr -name 'ssl.*'
```

This command may take some time to complete. If successful, you should see some output like this:

```
/usr/include/openssl/ssl.h
/usr/lib/libssl.so
/usr/lib/libssl.a
```

In this example, ssl.h is the include file, libssl.so is the shared version of the OpenSSL library, and libssl.a is the static version of the library.

If you can't find OpenSSL on your machine, you can attempt to find a binary package from your distribution. Be sure to install the OpenSSL development packages (usually named openssl-dev or openssl-devel); otherwise, you will probably not get the include files.

If you want to use a newer version of OpenSSL than your distribution ships with, or if you can't find a binary package, you can build OpenSSL yourself. You will see how to do this next.

Building and Installing OpenSSL from Source Code

OpenSSL, Postfix, and the TLS patch kit are under constant development. Because the TLS patch kit depends on both Postfix and OpenSSL, you have to make sure that everything fits together when you download the source code and the patch kit.

CAUTION *Some Linux distributions ship with OpenSSL libraries that will break parts of your system if you overwrite the current OpenSSL installation on your system. If your machine has OpenSSL 0.9.6 or higher, you should stick with that version unless you know how to configure a newer version not to conflict with your existing installation.*

OpenSSL 0.9.6 or higher works fine with Postfix TLS. As an alternative, you can install the new library into a different place, thus avoiding the problem of overwriting the essential libraries.

The easiest way to get appropriate source code is to visit Lutz Jänicke's website at http://www.aet.tu-cottbus.de/personen/jaenicke/postfix_tls where you will find a TLS compatibility table. All you need to do is choose the Postfix, TLS patch kit, and OpenSSL sources from the same row of that table, and you will be prepared to begin building and installing your sources.

To install OpenSSL, do the following:

1. As a regular user, unpack the OpenSSL source with the **tar xzf openssl-***version***.tar.gz** command, where *version* is the OpenSSL version.

2. Change into the newly created directory containing the OpenSSL sources.

3. Read the INSTALL file, and decide whether you need any special options.

4. If you want to build shared libraries, run **configure** with **--shared**; shared libraries are not built by default. If you link Postfix statically against libopenssl.a, then you will need to recompile all of Postfix if you need to update OpenSSL due to security issues.

5. After running the configure script to build the Makefiles, run **make && make test**.

6. Become the superuser (root), and run **make install**. If you didn't build shared libraries, you're finished.

7. Verify the shared library path; the install process prints this directory just before terminating. The default path is /usr/local/ssl/lib.

8. Add the shared library path to your dynamic linker's runtime search path. On Linux, this means that you have to add the directory to the /etc/ld.so.conf file and run **ldconfig**. On Solaris, you need to run **crle**.

Building Postfix with TLS

After you've got the OpenSSL libraries and include files, you can build a new TLS-aware Postfix. You need the Postfix source code and the TLS patch kit.

CAUTION *Make sure you check the* README *and* INSTALL *files before doing anything; the procedure for installing TLS support may have changed since the date of publication.*

To build Postfix, follow these steps:

1. Unpack the Postfix source code and TLS patch kit as a regular user into *separate* directories.
2. Change into the Postfix source directory.
3. Run `patch -p1 < ../tls_dir/pfixtls.diff` to apply the patch, where `tls_dir` is the directory containing the TLS patch file named `pfixtls.diff`.
4. Set the build options, and then run `make makefiles` and `make` as follows, where `ssl_prefix` is your SSL base directory and `sasl2_prefix` is your SASL2 base directory.

```
$ CFLAGS="-DUSE_SSL -DUSE_SASL_AUTH -Isasl2_prefix/include -Issl_prefix/
  includes" AUXLIBS="-Lssl_prefix/lib -lssl -lcrypto -Lsasl_prefix/lib -
  lsasl2" ❶
$ make makefiles
$ make
```

❶ These options specify a Postfix build with TLS and SASL2 support. To add more options, read the relevant file in the `readme` directory of the Postfix source tree.

5. Switch to the superuser (`root`).
6. Run `make install` if this is the first installation from source code or `make upgrade` if you already had a working Postfix installation.
7. If you built OpenSSL as a shared library, run `ldd ` ` postconf -h daemon_directory` `/smtpd` to verify that the dynamic runtime linker can find all of the libraries that you used to compile Postfix.

After completing these steps, you should have a Postfix installation that supports Transport Layer Security.

Server-Side TLS

In server-side TLS, Postfix acts as a mail server (MTA), offering TLS to mail clients (see Figure 18-1). You can configure Postfix to encrypt the transport layer, hiding the entire SMTP communication session, to receive plaintext SMTP AUTH credentials safely, or to relay mail for clients based on the certificates that the clients present.

NOTE *Postfix does not offer* STARTTLS *to the sendmail command-line utility. This is a security feature; a TLS-aware sendmail would need to access the server's private key. However, the key is owned and is only readable by* root, *and the Postfix* sendmail *does not run as* root.

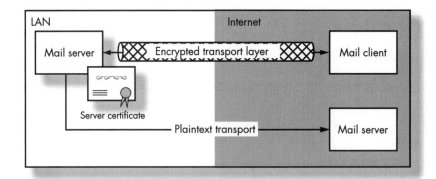

Figure 18-1: TLS for the Postfix mail server

Basic Server Configuration

To set up server-side TLS, you need to modify five parameters in your Postfix configuration files. You should also set two additional parameters to facilitate debugging (this not only helps you find problems, but is handy when tuning TLS sessions because Postfix gets to know mail clients that can and cannot use TLS).

The configuration steps are as follows:

1. Enable TLS in the main Postfix configuration file.
2. Tell Postfix where to find the certificates required for TLS.
3. Connect Postfix to a random source generator.
4. Increase the log level to get useful information as you learn to run TLS.
5. Add information to mail headers to further trace TLS.

Enabling Server-Side TLS

By default, TLS-capable Postfix servers do not have server-side TLS enabled, so Postfix does not offer TLS to clients, even if they ask for it. To enable server-side TLS, set the `smtpd_use_tls` parameter in `main.cf` to yes:

```
smtpd_use_tls = yes
```

After reloading the configuration, Postfix offers STARTTLS to mail clients in the SMTP dialog to inform them that they may negotiate a TLS session. However, enabling server-side TLS is not sufficient to get it working, because you haven't told Postfix where to find the server certificates essential to a TLS session. You will see a message like this in the mail log:

```
Dec  1 03:07:13 mail postfix/smtpd[741]: TLS engine: do need at least RSA _or_
  DSA cert/key data
```

Setting Certificate Paths

The next step is to add paths for the files or directories that hold your server certificates. At the very least, you must provide the server key and certificate that was signed by a certification authority and the corresponding private key used to create the certificate request. Both declarations appear in `main.cf`. Here is an example, where the certificates are in `/etc/postfix/certs`:

```
smtpd_tls_key_file = /etc/postfix/certs/postfix_private_key.pem ❶
smtpd_tls_cert_file = /etc/postfix/certs/postfix_public_cert.pem ❷
```

❶ `smtpd_tls_key_file` is the path to the private key.
❷ `smtpd_tls_cert_file` is the path to the server certificate.

NOTE *The preceding settings assume that your server certificate and private key are in separate files. If you decide to put both certificates in a single file, you can point one parameter to the other with a configuration line such as* smtpd_tls_cert_file = $smtpd_tls_key_file.

After setting these certificate parameters, you can run Postfix in server-side TLS mode, but you'll still have several errors and warnings in the log file. That's because Postfix can't transmit the CA's certificate and verify certificates sent by mail clients. You still need to configure the source for CA certificates.

Configuring the Postfix Certificate Root Store

As mentioned earlier in Chapter 17, OpenSSL does not have a default central root store, so you need to create a root store designed specifically for your mail system or to use a root store that already exists on your system. The configuration that you're about to see uses the `ca-bundle.crt` file that comes with the Apache `mod_ssl` module, which contains several CA certificates and servers for Apache.

NOTE *You may want to set up your own collection of CA certificates in order to make sure that they really stem from those certification authorities and weren't modified by some third party on their way to packaging. This is the safest way to proceed, because all TLS security efforts are in vain if the certificates on which this mechanism relies are fakes.*

When preparing to collect the CA certificates for your server, be prepared to spend a considerable amount of time in the process. When we researched this chapter, collecting the certificates turned out to be a very time-consuming task. Nearly all of the certification authorities seemed to hide the pertinent information on their websites.

To find the Apache mod_ssl ca-bundle.crt on your system, run **locate ca-bundle.crt** on the command line:

```
$ locate ca-bundle.crt
/usr/share/ssl/certs/ca-bundle.crt
```

If you do not have the `locate` command, you need to resort to the slower `find` command:

```
$ find / -name ca-bundle.crt
```

After you find or install your root store, you must configure Postfix to use it with the `smtpd_tls_CAfile` parameter in `main.cf`. Here's an example:

```
smtpd_tls_CAfile = /usr/share/ssl/certs/ca-bundle.crt
```

If you act as your own certification authority, you need to add your CA certificate to this root store. You can just append your certificate to the end of the preexisting root with a `cat` command, as in this example:

```
$ cat /usr/local/ssl/misc/demoCA/cacert.pem >> /usr/share/ssl/certs/ca-bundle.crt
```

NOTE *If your CA certificate is a link in a chain of certificates, add all of the CA certificates from your CA certificate down to the root CA certificate in the certificate chain.*

The `smtpd_tls_CAfile` parameter expects all certificates to be located in a single file. As an alternative, Postfix offers the `smtpd_tls_CApath` parameter, which you can set to a directory in which certificates are stored as separate files.

NOTE *The storage method isn't the only difference between `smtpd_tls_CAfile` and `smtpd_tls_CApath`. The files in `smtpd_tls_CApath` are consulted only when Postfix needs to verify a certificate. However, Postfix reads the files named by the `smtpd_tls_CAfile` parameter at startup, before Postfix enters the chroot jail. Therefore, if you decide to run Postfix in a chrooted environment, `smtpd_tls_CAfile` is the better choice, because you can place the certificate files outside the chroot jail.*

You might be better off setting both parameters, splitting some CA certificates into separate files from a main batch in a single file. Postfix reads files named by `smtpd_tls_CAfile` first, then consults `smtpd_tls_CApath` as a fallback.

Connecting Postfix to a Random Source Generator

TLS is a safe way to send mail not just because it encrypts the communication layer, but also because it never uses the same combination of numbers for any two ciphers. The TLS implementation does this by choosing a (pseudo) random number for all new TLS sessions.

OpenSSL does not generate its own random numbers because most Linux and BSD derivatives have built-in random number sources as system devices in `/dev`.

NOTE *If your system doesn't have built-in random number generation, you can use the pseudo-random number generator daemon (also by Lutz Jänicke). To configure Postfix to use this daemon, you set the `tls_random_exchange_name` parameter in `main.cf`. Have a look at `samples/sample-tls.cf` in your Postfix distribution for more details.*

The two sources for random numbers normally available on your system are `dev:/dev/random` and `dev:/dev/urandom`.

/dev/random

> The /dev/random generator provides high-quality random data, but you shouldn't use it on systems that use TLS heavily. The reason is that /dev/random can block if a TLS requests random data too quickly, draining the random source. If this happens, Postfix stops working until the systems gains enough entropy to provide numbers again.

/dev/urandom

> The /dev/urandom generator never blocks because it uses an internal pseudo-random number generator to create the entropy data. Use /dev/urandom for systems that start Postfix automatically.

> To connect Postfix to a random source generator, set the tls_random_source parameter in main.cf and reload your configuration:

```
tls_random_source = dev:/dev/urandom
```

NOTE *OpenSSL versions greater than 0.9.6 detect /dev/urandom automatically. If you use one of these versions, you do not need to set tls_random_source. OpenSSL 0.9.7 goes even further, detecting other random source generators. If you're using OpenSSL 0.9.7, look at its documentation for more details.*

Increasing the TLS Log Level

The TLS subsystem provides the smtpd_tls_loglevel parameter to control the amount of TLS-related information written to your mail log. The five levels described in Table 18-1 control how verbose the logging is.

Table 18-1: smtpd_tls_loglevel Levels for smtpd

Log Level	Description
0	No TLS logging; this is the default
1	Startup and certificate information
2	All of level 1, plus information about the various stages of TLS negotiation
3	All of level 2, plus hex and ASCII dumps of the negotiation process
4	All of level 3, plus hex and ASCII dumps of the complete transmission after the mail client sends STARTTLS

The first time you enable server-side TLS, set the log level to 2, which gives you enough information to start debugging if things don't work out as planned:

```
smtpd_tls_loglevel = 2
```

Adding Information to Mail Headers

You may also want your mail server to add TLS information to the Received header of each message sent using TLS. Do this by setting the smtpd_tls_received_header parameter in main.cf as follows.

```
smtpd_tls_received_header = yes
```

After a configuration reload, you should see something like this in your mail headers:

```
Received: from client.example.com (client.example.com [172.16.0.3])
        (using TLSv1 with cipher EDH-RSA-DES-CBC3-SHA (168/168 bits))
        (No client certificate requested)
        by mail.example.com (Postfix) with ESMTP id B637A7247
        for <tls-bounce@mail.examples.com>; Wed, 10 Dec 2003 23:37:02 +0100 (CET)
```

Testing Server-Side TLS

There are three things to test after you configure the TLS basics:

1. Check the log file to see if Postfix encountered any errors.
2. Check for STARTTLS in the SMTP dialog to see that Postfix is offering TLS.
3. Test TLS with the openssl program to prove that Postfix can initiate a TLS session using the certificates you provided in the basic configuration.

Checking the Log File

The first test is to look for TLS support by scanning the log file using a regular expression:

```
$ egrep '(reject|error|warning|fatal|panic):' /var/log/maillog
```

This command prints out all lines in /var/log/maillog that contain the words reject, error, warning, fatal, or panic followed by a colon (:).

If you did everything correctly, there shouldn't be any TLS-related errors. If problems do crop up, check the configuration file for typos and check the read permissions of the certificates.

Looking for STARTTLS in SMTP Communication

The next test you should do is run a telnet session to the Postfix server to verify that it offers TLS to mail clients. Look carefully at the following output for the STARTTLS keyword:

```
$ telnet localhost 25
220 mail.example.com ESMTP Postfix
EHLO client.example.com
250-mail.example.com
250-PIPELINING
```

```
250-SIZE 10240000
250-VRFY
250-ETRN
250-STARTTLS
250-AUTH NTLM LOGIN PLAIN OTP DIGEST-MD5 CRAM-MD5
250-XVERP
250 8BITMIME
QUIT
221 Bye
```

Simulating a TLS Mail Client–Server Session with OpenSSL

The final test is a simulation of a mail client-to-server session with the openssl s_client option. The OpenSSL client can connect to remote hosts with TLS/SSL, printing out plenty of diagnostic information in the process. If it succeeds, your TLS server configuration works, and you can now test with a mail client. If this test fails, you will get a wealth of useful debugging information for tracking down the error.

Here is an example of a successful session, where your CA path is /etc/postfix/certs:

```
# openssl s_client -starttls smtp -CApath /etc/postfix/certs/ -connect localhost:25
CONNECTED(00000003)
depth=1 /C=DE/ST=Bavaria/L=Munich/O=Postfix Book/OU=#Authoring/CN=mail.example.com/
emailAddress=postmaster@example.com
verify return:1
depth=0 /C=DE/ST=Bavaria/L=Munich/O=Postfix Book/OU=Mailserver/CN=mail.example.com/
emailAddress=postmaster@example.com
verify return:1
---
Certificate chain
 0 s:/C=DE/ST=Bavaria/L=Munich/O=Postfix Book/OU=Mailserver/CN=mail.example.com/
emailAddress=postmaster@example.com
   i:/C=DE/ST=Bavaria/L=Munich/O=Postfix Book/OU=#Authoring/CN=mail.example.com/
emailAddress=postmaster@example.com
 1 s:/C=DE/ST=Bavaria/L=Munich/O=Postfix Book/OU=#Authoring/CN=mail.example.com/
emailAddress=postmaster@example.com
   i:/C=DE/ST=Bavaria/L=Munich/O=Postfix Book/OU=#Authoring/CN=mail.example.com/
emailAddress=postmaster@example.com
---
Server certificate
-----BEGIN CERTIFICATE-----
MIID4DCCAOmgAwIBAgIBATANBgkqhkiG9w0BAQQFADCBnjELMAkGA1UEBhMCREUx
EDAOBgNVBAgTB0JhdmFyaWExDzANBgNVBAcTBk11bmljaDEVMBMGA1UEChMMUG9z
dGZpeCBCb29rMRMwEQYDVQQLFAojQXV0aG9yaW5nMRkwFwYDVQQDExBtYWlsLmV4
YW1wbGUuY29tMSUwIwYJKoZIhvcNAQkBFhZwb3N0bWFzdGVyQGV4YW1wbGUuY29t
MB4XDTAzMTAyMzIwMTky0VoXDTA0MTAyMjIwMTky0VowgZ4xCzAJBgNVBAYTAkRF
MRAwDgYDVQQIEwdCYXZhcmlhMQ8wDQYDVQQHEwZNdW5pY2gxFTATBgNVBAoTDFBv
```

```
c3RmaXggQm9vazETMBEGA1UECxMKTWFpbHNlcnZlcjEZMBcGA1UEAxMQbWFpbC5l
eGFtcGxlLmNvbTElMCMGCSqGSIb3DQEJARYWcG9zdG1hc3RlckBleGFtcGxlLmNv
bTCBnzANBgkqhkiG9w0BAQEFAAOBjQAwgYkCgYEA9wBRlv3EsemFDqoX5L/4DUCt
8oIpdlOXOpNMKqh/LnWuFXivCy52dMMbWtQgWaR+xRKaacyLeIdeyDx5LwzOgOd6
3zT+M2TAwGi6eQp+u8NpIuDF3eKYRBPoLGMuQiWkOcwNjagXg+U1Q9oVBseMgg/a
OVj8aNasi4qJ2N59sbcCAwEAAaOCASowggEmMAkGA1UdEwQCMAAwLAYJYIZIAYb4
QgENBB8WHU9wZW5TU0wwgR2VuZXJhdGVkIENlcnRpZmljYXRlMBOGA1UdDgQWBBQj
RXFGfepblNkc6G/57Et7xRI1eDCBywYDVR0jBIHDMIHAgBQJScWoXDhSbW76EWQI
GUMvoySuN6GBpKSBoTCBnjELMAkGA1UEBhMCREUxEDAOBgNVBAgTBOJhdmFyaWEx
DzANBgNVBAcTBk11bmljaDEVMBMGA1UEChMMUG9zdGZpeCBCb29rMRMwEQYDVQQL
FAojQXV0aG9yaW5nMRkwFwYDVQQDExBtYWlsLmV4YW1wbGUuY29tMSUwIwYJKoZI
hvcNAQkBFhZwb3N0bWFzdGVyQGV4YW1wbGUuY29tggEAMAOGCSqGSIb3DQEBBAUA
A4GBADUNOgZfc8ClIRir/9DboKup+MSijhlPi5bmMOj6OWNj6STiNrcjTaF8qH+6
LFxXbclJfWUHaEFvSLSeW79zh7KX67yOU46nVVYdF8+gHV/XnZK6f/6CpwcjOnQP
PI3GDtLoNXUlPqrngrJskWUuDcZwkQBlXinZlyMSs1gcSDSo
-----END CERTIFICATE-----
subject=/C=DE/ST=Bavaria/L=Munich/O=Postfix Book/OU=Mailserver/CN=mail.example.com/
emailAddress=postmaster@example.com
issuer=/C=DE/ST=Bavaria/L=Munich/O=Postfix Book/OU=#Authoring/CN=mail.example.com/
emailAddress=postmaster@example.com
---
No client certificate CA names sent
---
SSL handshake has read 2592 bytes and written 356 bytes
---
New, TLSv1/SSLv3, Cipher is DHE-RSA-AES256-SHA
Server public key is 1024 bit
SSL-Session:
    Protocol  : TLSv1
    Cipher    : DHE-RSA-AES256-SHA
    Session-ID: D341BF543EB5690DA873EFD0B0B4CB2EF210930812C14F3DBB85BD1AE92C6CB3
    Session-ID-ctx:
    Master-Key:
D4E3B4617214EDA8E1D2EAF54482FC65D1BD7BF5474F2FB2E2C0312BE098D8AF29ABC6603C4A89B7B413ED24D79375CD
    Key-Arg   : None
    Start Time: 1068108666
    Timeout   : 300 (sec)
    Verify return code: 0 (ok)
---
220 mail.example.com ESMTP Postfix (2.0.16-20030921)
QUIT
DONE
```

Server Performance Tuning

Cryptography puts a load on your processor. At the start of each TLS session, the client and server perform several private-key operations to sign the handshake messages—a computationally expensive process. A lot of simultaneous TLS sessions can seriously slow down a mail server.

By default, Postfix's smtpd memorizes the session key for its connections. However, Postfix also allows smtpd processes to terminate after a period of inactivity to save resources on the server and to load possible new configuration information. Unfortunately, this means that Postfix loses a session key after the smtpd terminates, so it must recalculate the key when a mail client returns to transmit another message.

To avoid the loss of session keys when an instance of smtpd dies, Postfix may maintain an out of process session key cache as described in the following section.

Configuring a TLS Session Key Cache

To head off the problem of computational load that TLS cryptography can create, you need to configure smtpd processes to store session keys in a database. After one smtpd stores the key, all smtpd processes have access to the key, regardless of whether they just started or have been running for a long time. A session-key cache significantly reduces CPU load.

To enable a session-key cache, set the smtpd_tls_session_cache_database parameter, and enable the tlsmgr daemon. The main.cf parameters look like this:

```
smtpd_tls_session_cache_database = sdbm:/etc/postfix/smtpd_scache
smtpd_tls_session_cache_timeout = 3600s
```

NOTE   *Session key caching requires concurrent write access to the key database. In Postfix, only the SDBM database type supports this. All TLS-enabled Postfix installations recognize this key type.*

By default, all session keys in the database expire after one hour (3,600 seconds). RFC 2246 recommends a maximum of timeout period of 24 hours. You can change the default behavior by setting a different value for smtpd_tls_session_cache_timeout, specified in seconds.

Maintaining the TLS Session-Key Cache with tlsmgr

Postfix needs to actively maintain its TLS session-key cache database. For security reasons, you must remove keys when they expire, and you also need to keep the database from growing without bounds. The tlsmgr daemon that is only present in TLS-capable Postfix installations performs these tasks. Here are the specifics on what tlsmgr does:

- Assists in creating random numbers on systems that do not have built-in random support

- Clears expired keys from the session cache database as defined by smtpd_tls_session_cache_timeout

- Rebuilds the database specified by smtpd_tls_session_cache_database from scratch when you restart Postfix

To run `tlsmgr`, you must verify that it is enabled in `master.cf`. On an installation built from source, you shouldn't need to change anything, but some distributions disable the daemon in their Postfix packages, so it never hurts to make sure that it is uncommented in your `master.cf`, as follows:

```
# ==========================================================================
# service type  private unpriv  chroot  wakeup  maxproc command + args
#               (yes)   (yes)   (yes)   (never) (100)
# ==========================================================================
...
tlsmgr    fifo  -       -       n       300     1       tlsmgr
...
```

CAUTION *Never put the TLS session cache database in the chroot jail. A compromised session cache database could be used to trick mail clients into believing that they are communicating with a safe mail server, allowing the clients to transmit sensitive information.*

You can run the `tlsmgr` daemon chrooted, because it opens the session-key database before it changes its root directory, and it is therefore able to read and write to the database while chrooted.

You must reload Postfix to start `tlsmgr` after making the appropriate changes in `master.cf`.

Server-Side Measures to Secure the SMTP AUTH Handshake

SMTP AUTH may offer plaintext security mechanisms, such as PLAIN and LOGIN. Certain mail clients, Microsoft Outlook and Outlook Express in particular, can use only those mechanisms at present. Although users are generally oblivious to security mechanisms, using plaintext for SMTP AUTH tends to make administrators nervous, because anyone capable of reading raw packets on the network can easily extract usernames and passwords.

You can protect against plaintext username and password submission by offering SMTP AUTH only in conjunction with TLS.

Offering SMTP AUTH with TLS Only

Postfix provides the `smtpd_tls_auth_only` parameter to offer SMTP AUTH only when an encrypted SMTP connection has been established. This parameter is not enabled by default; to turn it on, add this line to `main.cf` and reload your configuration:

```
smtpd_tls_auth_only = yes
```

Keep in mind that restricting SMTP AUTH to TLS sessions is a very strict approach to banning plaintext mechanisms from an unencrypted SMTP session, and it prohibits certain other (safer) mechanisms from regular SMTP communication.

To verify your TLS enforcement, ensure that the Postfix server does not offer SMTP AUTH for unencrypted sessions. Connect to your server on port 25, and start a handshake with `EHLO yourFQDN` as follows:

```
$ telnet mail.example.com 25
220 mail.example.com ESMTP Postfix
EHLO client.example.com
250-mail.example.com
250-PIPELINING
250-SIZE 10240000
250-VRFY
250-ETRN
250-STARTTLS
250 8BITMIME
QUIT
221 Bye
```

Notice that SMTP AUTH and its mechanisms do not appear in this SMTP session, so step one of this configuration works.

Testing with an Encrypted Transport Layer

Now you should check to see whether SMTP AUTH is offered in a TLS session. As you did when testing TLS earlier, run `openssl s_client` to connect to your server, and then issue `EHLO yourFQDN` as in the earlier telnet session. Although there is a lot more output this time, you should be able to pick out the SMTP AUTH information at the end:

```
# openssl s_client -starttls smtp -CApath /etc/postfix/certs/ -connect localhost:25
CONNECTED(00000003)
depth=1 /C=EX/ST=Examplia/L=Exampleton/O=Certification Authority Example Inc./
CN=mail.example.com/emailAddress=postmaster@example.com
verify return:1
depth=0 /C=EX/ST=Examplia/L=Exampleton/O=Example Inc./OU=MX Services/CN=mail.example.com/
emailAddress=postmaster@example.com
verify return:1
---
Certificate chain
 0 s:/C=EX/ST=Examplia/L=Exampleton/O=Example Inc./OU=MX Services/CN=mail.example.com/
emailAddress=postmaster@example.com
   i:/C=EX/ST=Examplia/L=Exampleton/O=Certification Authority Example Inc./CN=mail.example.com/
emailAddress=postmaster@example.com
 1 s:/C=EX/ST=Examplia/L=Exampleton/O=Certification Authority Example Inc./CN=mail.example.com/
emailAddress=postmaster@example.com
   i:/C=EX/ST=Examplia/L=Exampleton/O=Certification Authority Example Inc./CN=mail.example.com/
emailAddress=postmaster@example.com
---
Server certificate
```

```
-----BEGIN CERTIFICATE-----
MIID9jCCA1+gAwIBAgIBATANBgkqhkiG9w0BAQQFADCBpjELMAkGA1UEBhMCRVgx
ETAPBgNVBAgTCEV4YW1wbGlhMRMwEQYDVQQHEwpFeGFtcGxldG9uMSQwKwYDVQQK
EyRDZXJ0aWZpY2F0aW9uIEF1dGhvcml0eSBFeGFtcGxlIEluYy4xGTAXBgNVBAMT
EG1haWwuZXhhbXBsZS5jb20xJTAjBgkqhkiG9w0BCQEWFnBvc3RtYXN0ZXJAZXhh
bXBsZS5jb20wHhcNMDMxMTA5MjEyNTEzWhcNMDQxMTA4MjEyNTEzWjCBpDELMAkG
A1UEBhMCRVgxETAPBgNVBAgTCEV4YW1wbGlhMRMwEQYDVQQHEwpFeGFtcGxldG9u
MRUwEwYDVQQKEwxFeGFtcGxlIEluYy4xFDASBgNVBAsTC01YIFNlcnZpY2VzMRkw
FwYDVQQDExBtYWlsLmV4YW1wbGUuY29tMSUwIwYJKoZIhvcNAQkBFhZwb3N0bWFz
dGVyQGV4YW1wbGUuY29tMIGfMA0GCSqGSIb3DQEBAQUAA4GNADCBiQKBgQDL1OHc
H7lyo2bcDbafEeTvsSEGepsleBAmMsB1ohWLnjUcEmE5Rth9eF/TMYUABiWhnXOb
2HOKOalzuyjQqLtFHy4Bh6EcNeMdTtrEPZ2kYw+/ARkaGJrwzlNwfpzwuBhBr/qX
5FQstSG2cI4vMRkb2Vb9sq8aFneAMn+zH98v9QIDAQABo4IBMjCCAS4wCQYDVR0T
BAIwADAsBglghkgBhvhCAQ0EHxYdT3BlblNTCBHZW5lcmF0ZWQgQ2VydGlmaWNh
dGUwHQYDVR0OBBYEFJ42nZvtTjJzDoZVKv8bSfkcRxd1MIHTBgNVHSMEgcswgciA
FABSrbf6wu8BGp57D1fb3OSCWY0LoYGspIGpMIGmMQswCQYDVQQGEwJFWDERMA8G
A1UECBMIRXhhbXBsaWExEzARBgNVBAcTCkV4YW1wbGV0b24xLTArBgNVBAoTJEN1
cnRpZmljYXRpb24gQXV0aG9yaXR5IEV4YW1wbGUgSW5jLjEZMBcGA1UEAxMQbWFp
bC5leGFtcGxlLmNvbTElMCMGCSqGSIb3DQEJARYWcG9zdG1hc3RlckBleGFtcGxl
LmNvbYIBADANBgkqhkiG9w0BAQQFAAOBgQDOnDMeoWihd+TGQ+zJPF35RsZekYc2
OzayT4Ratkiv1GFKVRHVjr9iNgT3nywQonJzWVmqcm52LUBidtHhyY/VKLPhGCQM
VffjvUbVgBaygkV0XmVSrFq7w+A42ejqLCP/+Hi6o1RF9FfJoJPiyZ1LVStiIDYF
l2DRSfGKL4A+xw==
-----END CERTIFICATE-----
subject=/C=EX/ST=Examplia/L=Exampleton/O=Example Inc./OU=MX Services/CN=mail.example.com/
emailAddress=postmaster@example.com
issuer=/C=EX/ST=Examplia/L=Exampleton/O=Certification Authority Example Inc./
CN=mail.example.com/emailAddress=postmaster@example.com
---
Acceptable client certificate CA names
/C=EX/ST=Examplia/L=Exampleton/O=Certification Authority Example Inc./CN=mail.example.com/
emailAddress=postmaster@example.com
---
SSL handshake has read 2822 bytes and written 368 bytes
---
New, TLSv1/SSLv3, Cipher is DHE-RSA-AES256-SHA
Server public key is 1024 bit
SSL-Session:
    Protocol  : TLSv1
    Cipher    : DHE-RSA-AES256-SHA
    Session-ID: 01DFC00E443BBA8E4E9FE65C7F398702D7BB95367E62D9CBD12F217A97A9B8FC
    Session-ID-ctx:
    Master-Key:
E0F1C5F47787E3D9C9E236E38407555DE544C97BB9F81ACE3343C897DF8E50691AB432D03E2D79509F452DA7BB363CB8
    Key-Arg   : None
    Start Time: 1071223541
    Timeout   : 300 (sec)
    Verify return code: 0 (ok)
```

```
---
220 mail.example.com ESMTP Postfix
EHLO client.example.com
250-mail.example.com
250-PIPELINING
250-SIZE 10240000
250-VRFY
250-ETRN
250-AUTH NTLM LOGIN PLAIN OTP DIGEST-MD5 CRAM-MD5
250-AUTH=NTLM LOGIN PLAIN OTP DIGEST-MD5 CRAM-MD5
250-XVERP
250 8BITMIME
QUIT
DONE
```

With the preceding boldface-italic AUTH output, you can see that Postfix is indeed offering SMTP AUTH when encrypted. Now you can configure mail clients to use plaintext mechanisms in SMTP AUTH together with TLS.

Controlling SASL Mechanisms in TLS

A more sophisticated way to ban plaintext mechanisms in regular SMTP communication is to use the smtpd_sasl_tls_security_options parameter. As in the previous section, this parameter specifies that plaintext mechanisms must be protected in a TLS session, but also that non-plaintext mechanisms in unencrypted communication are permissible. A clever combination of the SASL smtpd_sasl_security_options parameter with the smtpd_sasl_tls_security_options parameter makes this possible:

```
smtpd_sasl_security_options = noanonymous, noplaintext
smtpd_sasl_tls_security_options = noanonymous
```

The first line says not to allow anonymous and plaintext authentication, but the second line overrides this, saying that plaintext is fine in a TLS session.

Testing SASL with TLS

As when barring all SMTP AUTH mechanisms, the first thing to test in the SASL configuration is to make sure Postfix does not offer the plaintext mechanisms in an unencrypted session. Connect to your server on port 25, issue EHLO yourFQDN, and observe the result:

```
$ telnet mail.example.com 25
220 mail.example.com ESMTP Postfix
EHLO client.example.com
250-mail.example.com
```

```
250-PIPELINING
250-SIZE 10240000
250-VRFY
250-ETRN
250-STARTTLS
250-AUTH NTLM OTP DIGEST-MD5 CRAM-MD5
250-AUTH=NTLM OTP DIGEST-MD5 CRAM-MD5
250 8BITMIME
QUIT
221 Bye
```

Notice that the SMTP AUTH lines are missing the plaintext LOGIN and PLAIN mechanisms, proving that the smtpd_sasl_security_options = noanonymous, noplaintext setting works.

Testing the Encrypted Transport Layer

After verifying that the smtpd_sasl_security_options setting works, check that your smtpd_sasl_tls_security_options = noanonymous setting functions as expected. Use openssl s_client to connect to your server, and issue EHLO yourFQDN as before. The result should look like this:

```
# openssl s_client -starttls smtp -CApath /etc/postfix/certs/ -connect localhost:25
CONNECTED(00000003)
depth=1 /C=EX/ST=Examplia/L=Exampleton/O=Certification Authority Example Inc./
CN=mail.example.com/emailAddress=postmaster@example.com
verify return:1
depth=0 /C=EX/ST=Examplia/L=Exampleton/O=Example Inc./OU=MX Services/CN=mail.example.com/
emailAddress=postmaster@example.com
verify return:1
---
Certificate chain
 0 s:/C=EX/ST=Examplia/L=Exampleton/O=Example Inc./OU=MX Services/CN=mail.example.com/
emailAddress=postmaster@example.com
   i:/C=EX/ST=Examplia/L=Exampleton/O=Certification Authority Example Inc./CN=mail.example.com/
emailAddress=postmaster@example.com
 1 s:/C=EX/ST=Examplia/L=Exampleton/O=Certification Authority Example Inc./CN=mail.example.com/
emailAddress=postmaster@example.com
   i:/C=EX/ST=Examplia/L=Exampleton/O=Certification Authority Example Inc./CN=mail.example.com/
emailAddress=postmaster@example.com
---
Server certificate
-----BEGIN CERTIFICATE-----
MIID9jCCA1+gAwIBAgIBATANBgkqhkiG9w0BAQQFADCBpjELMAkGA1UEBhMCRVgx
ETAPBgNVBAgTCEV4YW1wbGlhMRMwEQYDVQQHEwpFeGFtcGxldG9uMS0wKwYDVQQK
EyRDZXJ0aWZpY2F0aW9uIEF1dGhvcml0eSBFeGFtcGxlIEluYy4xGTAXBgNVBAMT
EG1haWwuZXhhbXBsZS5jb20xJTAjBgkqhkiG9w0BCQEWFnBvc3RtYXN0ZXJAZXhh
bXBsZS5jb20wHhcNMDMxMTA5MjEyNTEzWhcNMDQxMTA4MjEyNTEzWjCBpDELMAkG
A1UEBhMCRVgxETAPBgNVBAgTCEV4YW1wbGlhMRMwEQYDVQQHEwpFeGFtcGxldG9u
```

MRUwEwYDVQQKEwxFeGFtcGxlIEluYy4xFDASBgNVBAsTC01YIFNlcnZpY2VzMRkw
FwYDVQQDExBtYWlsLmV4YW1wbGUuY29tMSUwIwYJKoZIhvcNAQkBFhZwb3N0bWFz
dGVyQGV4YW1wbGUuY29tMIGfMA0GCSqGSIb3DQEBAQUAA4GNADCBiQKBgQDL1OHc
H7lyo2bcDbafEeTvsSEGepsleBAmMsB1ohWLnjUcEmE5Rth9eF/TMYUABiWhnXOb
2H0KOalzuyjQqLtFHy4Bh6EcNeMdTtrEPZ2kYw+/ARkaGJrwzlNwfpzwuBhBr/qX
5FQstSG2cI4vMRkb2Vb9sq8aFneAMn+zH98v9QIDAQABo4IBMjCCAS4wCQYDVR0T
BAIwADAsBglghkgBhvhCAQ0EHxYdT3BlblNTTCBHZW5lcmF0ZWQgQ2VydGlmaWNh
dGUwHQYDVR00BBYEFJ42nZvtTjJzDoZVKv8bSfkcRxd1MIHTBgNVHSMEgcswgciA
FABSrbf6wu8BGp57D1fb3OSCWYOLoYGspIGpMIGmMQswCQYDVQQGEwJFWDERMA8G
A1UECBMIRXhhbXBsaWExEzARBgNVBAcTCkV4YW1wbGV0b24xLTArBgNVBAoTJENl
cnRpZmljYXRpb24gQXV0aG9yaXR5IEV4YW1wbGUgSW5jLjEZMBcGA1UEAxMQbWFp
bC5leGFtcGxlLmNvbTElMCMGCSqGSIb3DQEJARYWcG9zdG1hc3RlckBleGFtcGxl
LmNvbYIBADANBgkqhkiG9w0BAQQFAAOBgQDOnDMeoWihd+TGQ+zJPF35RsZekYc2
OzayT4Ratkiv1GFKVRHVjr9iNgT3nywQonJzWVmqcm52LUBidtHhyY/VKLPhGCQM
VffjvUbVgBaygkVOXmVSrFq7w+A42ejqLCP/+Hi6o1RF9FfJoJPiyZ1LVStiIDYF
l2DRSfGKL4A+xw==
-----END CERTIFICATE-----
subject=/C=EX/ST=Examplia/L=Exampleton/O=Example Inc./OU=MX Services/CN=mail.example.com/
emailAddress=postmaster@example.com
issuer=/C=EX/ST=Examplia/L=Exampleton/O=Certification Authority Example Inc./
CN=mail.example.com/emailAddress=postmaster@example.com

Acceptable client certificate CA names
/C=EX/ST=Examplia/L=Exampleton/O=Certification Authority Example Inc./CN=mail.example.com/
emailAddress=postmaster@example.com

SSL handshake has read 2822 bytes and written 368 bytes

New, TLSv1/SSLv3, Cipher is DHE-RSA-AES256-SHA
Server public key is 1024 bit
SSL-Session:
    Protocol : TLSv1
    Cipher   : DHE-RSA-AES256-SHA
    Session-ID: 01DFC00E443BBA8E4E9FE65C7F398702D7BB95367E62D9CBD12F217A97A9B8FC
    Session-ID-ctx:
    Master-Key:
E0F1C5F47787E3D9C9E236E38407555DE544C97BB9F81ACE3343C897DF8E50691AB432D03E2D79509F452DA7BB363CB8
    Key-Arg   : None
    Start Time: 1071223541
    Timeout   : 300 (sec)
    Verify return code: 0 (ok)
---
220 mail.example.com ESMTP Postfix
EHLO client.example.com
250-mail.example.com
250-PIPELINING
250-SIZE 10240000
250-VRFY
250-ETRN

```
250-AUTH NTLM LOGIN PLAIN OTP DIGEST-MD5 CRAM-MD5
250-AUTH=NTLM LOGIN PLAIN OTP DIGEST-MD5 CRAM-MD5
250-XVERP
250 8BITMIME
QUIT
DONE
```

You can see that in a TLS session, Postfix offers the plaintext LOGIN and PLAIN mechanisms, proving that the `smtpd_sasl_tls_security_options = noanonymous` setting works. You can now proceed to configure mail clients to use plaintext mechanisms in SMTP AUTH together with TLS.

Server-Side Certificate-Based Relaying

Postfix's ability to permit relaying based on client certificates (see Figure 18-2) is an alternative to SMTP AUTH-based relaying. This is useful in a network where you cannot (or do not want to) use SMTP AUTH, or when you want to simplify the process of relaying and encrypting the transport layer by combining both processes into a single step.

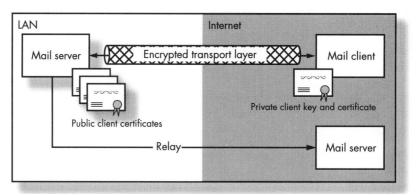

Figure 18-2: TLS for certificate-based relaying

The only drawback to this method is that the only known mail GUI that supports this kind of functionality is the Netscape/Mozilla mail client. In spite of this limitation, however, this approach is useful in a large network that has Postfix installations at several different locations, and when these locations have only dial-up access to the Internet and are limited to dynamic IP addresses. In this situation, it makes sense to have the dial-up Postfix servers relay their outgoing messages to a Postfix server that has a static IP address, using certificate-based relaying to make sure that the messages come from one of the dial-up servers and not some random third party. This approach also simplifies server setup, makes Postfix more secure by excluding SMTP AUTH, and protects the transport of in-house messages.

NOTE *As time goes on, fewer mail servers are accepting mail from dial-up and DSL lines, because lots of spam originates from those systems' IP addresses. Special DNS-based Blackhole Lists (DNSBLs) called Dial-Up User Lists (DULs) now ban complete subnets known to be used by dial-up machines.*

You need to perform the following steps for the server configuration:

1. Configure Postfix to ask for client certificates.
2. Configure Postfix to permit relaying for client certificates.

NOTE *Certificate-based relaying requires you to configure both server and client-side TLS. This section explains the server-side configuration; you'll see the client-side configuration later in this chapter.*

Configuring Postfix to Ask for Client Certificates

The first step in enabling certificate-based relaying is to instruct Postfix to ask explicitly for client certificates. This is necessary because mail clients usually do not automatically offer their certificates. The `smtpd_tls_ask_ccert` parameter takes care of this (it's not enabled by default):

```
smtpd_tls_ask_ccert = yes
```

This parameter is also useful for debugging, and you can always leave it on because the information added to the header of each message sent over TLS does not create any security risks.

NOTE *If no certificate is available, Netscape's mail client either complains or offers a number of client certificates from which to choose. This behavior is annoying, so this option is off by default. However, your SMTP server needs the certificate if you want to use certificate-based relaying.*

Configuring Postfix to Permit Relaying for Client Certificates

The Postfix TLS patch includes two additional restrictions that can control relaying with the `smtpd_recipient_restrictions` parameter. How you set up the restriction depends on your CA's certificate:

Client certificate–based relaying
You can build a map of client certificates that may relay mail through Postfix. This is the safe approach if your client certificates stem from more than one (official) CA.

Certification authority–based relaying
You can choose to permit relaying for all mail clients with certificates signed by your own CA, if you run your own CA and have full control over the certificates.

These two options are described in the following two sections.

Client Certificate—Based Relaying

If your setup requires that mail clients relay using certificates signed by one or more official CAs, you need to go through these steps:

1. Create a list of client certificate fingerprints.
2. Convert the list to a database.
3. Permit those clients to relay.

The first thing you need to do is collect the public certificates from the mail clients that are allowed to relay. For each certificate, you need to extract the MD5 fingerprint.

NOTE *If you don't want to do this manually, download and run **add_ccerts_to_relay_clientcerts.sh**. This script calculates the MD5 fingerprint, copies it to /etc/postfix/ relay_clientcerts, and builds an appropriate map from the contents of this file.*

Let's say that you have a client certificate named client_public_cert.pem. You can extract the MD5 fingerprint with this command:

```
# openssl x509 -noout -fingerprint -in client_public_cert.pem
```

The output should look something like this:

```
MD5 Fingerprint=00:8B:02:30:9D:18:F4:81:5D:2F:48:E4:5B:17:82:A7
```

The fingerprint is the string of hexadecimal numbers and colons. Add the fingerprint, along with the client hostname, to the /etc/postfix/ relay_clientcerts file, like this:

```
00:8B:02:30:9D:18:F4:81:5D:2F:48:E4:5B:17:82:A7 client_1.example.com
18:F4:81:5D:2F:82:A7:48:E4:5B:17:00:8B:02:30:9D client_2.example.org
...
```

Although Postfix's TLS implementation only requires the fingerprint, /etc/postfix/relay_clientcerts is a typical Postfix map, so you need two items per line. You can choose any string you want as the right-hand side; in this example it's the client's fully qualified domain name. Using the FQDN makes it easier to find and identify the fingerprint in the map.

TIP *You could also add the expiry date of the client certificate to the right side to speed up or automate the process of finding expired certificates.*

After adding the fingerprint, convert the relay_clientcerts file to a Postfix map with postmap:

```
# postmap hash:/etc/postfix/relay_clientcerts
```

This command creates /etc/postfix/relay_clientcerts.db, and you're finished with the list creation.

Now you need to add a parameter to `main.cf` that tells Postfix where to find the client map:

```
relay_clientcerts = hash:/etc/postfix/relay_clientcerts
```

Finally, expand the relay permissions by adding the `permit_tls_clientcerts` parameter to `smtpd_recipient_restrictions`:

```
smtpd_recipient_restrictions =
  ...
  permit_tls_clientcerts
  ...
```

Remember that the order of items in `smtpd_recipient_restrictions` is important. Make sure `permit_tls_clientcerts` appears early in your restrictions.

That's all you need to do to configure this version of certificate-based relaying. Reload Postfix to make the changes take effect.

Certification Authority–Based Relaying

If you want to relay only on the basis of a valid certificate, you must have full control over the client certificates. You must run your own certification authority (CA) and sign client certificates by yourself, and furthermore, your CA needs to be the only one that Postfix knows about. This is absolutely necessary, because with this feature, the *only* criterion that Postfix uses is successful certificate validation.

CAUTION   *If you use an official CA certificate or even a list of official CA certificates, any client on the Internet could get a certificate signed by one of those certification authorities, and would therefore be allowed to relay—your server would become an open relay.*

The relaying methods discussed earlier require you to build and maintain a list of client certificates that may relay; the advantage here is that you need just one CA certificate to make a decision.

To make Postfix relay for clients with certificates signed by your private CA, first reduce the list of CAs down to one, your own public CA certificate. As discussed earlier, the `smtpd_tls_CAfile` parameter controls the CA file, so your parameter line would look something like this in `main.cf`:

```
smtpd_tls_CAfile = /usr/share/ssl/certs/cacert.pem
```

After you're sure that Postfix recognizes only your own certificate, add the `permit_tls_all_clientcerts` parameter to `smtpd_recipient_restrictions`:

```
smtpd_recipient_restrictions =
  ...
  permit_tls_all_clientcerts
  ...
```

Finally, reload Postfix to make the changes effective.

Tightening the TLS Server

So far, you've seen how to configure Postfix to offer and process Transport Layer Security. This section shows how to enforce and reject TLS when the client does not submit a certificate.

CAUTION   *Be careful when using the following features, because they can break your mail system if used in an improper environment.*

Enforcing TLS

You can force all clients to use TLS. This feature is handy in a private network where you need to be sure that all message traffic is encrypted (for example, in a large company with distributed locations). To do so, set the smtpd_enforce_tls parameter in your main.cf file to yes (the default is no), and reload Postfix:

```
smtpd_enforce_tls = yes
```

CAUTION   *RFC 2487 states, "A publicly-referenced SMTP server MUST NOT require use of the STARTTLS extension in order to deliver mail locally. This rule prevents the STARTTLS extension from damaging the interoperability of the Internet's SMTP infrastructure."*

    Requiring TLS for every client on a public mail server is a bad idea in general, because it locks out clients that cannot use TLS or are not configured to do so. If you require TLS on a public mail server, expect that a large proportion of email will not be delivered to your network.

Requiring a Client Certificate

You can take TLS enforcement one step further and allow only clients that submit certificates. With this option, if a client does not send a certificate, Postfix refuses to go through with TLS. To make it work, add the smtpd_tls_req_ccert parameter to main.cf as follows, and reload Postfix:

```
smtpd_tls_req_ccert = yes
```

NOTE   *This setting does not keep a client from using unencrypted SMTP communication unless you enforce TLS with the smtpd_enforce_tls parameter described earlier. Use both parameters for a very strict policy.*

Client-Side TLS

Client-side TLS is used when Postfix is acting as a mail client that connects to mail servers that support TLS (see Figure 18-3). Depending on the configuration, Postfix can make (selective) use of TLS by sending SMTP AUTH credentials with plaintext mechanisms in TLS to acquire relay permission, or by presenting its own client certificate to be allowed relay access.

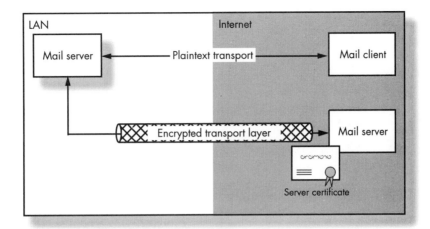

Figure 18-3: TLS for the Postfix mail client

Basic Client Configuration

You need to set three parameters in main.cf to enable basic TLS support for the Postfix mail client. You can also tweak an additional parameter to aid in debugging TLS sessions. These are the steps you need to go through:

1. Enable client-side TLS.
2. Configure Postfix to verify the server certificate.
3. Connect Postfix to a random source generator.
4. Log client-side TLS activity.

Enabling Client-Side TLS

All TLS-capable Postfix installations have client-side TLS, but they do not enable it by default. Postfix doesn't make use of STARTTLS with any server (even if the server enforces TLS) until you add the following parameter setting to main.cf on the client:

```
smtp_use_tls = yes
```

With this parameter in place, the Postfix smtp daemon initiates STARTTLS in the SMTP dialog if the mail server on the other side of a connection offers STARTTLS. However, enabling client-side TLS isn't enough to make the whole process work. The Postfix client doesn't yet know where to find CA certificates that it will need to verify the server certificate.

Verifying the Server Certificate

When the Postfix SMTP client starts TLS with a mail server, it attempts to validate the certificate that the server presents in the session. Postfix checks the cryptographic signature that a CA adds to the server's certificate by using the public key of the CA certificate. Therefore, your Postfix installation must have a repository of CA certificates where it can look for cryptographic signatures and compare them.

NOTE *As mentioned in Chapter 17, OpenSSL does not have a central root store for CA certificates. Therefore, you need to create a new root store. The configuration described shortly uses `ca-bundle.crt`, which is explained in the section "Configuring the Postfix Certificate Root Store." You may also want to create your own root store file, also in this section.*

Like the Postfix server, the client can use two different CA certificate storage types: a file with all CA certificates in a single file, or a directory containing many files, each containing a CA certificate.

For a chrooted mail client, you should keep all CA certificates in a single file, because Postfix reads the files at startup before running the chroot operation.

If you don't use chroot, you may as well keep the CA certificates in a directory, because it's easier to maintain. This is especially handy if you add CA certificates regularly, because you don't need to restart Postfix whenever you add a new CA certificate. However, don't use the directory approach for chrooted setups, because you will need to keep the certificates in the chroot jail, defeating the purpose chroot in the first place (keeping sensitive information away from the jail).

NOTE *As with the TLS server configuration, you can use both approaches at once. Set both of the parameters in the following sections, and separate some CA certificates from others. When Postfix searches for a CA certificate, it reads the file first, then turns to the directory if it can't find the certificate in the file.*

Concatenating All CA Certificates into a Single File

The simplest approach (and probably also the one that gets the most mileage) is to store all CA certificates in one file. As mentioned earlier, if you happen to run Apache with mod_ssl, you already have such a file, called ca-bundle.crt. Find it by executing `locate ca-bundle.crt` on the command line:

```
$ locate ca-bundle.crt
/usr/share/ssl/certs/ca-bundle.crt
```

Now tell the Postfix client to use this file by setting the `smtp_tls_CAfile` parameter to the `ca-bundle.crt` path in `main.cf`, and then reload Postfix:

```
smtp_tls_CAfile = /usr/share/ssl/certs/ca-bundle.crt
```

NOTE *If you run your own certification authority, add your CA certificate to this root store with a command like this:*

```
# cat /usr/local/ssl/misc/demoCA/cacert.pem >> /usr/share/ssl/certs/ca-
  bundle.crt
```

If your CA certificate is a link in a chain of certificates, add all of the CA certificates from your CA certificate up to the root CA certificate in the certificate chain.

Storing All CA Certificates in a Directory

For a directory-based approach to CA certificate access, set the smtp_tls_CApath parameter to a directory containing certificate files. The first thing you probably need to do with a new Postfix installation is create a directory for the certificate files:

```
# mkdir /etc/postfix/certs
```

Now put all of the CA certificates that you need for your setup into this directory, and build an index table for fast certificate lookup. Create the index with c_rehash, a program that comes with OpenSSL. Running this command builds the index and makes symbolic links to the CA certificates:

```
# c_rehash /etc/postfix/certs/
Doing /etc/postfix/certs/
cacert.pem => e0dc2d06.0
WARNING: postfix_private_key.pem does not contain a certificate or CRL: skipping
postfix_public_cert.pem => 6df723a3.0
```

NOTE *Don't forget to run c_rehash each time you add a new CA certificate.*

Once you've performed these steps, tell Postfix to use this directory as its CA root store, and then reload your configuration:

```
smtp_tls_CApath = /etc/postfix/certs
```

Connecting the Postfix Client to a Random Source Generator

To properly initialize the encryption, you need to connect Postfix to a random number source. See the discussion of the tls_random_source parameter in the earlier "Connecting Postfix to a Random Source Generator" section. The process is the same for the client and the server.

Logging Client-Side TLS Activity

Before you fire up Postfix to test your TLS client, increase the smtp_tls_ loglevel parameter setting to 2 so that you can see significant TLS events (the default is 0):

```
smtp_tls_loglevel = 2
```

See the discussion of the smtpd_tls_loglevel parameter in the earlier section "Increasing the TLS Log Level" for the meanings of the various log levels.

Testing Basic Client Functionality

To test basic client-side TLS, you need to perform only two steps:

1. Check the log file to see if the Postfix client detected any errors.
2. Send mail to a TLS-enabled server.

Checking the Log File for Errors

Run an **egrep** command to pick out TLS problems in the Postfix log file:

```
$ egrep '(reject|error|warning|fatal|panic):' /var/log/maillog
```

If there are any TLS-related glitches that Postfix can detect, this command should catch them. There shouldn't be any errors pointing to TLS-related issues, but if there are problems, check over your configuration to see if you mistyped something, and make sure that Postfix has read permission for the certificates.

Sending Mail to a TLS Server

Now try sending a message to a TLS-enabled mail server to see if the Postfix client uses TLS.

If you don't know of any TLS servers, Lutz Jänicke, developer of the TLS patch, has a public mail server that you can use for testing. Send a message to postfix_tls-bounce@serv01.aet.tu-cottbus.de, and the server should send the mail back to you, including headers added to your original message that indicate whether the message was transmitted over TLS. The header should look something like this:

```
Received: from mail.state-of-mind.de (mail.state-of-mind.de [212.14.92.89])
        (using TLSv1 with cipher EDH-RSA-DES-CBC3-SHA (168/168 bits))
        (Client did not present a certificate)
        by serv01.aet.tu-cottbus.de (Postfix) with ESMTP id 74C6B2330
        for <postfix_tls-bounce@serv01.aet.tu-cottbus.de>; Wed, 10 Dec 2003
   23:50:45 +0100 (MET)
```

Selective TLS Use

With selective TLS client configuration, you can enforce a security policy with certain servers but also keep messages from going into a black hole if a mail server that offers STARTTLS is somehow misconfigured.

NOTE *This happens quite often with Lotus Notes servers.*

You'll perform three steps:

1. Enable selective TLS in your Postfix configuration.
2. Build a policy map that tells the smtp client when to use TLS.
3. Configure Postfix to note when servers offer TLS.

Enabling Selective TLS

Turn on selective client-side TLS in `main.cf` by setting the `smtp_tls_per_site` parameter to a policy map. In this example, the map is `/etc/postfix/tls_per_site`:

```
smtp_tls_per_site = hash:/etc/postfix/tls_per_site
```

Building the TLS Policy Map

The TLS policy map has the same style as any other Postfix map; each line represents an entry with a key-value pair. Put the host or domain on the left side (the key) and the TLS policy on the right side (the value). The possible policies for the Postfix SMTP client are as follows:

NONE

> Disables client-side TLS.

MAY

> Allows the client to try TLS if the remote server offers STARTTLS, but it doesn't have to if it doesn't want to.

MUST

> Forces the Postfix client to use TLS when this server offers TLS with STARTTLS. Furthermore, Postfix checks the server certificate's CommonName parameter against the server's fully qualified domain name.

MUST_NOPEERMATCH

> A lesser version of the MUST policy. The Postfix client responds to START-TLS and verifies the server's certificate, but it ignores any differences between CommonName and the FQDN.

If you configure Postfix to use a TLS policy map, the settings in the map will always override your main.cf *settings. If you turned off TLS, it will use TLS for those hosts found in the map. Vice versa, if you turned TLS on in* main.cf *and the host cannot be found in the policy map, it will still use TLS.*

Start the map with a file named /etc/postfix/tls_per_site that looks something like this:

```
dom.ain               NONE
host.dom.ain          MAY
important.host        MUST
some.host.dom.ain     MUST_NOPEERMATCH
```

After writing this ASCII map, build the hash map with the postmap command to make it available to Postfix:

```
# postmap hash:/etc/postfix/tls_per_site
```

Identifying TLS Servers

Finding the servers that offer TLS is useful not only when debugging a TLS session, but also when you configure the selective TLS feature in Postfix. Set the smtp_tls_note_starttls_offer parameter to yes in your main.cf file:

```
smtp_tls_note_starttls_offer = yes
```

Now, as soon as your Postfix client connects to a mail server that offers STARTTLS, the client logs the server name to the mail log as follows:

```
client postfix/smtp[1504]: Host offered STARTTLS: [mail.example.com]
```

With this final configuration setting, your TLS client is ready to go.

Client Performance Tuning

The same performance considerations described for the Postfix TLS server in the section "Server Performance Tuning" apply to the TLS client. The client uses the same tlsmgr daemon described in that section to cache session keys for the client. However, because this is the client, the configuration parameter names are slightly different; change the smtpd to smtp.

Therefore, to enable caching, go through all of the steps described in "Server Performance Tuning," but use smtp_tls_session_cache_database and smtp_tls_session_cache_timeout in your main.cf instead:

```
smtp_tls_session_cache_database = sdbm:/etc/postfix/smtp_scache
smtp_tls_session_cache_timeout = 3600s
```

Securing Client SMTP AUTH

In the section "Server-Side Measures to Secure the SMTP AUTH Handshake," you saw how to secure SMTP AUTH communication on the server side with TLS. This section shows you how to do it on the client side. Just to recap, you do not want your client to send your username and password with the SMTP AUTH plaintext mechanisms over an unencrypted connection. If you have to use the plaintext mechanisms, the client should start a TLS session first.

With a combination of the `smtp_sasl_security_options` parameter for unencrypted connections and `smtp_sasl_tls_security_options` for TLS sessions, you can lock down SMTP AUTH:

```
smtp_sasl_security_options = noanonymous, noplaintext
smtp_sasl_tls_security_options = noanonymous
```

The first rule forbids anonymous and plaintext authentication mechanisms over an unencrypted transport layer, and the second allows plaintext mechanisms when talking to the server with TLS.

Client-Side Certificate-Based Relaying

Certificate-based relaying is a secure way of allowing servers to relay messages for clients, even if the clients aren't on a network that the server knows about. You saw the server configuration in the section "Server-Side Certificate-Based Relaying." However, the client configuration isn't like the server's relaying features; it's more like setting up the server itself, because you have to provide paths to the certificate that the client presents to the kernel and to the key that the client will use for initiating the connection.

Configuring Paths to the Postfix Client Certificate and Key

To make the Postfix client present a certificate to the server when a TLS session starts, you need to set the `smtp_tls_cert_file` parameter to the client certificate and the `smtp_tls_key_file` parameter to the client key in `main.cf`. Here's an example:

```
smtp_tls_cert_file = /etc/postfix/certs/postfix_public_cert.pem
smtp_tls_key_file = /etc/postfix/certs/postfix_private_key.pem
```

NOTE *If you also configured server-side TLS in your Postfix installation, reuse the server's certificate and key unless you want your Postfix server and client to have different "digital identities."*

Now, reload your Postfix configuration and start testing.

Testing Client-Side Certificate-Based Relaying

Testing involves three steps:

1. Check the log file for obvious errors.
2. Verify that the client sends its certificate.
3. Verify that the client can relay based on its certificate.

Checking the Log File

Checking the log files is a matter of running the egrep command that you've seen earlier in this chapter:

```
$ egrep '(reject|error|warning|fatal|panic):' /var/log/maillog
```

If you get any errors, the usual advice applies: check your configuration files for typos, and make sure the client has read permission for the certificates.

Verifying that the Client Certificate Is Sent

To get proof that the client sends its certificate, you have to send a mail to a TLS-enabled server and see whether it accepts the client certificate. If you send a client certificate to a Postfix mail server that has smtpd_tls_received_header = yes set, text like the following appears in your headers:

```
Received: from client.example.com (client.example.com [172.16.0.3])
    (using TLSv1 with cipher EDH-RSA-DES-CBC3-SHA (168/168 bits))
    (Client CN "client.example.com", Issuer "mail.example.com" (verified OK))
    by mail.example.com (Postfix) with ESMTP id 63AC77247
    for <tls-bounce@mail.example.com>; Thu, 11 Dec 2003 19:48:38 +0100 (CET)
```

The third line states that the mail client Client sent a certificate to the mail server. The certificate was signed by the mail.example.com CA, and the server was able to verify this.

NOTE *If things don't work as expected, and you don't know if it is the client or server that is causing problems, send a message to postfix_tls-bounce@serv01.aet.tu-cottbus.de. As described earlier, this service bounces the message back to you with TLS debugging enabled.*

Verifying that the Client Can Relay with Its Certificate

Now test your client's certificate-based relaying capabilities by sending a message through a TLS server. Make sure that the server relays messages based on your certificate with the following criteria.

1. Make sure your client is not part of the server's network, or any network that the server grants relay access to by other criteria, such as mynetworks.
2. Make sure your client does not use any features such as SMTP AUTH.
3. Make sure the recipient is not in the relayhosts list of final destinations.

Tightening Client-Side TLS

You can force the client to use TLS, or to take an even stricter stance, communicating with the server only if the client can verify the server's peer name. Enforcing TLS communication on the client side is useful only when you can control the servers with which the client communicates.

CAUTION   *Misconfiguring these features can break your outgoing mail system.*

The following prerequisites must hold in order to force TLS communication:

1. The server must offer TLS.
2. The values for CommonName in the certificate must match the server's fully qualified domain name.
3. The client must be able to verify the server's certificate with the CA's signature.

If even one of these conditions is not met, the client will not send the message to the server. Instead, the client holds the message in its queue and sends a 4xx error notice to the mail log.

NOTE   *Enforcing the SMTP client to use TLS is useful in private networks and when you know that your client relays all messages over one server.*

To force client-side TLS, set the smtp_enforce_tls parameter in your main.cf as follows:

```
smtp_enforce_tls = yes
```

If this mode is too strict for everyday use, you can allow transmission if the CommonName in the server's certificate does not match its fully qualified domain name. Do this by setting the smtp_tls_enforce_peername to no (this option is normally enabled when you set smtp_enforce_tls):

```
smtp_tls_enforce_peername = no
```

CAUTION   *This option presents the danger of a man-in-the-middle attack.*

19

A COMPANY MAIL SERVER

This chapter shows you how to build a complete mail system based on Postfix, Cyrus SASL, Courier maildrop, and Courier IMAP. These components will get configuration and authentication data from an OpenLDAP server that provides directory services.

We will go from a basic setup to an advanced setup. The basic setup will connect all applications to the central LDAP server. Once we got this going, we will make the system more complex. The advanced setup will add transport layer security wherever possible and will show you how to offer SMTP authentication based on LDAP queries.

You should have a profound understanding of LDAP schemas and OpenLDAP before you start to implement the company mail server we describe in this chapter. If you haven't dealt with OpenLDAP before, the *OpenLDAP Administrator's Guide,* http://www.openldap.org/doc/admin22, is a good starting point for reading.

Conceptual Overview

Figure 19-1 gives you an overview of the applications you will need to deal with in this chapter and how they will be linked to each other. You can see OpenLDAP is in the center of all the services. The application servers work as follows:

- Postfix hands authentication data to the LDAP server when mail clients seek to relay using SMTP AUTH. In addition, Postfix queries the LDAP server for local user and alias information when incoming mail arrives. Upon accepting a message, Postfix hands it to Courier maildrop.

- Courier maildrop is responsible for local delivery. It asks the LDAP server for the mailbox location, and it also looks for filter rules (for example, for placing messages marked as spam into a subfolder named .spam).

- The user connects to the Courier IMAP server to retrieve mail. This server queries the LDAP server for the user's credentials. LDAP also tells Courier where to find the mailbox and which UID and GID to use when accessing it.

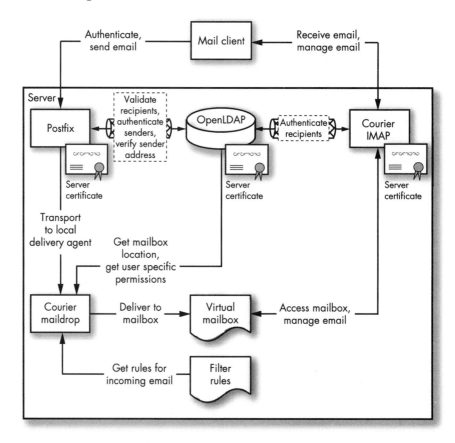

Figure 19-1: Architecture of a company mail server

The LDAP Directory Structure

The first thing you need to do to build the mail system is design your LDAP directory tree. This can be a difficult task; one reason why LDAP isn't more widespread is that it is daunting to design a directory from scratch. There are three key things to consider when you draw up the structure, schemata use, and attributes:

- The purpose of the directory
- Your organizational structure
- The requirements of the servers that use the LDAP directory

The primary purpose of the directory in this chapter is to show you how Postfix and other servers query an LDAP server. We will keep the structure as simple as possible so that you can focus on application configuration instead of getting lost in a directory quagmire.

We'll build the mail system in this chapter for an organization named Example Inc. This company got its start selling rocks and has grown large enough to have various departments. Among these are an IT department (run by a somewhat childish administrator named Bamm Bamm), a sales department, and a purchasing department. To keep it simple, we'll use just these three departments.

The directory service will provide Postfix, Cyrus SASL, Courier maildrop, and Courier IMAP with user and configuration data. This example will be based on the `authldap.schema` that comes with Courier IMAP because the other servers can use it without a problem.

NOTE *If you don't want to build your own directory, you can download an LDIF (LDAP Data Interchange Format) dump of Example Inc. from the* Book of Postfix *website at* `http://www.postfix-book.com`.

Figure 19-2 shows the directory tree, which starts at the node named `dc=example,dc=com` and spreads into two large branches.

The branch to the left contains authentication accounts for servers; we'll look at those later in the "Advanced Configuration" section when securing the LDAP data and connection.

The branch on the right is called `ou=people,dc=example,dc=com`. It has subnodes, such as `ou=it,ou=people,dc=example,dc=com`, that represent the organizational structure. As you go further down, you'll encounter more subnodes that hold user objects filled with attributes and values that hold all the information required to provide all user-related data for a complete mail system.

NOTE *You can do a lot more with a directory service. For example, you can add Postfix server configuration values for* mydestination, relayhost, virtual_domain, *and so on.*

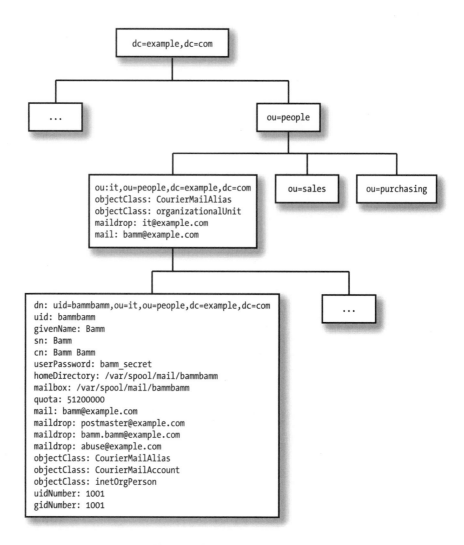

Figure 19-2: Organizational branch of Example Inc.

Choosing Attributes in a Postfix Schema

If you are an LDAP novice and were hoping for an easy solution, we have some bad news. There is no Postfix LDAP schema to drop in, fill with data, and let roll. You may be even more discouraged to hear that this is intentional, but there's a good reason for this. Nearly everything that Postfix needs for this solution comes in other schemata, such as the core.schema in OpenLDAP, or with applications like Courier IMAP, which comes with its own authldap.schema.

To choose the right schemata and attributes for your servers, you need to examine the requirements of the servers. For example, if Postfix uses LDAP for maps, you can set up the following entities.

Destinations, networks, and hosts

Destinations, networks, and hosts are represented by hostnames and IP addresses. Postfix looks these up to determine which domains it should accept mail and allow relay access for, and it may also use them when it applies host and network restrictions.

Your directory must contain attributes that describe hosts and networks and that perhaps allow for multivalue addition in a single LDAP object. You'll find appropriate attributes in network-related schemata, such as the CORE or NIS schema examples.

Recipients and senders

When Postfix looks up recipients and senders, it looks for *username@hostname* by default. There are many available schemata containing attributes like this. For example, you could look at core.schema and other mail-related schemata like the ones for Sendmail or qmail. However, don't forget the delivery side of the mail system. Many POP and IMAP servers come with their own schemata, all with attributes for defining sender and recipient addresses.

Aliases

A user may have more than one alias. The attribute you choose must allow for multiple addition to an object. Most mail-related schemata have an alias attribute. The schema that you plan to use for sender and recipient addresses is probably appropriate.

Lists

Lists consist of a single alias entry and multiple recipient addresses. If you have a schema with both attributes, you have everything that you need for a list.

Before you undertake to write your own Postfix schema you should rather adapt the schemata for other servers to Postfix. This approach lessens the load and complexity of your LDAP service, and it gives you more flexibility when expanding your directory or the servers that use it.

As mentioned before, this chapter's example is based primarily on the authldap.schema that comes with Courier IMAP because it has almost everything necessary for a complete directory.

Branch Design

We will split the directory in two major branches (see Figure 19-2). The left branch will contain application accounts, which we will use later in the "Advanced Configuration" section to implement access control for applications querying the directory.

The right branch will contain user-related information. It will be split into smaller subunits according to the department structure. We will use the organizationalUnit object to create the subunits, and later we will configure the organizationalUnit objects to hold information for simple mailing lists.

With the branches in place, we can turn to creating an actual user object.

Building User Objects

You can build user objects from three object classes, `inetOrgPerson`, `CourierMailAccount`, and `CourierMailAlias`, which you can find in `inetorgperson.schema`, `authldap.schema` (Courier IMAP), and `nis.schema`. Usage of the `nis.schema` is necessary because `authlap.schema` depends on some of its attributes.

Using attributes from all three schemata, we will describe a single user object. A complete object for Bamm Bamm in the IT department as we use it in this chapter looks like this:

```
dn: uid=bammbamm,ou=it,ou=people,dc=example,dc=com
uid: bammbamm
givenName: Bamm
sn: Bamm
cn: Bamm Bamm
userPassword: bamm_secret
homeDirectory: /var/spool/mail/bammbamm
mailbox: /var/spool/mail/bammbamm/Maildir
quota: 51200000S
mail: bamm@example.com
maildrop: postmaster@example.com
maildrop: bamm.bamm@example.com
maildrop: abuse@example.com
objectClass: CourierMailAlias
objectClass: CourierMailAccount
objectClass: inetOrgPerson
uidNumber: 1003
gidNumber: 1003
```

You may wonder where all of these attributes came from. The following sections explain their origins.

Creating the Sender and Recipient

You need to create an object to carry all user related attributes and values. We'll use `inetorgperson.schema`, because it provides extra attributes that allow for a company-wide address book.

You can create a unique user object with the `uid` attribute. `inetorgperson.schema` also gives you access to the `mail` attribute, which you can use for local recipient addresses and valid sender addresses. These two attributes look like this in the `inetorgperson.schema`:

```
attributetype ( 0.9.2342.19200300.100.1.1
    NAME ( 'uid' 'userid' )
    DESC 'RFC1274: user identifier'
    EQUALITY caseIgnoreMatch
    SUBSTR caseIgnoreSubstringsMatch
    SYNTAX 1.3.6.1.4.1.1466.115.121.1.15{256} )
```

```
attributetype ( 0.9.2342.19200300.100.1.3
    NAME ( 'mail' 'rfc822Mailbox' )
    DESC 'RFC1274: RFC822 Mailbox'
    EQUALITY caseIgnoreIA5Match
    SUBSTR caseIgnoreIA5SubstringsMatch
    SYNTAX 1.3.6.1.4.1.1466.115.121.1.26{256} )
```

NOTE   *You can add the mail attribute to an object more than once. You'll see later that this comes in handy for creating mailing list members.*

Let's say that we want to create an object. In this chapter, we'll use the concatenation of the user's first and last names as the uid attribute.

Defining Aliases

You can find a good attribute for defining aliases in authldap.schema from Courier IMAP. There's an auxiliary class there named CourierMailAlias with a maildrop attribute that defines a RFC 822 mailbox for a mail alias:

```
attributetype ( 1.3.6.1.4.1.10018.1.1.4 NAME 'maildrop'
        DESC 'RFC822 Mailbox - mail alias'
        EQUALITY caseIgnoreIA5Match
        SUBSTR caseIgnoreIA5SubstringsMatch
        SYNTAX 1.3.6.1.4.1.1466.115.121.1.26{256} )
```

NOTE   *The CourierMailAlias object class is an auxiliary class, which means that you can't add it to a directory by itself. You need to add it in conjunction with a structural class. This is fine, because the inetOrgPerson class that we're already using is a structural class.*

Creating List Objects

The simplest kind of list that Postfix supports without the help of a list manager (such as Mailman) are just aliases that map to a list of recipients. At this point, we already have all of the attributes we need, so we just need to come up with a suitable list object—anything without a userPassword attribute should do.

In fact, you don't need to create an extra object for lists. Just add the CourierMailAlias object class to the organizationalUnit class used to create the original branches.

The CourierMailAlias object gives us access to the maildrop and mail attributes. Now you can assign an alias name, such as all@example.com, to a maildrop attribute of ou=people,dc=example,dc=com, and add mail entries for every member in the organization. A complete list object might look like this:

```
dn: ou=people,dc=example,dc=com
ou: people
description: All employees
objectClass: CourierMailAlias
objectClass: organizationalUnit
```

```
maildrop: all@example.com
mail: bamm@example.com
mail: pebble@example.com
mail: mcbricker@example.com
mail: flintstone@example.com
mail: rubble@example.com
```

At this point, the LDAP server has the recipients and aliases that Postfix needs, so you can turn your attention to the other servers.

Adding Attributes for the Remaining Servers

When Postfix finishes processing an email, it sends it to a local delivery agent (LDA), such as Courier maildrop. The LDA needs to know the location of the mailbox and the user and permissions that it should use. Mail transport agents such as Courier IMAP also need to know where the mailbox is located.

We'll specify the mailbox location with the `mailbox` attribute from Courier's `authldap.schema`:

```
attributetype ( 1.3.6.1.4.1.10018.1.1.1 NAME 'mailbox'
    DESC 'The absolute path to the mailbox for a mail account in a non-default
location'
        EQUALITY caseExactIA5Match
        SYNTAX 1.3.6.1.4.1.1466.115.121.1.26 SINGLE-VALUE )
```

This schema also defines a quota attribute that can define the maximum size of a mailbox:

```
attributetype ( 1.3.6.1.4.1.10018.1.1.2 NAME 'quota'
    DESC 'A string that represents the quota on a mailbox'
        EQUALITY caseExactIA5Match
        SYNTAX 1.3.6.1.4.1.1466.115.121.1.26 SINGLE-VALUE )
```

However, `authldap.schema` refers to `nis.schema` for the following attributes that Courier needs while accessing mailboxes:

```
attributetype ( 1.3.6.1.1.1.1.0 NAME 'uidNumber'
    DESC 'An integer uniquely identifying a user in an administrative domain'
    EQUALITY integerMatch
    SYNTAX 1.3.6.1.4.1.1466.115.121.1.27 SINGLE-VALUE )
attributetype ( 1.3.6.1.1.1.1.1 NAME 'gidNumber'
    DESC 'An integer uniquely identifying a group in an administrative domain'
    EQUALITY integerMatch
    SYNTAX 1.3.6.1.4.1.1466.115.121.1.27 SINGLE-VALUE )
attributetype ( 1.3.6.1.1.1.1.3 NAME 'homeDirectory'
    DESC 'The absolute path to the home directory'
    EQUALITY caseExactIA5Match
    SYNTAX 1.3.6.1.4.1.1466.115.121.1.26 SINGLE-VALUE )
```

The `uidNumber` and `gidNumber` attributes contain the numbers for the mailbox user ID and group ID. Courier maildrop needs them to get the correct permissions for writing messages to a mailbox, and Courier IMAP needs them when reading and deleting messages. In addition, Courier maildrop needs the `homeDirectory` attribute to read filtering rules.

Basic Configuration

This section shows you how to integrate LDAP support into Postfix and other servers. We'll look at only the basic functionality here. The "Advanced Configuration" section later in the chapter will explain how to secure your data.

Configuring Cyrus SASL

One of the stranger twists of the software installed for the company mail server is that the Cyrus SASL ldapdb plug-in requires the OpenLDAP development libraries. However, to be able to talk to Cyrus SASL, OpenLDAP requires the Cyrus SASL development libraries. If you want to build both from source code, this cross-reference can be tricky.

NOTE *The ldapdb plug-in requires OpenLDAP either later than 2.1.27 or later than 2.2.6. If you already have an appropriate OpenLDAP installation that supports SASL, you may only need to install the OpenLDAP development libraries when you build SASL with ldapdb support.*

To get around this problem, you have to build and install Cyrus SASL twice. The first time, you'll do it without ldapdb, so that OpenLDAP can link against the SASL libraries. Later in this chapter, you'll need to rebuild Cyrus SASL with your newly installed OpenLDAP library, so that you can get the ldapdb plug-in. If you don't need Cyrus SASL for other applications on your server, you can use the following configuration command to get the minimum SASL required to build OpenLDAP:

```
# ./configure \
    --with-plugindir=/usr/lib/sasl2 \
    --disable-java \
    --disable-krb4 \
    --with-dblib=berkeley \
    --with-saslauthd=/var/state/saslauthd \
    --without-pwcheck \
    --with-devrandom=/dev/urandom \
    --enable-cram \
    --enable-digest \
    --enable-plain \
    --enable-login \
    --disable-otp
```

Now you can turn your attention to building OpenLDAP.

Configuring OpenLDAP

If you don't have OpenLDAP on your system, get a version newer than 2.1.27 or 2.2.6 (this version uses a different BerkeleyDB) from a package, or download the source code from http://www.openldap.org/software/download. Read the following section "Installing OpenLDAP from Source" if you're building from source code.

Installing OpenLDAP from Source

As a regular user, unpack the archive and change into the newly created directory. Run **configure** with at least the following options:

```
$ ./configure  --prefix=/usr --exec-prefix=/usr --bindir=/usr/bin \
  --sbindir=/usr/sbin --sysconfdir=/etc --datadir=/usr/share \
  --includedir=/usr/include --libdir=/usr/lib --libexecdir=/usr/libexec \
  --localstatedir=/var --sharedstatedir=/usr/com --mandir=/usr/share/man \
  --infodir=/usr/share/info --with-slapd --with-slurpd --without-ldapd \
  --with-threads=posix --enable-static --enable-dynamic --enable-local \
  --enable-cldap --enable-rlookups --with-tls --with-cyrus-sasl \
  --enable-wrappers --enable-passwd --enable-cleartext --enable-crypt \
  --enable-spasswd --enable-modules --disable-sql --libexecdir=/usr/sbin \
  --localstatedir=/var/run --enable-ldbm --with-ldbm-api=berkeley \
  --enable-bdb --enable-ldap --enable-meta --enable-monitor \
  --enable-null --enable-rewrite --disable-shared --with-kerberos=k5only
```

After the configuration script finishes, run **make depend**, **make**, and **make test**, and then become root, and run **make install**. You're now ready to configure OpenLDAP.

Configuring the LDAP Server

To configure the OpenLDAP server, slapd, change to the configuration directory (for example, /etc/openldap) and edit the slapd.conf file. You need to add the following configuration:

```
# SCHEMATA
include     /etc/openldap/schema/core.schema
include     /etc/openldap/schema/cosine.schema
include     /etc/openldap/schema/inetorgperson.schema
include     /etc/openldap/schema/misc.schema
include     /etc/openldap/schema/nis.schema
include     /etc/openldap/schema/authldap.schema
# RUNTIME
pidfile     /usr/var/slapd.pid
argsfile    /usr/var/slapd.args
# DATABASE DEFINITIONS
database    ldbm
suffix      "dc=example,dc=com"
```

```
rootdn        "cn=Manager,dc=example,dc=com"
rootpw        {CRYPT}SHXa4LHVH8y3A
directory     /usr/var/openldap-data
# INDICES
index   objectClass                           eq
index   cn                                    eq
index   mail,maildrop                         pres
index   mailbox,quota,uidNumber,gidNumber eq
```

The SCHEMATA section of slapd.conf specifies the schemata to load during startup.

The DATABASE DEFINITIONS section sets "dc=example,dc=com" as the suffix defining the top branch of your directory tree. It assigns a rootdn set of attribute values ("cn=Manager,dc=example,dc=com") and a rootpw value to give the user defined by rootdn read-write access to the directory. Use the slappasswd(8) command to create an encrypted password.

The INDICES section defines attributes that should be indexed. When you index an attribute, it is much quicker to look up.

Controlling SASL Authentication in OpenLDAP

Because OpenLDAP has SASL support, it may use SASL during authentication to bind users to the server. Although it will not use plaintext mechanisms to process authentication, it might offer GSSAPI among the remaining mechanisms.

Because we're not going to configure a full-blown Kerberos server just to use this mechanism, it's best to disable it now so that clients don't try to use it. Do this by listing only the mechanisms you want in a special SASL configuration file for OpenLDAP. Create a /usr/lib/sasl2/slapd.conf file with this setting:

```
mech_list: DIGEST-MD5
```

See Chapter 15 for more information about SMTP authentication.

Importing the Directory

Now it's time to fill the LDAP database with data. There are a lot of ways to do this, but in our case, slapd probably isn't running yet. This means that you can use the slapadd utility on an LDIF file like this:

```
# slapadd -v -c -b "dc=example,dc=com" -l example.com.ldif
```

CAUTION   *Don't run slapadd when slapd is running. The utility writes directly to the database, and it might cause slapd to crash and corrupt your database.*

After successfully importing the LDIF file, start slapd. If you experience problems with the import, read slapadd(8) to see if you need any other parameters (or, if things are really bad, turn on debugging).

Configuring the LDAP Client

To test your `slapd` configuration and get it working with Courier IMAP, you need to configure the OpenLDAP client. Normally, you need to adjust some settings in the `/etc/openldap/ldap.conf` file. For the basics, enable the following parameters:

```
URI ldap://mail.example.com
BASE dc=example,dc=com
```

The `URI` and `BASE` parameters specify which LDAP server to access and where in the tree to start queries. Once you set these parameters correctly, you can test the directory.

Testing LDAP

The easiest way to test the LDAP server is to run the client tools that come with OpenLDAP. From the command line, run **ldapsearch** to connect the LDAP client to the server and make a query to the directory. Here's a successful example:

```
# ldapsearch -x -LLL -b "uid=bammbamm,ou=it,ou=people,dc=example,dc=com" "(objectclass=*)"
dn: uid=bammbamm,ou=it,ou=people,dc=example,dc=com
uid: bammbamm
givenName: Bamm
sn: Bamm
cn: Bamm Bamm
homeDirectory: /var/spool/mail/bammbamm
maildrop: postmaster@example.com
maildrop: bamm.bamm@example.com
maildrop: abuse@example.com
objectClass: CourierMailAlias
objectClass: CourierMailAccount
objectClass: inetOrgPerson
mailbox: /var/spool/mail/bammbamm/Maildir
quota: 5120000S
userPassword:: YmFtbV9zZWNyZXQ=
uidNumber: 1003
gidNumber: 1003
mail: bamm@example.com
```

If you get this output, you know that you can access the directory and that it is stored as intended. If you don't get any output, configure the loglevel parameter as described in slapd.conf(5), and see what more debugging information can tell you.

Configuring Postfix and LDAP

To check whether your Postfix already has LDAP and SASL support enabled, try this command:

```
$ ldd `/usr/sbin/postconf -h daemon_directory`/smtpd
        linux-gate.so.1 =>  (0x00bad000)
        libldap.so.2 => /usr/lib/libldap.so.2 (0x00882000)
        liblber.so.2 => /usr/lib/liblber.so.2 (0x00646000)
        libsasl2.so.2 => /usr/lib/libsasl2.so.2 (0x0098a000)
        libdb-4.2.so => /lib/tls/libdb-4.2.so (0x00a73000)
        libnsl.so.1 => /lib/libnsl.so.1 (0x00835000)
        libresolv.so.2 => /lib/libresolv.so.2 (0x00655000)
        libc.so.6 => /lib/tls/libc.so.6 (0x004e6000)
        libdl.so.2 => /lib/libdl.so.2 (0x00603000)
        libssl.so.4 => /lib/libssl.so.4 (0x0084c000)
        libcrypto.so.4 => /lib/libcrypto.so.4 (0x04377000)
        libpthread.so.0 => /lib/tls/libpthread.so.0 (0x0061c000)
        /lib/ld-linux.so.2 => /lib/ld-linux.so.2 (0x004cd000)
        libgssapi_krb5.so.2 => /usr/lib/libgssapi_krb5.so.2 (0x00d09000)
        libkrb5.so.3 => /usr/lib/libkrb5.so.3 (0x006da000)
        libcom_err.so.2 => /lib/libcom_err.so.2 (0x058fd000)
        libk5crypto.so.3 => /usr/lib/libk5crypto.so.3 (0x05902000)
        libz.so.1 => /usr/lib/libz.so.1 (0x00609000)
```

The lines with the ldap and sasl2 libraries indicate that LDAP and SASL support have been compiled into Postfix.

You learned how to configure SASL support in Chapter 15. Now you need support for LDAP in addition to SASL. You can get this support by combining the environment variables CCARGS and AUXLIBS that the build process uses in a sensible fashion. First, recall that you built for SASL like this:

```
$ CCARGS="-DUSE_SASL_AUTH -I/usr/local/include AUXLIBS="-L/usr/local/lib
 -lsasl2" make makefiles
```

To build the Cyrus SASL libraries with LDAP support, you need to find the LDAP libraries and header files on your system. If you don't know where they are, search for the libraries like this:

```
# find /usr -name 'libldap*.*'
/usr/local/lib/libldap.so.2
/usr/local/lib/libldap.so.2.0.122
/usr/local/lib/libldap_r.so.2
/usr/local/lib/libldap_r.so.2.0.122
/usr/local/lib/libldap.so
/usr/local/lib/libldap.a
```

```
/usr/local/lib/libldap_r.so
/usr/local/lib/libldap_r.a
# find /usr -name 'liblber*.*'
/usr/local/lib/liblber.so.2.0.122
/usr/local/lib/liblber.so.2
/usr/local/lib/liblber.so
/usr/local/lib/liblber.a
```

This output shows that the LDAP libraries are in /usr/local/lib; the /usr/lib and /usr/include paths are searched by the compiler, preprocessor, and linker automatically. Take a note of this location, and then search for the corresponding include files with this command:

```
# find /usr -name '*ldap*.h'
/usr/local/include/ldap.h
/usr/local/include/ldap_cdefs.h
/usr/local/include/ldap_schema.h
/usr/local/include/ldap_utf8.h
/usr/local/include/ldap_features.h
```

NOTE *If you can't find the include files for LDAP on your system, but the libraries are there, you probably need to install the LDAP developer packages from your operating system. You're looking for packages that end in -dev or -devel.*

Now that you know where to look for both LDAP and SASL support, unpack the Postfix source as a regular user, and change to the Postfix source directory. Configure and build Postfix with options for both SASL (-DUSE_SASL_AUTH) and LDAP (-DHAS_LDAP) like this:

```
$ CCARGS="-DHAS_LDAP -DUSE_SASL_AUTH -I/usr/local/include" AUXLIBS="-lldap
  -llber -L/usr/local/lib -lsasl2"
$ make makefiles
$ make
```

After the build completes, become the superuser (root) and run **make install** or **make upgrade** as appropriate. Finally, verify that you have SASL and LDAP support as described at the beginning of this chapter.

LDAP Lookups

There aren't many LDAP-related questions on the Postfix mailing lists, especially compared to the number asking about database backends. Many people think that running Postfix (or anything else, for that matter) with LDAP is akin to voodoo and try to avoid it at all costs. However, this just isn't the case. The configuration steps for LDAP queries always go as follows.

1. Create a directory for the LDAP configuration files.
2. Create a Postfix configuration file for LDAP.

3. Test an LDAP query.

4. Configure Postfix to use the LDAP query configuration.

You will iterate over these steps twice in the following subsections. First you will configure a query for local recipients and as a second step you will configure a query for mail aliases.

Creating an LDAP Configuration Directory

A well-configured LDAP server rejects queries for security-related directory data. The directory requires users that want to retrieve such data to authenticate ("bind") to the LDAP server first. You'll learn how to create a binding user for Postfix in the "Advanced Configuration" section later in the chapter, but you need to take the first step of creating the extra configuration directory now. This is because Postfix bind credentials must be stored in Postfix-specific configuration files, but you don't want to put them into your main.cf file, because that would make them world-readable.

CAUTION *Creating LDAP configurations in external files requires Postfix 2.x. You can configure LDAP query parameters entirely in* main.cf, *but because this requires that the passwords for LDAP users be in* main.cf, *it's not very secure—any user on the Unix system that Postfix runs on can read them.*

If you really want to use the main.cf *file to store the credentials, read the "Backwards Compatibility" section in the* ldap_table(5) *manual page.*

To create the configuration directory, create an /etc/postfix/ldap directory accessible only to root and postfix. You'll store all LDAP map configuration files there and reference them from main.cf.

```
# mkdir /etc/postfix/ldap
# chgrp postfix /etc/postfix/ldap
# chmod 750 /etc/postfix/ldap
```

Adding LDAP Queries for Local Recipients

Let's look now at the basic Postfix parameters for querying an LDAP server. We will start off by disabling LDAP bind operations. Then we will create a set of parameters that will give us information to verify to local recipients.

Disabling LDAP Bind

By default, Postfix tries to authenticate via LDAP bind to the server before running a query. When you're first starting out, it's a good idea to disable this authentication in order to keep things as simple as possible. Create an LDAP query configuration file named /etc/postfix/ldap/local_recipients.cf with the following configuration parameter, which turns off the bind:

```
bind = no
```

Configuring the LDAP Host

You can tell Postfix where to find the directory service with the `server_host` and `server_port` configuration parameters. The `server_host` parameter defines the connection type (`ldap://`, `ldaps://`, or `ldapi://`) as a part of one or more LDAP server URLs that may include the server port. This parameter defaults to `server_host = ldap://localhost:389`.

Optionally, you can set `server_port` (whose default port is 389) to define the LDAP server port, but this makes sense only if all of your LDAP servers listen on the same port. Otherwise, you can just append the port on a per-URL basis, like this:

```
server_host = ldap://mail.example.com:389, ldaps://auth.example.com:636
```

In this chapter, the LDAP server runs on the same host as the other servers and listens on the default LDAP port (389). In this case, you can set `server_host` as follows:

```
server_host = ldap://mail.example.com
```

Specifying a Branch

The next thing to do is set Postfix's starting branch for searches with the `search_base` parameter. There is no default value, so you always have to set it. Add the dn piece of the branch for the user objects, like this:

```
search_base = ou=people,dc=example,dc=com
```

Defining LDAP Result Attributes

To complete the LDAP map configuration, you need to define the attribute that holds the key that Postfix accesses upon lookups. The logic is exactly as in any other map that you have seen so far. The parameter names for the keys and values compared to indexed maps are shown in Table 19-1.

Table 19-1: How Fields of Indexed Maps Correspond to LDAP Query Parameters

Map Type	LHS	RHS	Conditions
indexed map	key	value	-
LDAP query	query_filter	result_attribute, result_filter	special_result_attribute

As you can see, you define the query key attribute with the `query_filter` parameter. Following the example from the Example Inc. directory, specify the attribute for local recipient mail addresses (the `mail` attribute), and define the part of the fully qualified mail address that Postfix should submit to the LDAP server. The substitutions are as follows.

%s   The complete mail address (for example, `bamm@example.com`)

%u   The localpart without the @ and the domain (for example, `bamm`)

%d   The domain part without the localpart and the @ (for example, `example.com`)

Because the directory entries in this chapter contain only fully qualified mail addresses, such as `bamm@example.com`, we'll use `%s`. Configure Postfix to query based on the full domain name as follows:

```
query_filter = (mail=%s)
```

NOTE   *The standard syntax for LDAP queries and results is defined in RFC 2254 (`http://www.rfc-editor.org/rfc/rfc2254.txt`). You can specify your query in any way that you like. For example, if you have an attribute named `mailboxActive` in your schema that denotes an active (not disabled) mailbox, you could form the query parameter as follows:*

```
query_filter = (&(mail=%s)(mailboxActive=1))
```

Now you need to define the attribute Postfix will use to query for a result. There are two parameters at your disposal: `result_attribute` for configuring the actual attribute, and `result_filter` for filtering out parts of the LDAP query result that you may not need.

In this chapter, you need only verify the existence of a local mail address because Courier maildrop is the delivery agent in this chapter, not Postfix. Postfix simply needs to know whether the local recipient address is valid, so you can use any attribute returned.

NOTE   *This means that Postfix accepts any value that the LDAP server returns as proof that the local recipient exists for an incoming message. If the LDAP server doesn't return a value, Postfix rejects the message.*

Choose a simple attribute that's easy to identify when testing the query. In our case, `uid` fits the bill, so here's how to configure it as the result attribute in the Postfix `local_recipients.cf` configuration file:

```
result_attribute = uid
```

Activating the Query Map

When you're happy with your `/etc/postfix/ldap/local_recipients.cf` file, you need to activate this map in the main Postfix configuration. Set the `local_recipient_maps` parameter in your `main.cf` file to a list of maps that Postfix will consult when looking for local recipients. Use `proxymap` (described in Chapter 5) to improve LDAP query performance, as follows:

```
local_recipient_maps = proxy:ldap:/etc/postfix/ldap/local_recipients.cf
```

Each proxymap process asks queries on behalf of multiple clients, and may, but does not have to, cache lookup results.

With the new map in place, reload your Postfix configuration and start testing.

Testing LDAP Recipients

At this point, the only test you can perform is checking whether Postfix can look up a valid local recipient. You won't be able to send a test message because local delivery hasn't been configured.

Use the postmap command to query the LDAP server for a known local recipient, such as bamm@example.com. However, before you do this you need to switch to the postfix user on your system, because you must make sure that this user is allowed to read the LDAP configuration file and run the query. A successful test looks like this:

```
# su - postfix
$ /usr/sbin/postmap -q "bamm@example.com" ldap:/etc/postfix/ldap/
  local_recipients.cf
bammbamm
```

The query here returns the uid value for bamm@example.com; in this case, the value for that attribute is bammbamm, so the configuration works. If it doesn't work, add a -v parameter to the postmap command for verbose output. In addition, you can add the debuglevel parameter to the LDAP query configuration file:

```
debuglevel = 1
```

NOTE *You can increase the debug level to 3, which should give you all information necessary to fix a problem.*

Querying LDAP for Mail Aliases

To configure Postfix to query the LDAP server for mail aliases, you'll follow the same basic configuration steps that were shown in the earlier "Adding LDAP Queries for Local Recipients" section, except that this time you must specify a different result_attribute parameter for the query result, and you must use the query_filter parameter to extract a specific attribute from the results.

Alias names in the example directory server are assigned to the maildrop attribute of an entry. Therefore, a configuration file for aliases (for example, /etc/postfix/ldap/virtual_aliases.cf) would look like the following.

```
bind = no
server_host = ldap://mail.example.com
search_base = ou=people,dc=example,dc=com
query_filter = (maildrop=%s)
result_attribute = mail
```

Configuring Postfix for LDAP Alias Query Maps

With the LDAP alias query configuration file in place, you need to connect it to your Postfix configuration by setting the virtual_alias_maps parameter in main.cf. The syntax is the same as in the recipient maps described in the earlier "Activating the Query Map" section:

```
virtual_alias_maps = proxy:ldap:/etc/postfix/ldap/virtual_aliases.cf
```

Reload your configuration and start testing.

Testing LDAP Alias Query Maps

As before, you can't send a message to test the LDAP query configuration, but you can use the postmap command. Recall that postmaster@example.com is an alias for bamm@example.com in the directory. Switch to the postfix user, and see if the alias map works like this:

```
# su - postfix
$ /usr/sbin/postmap -q "postmaster@example.com" ldap:/etc/postfix/ldap/virtual_aliases.cf
bamm@example.com
```

If you don't get any output from this command, add a -v parameter to the postmap command for verbose output. You can also add the debuglevel parameter to the LDAP query configuration file (and you can increase the debug level up to 3, depending on the amount of information you need):

```
debuglevel = 1
```

Testing Lists

You may recall that the simple list design described in the "Creating List Objects" section earlier in the chapter uses aliases. Therefore, you should be able to retrieve multiple recipients of an alias by running a postmap query on the list name:

```
# su - postfix
$ /usr/sbin/postmap -q "all@example.com" ldap:/etc/postfix/ldap/virtual_aliases.cf
bamm@example.com,pebble@example.com,mcbricker@example.com,flintstone@example.com,rubble@example.com
```

When the LDAP server returns multiple results, Postfix collects all of them and transforms them into a comma-separated list, as in the preceding example.

Delegating Transport to Courier Maildrop

The configuration in this chapter does not use any of the Postfix delivery agents (the local, maildrop, and virtual daemons). One reason for this is that third-party delivery agents offer features such as filtering rules and quotas. For example, the user bammbamm could place all messages for postmaster@example.com in a subfolder. This section shows you how to configure Postfix to delegate the task of local message delivery to Courier maildrop.

Creating a Local Transport

Start out by defining a new transport service in your master.cf file. Don't worry about breaking your current LDA (if you even have a working one), because Postfix won't use the new service until you make a corresponding change in your main.cf file. The new transport will be a pipe transport called maildrop. Add the following configuration lines to your master.cf file:

```
maildrop  unix  -      n      n      -      -      pipe
    flags=DRhu user=vmail argv=/usr/local/bin/maildrop -d ${recipient} -w 75
```

The flags of this pipe(8) transport operate as follows:

D   Prepends a Delivered-To recipient message header with the envelope recipient address. This mimics the Postfix local daemon and serves as a precaution against mail loops.

R   Prepends a Return-Path message header containing the envelope sender address. The Postfix local daemon is required to this by RFC 2821.

h   Converts the domain name of the command-line $recipient address and the $nexthop hostname to lowercase.

u   Converts the localpart of the command-line $recipient address to lowercase.

user   user=vmail specifies that /usr/local/bin/maildrop -d ${recipient} should run as the user vmail, a user that you'll see later when setting up Courier maildrop.

-w   Sets the warning level for deliverquota(8) to 75 percent of the mail directory quota. Omit this if you don't want to enforce a quota.

After you add the service, edit your main.cf file to tell Postfix to use it as the local transport:

```
local_transport = maildrop
```

CAUTION   *There are two side effects of using maildrop instead of the local delivery agent. First local looks at the alias maps, but Courier maildrop can't do this. However, you already addressed this problem in the earlier "Configuring Postfix for LDAP Alias Query Maps"* *section when you set the* virtual_alias_maps *parameter. The second limitation is that maildrop will not take care of Delivered-To loops unless you configure a filter rule. This will be taken care of in the section "Creating a Mail Filter."*

Limiting Concurrent Messages

Before testing your new transport, you need to make sure it is configured to deliver to only one user at a time. Don't fret over any performance loss from this, because it's normal for most mail servers. Even the Postfix local transport is limited to one message at a time with the local_destination_ recipient_limit parameter.

The parameter syntax for creating a limit for other LDAs is *servicename_* destination_recipient_limit, with *servicename* equal to the first field in master.cf. Add the following line to main.cf for the Courier maildrop service that you just defined:

```
maildrop_destination_recipient_limit = 1
```

Now reload Postfix and start testing.

Testing the LDA

To test the LDA, just send a message to one of the addresses in your recipient map and watch the mail log. You should be able to see Postfix using the new maildrop transport like this:

```
# echo foo | /usr/sbin/sendmail -f "" postmaster@example.com
# tail -f /var/log/maillog
Jun 29 14:39:13 mail postfix/pickup[5122]: AC7B94400C: uid=0 from=<>
Jun 29 14:39:13 mail postfix/cleanup[5127]: AC7B94400C:
    message-id=<20040629123913.AC7B94400C@mail.example.com>
Jun 29 14:39:13 mail postfix/qmgr[5123]: AC7B94400C:
    from=<>, size=285, nrcpt=1 (queue active)
Jun 29 14:39:13 mail postfix/pipe[5130]: AC7B94400C:
    to=<bamm@example.com>, orig_to=<postmaster@example.com>,
    relay=maildrop, delay=0, status=sent (example.com)
Jun 29 14:39:13 mail postfix/qmgr[5123]: AC7B94400C: removed
```

If you don't see a maildrop transport in the log, turn on verbose logging for smtpd in master.cf, reload your configuration, and send another message.

Configuring Courier Maildrop

Courier maildrop is an LDA that takes messages from a transfer agent such as Postfix and stores them in a recipient's mailbox in Maildir format. Maildrop can also apply filters to messages. One more interesting capability is the enforcement of quotas on directories (messages in Maildir format are stored as separate files in a directory).

Preparing Your System

Courier maildrop prohibits unauthorized users from writing to mailboxes. You need to choose trusted users and groups before you build the binaries. Create at least one new user with user ID and group ID numbers matching the values that you gave to the `uidNumber` and `gidNumber` attributes in your LDAP directory. Courier maildrop and IMAP retrieve these attributes from the directory when accessing the mailbox.

The example configuration in this chapter uses the following user ID and group ID:

```
uidNumber: 1003
gidNumber: 1003
```

If you haven't done so yet, create a user and group to match these values. For example, these commands add a user and group named `vmail` on a Linux system:

```
# useradd -u 1003 vmail
# groupadd -g 1003 vmail
```

Installing Courier Maildrop

LDAP support in Courier maildrop is in beta testing as we're writing this. It runs well when correctly configured, but it won't tell you what went wrong if it catches an error. Considering the speed at which Courier maildrop evolves, this will probably be fixed by the time you read this book. To get LDAP support, download the development snapshot of maildrop from `http://www.courier-mta.org/download.php#maildrop`.

Extract the archive as a regular user, and change to the newly created directory. Courier maildrop uses GNU Autoconf, so the build options are specified as follows:

```
$ ./configure --enable-restrict-trusted=1 --enable-trusted-users='root vmail'
  --enable-trusted-groups='root vmail' --enable-maildirquota --with-trashquota
  --enable-maildropldap
```

Make sure that you specify `--enable-maildropldap` for LDAP support. If you want quota support, include `--enable-maildirquota` and `--with-trashquota`, but have a look at the section "Preparing Maildir Quotas" first. After the configuration script finishes, run **make**. If everything goes smoothly, become `root` and run **make install-strip install-man** to install stripped binaries and manual pages.

Now that you have `maildrop` installed, you need to do something about the Postfix `pipe` daemon, which refuses to run any process as `root`. To get around this, change the `maildrop` binary to setuid `root`.

```
# chmod 750  /usr/local/bin/maildrop
# chmod u+s /usr/local/bin/maildrop
# chown root:vmail /usr/local/bin/maildrop
# ls -l /usr/local/bin/maildrop
-rwsr-x---  1 root   vmail  165552 Jun 25 12:48 /usr/local/bin/maildrop
```

Don't worry about circumventing the normal Postfix security policies. The pipe daemon runs maildrop, which immediately starts running as root, but upon getting the correct user ID and group ID from LDAP, maildrop switches to that user and group.

Configuring Courier Maildrop

The easiest way to set up the maildrop configuration for LDAP is to copy the sample file named maildropldap.config from the maildrop source directory to /etc/maildropldap.config (this is where Courier maildrop looks for an LDAP configuration file by default). Edit the file to match your configuration.

Here's how it would look for the example in this chapter:

```
hostname                mail.example.com
basedn                  dc=example,dc=com
filter                  &(objectclass=inetorgperson)
timeout                 5
search_method           mail
mail_attr               mail
uid_attr                uid
uidnumber_attr          uidNumber
gidnumber_attr          gidNumber
maildir_attr            mailbox
homedirectory_attr      homeDirectory
quota_attr              quota
```

Creating Maildir Mailboxes

All users in this company mail server are virtual users. They are in no relation to local user accounts, and when you created users in your LDAP directory, no script automatically created a home directory or a mailbox.

Before testing the maildrop program, you need to create the user mailboxes. You'll have to do this by hand for now (you can automate it later with scripts, of course). Courier maildrop comes with a utility called maildirmake that creates a Maildir mailbox and a few default subfolders.

Maildrop looks at the homeDirectories attribute on the LDAP server to locate a mailbox. However, because you switched to virtual users, you can create a skeleton directory in a place such as /home/mailskel, which you can simply copy to user home directories without worrying about specific user permissions.

Here's how to create the outer mail skeleton directory:

```
# mkdir /home/mailskel
# chgrp vmail /home/mailskel
# chmod 770 /home/mailskel
# ls -dall /home/mailskel
drwxrwx---    6 root     vmail       4096 Jun 28 17:52 /home/mailskel
```

Now you can create another directory named /home/mailskel/.templateDir and give ownership to vmail:

```
# mkdir /home/mailskel/.templateDir
# chown vmail /home/mailskel/.templateDir/
# chgrp vmail /home/mailskel/.templateDir/
# chmod 700 /home/mailskel/.templateDir/
# ls -dall /home/mailskel/.templateDir
drwx------    2 vmail     vmail       4096 Jun 29 22:27 /home/mailskel/.templateDir
```

You're now ready to build the actual mail directory. However, before running maildirmake to create the basic Maildir directory structure, you need to switch to the vmail user so that maildrop will be able to access an exact copy of it later:

```
# su - vmail
$ maildirmake /home/mailskel/.templateDir/Maildir
```

Verify that maildirmake created the directory as follows:

```
$ ls -la /home/mailskel/.templateDir/Maildir
total 20
drwx------    5 vmail     vmail       4096 Jun 29 22:31 .
drwx------    3 vmail     vmail       4096 Jun 29 22:31 ..
drwx------    2 vmail     vmail       4096 Jun 29 22:31 cur
drwx------    2 vmail     vmail       4096 Jun 29 22:31 new
drwx------    2 vmail     vmail       4096 Jun 29 22:31 tmp
```

As you can see, you now have a directory called Maildir containing the three subdirectories cur, new, and tmp, where inbox messages reside (depending on their status).

Run maildirmake a few more times to create subfolders named Drafts, Trash, and Spam:

```
$ maildirmake -f Drafts /home/mailskel/.templateDir/Maildir
$ maildirmake -f Trash /home/mailskel/.templateDir/Maildir
$ maildirmake -f Spam /home/mailskel/.templateDir/Maildir
$ ls -la /home/mailskel/.templateDir/Maildir
```

```
total 32
drwx------    8 vmail    vmail    4096 Jun 29 22:39 .
drwx------    3 vmail    vmail    4096 Jun 29 22:31 ..
drwx------    2 vmail    vmail    4096 Jun 29 22:31 cur
drwx------    5 vmail    vmail    4096 Jun 29 22:39 .Drafts
drwx------    2 vmail    vmail    4096 Jun 29 22:31 new
drwx------    5 vmail    vmail    4096 Jun 29 22:39 .Spam
drwx------    2 vmail    vmail    4096 Jun 29 22:31 tmp
drwx------    5 vmail    vmail    4096 Jun 29 22:39 .Trash
```

Notice that each of these subdirectories has cur, new, and tmp subdirectories.

Your mail directory template is now available as a skeleton to use when creating virtual Maildir mailboxes for other users. Use cp -pR as the superuser to preserve ownership and permissions when copying the template. For example, you can create the mailbox for bammbamm as follows:

```
# cp -pR /home/mailskel/.templateDir/ /var/spool/mail/bammbamm
# ls -all /var/spool/mail/bammbamm
total 12
drwx------    3 vmail    vmail    4096 Jun 29 22:31 .
drwxrwx---    9 root     vmail    4096 Jun 29 22:55 ..
drwx------    8 vmail    vmail    4096 Jun 29 22:39 Maildir
# ls -all /var/spool/mail/bammbamm/Maildir/
total 32
drwx------    8 vmail    vmail    4096 Jun 29 22:39 .
drwx------    3 vmail    vmail    4096 Jun 29 22:31 ..
drwx------    2 vmail    vmail    4096 Jun 29 22:31 cur
drwx------    5 vmail    vmail    4096 Jun 29 22:39 .Drafts
drwx------    2 vmail    vmail    4096 Jun 29 22:31 new
drwx------    5 vmail    vmail    4096 Jun 29 22:39 .Spam
drwx------    2 vmail    vmail    4096 Jun 29 22:31 tmp
drwx------    5 vmail    vmail    4096 Jun 29 22:39 .Trash
```

Don't create directories for the rest of your users yet; have a look at the next section first.

Creating a Mail Filter

After creating a Maildir template directory, you can create a default set of delivery filters for Courier maildrop. To get started, configure a global set of rules in /etc/maildroprc that apply to every mail recipient on your server. For debugging purposes, you may find it handy to put a log file into each user's home directory with this rule:

```
logfile "$HOME/maildrop.log"
```

Now you can turn your attention to filter rules. The first rule in the following example will prevent a Delivered-To loop as mentioned in the section "Creating a Local Transport." It should always be at the beginning of your `maildroprc` file to catch before any other actions are carried out. The second rule tells maildrop to put any message with X-Spam-Status: Yes in the message header into the `.spam` subfolder of the recipients mailbox ($DEFAULT):

```
logfile "$HOME/maildrop.log"
if ( /^Delivered-To: $LOGNAME@mail.example.com/:h )
{
  echo "This message is looping, it already has my Delivered-To: Header!"
  EXITCODE = 1
  exit
}
if (/^X-Spam-Status: Yes/)
{
    to $DEFAULT/.spam/
}
```

You can filter on a per-user basis by adding a `.mailfilter` file with additional rules to a recipient's home directory. You must use a strict set of permissions, or maildrop will refuse to use instructions from `.mailfilter`. Here's how to create it for bammbamm:

```
# su - vmail
$ cd /var/spool/mail/bammbamm
$ touch .mailfilter
$ chmod 600 .mailfilter
```

Recall that the preceding user is also the postmaster. Therefore, the following `.mailfilter` filter rule files messages with postmaster@example.com as the recipient in the message header to the `.postmaster` directory:

```
if (/^To.*postmaster@example\.com/)
{
  to "$DEFAULT/.postmaster/"
}
```

NOTE   *Global filter rules take precedence over per-user rules.*

Of course, you haven't created the `.postmaster` folder yet, so before you can use this rule, you must create it. Become vmail and run **maildirmake** as follows:

```
# su - vmail
$ cd /var/spool/mail/bammbamm
$ maildirmake -f postmaster Maildir
```

Maildrop filtering rules can make life a lot easier for users because they don't have to rely on their mail client. To learn more about maildrop's filtering capabilities, refer to the maildropfilter(5) manual page, and pay special attention to the examples listed for `http://www.dotfiles.com` in the "Other" section.

Preparing Maildir Quotas

Quotas seem like a nice feature to have, but before you decide to turn them on, you should be aware that the maildrop quota system is somewhat controversial because Maildir quotas are not reliable all the time. The following statement by Victor Duchovni summarizes a Postfix developer's point of view:

> The real sticking point is that the users of "maildir++" don't want robust quota code that is guaranteed to work all the time! They are willing to trade robustness (quota state files never need to be rebuilt, user always under quota, . . .) for ease of use (no filesystem quota interface to worry about, quotas can be soft allowing for configurable limited functionality when over quota).

Of course, this aspect of the quotas is known (see `http://www.inter7.com/courierimap/README.maildirquota.html`), but many administrators still prefer to take the advantages of Courier maildrop along with some slight disadvantages. Every situation is different, so you need to decide on the matter of quotas for yourself.

If you want to go for it, first add `-w 75` to the maildrop service line in the earlier "Creating a Local Transport" section to generate a warning message when the mail directory is at 75 percent capacity (a "soft" limit). You will need to come up with the warning message template yourself. Create the template as a plaintext file named `/usr/local/etc/quotawarnmsg` containing a message something like this:

```
From: MAILER-DAEMON <>
To: Valued Customer:;
Subject: Mail quota warning
Mime-Version: 1.0
Content-Type: text/plain; charset=iso-8859-1
Content-Transfer-Encoding: 7bit

Your mailbox on the server is now more than 75% full. So that you can continue
to receive mail you need to remove some messages from your mailbox.
```

Maildrop adds `Message-ID` and `Date` headers when storing the quota warning in the recipient's mailbox.

Testing Courier Maildrop

It's now time to test your Courier maildrop installation. There are four steps in the testing:

1. Test that Courier maildrop works without Postfix.
2. Use the sendmail program that comes with Postfix to deliver a message to Courier maildrop.

3. Test that the filters work.

4. Test that the quotas work (if you chose to use them).

Testing Stand-Alone Courier Maildrop

Switch to the vmail user and execute the `maildrop` command as Postfix would:

```
# su - vmail
$ /usr/local/bin/maildrop -d bamm@example.com
this is a test message
```

Enter CTRL-D on a line by itself to send the message. Check whether maildrop terminated cleanly by looking at the exit code, as follows:

```
$ echo $?
0
```

An exit code of zero indicates successful execution and delivery. Of course, you could also verify that maildrop created a new file in bamm's mail directory:

```
$ ls -l /var/spool/mail/bammbamm/Maildir/new
total 4
-rw-------   1 vmail    vmail          23 Jun 30 12:12
  1088590342.M975018P6589V0000000000000302I0001840E_0.mail.example.com,S=4
```

If you enabled Courier maildrop logging, you will find this proof of delivery in the log:

```
Date: Mon Aug  9 09:05:56 2004
From:
Subj:
File: /var/spool/mail/bammbamm/Maildir                                   (12)
```

Testing Courier Maildrop with Postfix

To test Postfix with maildrop, use the Postfix `sendmail` binary and inspect your mail log as follows:

```
# echo foo | /usr/sbin/sendmail -f rubble@example.com bamm@example.com
# tail -f /var/log/maillog
Jul 26 23:20:58 mail postfix/pickup[27883]: 608DD229EF5: uid=0
  from=<rubble@example.com>
Jul 26 23:20:58 mail postfix/cleanup[28429]: 608DD229EF5:
  message-id=<20040726212058.608DD229EF5@mail.example.com>
Jul 26 23:20:58 mail postfix/qmgr[27882]: 608DD229EF5:
  from=<rubble@example.com>, size=288, nrcpt=1 (queue active)
```

```
Jul 26 23:20:58 mail postfix/pipe[28432]: 608DD229EF5: to=<bamm@example.com>,
  relay=maildrop, delay=0, status=sent (example.com)
Jul 26 23:20:58 mail postfix/qmgr[27882]: 608DD229EF5: removed
```

The mail log here indicates that Postfix relayed the message to maildrop. If you enabled logging in /etc/maildroprc, you should find a log entry like the following in Bamm Bamm's maildrop.log file:

```
Date: Mon Jul 26 23:24:42 2004
From: rubble@example.com (root)
Subj:
File: /var/spool/mail/bammbamm/Maildir                          (345)
```

This entry states that a message from rubble@example.com (identified by Postfix as root) was delivered to /var/spool/mail/bammbamm/Maildir, which happens to be Bamm Bamm's inbox.

Testing Courier Maildrop Filters

To test filtering, create and send a file named testmessage with something to trigger the filter rules in /etc/maildroprc. Here's a message that should work with the spam filtering rule from the section "Creating a Mail Filter":

```
From: Barney <rubble@example.com>
To: Bamm Bamm <bamm@example.com>
Subject: Test message tagged as SPAM
X-Spam-Status: Yes
foo bar
```

Send the message with sendmail as follows:

```
# /usr/sbin/sendmail -f rubble@example.com bamm@example.com < testmessage
```

In addition to checking the spam subfolder to verify that it works, check the maildrop.log file. It should look like this:

```
Date: Mon Jul 26 22:29:24 2004
From: Barney <rubble@example.com>
Subj: Test message tagged as SPAM
File: /var/spool/mail/bammbamm/Maildir/.spam/                   (412)
```

The message was delivered to the subfolder .spam, so the global filters work.

Now alter your test message as follows to see if local filters work:

```
From: Barney <rubble@example.com>
To: Postmaster <postmaster@example.com>
Subject: Test message for Postmaster
```

Send this message to postmaster@example.com:

```
# /usr/sbin/sendmail -f rubble@example.com postmaster@example.com < testmessage
```

The `maildrop.log` file should look like the following, confirming that the message went to the Postmaster's folder:

```
Date: Mon Jul 26 23:36:48 2004
From: Barney <rubble@example.com>
Subj: Test message for Postmaster
File: /var/spool/mail/bammbamm/Maildir/.postmaster          (391)
```

Testing Courier Maildrop Quotas

Finally, if you configured maildrop to use Maildir quotas, you need to test whether the soft limit and hard limit work. Create a `testmessage` that has a size of 5MB like this:

```
#  dd if=/dev/zero of=/root/testmessage bs=5M count=1
1+0 records in
1+0 records out
# ls -all testmessage
-rw-r--r--  1 root root 5242880 Jul 27 09:25 testmessage
```

Next, use `ldapmodify` to set a lower quota for Bamm Bamm. It should reach `softlimit` after one `testmessage` and `hardlimit` after the second. Create a file, such as `modify_bammbamm_quota.ldif`, including your changes:

```
dn: uid=bammbamm,ou=it,ou=people,dc=example,dc=com
changetype: modify
replace: quota
quota: 6990507S
```

Then run **ldapmodify**, and import the changes from `modify_bammbamm_quota.ldif`:

```
# ldapmodify -x -D "cn=Manager,dc=example,dc=com" -w secret -f modify_bammbamm_quota.ldif
```

When all of this is set up, you can send the first of the two test messages off to bamm@example.com:

```
# /usr/sbin/sendmail -f rubble@example.com bamm@example.com < /root/testmessage
```

Check whether the message was delivered to Bamm Bamm's mailbox:

```
# ls -la
-rw-------  1 vmail vmail 5243221 Jul 27 09:38 1090913892.\
    M24019P29629V0000000000000302I00229EF6_0.mail.example.com,S=5243221
-rw-r-----  1 vmail vmail     447 Jul 27 09:38 1090913893.\
    M932062P29629V0000000000000302I00229F00_warn.mail.example.com,S=447
```

You can see an additional message that carries the string warn in its filename. Use cat to have a look at it:

```
# cat 1090913893.M932062P29629V0000000000000302I00229F00_warn.mail.example.com\,S\=447
From: MAILER-DAEMON <>
To: Valued Customer:;
Subject: Mail quota warning
Mime-Version: 1.0
Content-Type: text/plain; charset=iso-8859-1
Content-Transfer-Encoding: 7bit

Your mailbox on the server is now more than 75% full. So that you can
continue to receive mail you need to remove some messages from your mailbox.
```

Maildrop has delivered the message, and it created a mail quota warning message in the recipient's mailbox. Because the mailbox is said to be 75 percent full, your next message will saturate the hardlimit; maildrop will have to bounce the message back to rubble@example.com:

```
# /usr/sbin/sendmail -f rubble@example.com bamm@example.com < /root/testmessage
```

In the mail log, you should see that the message was bounced back to the sender:

```
# tail -f /var/log/maillog
Jul 27 09:59:18 mail postfix/pickup[29788]: 4C083229F09: uid=0
  from=<rubble@example.com>
Jul 27 09:59:18 mail postfix/cleanup[29793]: 4C083229F09:
  message-id=<20040727075918.4C083229F09@mail.example.com>
Jul 27 09:59:18 mail postfix/qmgr[29789]: 4C083229F09:
  from=<rubble@example.com>, size=5250843, nrcpt=1 (queue active)
Jul 27 09:59:19 mail postfix/pipe[29795]: 4C083229F09: to=<bamm@example.com>,
  relay=maildrop, delay=1, status=bounced (permission denied. Command output:
  maildrop: maildir over quota. )
```

The bounce notifies the sender, rubble@example.com, that delivery was not possible due to the following reason: <bamm@example.com>: permission denied. Command output: maildrop: maildir over quota.

Configuring Courier IMAP

The last server that you need to configure is Courier IMAP. If you're not familiar with it already, Courier supports the Maildir format and offers POP, POP-SSL, IMAP, and IMAP-SSL services to clients.

Installing Courier IMAP

To install the Courier IMAP server, download the source code from http://www.courier-mta.org/download.php#imap. As a normal user, extract the archive, change to the new directory, and run configure as follows.

```
$ ./configure --enable-workarounds-for-imap-client-bugs --enable-unicode
  --without-authpgsql --without-socks
$ make
```

The configuration process automatically detects LDAP libraries on your machine.

NOTE *If you're running Red Hat, add --with-redhat to the configuration options to enable a Red Hat–specific workaround.*

After the configuration is complete, switch to root and run `make install install-configure` to install the software and the documentation.

Configuring Courier IMAP to Use Its LDAP Authentication Daemon

Courier uses a modular authentication backend (the modules are located in `/usr/lib/courier-imap/libexec/authlib` if you compiled Courier IMAP with the default options). To configure the Courier authentication daemon (`authdaemon`) for exclusive LDAP authentication, change the value of the `authmodulelist` parameter in `/usr/lib/courier-imap/etc/authdaemonrc` to read as follows:

```
authmodulelist="authldap"
```

For consistency, you should remove all other module names from the `authmodulelist`.

While still editing the `authdaemonrc` file, go to the end of the file and change or add the version parameter to include only `authdaemond.ldap` (otherwise, `authdaemon` chooses the first `authdaemond.*` module that it finds):

```
version="authdaemond.ldap"
```

Configuring the Authentication Backend

You now need to tell the authentication backend about your LDAP server and directory. To configure the `authdaemond.ldap` module, change the default entries in `/usr/lib/courier-imap/etc/authldaprc` to match your server and directory. To make it work with the example in this chapter, specify the following parameters:

LDAP_SERVER	mail.example.com
LDAP_BASEDN	dc=example,dc=com
LDAP_MAIL	mail
LDAP_FILTER	(objectClass=inetorgperson)
LDAP_HOMEDIR	homeDirectory
LDAP_MAILDIR	mailbox
LDAP_MAILDIRQUOTA	quota

```
LDAP_CLEARPW          userPassword
LDAP_UID              uidNumber
LDAP_GID              gidNumber
```

NOTE *The comments in authldaprc are quite helpful for explaining the parameters.*

Creating the IMAP Certificate

The only thing left to do is to create a security certificate for Courier IMAP. Although Courier creates one automatically upon starting up imapd-ssl (and it comes with the mkimapdcert utility), we can't really use it because it isn't signed by our certification authority.

Follow these steps to create the certificate:

1. Assuming that you set up your own CA as described in Chapter 17, you can create an imapd certificate as follows:

    ```
    # openssl req -new -nodes -keyout imapd_private_key.pem -out
      imapd_private_key.pem -days 365
    ```

2. Sign the key with your CA, creating the public certificate:

    ```
    # openssl ca -policy policy_anything -out imapd_public_cert.pem -infiles
      imapd_private_key.pem
    ```

3. Creating the certificate file for Courier IMAP is a little different than for Postfix TLS and OpenLDAP. Concatenate both key files to create an imapd.pem file:

    ```
    # cat imapd_private_key.pem imapd_public_cert.pem > imapd.pem
    ```

4. Copy the certificate to where Courier can find it, and set the correct permissions to protect the private key inside the file:

    ```
    # cp imapd.pem /usr/lib/courier-imap/share/imapd.pem
    # chmod 600 /usr/lib/courier-imap/share/imapd.pem
    # chown root /usr/lib/courier-imap/share/imapd.pem
    ```

5. Start the SSL instance of imapd:

    ```
    # /usr/lib/courier-imap/libexec/imapd-ssl.rc start
    ```

6. Use ps to make sure that it started:

    ```
    # ps auxwww | grep imapd-ssl
    root  1676  0.0  0.3  1940  500 ?  S  16:08  0:00 /usr/lib/ \
    ```

```
courier-imap/libexec/couriertcpd -address=0 \
-stderrlogger=/usr/lib/courier-imap/sbin/courierlogger \
-stderrloggername=imapd-ssl -maxprocs=40 -maxperip=4 \
-pid=/var/run/imapd-ssl.pid -nodnslookup -noidentlookup 993 \
/usr/lib/courier-imap/bin/couriertls \
root  1680  0.0  0.2  1952  340 ?  S  16:08  0:00 /usr/lib/ \
courier-imap/sbin/courierlogger imapd-ssl
root  1810  0.0  0.4  4600  564 pts/0  S  17:24  0:00 grep imapd-ssl
```

NOTE *You can use the scripts in /usr/lib/courier-imap/libexec and copy them to your init.d directory to have Courier started and stopped automatically when you change runlevels.*

Testing the IMAP Server

To verify that your IMAP server is accessible and that users can log in, connect to port 143 of your server and carry out a session. Connect to the server as follows:

```
# telnet mail.example.com 143
* OK [CAPABILITY IMAP4rev1 UIDPLUS CHILDREN NAMESPACE \
    THREAD=ORDEREDSUBJECT THREAD=REFERENCES SORT QUOTA \
    IDLE ACL ACL2=UNION STARTTLS] Courier-IMAP ready. \
    Copyright 1998-2004 Double Precision, Inc.  \
    See COPYING for distribution information.
```

After you see the preceding greeting message, log in:

```
. login bammbamm bamm_password
. OK LOGIN Ok.
```

Now select the inbox to see whether the folder is working properly:

```
. select INBOX
* FLAGS (\Draft \Answered \Flagged \Deleted \Seen \Recent)
* OK [PERMANENTFLAGS (\* \Draft \Answered \Flagged \Deleted \Seen)] Limited
* 5 EXISTS
* 0 RECENT
* OK [UIDVALIDITY 1089237749] Ok
* OK [MYRIGHTS "acdilrsw"] ACL
. OK [READ-WRITE] Ok
```

Finally, log out:

```
. logout
* BYE Courier-IMAP server shutting down
. OK LOGOUT completed
```

Testing IMAP over TLS

To test IMAP over TLS, use the s_client utility from OpenSSL instead of telnet. Let it connect to port 993 (the imaps port). This client displays quite a bit of certificate-checking output, but after the connection is established, you can use it just as you did with the preceding unencrypted session. Here's how it should look:

```
# openssl s_client -CAfile /usr/share/ssl/certs/cacert.pem -connect localhost:993
CONNECTED(00000003)
depth=1 /C=EX/ST=Examplia/L=Exampleton/O=Example Inc./OU=Certification
Authority/\
    CN=mail.example.com/emailAddress=certmaster@example.com
verify return:1
depth=0 /C=EX/ST=Examplia/L=Exampleton/O=Example Inc./OU=IMAP \
    services/CN=mail.example.com/emailAddress=postmaster@example.com
verify return:1
---
Certificate chain
 0 s:/C=EX/ST=Examplia/L=Exampleton/O=Example Inc./OU=IMAP services/\
    CN=mail.example.com/emailAddress=postmaster@example.com
   i:/C=EX/ST=Examplia/L=Exampleton/O=Example Inc./OU=Certification
    Authority/ CN=mail.example.com/emailAddress=certmaster@example.com
---
Server certificate
-----BEGIN CERTIFICATE-----
MIIEDDCCA3WgAwIBAgIBAzANBgkqhkiG9w0BAQQFADCBsDELMAkGA1UEBhMCRVgx
ETAPBgNVBAgTCEV4YW1wbGlhMRMwEQYDVQQHEwpFeGFtcGxldG9uMRUwEYDVQQK
EwxFeGFtcGxlIEluYy4xIDAeBgNVBAsTF0NlcnRpZmljYXRpb24gQXV0aG9yaXR5
MRkwFwYDVQQDExBtYWlsLmV4YW1wbGUuY29tMSUwIwYJKoZIhvcNAQkBFhZjZXJ0
bWFzdGVyQGV4YW1wbGUuY29tMB4XDTA0MDcxMzEzNTUzMloXDTA1MDcxMzEzNTUz
MlowgaYxCzAJBgNVBAYTAkVYMREwDwYDVQQIEwhFeGFtcGxpYTETMBEGA1UEBxMK
RXhhbXBsZXRvbjEVMBMGA1UEChMMRXhhbXBsZSBJbmMuMRYwFAYDVQQLEw1JTUFQ
IHNlcnZpY2VzMRkwFwYDVQQDExBtYWlsLmV4YW1wbGUuY29tMSUwIwYJKoZIhvcN
AQkBFhZwb3N0bWFzdGVyQGV4YW1wbGUuY29tMIGfMA0GCSqGSIb3DQEBAQUAA4GN
ADCBiQKBgQC95UUtw3dVVGghNLPEN3YBw/iKMkXtNhXllLAUEshZEIDGGjB1q9W8
QC4mLBOsWTYLTXWUbvoJHmBCmf6tzVv0i932r4KTDzanLP7EDc4tvg8ouhFxUEka
lVA+1g3l5oY8v1LIOYWxS8fpmRQENYHWncoShmXRPjg4wO6/2pZaawIDAQABo4IB
PDCCATgwCQYDVR0TBAIwADAsBglghkgBhvhCAQOEHxYdT3BlblNTTCBHZW5lcmF0
ZWQgQ2VydGlmaWNhdGUwHQYDVR0OBBYEFFK61+FMcqcC3M/Em3X2I8JCn8JuMIHd
BgNVHSMEgdUwgdKAFMNGZ7/NorS6WpJQJZ2IhDno97iXoYG2pIGzMIGwMQswCQYD
VQQGEwJFWDERMA8GA1UECBMIRXhhbXBsaWExEzARBgNVBAcTCkV4YW1wbGV0b24x
FTATBgNVBAoTDEV4YW1wbGUgSW5jLjEgMB4GA1UECxMXQ2VydGlmaWNhdGlvbiBB
dXRob3JpdHkxGTAXBgNVBAMTEG1haWwuZXhhbXBsZS5jb20xJTAjBgkqhkiG9w0B
CQEWFmNlcnRtYXN0ZXJAZXhhbXBsZS5jb22CAQAwDQYJKoZIhvcNAQEEBQADgYEA
iqd/nOvihp1EWF+K7hgbptl9v13tzyuE3TMSI3oXtGnQtYNLTvx3eaYDBecUQaI1
q1ocQBsvz17+noz9jwD69UlBWUANwxDuObPHmnr7CeePVnv6fAyZ4Jg9x8vAPzDD
Nu/Tu88M0kEVQ2XT35oPM+gDy3Mw44NrYB2xhky8Ptg=
-----END CERTIFICATE-----
```

```
subject=/C=EX/ST=Examplia/L=Exampleton/O=Example Inc./OU=IMAP services/\
    CN=mail.example.com/emailAddress=postmaster@example.com
issuer=/C=EX/ST=Examplia/L=Exampleton/O=Example Inc./OU=Certification
Authority/\
    CN=mail.example.com/emailAddress=certmaster@example.com
---
No client certificate CA names sent
---
SSL handshake has read 1202 bytes and written 340 bytes
---
New, TLSv1/SSLv3, Cipher is AES256-SHA
Server public key is 1024 bit
SSL-Session:
    Protocol  : TLSv1
    Cipher    : AES256-SHA
    Session-ID:
7AA6E031976D8B3846F1B2C8FCBEBEB777C89BAD16E548C0D8FE0B170BF1D49B
    Session-ID-ctx:
    Master-Key: E41CE39B98EFF3395936404F7142D2804FA7BBE63ADB6A57F3FB51\
    3A756E6D55F548A5765AC27F99F862F46664131C72
    Key-Arg   : None
    Krb5 Principal: None
    Start Time: 1089732738
    Timeout   : 300 (sec)
    Verify return code: 0 (ok)
---
* OK [CAPABILITY IMAP4rev1 UIDPLUS CHILDREN NAMESPACE THREAD=ORDEREDSUBJECT \
    THREAD=REFERENCES SORT QUOTA IDLE AUTH=PLAIN ACL ACL2=UNION] Courier-IMAP
    ready. \
    Copyright 1998-2004 Double Precision, Inc.  See COPYING for distribution
    information.
. login bamm@example.com bamm_secret
. OK LOGIN Ok.
. logout
* BYE Courier-IMAP server shutting down
. OK LOGOUT completed
closed
```

Congratulations! You now have a working LDAP-based mail server. But there still are a few things to do.

Advanced Configuration

Your mail server is functional, but you still have more work to do. At the moment, anyone who can connect to the LDAP server can retrieve security-related data, such as the userPassword attribute. Furthermore, all data retrieved by the various servers (including Postfix) conduct their LDAP sessions in plaintext.

Your first priority should be to address these security issues by tightening things up. This section shows you how to use bind users in an LDAP server so that you can limit what the LDAP server can send to a client. In addition, you'll see how to encrypt the LDAP session itself. As an added bonus, you'll configure ldapdb-based SMTP authentication and use it to enforce a company policy that prevents potential abuse of sender addresses.

Expanding the Directory

Controlling access to an LDAP directory and enforcing SMTP authentication require you to set up accounts for all servers that depend on the directory. To do this, you need to expand the directory tree to add another top branch that will keep servers separate from mail users. Figure 19-3 illustrates the new branch called ou=auth,dc=example,dc=com, which holds objects of the class account.

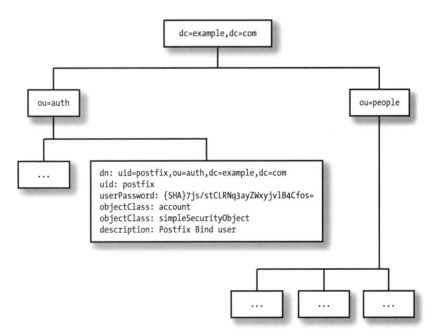

Figure 19-3: Authentication branch of Example Inc.

In the plaintext directory, you will use these attributes and schemata:

```
dn: ou=auth,dc=example,dc=com
ou: auth
objectClass: organizationalUnit
dn: uid=postfix,ou=auth,dc=example,dc=com
uid: postfix
objectClass: account
```

```
objectClass: simpleSecurityObject
description: Postfix Bind user
userPassword: {CRYPT}9lGRsJNHN5DrI
dn: uid=couriermaildrop,ou=auth,dc=example,dc=com
uid: couriermaildrop
objectClass: account
objectClass: simpleSecurityObject
description: Courier Maildrop Bind user
userPassword: {CRYPT}lA8iQdmwZRC86
dn: uid=courierimap,ou=auth,dc=example,dc=com
uid: courierimap
objectClass: account
objectClass: simpleSecurityObject
description: Courier IMAP Bind user
userPassword: {CRYPT}S1t1/3ENmjk1s
dn: uid=ldapdb,ou=auth,dc=example,dc=com
uid: ldapdb
objectClass: inetOrgPerson
givenName: ldapdb
sn: ldapdb
cn: ldapdb
userPassword: AvaAgO7i
mail: ldapdb
saslAuthzTo: ldap:///
ou=people,dc=example,dc=com??sub?(objectclass=inetOrgPerson)
```

Each server that accesses the LDAP directory (Postfix, Courier maildrop, Courier IMAP, and Cyrus SASL) through the ldapdb module will have its own account. The attributes in the uid=ldapdb,ou=auth,dc=example,dc=com object differ from the others as follows:

- The password is stored in plaintext format to enable the DIGEST-MD5 shared-secret authentication mechanism (this mechanism can't access encrypted passwords).
- The new mail attribute will be used instead of uid to authenticate users.
- The saslAuthzTo attribute defines where ldapdb can take another user's identity.

Adding Authentication to Servers

The first feature that we'll implement is mail relaying through SMTP authentication so that mobile and remote users with IP addresses outside the local trusted network can send mail. You already saw how to do this without LDAP in Understanding SMTP authentication, but this time we'll build and configure Cyrus SASL with the ldapdb plug-in. You could always do it with the saslauthd stand-alone daemon, but unfortunately, this daemon is limited to plaintext mechanisms. When you're through with this section, your Postfix server should be able to offer plaintext mechanisms (PLAIN, LOGIN) and shared-secret mechanisms (CRAM-MD5, DIGEST-MD5) to mail clients.

The authentication process differs slightly from what is described in Chapter 16, which discusses Postfix and Cyrus SASL interaction, because it uses an authorization ID to verify authentication. This identifier stems from the Cyrus IMAP project, where it is possible to allow a group of users to act on behalf of one user. For example, you can set Cyrus IMAP up to allow others to read a vacationing user's mail without exchanging any passwords.

The ldapdb authentication process works as follows:

1. A mail client using SMTP authentication connects to the Postfix server and transmits the username (and a passphrase if a plaintext mechanism is in use). This username is the *authentication ID* in the context of SASL.

2. The Postfix smtpd asks the SASL library to verify the credentials. The SASL library delegates this task to the ldapdb plug-in, which will get in contact with the LDAP server.

3. The ldapdb configuration for the Postfix smtpd daemon contains another username and passphrase (ldapdb transmits the passphrase only when the client uses a plaintext mechanism). This username is called the *authorization ID* in the context of SASL because it has permission to retrieve the passphrase from the mail user (the authentication ID).

4. If ldapdb succeeds in retrieving the passphrase from the LDAP server, it compares the string to the passphrase given by the mail client. The exact method of verification depends on the mechanism that the mail client used. Plaintext mechanisms mean that a simple comparison of strings will be performed, but shared-secret mechanisms cause ldapdb to calculate strings using the passphrase and to compare the strings.

   If either method succeeds, authentication was successful, and ldapdb transmits the information back to SASL, which then tells Postfix that it may grant relay access.

Applying the ldapdb Patch

The ldapdb plug-in was contributed to Cyrus SASL by OpenLDAP architect Howard Chu to enable shared-secret mechanisms to SASL authentication. Though ldapdb has been scheduled to be part of future Cyrus SASL versions, it hasn't made its way into the current release (as of Cyrus SASL 2.1.19). To make it easier to get ldapdb support for Cyrus SASL, we've created a patch that you can download from the http://www.postfix-book.com website.

To apply the patch to the Cyrus SASL source files, unpack a fresh SASL distribution and change into the new directory. Apply the patch as shown in the following example.

```
# patch -p1 < ../cyrus-sasl-2.1.19-ldapdb.patch
patching file config/openldap.m4
patching file configure.in
patching file doc/install.html
patching file doc/options.html
patching file doc/readme.html
patching file doc/sysadmin.html
patching file lib/staticopen.h
patching file plugins/ldapdb.c
patching file plugins/Makefile.am
patching file plugins/makeinit.sh
```

If the patch goes cleanly, build Cyrus SASL like this (notice the --with-ldap* options):

```
# ./configure \
  --with-plugindir=/usr/lib/sasl2 \
  --disable-java \
  --disable-krb4 \
  --with-dblib=berkeley \
  --with-saslauthd=/var/state/saslauthd \
  --without-pwcheck \
  --with-devrandom=/dev/urandom \
  --enable-cram \
  --enable-digest \
  --enable-plain \
  --enable-login \
  --disable-otp \
  --with-ldap=/usr \
  --with-ldapdb
```

After the configuration process completes, you can install or upgrade your current version of SASL by running **make install**. If you have not already done so, create a symbolic link from /usr/local/lib/sasl2 to /usr/lib/sasl2, because SASL will expect to find the libraries in that directory with these particular configuration options.

When you are finished, you should see these new ldapdb libraries in /usr/lib/sasl2:

```
# ls -la libldapdb.*
-rwxr-xr-x  1 root root    702 Jul 16 20:43 libldapdb.la
lrwxrwxrwx  1 root root     19 Jul 16 20:43 libldapdb.so -> libldapdb.so.2.0.19
lrwxrwxrwx  1 root root     19 Jul 16 20:43 libldapdb.so.2 -> libldapdb.so.2.0.19
-rwxr-xr-x  1 root root  94948 Jul 16 20:43 libldapdb.so.2.0.19
```

Configuring ldapdb

As explained earlier in the "Adding Authentication to Servers" section, you must create a SASL configuration for the Postfix smtpd daemon in /usr/lib/sasl2/smtpd.conf to make SASL available to Postfix.

Here's an example:

```
pwcheck_method: auxprop
auxprop_plugin: ldapdb
mech_list: PLAIN LOGIN DIGEST-MD5 CRAM-MD5
ldapdb_uri: ldap://mail.example.com
ldapdb_id: proxyuser
ldapdb_pw: proxy_secret
ldapdb_mech: DIGEST-MD5
log_level: 7
```

The additional LDAP-related configuration parameters are `ldapdb_id` and `ldapdb_pw`. The username here is the authorization ID. (Remember that the ldapdb plug-in requires smtpd to use the authorization ID before it can become the identity of the mail user and reauthenticate.)

Configuring the OpenLDAP Authorization Policy

You now have Postfix set up to bind to the OpenLDAP server, but you still need to configure the OpenLDAP `slapd` to authenticate the user and authorize it to become another user. First, select a policy that defines how `slapd` should handle the authenticated users. Set the `sasl-authz-policy` parameter in your `slapd.conf` file to one of the following choices:

none Disables authorization. This is the default setting.

from Requires each LDAP user to explicitly permit one or more users to act as the authorization ID. To allow authorization, they need to add the `saslAuthzFrom` attribute to their own user object. This attribute contains the `dn` (distinguished name) of the user that may take their identity.

to Permits all users to act as an authorization ID by default. With this policy, a user adds the `saslAuthzTo` attribute to their own user object, which defines where it is permissible to take another user's identity. The LDAP directory administrator must create a rule that allows only a limited number of users to assume other identities (to prevent abuse).

both Activates both of the `from` and `to` policies.

NOTE *You will find more detailed information in Chapter 10 of the "OpenLDAP Administrator's Guide" (http://www.openldap.org/doc/admin22/ sasl.html#SASL%20Proxy%20Authorization).*

We'll use to as the policy in this book because we believe it is easier for the administrator to limit who may take another identity than to add a new attribute to each user object. To configure the policy for the example in this chapter, add the following line to `slapd.conf`:

```
sasl-authz-policy        to
```

Configuring SASL OpenLDAP Binds

For the last step in enabling SASL-based binds to the OpenLDAP server, you need to configure `slapd` with the directory branch where credentials are stored. You also need to specify the query attribute for the given authentication ID. This is handled with a search filter called `sasl-regexp` that defines where the `smtpd` bind (authorization ID) should search for users it wants to authenticate.

Put the filter in your `slapd.conf` configuration file as follows:

```
sasl-regexp
    uid=(.*),cn=.*,cn=auth
    ldap:///dc=example,dc=com??sub?(&(objectclass=inetOrgPerson)(mail=$1))
```

NOTE   *The preceding regular expression does not look for a uid (login name), but rather, a mail address. This is intentional; many ISPs and mail service providers use the email address as the login name. There are many reasons for using the email address as the login, but the top two are that users need to memorize one less value, and it's easier to share authentication data with other systems, such as Radius servers.*

After your filter is in place, restart your OpenLDAP server, check the log for problems, and start testing.

Testing the ldapdb Plug-In

There are three points that you need to check in your ldapdb configuration:

- The mechanism limitation
- Direct SASL-based binding
- ldapdb-based authentication

Testing the Mechanism Limitation

Make sure that the `mech_list` parameter in your `/usr/lib/sasl2/slapd.conf` configuration is effective. Run **ldapsearch** as follows to list the mechanisms that `slapd` offers to clients:

```
# ldapsearch -LLL -x -s base -b "" "(objectClass=*)" supportedSASLMechanisms
dn:
supportedSASLMechanisms: DIGEST-MD5
```

If your output looks like this, you're in good shape. Otherwise check your `slapd.conf` file for typos.

Testing Direct SASL Binds

Verify that a user in your directory can bind directly to `slapd` using SASL (without the ldapdb plug-in) by using the `ldapwhoami` command.

```
# ldapwhoami -U bamm@example.com
SASL/DIGEST-MD5 authentication started
Please enter your password:
SASL username: bamm@example.com
SASL SSF: 128
SASL installing layers
dn:uid=bammbamm,ou=it,ou=people,dc=example,dc=com
```

This test verifies that you can actually authenticate as a user. If it fails, you're not going to get any further. Refer back to the section "Configuring SASL OpenLDAP Binds" to see if you made any mistakes.

Testing ldapdb Authentication

Cyrus SASL comes with utilities named server and client that allow you to test authentication independent of other servers. Using them eliminates any side effects that packages such as Postfix might introduce, and it allows you to zero in on SASL-based problems, including those that involve ldapdb.

To test authentication, first create a symlink from smtpd.conf to sample.conf for use by server:

```
# cd /usr/lib/sasl2/
# ln -s smtpd.conf sample.conf
```

Now, open a terminal window and start server:

```
# ./server -s rcmd -p 23
trying 10, 1, 6
socket: Address family not supported by protocol
trying 2, 1, 6
```

Open a second terminal window, and start client with the LDAP uid of a user in your LDAP server. This program asks you for the authentication ID and the authorization ID. Here's how you would do it for bammbamm (dn: uid=bammbamm,ou=it,ou=people,dc=example,dc=com):

```
# ./client -s rcmd -p 23 -m PLAIN mail.example.com
receiving capability list... recv: {31}
LOGIN PLAIN DIGEST-MD5 CRAM-MD5
LOGIN PLAIN DIGEST-MD5 CRAM-MD5
please enter an authentication id: bammbamm
please enter an authorization id: bammbamm
Password:
send: {5}
PLAIN
send: {1}
Y
```

```
send: {29}
bammbamm[0]bammbamm[0]bamm_secret
successful authentication
closing connection
```

NOTE *The authorization ID will be replaced by the value specified by the* `ldapdb_id` *parameter in your* `sample.conf` *file, but you still need to provide something at the prompt.*

If you see `successful authentication` (as in the preceding output), ldapdb-based authentication works. Otherwise, take a look at your authentication log and the Cyrus SASL logs to figure out what went wrong.

Protecting Directory Data

For security reasons, you don't want to make all data on your LDAP server readable by anyone who queries the server. You can restrict read access on a server by putting access control lists (ACLs) on users that bind to the LDAP server. It's a two-step process:

1. Configure the LDAP server to limit read access.
2. Configure the LDAP-dependent packages to bind to the LDAP server.

Limiting Directory Read Access

In the earlier "Expanding the Directory" section, you added bind users to your directory. Now you must tell `slapd` what parts of the directory the bind users may access, as well as what other users (such as anonymous users) may do.

Add the following rules to your /etc/openldap/slapd.conf file:

```
# Access rules for saslAuthzTo
access to dn.subtree="dc=example,dc=com" attr=saslAuthzTo
    by dn.base="cn=Manager,dc=example,dc=com"                 write
    by *                                                       read
# Access rules for userPassword
# authenticated users (self) and the directory Manager may
# change their (own) password.
# anybody else may access the passwords during authentication
access to dn.subtree="dc=example,dc=com"
    attr=userPassword
    by self                                                   write
    by dn.base="cn=Manager,dc=example,dc=com"                 write
    by dn.base="uid=courierimap,ou=auth,dc=example,dc=com"    read
    by *                                                       auth
# Access rules for uidNumber, gidNumber, mailbox, homeDirectory, quota
# The only one to change their values is Manager.
# Applications that need these values may read them.
# Authenticated users may read their own data.
# Anybody else may not access these data.
```

```
access to dn.subtree="dc=example,dc=com"
    attr=uidNumber attr=gidNumber attr=mailbox attr=homeDirectory attr=quota
    by dn.base="cn=Manager,dc=example,dc=com"                      write
    by dn.base="uid=courierimap,ou=auth,dc=example,dc=com"         read
    by dn.base="uid=couriermaildrop,ou=auth,dc=example,dc=com"     read
    by dn.base="uid=postfix,ou=auth,dc=example,dc=com"             read
    by self                                                        read
    by *                                                           none
# Access rules for attributes mail, uid and maildrop
# Applications may access these attributes.
# Authenticated users may do so as well
# Anybody else may read them as well
access to dn.subtree="dc=example,dc=com"
    attrs=mail attr=uid attr=maildrop
    by dn.base="uid=courierimap,ou=auth,dc=example,dc=com"         read
    by dn.base="uid=postfix,ou=auth,dc=example,dc=com"             read
    by dn.base="uid=ldapdb,ou=auth,dc=example,dc=com"              read
    by self                                                        read
    by *                                                           read
# Fallback rule
# Any attribute that wasn't addressed above may be read by anyone.
access to * by * read
```

Restart your LDAP server after adding the rules.

This is a relatively simple ACL rule set that works well with the schema and applications in this chapter. You can create finer access rules; have a look at the slapd.access(5) manual page, or get one of the current LDAP books.

Configuring Bind Users in LDAP Clients

With the OpenLDAP ACLs in place, you need to configure each of your packages that access the LDAP server to connect as a bind user.

Configuring Postfix as a Bind User

To make Postfix connect to an LDAP server as a bind user, you must change three parameters in the configuration files in /etc/postfix/ldap. The parameters are bind, bind_dn, and bind_pw:

- The bind parameter must be set to yes to enable the bind user.
- The bind_dn parameter sets the distinguished name of the bind user. In this chapter's example, you can set bind_dn = uid=postfix,ou=auth, dc=example,dc=com.
- The bind_pw parameter sets the password (in plaintext).

NOTE   *You can see that you need to secure this data, because it contains a password. This is the reason why we created a separate directory for LDAP query configuration files at the beginning of this chapter.*

After you're finished, all of your configuration files in /etc/postfix/ldap should contain lines like this:

```
bind = yes
bind_dn = uid=postfix,ou=auth,dc=example,dc=com
bind_pw = Yanggt!
```

Configuring Courier Maildrop as a Bind User

The Courier maildrop parameters are almost the same as those for Postfix, except that there is no parameter to switch the bind system on (if you do not specify a bind distinguished name, Courier won't try to bind). The parameters that you'll place in your /etc/maildropldap file are binddn and bindpw; the configuration should look something like this:

```
binddn    uid=couriermaildrop,ou=auth,dc=example,dc=com
bindpw    Yrj6Hl6r
```

CAUTION   *Now that you have a password in plaintext, verify that /etc/maildropldap is accessible only to root.*

Configuring Courier IMAP as a Bind User

The last client that you need to configure as a bind user is Courier IMAP. As with Courier maildrop, there are only two parameters that you need to set in your /usr/lib/courier-imap/etc/authldaprc file—LDAP_BINDDN and LDAP_BINDPW:

```
LDAP_BINDDN    uid=courierimap,ou=auth,dc=example,dc=com
LDAP_BINDPW    X5mYpl6p
```

CAUTION   *As before, make sure that your IMAP LDAP configuration file (/usr/lib/courier-imap/etc/authldaprc) is accessible only by root.*

Testing Server Restrictions

To test the servers, refer back to the section "Testing LDAP Recipients"; all you need to do is make sure that each component can retrieve data from the LDAP server. If you run into problems, check your log files. In particular, have a close look at the slapd log file. If you need to adjust the slapd logging level, adjust the loglevel parameter as described in the slapd.conf(5) manual page.

Encrypting LDAP Queries

Although you are now protecting the data on your LDAP server from unauthorized users, you still haven't done anything about keeping the data safe when it is being transmitted over an insecure network. This section shows you how to use TLS to protect the communication layer.

Configuring TLS for OpenLDAP

Before you try to configure TLS for your installation of LDAP, verify that slapd supports TLS. Running ldd on slapd usually shows dependencies on the SSL library if TLS is supported:

```
# ldd /usr/sbin/slapd
        libslapd_db-4.1.so => /usr/lib/libslapd_db-4.1.so (0x00116000)
        libsasl2.so.2 => /usr/lib/libsasl2.so.2 (0x00101000)
        libkrb5.so.3 => /usr/lib/libkrb5.so.3 (0x00a6f000)
        libk5crypto.so.3 => /usr/lib/libk5crypto.so.3 (0x00ad8000)
        libcom_err.so.2 => /lib/libcom_err.so.2 (0x00a6a000)
        libssl.so.4 => /lib/libssl.so.4 (0x00b11000)
        libcrypto.so.4 => /lib/libcrypto.so.4 (0x00977000)
        libcrypt.so.1 => /lib/libcrypt.so.1 (0x008d0000)
        libresolv.so.2 => /lib/libresolv.so.2 (0x00965000)
        libdl.so.2 => /lib/libdl.so.2 (0x008b8000)
        libwrap.so.0 => /usr/lib/libwrap.so.0 (0x00bfe000)
        libpthread.so.0 => /lib/libpthread.so.0 (0x00912000)
        libc.so.6 => /lib/libc.so.6 (0x0076e000)
        libgssapi_krb5.so.2 => /usr/lib/libgssapi_krb5.so.2 (0x00afc000)
        libz.so.1 => /usr/lib/libz.so.1 (0x008bd000)
        /lib/ld-linux.so.2 => /lib/ld-linux.so.2 (0x00759000)
        libnsl.so.1 => /lib/libnsl.so.1 (0x008fe000)
```

You will need to perform the following steps to configure slapd with TLS:

1. Create X509 certificates for slapd.
2. Configure slapd to offer TLS.
3. Configure the LDAP clients to use TLS.

Creating X509 Certificates for slapd

As with any server that offers SSL-derived encryption, you must create certificates for slapd that contain public and private keys. Chapter 17 explains how to create the certificates.

Assuming that you run your own CA, you could create a private key file named slapd_private_key.pem for slapd as follows:

```
# openssl req -new -nodes -keyout slapd_private_key.pem -out \
  slapd_private_key.pem -days 365
```

The corresponding command to create a public key named slapd_public_cert.pem is as follows:

```
# openssl ca -policy policy_anything -out slapd_public_cert.pem -infiles \
  slapd_private_key.pem
```

Now create a subdirectory named certs for your keys in /etc/openldap. After copying the .pem files into the subdirectory, it should look like this:

```
# ls -la /etc/openldap/certs/
total 24
drwx------    2 ldap     ldap         4096 Jun 21 22:31 .
drwxr-xr-x    4 root     root         4096 Jun 21 23:12 ..
-rw-------    1 ldap     ldap         1624 Jun 21 22:31 slapd_private_key.pem
-rw-------    1 ldap     ldap         3807 Jun 21 22:31 slapd_public_cert.pem
```

CAUTION *Make sure that you change the ownership and permissions of the files so that they are accessible only to the user that runs slapd.*

Configuring slapd to Offer TLS

To tell slapd about your new certificate files, you need to add four parameters to your slapd.conf file:

```
TLSCACertificateFile /usr/share/ssl/certs/cacert.pem
TLSCertificateFile /etc/openldap/certs/slapd_public_cert.pem
TLSCertificateKeyFile /etc/openldap/certs/slapd_private_key.pem
TLSVerifyClient demand
```

The TLSCACertificateFile parameter specifies the location of the CA certificate. In this example, slapd looks at a single file for this certificate, but you may need more than one file. If this is the case, you can omit the filename and have slapd search the entire directory. You will also need to use c_rehash from the OpenSSL utilities to index the directory, as described in Chapter 18.

NOTE *Your CA certificates should be in a location that the rest of the LDAP clients can access.*

You can set the TLSVerifyClient parameter to one of never, allow, try, or demand to restrict access for certain kinds of authentication. You need to make sure that the TLS settings work on the client side, so set this parameter to demand to force clients to use TLS. This makes it easy to find out whether the clients support it.

Configuring TLS for LDAP Clients

This section shows you how to turn on client-side LDAP support in Postfix and Courier IMAP. At the moment, Courier maildrop cannot do TLS, but this isn't really a problem, because the LDA doesn't need to know any user passwords.

Turning On Postfix LDAP Support

Postfix needs its own public certificate and private key to access the LDAP server over TLS. You should have already created the key files in Chapter 17, so you can reuse them.

To enable TLS over LDAP, you must add the following parameters to all LDAP query configuration files in /etc/postfix/ldap:

```
version = 3
tls_ca_cert_file = /usr/share/ssl/certs/cacert.pem
tls_cert = /etc/postfix/certs/postfix_public_cert.pem
tls_key = /etc/postfix/certs/postfix_private_key.pem
start_tls = yes
```

The parameters work as follows:

version

Sets the version of the LDAP protocol. By default, Postfix uses version 2, but TLS requires version 3.

tls_ca_cert_file

Specifies the CA certificate.

tls_cert

Specifies the public certificate for Postfix.

tls_key

Specifies the private key for Postfix.

start_tls

Enables TLS.

Enabling LDAP Queries for Courier IMAP

To enable LDAP over TLS for Courier IMAP, you need to follow a configuration strategy different from that of Postfix because Courier does not come with its own LDAP client, but rather uses the one that comes with OpenLDAP. You need to configure the OpenLDAP client to use TLS, and then tell Courier IMAP to request LDAP over TLS from the OpenLDAP client.

The OpenLDAP client configuration file is usually /etc/openldap/ldap.conf. You need to add the following TLS_* parameters to enable TLS support:

```
URI ldap://mail.example.com
BASE dc=example,dc=com
TLS_CACERT /usr/share/ssl/certs/cacert.pem
TLS_CERT /etc/openldap/certs/slapd_public_cert.pem
TLS_KEY /etc/openldap/certs/slapd_private_key.pem
TLS_REQCERT demand
```

The parameters are similar to the ones for Postfix:

TLS_CACERT

Specifies the CA certificate that the rest of the packages in this chapter use.

TLS_CERT

Specifies the client's public certificate.

TLS_KEY

Specifies the client's private key. If you like, you can reuse the slapd certificate and key.

TLS_REQCERT

Specifies the policy for requesting the server certificate. Set it to demand in order to force TLS or drop the connection.

Because you already told the OpenLDAP client about the certificate and keys, you just need to tell Courier IMAP to request TLS for LDAP in your /usr/lib/courier-imap/etc/authldaprc file:

```
LDAP_TLS          1
```

With this final piece in place, you can restart Courier IMAP and test it.

Testing TLS

The TLS parameters that you just added to your configuration added a lot of complexity, so it's important that you test it carefully.

1. Test the application all others turn to—the LDAP server. Test the LDAP server's own client.

2. If that works, turn to Postfix and see if it can connect. Verify that Courier IMAP is able to use the LDAP client to get SSL.

Testing the OpenLDAP Server

The first test is to make sure that the OpenLDAP server offers TLS certificates. There really isn't any simple command for checking this on port 389 (where you normally find TLS1 for LDAP). We'll see if we can go to port 636 (where OpenLDAP offers SSL) to see if slapd will be satisfied with the certificates.

Use the s_client utility to connect to the server as follows:

```
# openssl s_client -CAfile /usr/share/ssl/certs/cacert.pem -connect localhost:636
CONNECTED(00000003)
depth=1 /C=EX/ST=Examplia/L=Exampleton/O=Example Inc./OU=Certification
Authority/\
    CN=mail.example.com/emailAddress=certmaster@example.com
verify return:1
depth=0 /C=EX/ST=Examplia/L=Exampleton/O=Example Inc./OU=LDAP services/\
    CN=mail.example.com/emailAddress=ldapmaster@example.com
verify return:1
---
Certificate chain
 0 s:/C=EX/ST=Examplia/L=Exampleton/O=Example Inc./OU=LDAP services/\
    CN=mail.example.com/emailAddress=ldapmaster@example.com
   i:/C=EX/ST=Examplia/L=Exampleton/O=Example Inc./OU=Certification Authority/\
    CN=mail.example.com/emailAddress=certmaster@example.com
 1 s:/C=EX/ST=Examplia/L=Exampleton/O=Example Inc./OU=Certification Authority/\
```

```
          CN=mail.example.com/emailAddress=certmaster@example.com
      i:/C=EX/ST=Examplia/L=Exampleton/O=Example Inc./OU=Certification Authority/\
        CN=mail.example.com/emailAddress=certmaster@example.com
---
Server certificate
-----BEGIN CERTIFICATE-----
MIIEDDCCA3WgAwIBAgIBAjANBgkqhkiG9w0BAQQFADCBsDELMAkGA1UEBhMCRVgx
ETAPBgNVBAgTCEV4YW1wbGlhMRMwEQYDVQQHEwpFeGFtcGxldG9uMRUwEwYDVQQK
EwxFeGFtcGxlIEluYy4xIDAeBgNVBAsTF0NlcnRpZmljYXRpb24gQXV0aG9yaXR5
MRkwFwYDVQQDExBtYWlsLmV4YW1wbGUuY29tMSUwIwYJKoZIhvcNAQkBFhZjZXJ0
bWFzdGVyQGV4YW1wbGUuY29tMB4XDTA0MDcxMzEzNTQwNloXDTA1MDcxMzEzNTQw
NlowgaYxCzAJBgNVBAYTAkVYMREwDwYDVQQIEwhFeGFtcGxYTETMBEGA1UEBxMK
RXhhbXBsZXRvbjEVMBMGA1UEChMMRXhhbXBsZSBJbmMuMRYwFAYDVQQLEw1MREFQ
IHNlcnZpY2VzMRkwFwYDVQQDExBtYWlsLmV4YW1wbGUuY29tMSUwIwYJKoZIhvcN
AQkBFhZsZGFwbWFzdGVyQGV4YW1wbGUuY29tMIGfMA0GCSqGSIb3DQEBAQUAA4GN
ADCBiQKBgQDcqVcyPn4qhI65sAdPgu+Et2vzWsyHT/IT39mZ6Gqrh15Oa/eQA7Lz
GmUKR/t/W4ol28ygN/udpkHZiTUDjUC5ENF7kqk4vnx/4DpwmDmOjNgO7JJErOFL
cOJl/KqZzAItBh32KtIhV8BQcdlfzdoxEqO7MkxRw1pu7LyLo5qOkwIDAQABo4IB
PDCCATgwCQYDVR0TBAIwADAsBglghkgBhvhCAQOEHxYdT3BlblNTTCBHZW5lcmF0
ZWQgQ2VydGlmaWNhdGUwHQYDVR0OBBYEFCKdRZglsm4/1io2sltD1riyCE+KMIHd
BgNVHSMEgdUwgdKAFMNGZ7/NorS6WpJQJZ2IhDno97iXoYG2pIGzMIGwMQswCQYD
VQQGEwJFWDERMA8GA1UECBMIRXhhbXBsaWExEzARBgNVBAcTCkV4YW1wbGV0b24x
FTATBgNVBAoTDEV4YW1wbGUgSW5jLjEgMB4GA1UECxMXQ2VydGlmaWNhdGlvbiBB
dXRob3JpdHkxGTAXBgNVBAMTEG1haWwuZXhhbXBsZS5jb20xJTAjBgkqhkiG9w0B
CQEWFmNlcnRtYXN0ZXJAZXhhbXBsZS5jb22CAQAwDQYJKoZIhvcNAQEEBQADgYEA
AZCH5A23WVdIdO9NkD23Bz3HF+MyOf8fUx1CaQbLwo572mjgB/O3H7K969bU/te2
BeLOjifMo/vexXPMeajwzDnIKm/yJO7eNt85eeKciI6MZJVhvuPvtp/Rc5vArcas
HNqpmm7oDAEFIRclHsfhsyAHwsTTr18UGndfL3Hetkw=
-----END CERTIFICATE-----
subject=/C=EX/ST=Examplia/L=Exampleton/O=Example Inc./OU=LDAP services/\
    CN=mail.example.com/emailAddress=ldapmaster@example.com
issuer=/C=EX/ST=Examplia/L=Exampleton/O=Example Inc./OU=Certification
Authority/CN=mail.example.com/emailAddress=certmaster@example.com
---
Acceptable client certificate CA names
/C=EX/ST=Examplia/L=Exampleton/O=Example Inc./OU=Certification Authority/\
    CN=mail.example.com/emailAddress=certmaster@example.com
---
SSL handshake has read 2402 bytes and written 352 bytes
---
New, TLSv1/SSLv3, Cipher is AES256-SHA
Server public key is 1024 bit
SSL-Session:
    Protocol  : TLSv1
    Cipher    : AES256-SHA
    Session-ID:
21430E35213A797176B28B16BF24D20EC9019902B5B09FCEDDA0333682FD6F7D
    Session-ID-ctx:
    Master-Key:
45636217FD3136A536CE62618DBC1CA92E6E0B1E773F75120632F761C289943BB\
    85F78369C622A0D78DB60726147465F
    Key-Arg   : None
```

```
      Krb5 Principal: None
      Start Time: 1089733870
      Timeout   : 300 (sec)
      Verify return code: 0 (ok)
---
QUIT
DONE
```

If you get a return code of 0 (ok), the certificates check out. Now you can test whether you can use the LDAP client to query the server over TLS.

Testing the OpenLDAP Client

To see whether the OpenLDAP client works, try to retrieve data with the ldapsearch command as follows:

```
# ldapsearch -ZZ -x -LLL "(mail=bamm@example.com)" userPassword
dn: ou=people,dc=example,dc=com
dn: ou=it,ou=people,dc=example,dc=com
dn: uid=bammbamm,ou=it,ou=people,dc=example,dc=com
userPassword:: YmFtbV9zZWNyZXQ=
```

This ldapsearch command is particularly useful because it reads the default settings in ldap.conf; recall that the Courier IMAP TLS/LDAP configuration depends on these. Furthermore, this query mimics a Courier IMAP query. The -ZZ option forces ldapsearch to use TLS.

If this command doesn't work, have a close look at your ldap.conf file and your logs.

Testing Postfix

To test Postfix's LDAP over TLS support, run a **postmap** command to query the directory for a known recipient. Here's an example from this chapter:

```
# postmap -q "bamm@example.com" ldap:/etc/postfix/ldap/local_recipients.cf
bammbamm
```

If this doesn't work, see if it works without TLS support. After you've got it working, re-enable the TLS settings and set the debuglevel in your Postfix LDAP configuration file (for example, /etc/postfix/ldap/local_recipients.cf) to at least 1, so that you can pore over some descriptive logging information.

Testing Courier IMAP

You just tested some of the underpinnings of the Courier IMAP configuration in the "Testing the OpenLDAP Client" section. To verify that everything works, connect to the IMAP port and log in as you did in the section "Testing the IMAP Server." A successful login looks like this:

```
# telnet mail.example.com 143
* OK [CAPABILITY IMAP4rev1 UIDPLUS CHILDREN NAMESPACE \
    THREAD=ORDEREDSUBJECT THREAD=REFERENCES SORT QUOTA \
```

```
        IDLE ACL ACL2=UNION STARTTLS]
        Courier-IMAP ready. Copyright 1998-2004 Double Precision, Inc.\
        See COPYING for distribution information.
. login bamm@example.com bamm_secret
. OK LOGIN Ok.
. logout
* BYE Courier-IMAP server shutting down
. OK LOGOUT completed
```

Enforcing Valid Sender Addresses

Once users successfully connect to the Postfix server with SMTP authentication, they can relay messages through your server using any sender address that they desire. If you don't really trust your users that much, you can use a restriction called reject_authenticated_sender_login_mismatch, introduced in Postfix 2.1, that tells Postfix to enforce valid sender addresses. It works like this:

1. The user connects with a username using SMTP authentication.
2. When the user attempts to send a message, Postfix extracts the envelope-sender.
3. Postfix looks up the envelope sender in the maps configured with smtpd_sender_login_maps. Ideally, this is an LDAP-based map.
4. If the lookup returns the same username that was used for SMTP authentication, Postfix accepts the message. Otherwise Postfix rejects the message.

Creating the LDAP Map

You already have all of the data for the smtpd_sender_login_maps map in your directory, so it makes sense to reuse it, not only because you need no additional data, but also because there is no additional maintenance work. To set up the map, create a new file in /etc/postfix/ldap with the settings that you need for the query.

When you specify the attributes to be retrieved from the LDAP server as usernames, you can choose to permit only mail addresses used in mail attributes or to also allow senders to use their aliases (which are stored in the maildrop attribute).

Let's say that you want to create a configuration that permits both in the query file named /etc/postfix/ldap/mail_from_login.cf. Assuming that you have TLS enabled, the complete file should look like this:

```
version = 3
debuglevel = 0
server_host = ldap://mail.example.com
tls_ca_cert_file = /usr/share/ssl/certs/cacert.pem
tls_cert = /etc/postfix/certs/postfix_public_cert.pem
```

```
tls_key = /etc/postfix/certs/postfix_private_key.pem
tls_random_file = /dev/urandom
start_tls = yes
bind = yes
bind_dn = uid=postfix,ou=auth,dc=example,dc=com
bind_pw = Yanggt!
search_base = ou=people,dc=example,dc=com
query_filter = (|(mail=%s)(maildrop=%s))
result_attribute = mail
```

The only two parameters here that should be different from the other files in /etc/postfix/ldap are query_filter and result_attribute.

With the query map file in place, set the smtpd_sender_login_maps parameter in your main.cf file as follows:

```
smtpd_sender_login_maps = ldap:/etc/postfix/ldap/mail_from_login.cf
```

Configuring the smtpd Restriction

Finally, put everything in place for restricting senders to their own mail addresses by adding the reject_authenticated_sender_login_mismatch parameter to the list of restrictions in your main.cf file:

```
smtpd_recipient_restrictions =
    permit_mynetworks
    reject_authenticated_sender_login_mismatch
    permit_sasl_authenticated
    reject_unauth_destination
```

NOTE *This restriction applies only to users that have authentication, but it does not apply to anyone else. Therefore, users in your trusted networks can send mail as anyone they please. Furthermore, incoming mail from the rest of the Internet still works.*

Testing the smtpd Restriction

To test your new configuration, first see if the map works. Use postmap to match a regular recipient as follows:

```
# postmap -q "bamm@example.com" ldap:/etc/postfix/ldap/mail_from_login.cf
bammbamm
```

If you are permitting aliases as sender addresses, use postmap to query for an alias:

```
# postmap -q "postmaster@example.com" ldap:/etc/postfix/ldap/mail_from_login.cf
bammbamm
```

If this works, the last thing you need to test is an actual SMTP session. First, prepare a base64-encoded authentication string for the first stage of the connection:

```
# perl -MMIME::Base64 -e \
'print encode_base64("bamm\@example.com\0bamm\  @example.com\0bamm_secret");'
YmFtbUBleGFtcGxlLmNvbQBiYW1tQGV4YW1wbGUuY29tAGJhbW1fc2VjcmV0
```

Now, connect from a remote host to your Postfix server and authenticate using this string:

```
# telnet mail.example.com 25
220 mail.example.com ESMTP Postfix
EHLO client.example.com
250-mail.example.com
250-PIPELINING
250-SIZE 10240000
250-VRFY
250-ETRN
250-AUTH PLAIN LOGIN CRAM-MD5 DIGEST-MD5
250-AUTH=PLAIN LOGIN CRAM-MD5 DIGEST-MD5
250 8BITMIME
AUTH PLAIN YmFtbUBleGFtcGxlLmNvbQBiYW1tQGV4YW1wbGUuY29tAGJhbW1fc2VjcmV0
235 Authentication successful
```

Now, try to send a message as a different user (recall that you authenticated as Bamm Bamm):

```
MAIL FROM: <rubble@example.com>
250 Ok
RCPT TO: <wietse@porcupine.org>
553 <rubble@example.com>: Sender address rejected: not owned by user
bamm@example.com
```

Postfix detects the mismatch in the RCPT TO stage, because this is where the smtpd_recipient_restrictions parameter takes effect.

You should also try sending as the real user as well. If this works, there's nothing left to do. You're finished. Have fun!

20

RUNNING POSTFIX IN A CHROOT ENVIRONMENT

The chroot feature adds just another barrier against intrusion;
that barrier is meaningful only when the host is already running
in a hardened configuration.—Wietse Venema

Running Postfix in a chroot jail isolates it from the entire directory structure of the operating system. The goal is to protect the system from the intruder who manages to break into Postfix. In order to use this feature, you must lock a minimal number of files, applications, and other resources into a chroot jail directory.

Setting up a chroot jail requires no external programs. The distribution contains helper scripts that set up an appropriate chroot environment. This chapter both describes the theory of chroot environments and provides an SASL/TLS example that shows how chroot and Postfix actually work together.

The chroot scripts that come with Postfix can be found in the examples/ chroot-setup directory of the source tree. If you use prepackaged Postfix binaries, the packager probably added a few scripts that keep the contents of the chroot jail directory in sync with the filesystem outside of the jail.

The foolproof procedure for setting up a chroot jail is as follows:

1. Get things working without using chroot.
2. Convert Postfix daemons to a chroot setup, one at a time.

If you use this procedure, you can easily identify any daemons that break when chrooted and adjust the contents of the jail directory accordingly.

How Does a chroot Jail Work?

Imagine a burglar breaking a window to get into your house, but that window belongs to a high-security room. Not only does the room contain nothing of value, but the items in the room will not help the burglar get further into the house. The burglar has no choice but to give up.

For this to work, the architect must make sure that only things that are absolutely necessary are located in this high-security room. Furthermore, these items must be properly secured so they cannot be turned against the high-security room itself.

A chroot jail under Unix is much like this high-security room.

Basic Principles of a chroot Setup

These are the basic principles of a chroot setup:

Use the lowest privileges required to run applications
The more powerful the user, the more they can harm the system. In particular, root and programs running as root can break out of the chroot jail fairly easily. Therefore, programs running in the chroot jail should not run with superuser privileges, but with the lowest privilege level required to get their jobs done.

Drop privileges correctly
An application that provides a service offered on a low-numbered port, such as port 25, may need to be started as root in order to get access to the port. However, after the application gets what it needs, it should drop special access privileges correctly.

Keep the jail small and bare
Keep only the bare minimum of files in a chroot jail. The fewer there are, the less likely it is that you will provide an intruder with something to abuse.

Make the files in the jail owned by root and writable by root only
Applications running in the chroot jail should not be able to alter files within the jail. Change ownership and write permissions to root only.

Link configuration files from the outside

Symbolic links from inside the jail to files outside of it will not work for the system running inside the jail. Some systems share a configuration file between the jailed daemon and other utilities that are run from user mode. This requires all of the daemons to be able to access the configuration file, whether they are inside or outside the jail. Rather than rebuilding these utilities to use a special path (such as /chroot/named/etc/named.conf) you can create a symbolic link *from outside to inside* the jail, as in this example:

```
# ln -s /chroot/named/etc/named.conf /etc/named.conf
```

This allows most of the tools to operate normally, but you have to be a little more careful when editing files such as /etc/named.conf, because when you do so, you're affecting a jailed system.

Technical Implementation

The daemons chroot and drop privileges by themselves. This allows them to access /etc/postfix files (and open maps) before going to jail.

The chroot() system call alters how a process—after entering the chroot jail—perceives the filesystem to a process. Here's how it works:

1. The master daemon calls chdir(queue_directory).
2. The master daemon invokes the other Postfix daemons, telling each of them whether or not it should change the file system root or drop its privileges.

Except in very limited circumstances, it's impossible to escape this jail.

How Does chroot Affect Postfix?

When you run Postfix in a chroot jail, it affects the way Postfix sees the filesystem. Let's say that you chrooted to /var/spool/postfix. Although any other application may be able to see /var/spool/postfix (the queue directory) and anything else on the system, the Postfix daemons consider /var/spool/postfix to be / once they start chrooted. They can't access anything else outside of /var/spool/postfix.

This may require you to copy several files into the Postfix jail that are out of reach to the daemons that run chrooted:

Binaries (daemons)

You don't need to copy daemons into the chroot jail, because they are launched by the master daemon, which isn't chrooted.

Libraries needed by binaries

Programs load libraries before going to the jail, so you won't need to copy them to the jail.

Maps

Programs open static maps before going into the jail. However, you may need to create a socket in the chroot jail for database-driven maps (see the sockets point in this list).

Configuration files

The daemons read configuration files before going to the jail. There's no need to copy them into the jail.

Sockets

Socket files, such as the mysql socket or the SASL socket, need to be accessible to daemons inside the jail. Keep in mind that the MySQL client library may look for the socket in a place such as `/var/run/mysql.socket`, so you will need to put it in a place such as *queue_directory/*`var/run/mysql.socket`.

Files needed by libraries

The C library needs to look at files such as `/etc/resolv.conf` and `/etc/localtime` to work properly. You need to install copies of these files in `/var/spool/postfix`.

Helper Scripts for chroot

Postfix comes with several helper scripts in the `examples/chroot-setup` directory of the source tree. These scripts assist you in setting up a chroot jail for your particular operating system.

When you run Postfix chrooted, it checks that the basic required files, such as `/var/spool/postfix/etc/resolv.conf`, are present and up-to-date in the chroot jail. Postfix writes warnings to the log file if files inside and outside the chroot jail are out of sync. It's very important that you heed these warnings and act to fix the inconsistencies.

chrooted Daemons

Because the `master` daemon starts the rest of the Postfix daemons, it is the one that tells the daemons to run chrooted or not. You control chroot invocation in `/etc/postfix/master.cf`.

Enabling chroot

To run a daemon chrooted, you need to identify the service that invokes it in the `master.cf` file. Check the chroot column in `master.cf` to find the current chroot state of the daemon. Postfix SOURCE ships with every daemon set to n, but some distributions change that in their Postfix packages. That is, none of the daemons in a stock installation runs chrooted. To change it, change the chroot option from n or - to y.

For example, if you want to chroot the smtpd daemon, your configuration file might look like this:

```
# ==========================================================================
# service type  private unpriv  chroot  wakeup  maxproc command + args
#               (yes)   (yes)   (yes)   (never) (100)
# ==========================================================================
smtp      inet  n       -       y       -       -       smtpd
#smtps    inet  n       -       n       -       -       smtpd
#   -o smtpd_tls_wrappermode=yes -o smtpd_sasl_auth_enable=yes
...
pickup    fifo  n       -       n       60      1       pickup
cleanup   unix  n       -       n       -       0       cleanup
...
```

Notice that the chroot column entry for the smtp service has been changed to y. The master daemon will run this service chrooted after you reload Postfix.

chroot Limitations and Task Delegation

The documentation within master.cf indicates that you can run almost any daemon chrooted "*except* for the pipe, virtual, and local daemons":

pipe

> The pipe daemon spawns external programs, usually located outside the Postfix queue directory, and it therefore usually need files outside the queue directory.

local

> The local daemon takes care of local delivery and needs to have access to user home directories. It doesn't make much sense to run local chrooted, because this would imply that the home directories are below /var/spool/postfix, inside the chroot jail, where an intruder could possibly gain access to them.

virtual

> The virtual daemon takes care of local delivery, just like the local daemon. The logic against running the local daemon chrooted holds for this daemon too.

When using a chroot environment, other daemons may need to use the proxymap daemon in order to gain access to configuration data. For example, if a chrooted SMTP server needs access to the system passwd file in order to reject mail for nonexistent local addresses, it wouldn't be practical to maintain a copy of the passwd file in the chroot jail, because this would undermine the whole idea of running Postfix chrooted.

To keep security-related maps out of the jail, you can delegate lookups to the proxymap daemon (again, not running chrooted) with this configuration parameter:

```
local_recipient_maps = proxy:unix:passwd.byname $alias_maps
```

Keep in mind that because proxymap goes through the barrier of the jail, proxymap cannot proxy maps used in a security relevant context.

chroot Libraries, Configuration Files, and Other Files

Many programs need external files to function correctly. These files include:

- Libraries and other shared objects
- Configuration files
- Other files, such as socket devices

There are several ways of finding out which files a program needs. To find shared library dependencies, you can use ldd or chatr on most Unix variants. However, this will not be a problem with a standard Postfix installation, because all daemons are started and load their libraries before going into the chroot jail.

To find out what configuration files you need, use a program such as strace (on Linux), truss (on Solaris), or ktrace (on other Unix variants). One way of using strace is to start a program like this:

```
# strace -o ouputfile program
```

Then inspect the file output for open() calls:

```
# grep open outputfile | grep ENOENT
open("/etc/ld.so.preload", O_RDONLY)    = -1 ENOENT (No such file or directory)
open("/usr/share/locale/C/libdst.cat", O_RDONLY) = -1 ENOENT (No such file or directory)
open("/usr/share/locale/C/LC_MESSAGES/libdst.cat", O_RDONLY) = -1 ENOENT (No such file or directory)
open("/usr/share/locale/C/libdst.cat", O_RDONLY) = -1 ENOENT (No such file or directory)
open("/usr/share/locale/C/LC_MESSAGES/libdst.cat", O_RDONLY) = -1 ENOENT (No such file or directory)
open("/usr/share/locale/C/libisc.cat", O_RDONLY) = -1 ENOENT (No such file or directory)
open("/usr/share/locale/C/LC_MESSAGES/libisc.cat", O_RDONLY) = -1 ENOENT (No such file or directory)
open("/usr/share/locale/C/libisc.cat", O_RDONLY) = -1 ENOENT (No such file or directory)
open("/usr/share/locale/C/LC_MESSAGES/libisc.cat", O_RDONLY) = -1 ENOENT (No such file or directory)
open("/usr/share/locale/C/libdns.cat", O_RDONLY) = -1 ENOENT (No such file or directory)
open("/usr/share/locale/C/LC_MESSAGES/libdns.cat", O_RDONLY) = -1 ENOENT (No such file or directory)
open("/usr/share/locale/C/libdns.cat", O_RDONLY) = -1 ENOENT (No such file or directory)
open("/usr/share/locale/C/LC_MESSAGES/libdns.cat", O_RDONLY) = -1 ENOENT (No such file or directory)
```

Keep in mind that a program may try to open several versions of a configuration file before finding the correct one.

Alternatively, you can attach `strace` to a running process to see what it is trying to do. For example, if you'd like to see what the `master` daemon is doing, try something like this:

```
# ps auxwww|grep master
root  9004  0.0  0.3  3452  940 ?  S    07:49   0:00 /usr/lib/postfix/master
# strace -p 9004
Process 9004 attached - interrupt to quit
select(76, [10 11 12 15 17 18 21 23 24 26 27 29 30 32 33 35 36 38 39 41 42 44
45 47 48 50 51 53 54 56 57 59 60 62 63 65 66 68 69 71 72 74 75], [], [10 11 12
15 17 18 21 23 24 26 27 29 30 32 33 35 36 38 39 41 42 44 45 47 48 50 51 53 54
56 57 59 60 62 63 65 66 68 69 71 72 74 75], {22, 790000} <unfinished ...>
Process 9004 detached
```

Overcoming chroot Restrictions

The scripts that help you set up a chroot jail in the Postfix source distribution (in `examples/chroot-scripts`) can also tell you which system files you might need to copy into your chroot jail, such as the time zone files required by the C library. The following is an overview of the files you will need.

DNS

The C library needs certain files to implement name resolution correctly; for example, you need `/etc/resolv.conf`, `/etc/nsswitch.conf`, and `/etc/hosts` on a Linux system. These need to be inside the chroot jail, and the helper scripts can copy them for you.

Time settings

If you find that the logging produced by your Postfix daemon is off by several hours, you need to copy the time zone information (`/etc/localtime`) into the chroot jail.

Sockets

You can configure Postfix and saslauthd easily to work inside a Postfix chroot environment. All you need to do is configure Postfix and saslauthd with different paths for saslauthd's socket.

In the Postfix chroot jail (usually `/var/spool/postfix`), first create all required `run_path` subdirectories:

```
# mkdir /var/spool/postfix/var
# mkdir /var/spool/postfix/var/run
# mkdir /var/spool/postfix/var/run/saslauthd
# chmod 750 /var/spool/postfix/var/run/saslauthd
# chgrp postfix /var/spool/postfix/var/run/saslauthd
```

Now, add the saslauthd_path parameter to /usr/lib/sasl/smtpd.conf, which tells the chrooted smtpd where to look for the socket. Cut off the path that leads to the jail (that is, leave off /var/spool/postfix), and provide the path of the run_path, including the socket name (mux) as the value:

```
saslauthd_path: /var/run/saslauthd/mux
```

Finally, start saslauthd with the -m option, which defines where to create the socket. Give it the full path as seen outside the jail:

```
# /usr/sbin/saslauthd -m /var/spool/postfix/var/run/saslauthd/mux -a shadow
```

This way, both applications use the same socket to communicate, even though Postfix is running chrooted.

PART IV

TUNING POSTFIX

This part of the book provides hints on how to improve the performance of your server. Starting from commonplace problems, such as DNS caching and being an open relay, we progress to advanced concepts, including how to avoid bouncing undeliverable mail and setting up dedicated transports. You can employ blacklists to reduce the inflow of mail, and the experimental rate-limiting features of Postfix 2.1 are also worth looking at.

Remote Client Concurrency and Request Rate Limiting
Chapter 21 shows you a new feature for limiting the rate of client connections. This is a countermeasure for protecting Postfix from SMTP clients that inundate the `smtpd` daemon with too many connections at once.

Performance Tuning
Postfix is fast, but sometimes you can tune it to become even faster. You should read Chapter 22 if your Postfix does not perform as well as you think it should.

21

REMOTE CLIENT CONCURRENCY AND REQUEST RATE LIMITING

Postfix 2.1 and 2.2 implement remote client concurrency and rate limits. Rate limiting is a countermeasure for protecting Postfix from SMTP clients that inundate the smtpd daemon with too many connections at once. This chapter illustrates several instances where rate limiting is useful and shows you how to configure it.

The Basics of Rate Limiting

Even a well-tuned Postfix installation can handle only a finite amount of email traffic at one time. A server's capacity depends on parameters such as disk I/O throughput, CPU speed, and the speed of any virus scanners that are connected to Postfix. Before Postfix 2.1, it was possible for a single client to use all of the available smtpd Postfix server processes, locking out all other clients trying to deliver mail.

Hardware limitations, clients eating up connections, and complex configurations are enough to justify limiting the amount of incoming mail. However, there are other situations where rate limiting prevents mail deferral or otherwise lessens the ill effects on Postfix:

Virus and worm outbreaks

New viruses and worms spreading across a network normally attempt to propagate themselves as quickly as possible. Rate limiting slows the spread of malicious software by throttling the propagation speed.

Mail bombs

Mail bombs are large, continuous bursts of mail, usually sent from a single system to your system. Usually this happens with malicious intent, but it can also happen by accident. (For example, we've seen an antivirus product send one message per infected file—when this happens on a thoroughly infected system, your mail server may be flooded with more than 100 messages per minute.)

Runaway clients

The term "runaway client" is a generalization that includes virus or worm outbreaks and mail bombs; it refers to any client that is out of control, sending continuous stream of mails to your system. The client is not necessarily malicious—the problem could be caused by a programming or configuration error.

Spam from open proxies

Open proxies are popular with spammers as a tool to disguise the origin of their mail. When rate limiting restricts messages from an open proxy, Postfix refuses incoming messages from an open proxy with a temporary error code. Because the proxy has no queuing mechanisms of its own, it does not retry delivery, so large inflows of spam from open proxies do not make it to your system.

To use rate limiting, you must gather statistics and adjust several parameters to influence how many successive and simultaneous connections clients may make to the smtpd daemon. You'll see how to do this in the following sections.

Gathering Rate Statistics

Before you can start limiting client connections, you must know which clients connect and how many successive and simultaneous connections they initiate during normal operation. The anvil daemon keeps track of clients for you, maintaining connection statistics and recording maximum connection counts and rates.

NOTE   *Recording client-connection statistics is useful beyond the implementation of rate limiting. For example, you can read this information into a log-watching program that in turn updates firewall rules to block those runaway clients. Rate limiting is relatively new to Postfix, so as of this writing there are no popular programs that do this.*

Running the anvil Daemon

Like other Postfix daemons, anvil is controlled by the master daemon.
Although anvil is enabled by default, you should examine your master.cf file
to verify that the line that configures anvil is not commented out:

```
# ========================================================================
# service type  private unpriv  chroot  wakeup   maxproc command + args
#               (yes)   (yes)   (yes)   (never)  (100)
# ========================================================================
anvil     unix  -       -       n       -        1       anvil
```

The anvil daemon is started on demand, and it writes all data it gathers
to the mail log at fixed intervals. These log messages appear as follows:

```
Dec 20 01:19:16 mail postfix/anvil[8991]: statistics: max connection count 4
    for (10.0.0.1:smtp:216.129.165.190) at Dec 20 01:18:35
Dec 20 01:29:16 mail postfix/anvil[8991]: statistics: max connection rate 9/
    60s for (10.0.0.1:smtp:62.243.72.19) at Dec 20 01:22:11
Dec 20 01:29:16 mail postfix/anvil[8991]: statistics: max connection count 2
    for (10.0.0.1:smtp:62.243.72.19) at Dec 20 01:22:09
Dec 20 01:39:16 mail postfix/anvil[8911]: statistics: max connection rate 3/
    60s for (10.0.0.1:smtp:146.82.138.6) at Dec 20 01:37:04
Dec 20 01:49:16 mail postfix/anvil[8991]: statistics: max connection rate 2/
    60s for (10.0.0.1:smtp:218.18.32.248) at Dec 20 01:46:35
Dec 20 01:49:16 mail postfix/anvil[8991]: statistics: max connection count 2
    for (10.0.0.1:smtp:218.18.32.248) at Dec 20 01:46:35
Dec 20 01:59:16 mail postfix/anvil[8991]: statistics: max connection rate 3/
    60s for (10.0.0.1:smtp:146.82.138.6) at Dec 20 01:50:58
Dec 20 01:59:16 mail postfix/anvil[8991]: statistics: max connection count 2
    for (10.0.0.1:smtp:171.67.16.117) at Dec 20 01:55:33
Dec 20 02:09:16 mail postfix/anvil[8991]: statistics: max connection rate 2/
    60s for (10.0.0.1:smtp:216.136.204.119) at Dec 20 02:03:38
Dec 20 02:19:16 mail postfix/anvil[8991]: statistics: max connection rate 2/
    60s for (10.0.0.1:smtp:63.161.42.51) at Dec 20 02:09:29
Dec 20 02:19:16 mail postfix/anvil[8991]: statistics: max connection count 2
    for (10.0.0.1:smtp:130.149.17.13) at Dec 20 02:11:52
```

Changing the anvil Log Interval

By default, anvil writes statistic reports to the mail log every ten minutes,
or when the daemon terminates (for example, if you reload Postfix, or if the
daemon terminates itself after max_idle seconds). If you need to increase or
decrease this interval, set the client_connection_status_update_time parameter
in main.cf:

```
client_connection_status_update_time = 10m
```

Your changes take effect as soon as you reload Postfix.

NOTE   *This log interval is a diagnostic tool that is independent of the anvil daemon's internal operation. Decreasing the interval does not cause anvil to collect statistics more often; the Postfix programs access all current anvil data through interprocess communication. They do not look at the log files.*

Limiting Client-Connection Frequency

By default, Postfix does not impose a limit on the number of successive times that a client may connect. Therefore, if you do not change anything, a client can connect and disconnect as often as it likes, making smtpd waste precious resources performing DNS lookups, doing TLS handshakes, and so on.

To impose a client-connection frequency limit, Postfix must count the number of connections in a specific period of time. This interval is known as the rate time unit, and you can define it with the client_connection_rate_time_unit parameter. The default is one minute (60 seconds):

```
client_connection_rate_time_unit = 60s
```

Now you can set a limit on the number of connections permitted from a single client during this rate time unit with the smtpd_client_connection_rate_limit parameter. For example, the following setting, in conjunction with the preceding default rate time unit, allows one client to connect a maximum of 30 times in 60 seconds:

```
smtpd_client_connection_rate_limit = 30
```

Testing Client-Connection Rate Limits

The easiest way to test rate limits is to apply the settings and then observe the logs for a few days. Incorrect settings cannot cause you to lose mail or harm your system, because Postfix refuses rate-limited clients with temporary error codes. A properly configured client will retry delivery; for example, Postfix retries for five days by default (see the maximal_queue_lifetime parameter).

If you want an immediate test, try the following:

1. Generate lots of mail traffic with a program such as smtp-source.
2. Send mail from an IP address that is not exempt from the rate limits.

NOTE   *During testing, you can also reduce the client_connection_status_update_time parameter to one minute to gather connection statistics more frequently.*

To carry out the test, use the following settings in your master.cf file and reload your server configuration:

```
smtpd_client_event_limit_exceptions= ❶
client_connection_rate_time_unit = 60s
```

```
smtpd_client_connection_rate_limit = 1 ❷
client_connection_status_update_time = 1m ❸
```

❶ Setting this parameter to empty specifies that all clients are subject to rate limiting; use this setting only for testing.

❷ This limit is set gratuitously low for testing purposes. You really don't want an email server that allows only one connection from a client per minute.

❸ This setting generates statistic logs every minute, so that you don't have to wait ten minutes for a status report. Again, use this only for testing.

Now you need to generate enough traffic to activate the rate limiter. Use the smtp-source command on your Postfix server like this:

```
$ smtp-source -m 10 -f sender@example.com -t recipient@example.com 127.0.0.1:25
```

NOTE   *If* smtp-source *isn't part of your distribution, grab it from the Postfix source files.*

The preceding command sends ten test messages from sender@example.com to recipient@example.com via the SMTP server on 127.0.0.1 (localhost). Because you set the per-client limit to one connection every 60 seconds, this command easily exceeds that limit.

You will see this error output from smtp-source:

```
smtp-source: fatal: bad startup: 450 Too many connections from 127.0.0.1
```

Furthermore, your log will show this:

```
Jan  9 09:04:16 mail postfix/smtpd[26530]: connect from localhost[127.0.0.1]
Jan  9 09:04:16 mail postfix/smtpd[26530]: 12AA515C06F:
  client=localhost[127.0.0.1]
Jan  9 09:04:16 mail postfix/smtpd[26530]: disconnect from localhost[127.0.0.1]
Jan  9 09:04:16 mail postfix/smtpd[26530]: connect from localhost[127.0.0.1]
Jan  9 09:04:17 mail postfix/smtpd[26530]: warning: Too frequent connections:
  2 from 127.0.0.1 for service localhost:smtp
Jan  9 09:04:17 mail postfix/smtpd[26530]: disconnect from localhost[127.0.0.1]
```

Here is another example, where the smtpd_client_connection_rate_limit parameter was set to 30. Postfix refused all clients exceeding that maximum allowed frequency with a 450 status code, disconnected, and produced a warning with the client name and address and daemon name:

```
Dec 20 02:39:03 mail postfix/smtpd[18431]: warning: Too frequent connections:
  31 from 81.199.6.44 for service 10.0.0.1:smtp ❶
Dec 20 02:39:04 mail postfix/smtpd[17840]: warning: Too frequent connections:
  32 from 81.199.6.44 for service 10.0.0.1:smtp
Dec 20 02:39:04 mail postfix/smtpd[17878]: warning: Too frequent connections:
  33 from 81.199.6.44 for service 10.0.0.1:smtp
...
Dec 20 02:39:15 mail postfix/smtpd[18440]: warning: Too frequent connections:
  65 from 81.199.6.44 for service 10.0.0.1:smtp
```

```
Dec 20 02:39:15 mail postfix/smtpd[18432]: warning: Too frequent connections:
    66 from 81.199.6.44 for service 10.0.0.1:smtp
Dec 20 02:39:16 mail postfix/anvil[8991]: statistics: max connection rate 72/
    60s for (10.0.0.1:smtp:81.199.6.44) at Dec 20 02:39:15 ❷
```

❶ The client running on 81.199.6.44 exceeded the 30-connections-per-minute limit, causing the Too frequent connections warning in the log.

❷ This particular client (81.199.6.44) set the connection rate record with 72 connections in 60 seconds, as anvil reports here.

Restricting Simultaneous Client Connections

By default, the number of simultaneous connections per client is limited to half the default process limit. As a result, two clients can occupy all of the smtpd processes that Postfix is permitted to run. The smtpd_client_connection_count_limit parameter controls the number of simultaneous connections per client. For example, the following configuration setting in main.cf limits a client to 25 concurrent connections:

```
smtpd_client_connection_count_limit = 25
```

CAUTION *The process limit for smtpd or the default_process_limit parameter should be considerably larger than smtpd_client_connection_count_limit; otherwise one client might hog all available smtpd processes.*

Testing Simultaneous Client-Connection Limits

As was the case with connection frequency limits, the easiest way to test concurrent session limits is to apply the settings and observe the logs for a few days. However, if you'd like an immediate test, generate lots of simultaneous connections with the smtp-source command from an IP address that is not exempt from rate limits.

During testing, you should probably reduce client_connection_status_update_time to one minute.

To carry out the test, set the rate-limiting parameters in your master.cf file as follows, and reload the configuration:

```
smtpd_client_connection_limit_exceptions = ❶
client_connection_rate_time_unit = 60s
smtpd_client_connection_count_limit = 1 ❷
client_connection_status_update_time = 1m ❸
```

❶ All clients are being subjected to rate limiting; do this only for testing.

❷ This limit is far too low; use this only for testing. You don't want to use an email server that only allows one connection from one client every 60 seconds.

❸ Produce log reports every minute so that you don't have to wait ten minutes for a status report; use this only for testing.

You can open several simultaneous connections with the `smtp-source` command. Try running this on your Postfix server:

```
$ smtp-source -s 10 -m 10 -f sender@example.com -t recipient@example.com 127.0.0.1:25
```

The `-m 10` option says to send ten test messages, and the `-s 10` option specifies ten simultaneous SMTP sessions. With a limit of one connection per client, you should easily trip the limit and generate this error message from `smtp-source`:

```
smtp-source: fatal: bad startup: 450 Too many connections from 127.0.0.1
```

The log should show something like this:

```
Jan  9 09:14:15 mail postfix/smtpd[28438]: warning: Too many connections:
 2 from 127.0.0.1 for service localhost:smtp
Jan  9 09:14:15 mail postfix/smtpd[28438]: disconnect from localhost[127.0.0.1]
Jan  9 09:14:15 mail postfix/smtpd[28437]: warning: Too many connections:
 2 from 127.0.0.1 for service localhost:smtp
Jan  9 09:14:15 mail postfix/smtpd[28437]: disconnect from localhost[127.0.0.1]
Jan  9 09:14:15 mail postfix/smtpd[28439]: warning: Too many connections:
 3 from 127.0.0.1 for service localhost:smtp
Jan  9 09:14:15 mail postfix/smtpd[28439]: disconnect from localhost[127.0.0.1]
Jan  9 09:14:15 mail postfix/smtpd[28440]: warning: Too many connections:
 4 from 127.0.0.1 for service localhost:smtp
Jan  9 09:14:15 mail postfix/smtpd[28440]: disconnect from localhost[127.0.0.1]
```

For the log messages that follow, `smtpd_client_connection_count_limit` was set to 25. As was the case with frequency limits, Postfix sends a 450 status code to a client making too many simultaneous connections, disconnects, and logs a warning with the client name and address:

```
Dec  3 09:12:53 mail postfix/smtpd[19883]: warning: Too many connections:
 26 from 213.165.64.165 for service 10.0.0.1:smtp ❶
Dec  3 09:12:53 mail postfix/smtpd[19884]: warning: Too many connections:
 27 from 213.165.64.165 for service 10.0.0.1:smtp
...
Dec  3 09:13:15 mail postfix/smtpd[19894]: warning: Too many connections:
 35 from 213.165.64.165 for service 10.0.0.1:smtp
...
Dec  3 09:16:47 mail postfix/anvil[7958]: statistics: max connection count
 37 for (10.0.0.1:smtp:213.165.64.165) at Dec  3 09:12:3 ❷
```

❶ `213.165.64.165` exceeds the limit of 25 connections, causing the `Too many connections` warning in the log.

❷ `213.165.64.165` set the record with 37 connections targeted to `smtpd`.

Exempting Clients from Limits

You can use the smtpd_client_connection_limit_exceptions parameter to exclude authorized hosts and networks from the client limitations in this chapter. The notation includes network/netmask expressions, hostnames, and domain names.

By default, Postfix grants client-limit exemptions to all hosts in mynetworks. If you want to use a more restrictive setting, you can take a look at sample-smtpd.cf, smtpd(8), and anvil(8).

Here is an example that allows hosts in $mynetworks, the subnet 10.45.207.0/24, and the domain example.com to connect as much and as often as they please:

```
smtpd_client_connection_limit_exceptions =
  $mynetworks,
  10.45.207.0/24,
  .example.com
```

22

PERFORMANCE TUNING

Postfix is fast out of the box, but like other packages, you can usually tune it to work even faster. Furthermore, there are situations where Postfix may not perform as well as you expected, whether because of hardware or software limitations on the server system or other adverse conditions, such as a big influx of spam or undeliverable mail.

This chapter shows you how to find and analyze the most common performance problems.

Basic Enhancements

We will first look at a few elementary tweaks that still may not be terribly obvious. Think of the suggestions here as a checklist for solving or avoiding simple problems. Above all, keep in mind that many performance problems are actually caused by a flawed setup, such as a bad /etc/resolv.conf file. The following points appear in no particular order; they're all of equal importance.

Speeding Up DNS Lookups

Postfix does a lot of DNS queries because SMTP requires lookups for MX and A records. Furthermore, many of the Postfix restrictions use DNS lookups to verify a client's hostname or to perform a blacklist lookup. Therefore, it's critical that your server be able to look up DNS records quickly, especially if you have a high amount of traffic.

Testing DNS Lookups

The most common problem with DNS name resolution is that queries take too long. You can use the dig command to perform a DNS lookup and display detailed information about the query's execution:

```
$ dig www.example.com
; <<>> DiG 9.2.3rc4 <<>> www.example.com
;; global options:  printcmd
;; Got answer:
;; ->>HEADER<<- opcode: QUERY, status: NOERROR, id: 48136
;; flags: qr rd ra; QUERY: 1, ANSWER: 1, AUTHORITY: 0, ADDITIONAL: 0
;; QUESTION SECTION:
;www.example.com.                IN      A
;; ANSWER SECTION:
www.example.com.        172800  IN      A       192.0.34.166
;; Query time: 174 msec
;; SERVER: 127.0.0.1#53(127.0.0.1)
;; WHEN: Mon Oct  6 09:40:52 2003
;; MSG SIZE  rcvd: 49
```

In this example, the query took 174 milliseconds. Now, let's run the query again:

```
$ dig www.example.com
; <<>> DiG 9.2.3rc4 <<>> www.example.com
;; global options:  printcmd
;; Got answer:
;; ->>HEADER<<- opcode: QUERY, status: NOERROR, id: 6398
;; flags: qr rd ra; QUERY: 1, ANSWER: 1, AUTHORITY: 0, ADDITIONAL: 0
;; QUESTION SECTION:
;www.example.com.                IN      A
;; ANSWER SECTION:
www.example.com.        172765  IN      A       192.0.34.166
;; Query time: 18 msec
;; SERVER: 127.0.0.1#53(127.0.0.1)
;; WHEN: Mon Oct  6 09:41:27 2003
;; MSG SIZE  rcvd: 49
```

This subsequent query for the same host took only 18 milliseconds, approximately ten times faster. The reason that this second query was so quick is that this particular machine is accessing a caching DNS server.

If the lookups take significantly longer (or worse, time out), then you're having DNS problems. There are several possible reasons:

`resolv.conf` settings

If you run Postfix in a chroot jail, you may have changed /etc/resolv.conf but forgotten to copy the updated file to the chroot jail (usually /var/spool/postfix/etc/resolv.conf).

The nameservers listed in /etc/resolv.conf could be slow or not servicing requests at all. Verify that the specified servers answer your DNS queries in a timely manner for each server line in /etc/resolv.conf using the dig command.

Network problems

Your uplink to the Internet might not be working as it should, or it could be saturated. If this is the case, you should consider getting more bandwidth or using traffic shaping to give priority to nameserver queries.

Firewall settings

A firewall can block nameserver packets moving to and from your mail server.

Malfunctioning caching nameserver

If you're running a caching nameserver locally, make sure that it's actually working.

Improving DNS Lookup Performance

If your /etc/resolv.conf settings, your network, and your firewall all seem fine, yet you still need to speed up your DNS queries, you should consider running a local caching server, such as djbdns dnscache or an instance of BIND on your server or network. The cache significantly speeds up the lookup process and decreases network utilization at the same time because recurring lookups don't result in outgoing packets.

Confirming That Your Server Is Not Listed as an Open Relay

If you're running an open relay, you can expect that many mail servers will refuse any mail from your servers. In addition, spammers will use your system to send their mail, increasing the load on your system, because your system is handling your users as well as your abusers.

Your system will typically end up on a blacklist after the open relay has been confirmed. It can be a royal pain to get off a blacklist, and it may take days or even weeks. Therefore, it's essential that you make sure that your system is not an open relay or open proxy. Look up your IP address on http://openrbl.org. If you're listed, close the open relay immediately. Allow users to relay in only one of these situations:

- The user's client is listed in the mynetworks parameter.
- The user's client successfully performed SMTP authentication.
- The user's client successfully authenticated itself using a TLS client certificate.

Refusing Messages to Nonexistent Users

It's a good idea to refuse messages for recipients that don't exist in your system. If Postfix were to accept such mail, it would have to send a non-delivery notification to the sender address. In the case of spam or viruses, that sender address is almost certainly not the true origin of the mail. The resulting MAILER-DAEMON notifications will clog the queue for several days.

This shouldn't be too much of a problem by itself, but if you accept mail for users that do not exist on your system, your system can store the messages in a place that can eventually fill up, or if you run a relaying system (see Chapter 13), the ultimate target of the message will eventually have to send a bounce back to the envelope sender of the message (to the Return-Path in the message header). Furthermore, this bounce may turn out to be undeliverable itself, because the domain used as the sender domain probably won't accept anything.

In any case, these bounces will clutter your queue or go to the mailbox specified by double_bounce_recipient (which may be your postmaster account). If you see something like this in your mail queue, you may be having this problem:

```
$ mailq
-Queue ID- --Size-- ----Arrival Time---- -Sender/Recipient-------
63BE9CF331    10658 Mon Jan 12 14:38:30  MAILER-DAEMON
         (connect to mail3.quickspress.com[63.89.113.198]: Connection timed out)
                                     platinum@quickspress.com
1C932CF30E     3753 Sat Jan 10 16:16:38  MAILER-DAEMON
         (connect to mx.unrealdeals.biz[69.5.69.110]: Connection refused)
                                     EntrepreneurCareers@unrealdeals.biz
98EC3CF3F9     5505 Sat Jan 10 20:25:06  MAILER-DAEMON
        (connect to fhweb8.ifollowup.com[216.171.193.38]: Connection refused)
                                     root@fhweb8.ifollowup.com
50B14CF31E     5196 Mon Jan 12 11:35:11  MAILER-DAEMON
      (connect to mail.refilladvice.net[218.15.192.166]: Connection timed out)
                                     clintoncopeland@refilladvice.net
F4009CF39D     5452 Sun Jan 11 01:58:27  MAILER-DAEMON
        (connect to fhweb9.ifollowup.com[216.171.193.39]: Connection refused)
                                     root@fhweb9.ifollowup.com
-- 30 Kbytes in 5 Requests.
```

Here you can see five messages that are being bounced back to the original senders (notice that the sender is MAILER_DAEMON), but in each case, the recipient's mail server is unreachable.

To refuse messages for nonexistent recipients on your system, set the `local_recipient_maps` and `relay_recipient_maps` parameters (the latter if you're running a gateway that just relays mail to internal mail servers) to maps containing valid recipients.

If bounces really get out of hand, you can also employ RHSBL-style blacklists (see Chapter 8) to reject mail from servers that don't accept bounces at all (because all bounces that need to be sent back to these servers remain in your mail queue for several days). There's an RHSBL-style blacklist at RFC-Ignorant.Org (`http://rfc-ignorant.org`) that you can use like this:

```
check_rhsbl_sender dsn.rfc-ignorant.org
```

Blocking Messages from Blacklisted Networks

There are many different kinds of blocklists and DNS blacklists available that list individual IP addresses, whole IP ranges, and even sender domains for all sorts of reasons. There's at least one list for every kind of perceived misbehavior.

The most useful of these list open relays and open proxies, because they can be tested automatically in an objective manner. Here are just a few of the blacklists:

- `relays.ordb.org`
- `list.dsbl.org`
- `cbl.abuseat.org`
- `dul.dnsbl.sorbs.net`

NOTE *Few things change faster than blacklists. Today's hot blacklist may be out of service tomorrow.*

These blacklists have low probabilities of false positives because they provide clear criteria for listing addresses. Running an open proxy or open relay is generally considered wrong, so using these lists puts social pressure on the administrators of the misconfigured systems. (Of course, they may be clueless or just not care.)

Refusing Messages from Unknown Sender Domains

If possible, do not accept messages containing an envelope sender from an invalid domain. If there's a problem during delivery, the error report always goes back to the envelope sender, and if this address contains a nonexistent domain, there's nowhere to send the error report.

Postfix tries to send the error report, finds it to be undeliverable, and then (since it cannot be bounced, because the envelope sender is empty) sends it to `2bounce_notice_recipient`.

You can avoid this by adding reject_unknown_sender_domain to smtpd_
sender_restrictions or smtpd_recipient_restrictions, as discussed at length
in Chapter 8.

Reducing the Retransmission Attempt Frequency

If you have a lot of mail that your server can't deliver on the first few
attempts, consider using a fallback relay (with the fallback_relay parameter)
or increasing the backoff time (maximal_backoff_time) to reduce the frequency
with which deferred mail reenters the active queue.

Without a fallback relay, Postfix spends precious time trying to deliver
mail to sites that are down or unreachable. Each of these delivery attempts
ties up one smtp process that has to wait until the timeout is reached. A fallback relay can do the dirty work of retrying transmission for messages that
can't be delivered on the first try. This means your regular mail server can
operate with the default timeouts or even with reduced timeout values,
speeding up delivery.

On the other hand, increasing the maximal_backoff_time parameter bumps
up the maximum time that the server ignores a certain destination after a
delivery problem occurs. Therefore, Postfix makes fewer attempts to contact
problematic servers.

Finding Bottlenecks

This section describes how you can identify bottlenecks in your system.
Before reading through this material, you may want to review Chapter 5 to
get an idea of which daemons do what.

Because all of the Postfix daemons have to access one or more queues in
order to do their work, knowing the status of queues can come in really
handy. Here are a few of the queues that you need to worry about:

- incoming
- deferred
- active
- maildrop

When a message enters the system, it becomes a queue file that Postfix
moves between the queues. If one of the queues has a lot of messages in it,
you may have an underlying performance problem. To get a handle on the
different queues, Victor Duchovni wrote a nifty utility called qshape to show
the distribution of messages among the previously mentioned queues. This
program reads the queue files directly, bypassing the mailq command, and
therefore, only root and the postfix user can run it. You can download it at
http://sbserv.stahl.bau.tu-bs.de/~hildeb/postfix/scripts. Recent Postfix
versions have this script included in the source tarball.

qshape displays a tabular view of the Postfix queue contents. The rows of the table show the number of messages bound for a particular destination, as well as the overall total. The columns show the age of the messages. For example, take a look at the following output for the hold queue (parameter hold), where you can see the top ten lines of the (mostly forged) sender domain distribution (parameter -s) for captured spam:

```
# qshape -s hold
```

	T	5	10	20	40	80	160	320	320+
TOTAL	12	0	0	0	0	2	2	0	6
hotmail.de	2	0	0	0	0	0	0	0	2
alb-24-194-161-132.nycap.rr.com	1	0	0	0	0	1	0	0	0
freeenet.de	1	0	0	0	0	0	1	0	0
x4u2.desy.de	1	0	0	0	0	0	0	0	1
csi.com	1	0	0	0	0	0	1	0	0
da.ru	1	0	0	0	0	0	0	0	1
freeuk.com	1	0	0	0	0	1	0	0	0
mx5.outrageouscourtiers.com	1	0	0	0	0	0	0	0	1
online.de	1	0	0	0	0	0	0	0	0
molgen.mpg.de	1	0	0	0	0	0	0	0	1
charite.de	1	0	0	0	0	0	0	0	0

The T column contains the total count of messages for each domain. The other columns show the counts for messages older than a certain age (measured in minutes) but not older than the age in the column to the right. In this case, there are two messages that purport to be from hotmail.de. Both are older than 320 minutes.

By default, qshape shows statistics for both the incoming and active queues because these are directly related to the overall performance. You can specify a different set of queues on the command line, as in these examples:

```
$ qshape deferred
$ qshape incoming active deferred
```

Now that you can track down busy queues, you can do something about them. The following sections explain how to clear up bottlenecks in each type of queue. We'll also cover the formulas you can use to calculate whether your system can handle a given amount of mail, and how and when to use fallback relays.

Incoming Queue Bottlenecks

As described in the previous section, "Finding Bottlenecks," the Postfix cleanup service stores all new mail in the incoming queue. New files get a permissions mode of 0600 until they are complete and are ready for further processing, when they get an access mode of 0700. Under normal conditions, the incoming queue is nearly empty and contains only files with a mode of 0600, because the queue manager should be able to import new messages into the active queue as soon as the cleanup service is done with them.

However, the incoming queue will grow when the message input rate spikes above the rate at which the queue manager can move messages into the active queue. At that stage, the only thing slowing down the queue manager is the trivial-rewrite service. If the queue manager is having trouble keeping up, you may be using slow lookup services—such as MySQL and LDAP—for transport lookups, or you may need to speed up the servers that provide the lookup services.

NOTE *If you're using high or variable latency IPC (interprocess communication) maps, such as LDAP and SQL, Postfix needs more time to receive mail. Thus, Postfix will be running more smtpd (and cleanup) processes, and will sooner hit the smtpd process limit. With these slow table lookups, a delivery agent (local, pipe, virtual, lmtp) will probably finish in less time than smtpd needs to receive mail, so Postfix will run fewer delivery agents than expected.*

One possible remedy with LDAP is to try to avoid binding to your LDAP server. Set bind = no in your LDAP query configuration files. This makes Postfix bind to the LDAP server anonymously, thus reducing the overhead for authentication and password verification.

In comparison to file-based maps, such as hash, btree, dbm, and cdb, IPC maps just takes longer to look up information, and therefore, the Postfix daemons can do nothing while waiting for the lookup to go through. If the lookup were faster, Postfix would be faster.

As discussed elsewhere, these maps do have their advantages, and that can outweigh the drawbacks. One of the most significant is that Postfix doesn't need to kill and restart a process to reopen a map when the contents have changed. You may want to try some database tuning instead.

If the bottleneck lies in the incoming queue, then the influx of messages is taking precedence over sending messages out. A way to prevent the inflow of mail from starving the outflow is to fool around with the in_flow_delay parameter to limit the input rate when the queue manager starts to fall behind. The cleanup service pauses for the number of seconds specified by in_flow_delay before creating a new queue file if it cannot obtain a token from the queue manager.

The reason that this works is that the number of cleanup processes is usually limited by the SMTP server (smtpd) concurrency. The input rate can exceed the output rate by at most the SMTP connection count divided by in_flow_delay messages per second. To find out the current number of incoming SMTP connections, use ps and grep as follows:

```
# ps auxww| grep smtpd | grep -v grep |  wc --lines
   22
```

There are 22 smtpd processes running on this system. This command counts all smtpd processes, so if you have multiple smtpd configurations (for example, if you're using a content filter that reinjects mail back into the queue with SMTP), then you need to use a more specific grep pattern to find the number of smtpd daemons accepting mail from the outside network:

```
# ps auxww| grep smtpd | grep -v grep | grep -v localhost | wc --lines
    9
```

With a default process limit of 100 and an in_flow_delay setting of one second, the coupling is strong enough to limit a single runaway injector to one message per second. However, it is not strong enough to deflect an excessive input rate from many sources at the same time.

If your server is under attack from multiple sources, your best option is to make the SMTP sessions as short as possible (a smtpd_error_sleep_time of zero, and a low smtpd_hard_error_limit, which will make Postfix hang up on connections that exceed this limit). Do this only if the incoming queue is growing even when the active queue isn't full and the trivial-rewrite service is using a fast transport lookup mechanism.

If you try these remedies and you're still having problems with a congested incoming queue but no active queue congestion, the problem is most likely your I/O subsystem: Mail is coming in and is written to disk, but the smtpd and qmgr processes need to access the same resource (the on-disk queue), and you're bound by the speed of the I/O subsystem.

In this case, it's time to either add a *lot* of memory to your mail server (in order to increase the disk caching pool for the operating system), or move the queue directory to one of these:

- A striping RAID system
- A battery-backed RAM disk (this is for the daring people out there, because you'll lose mail in the case of a system crash)

Maildrop Queue Bottlenecks

Messages that are submitted via the Postfix sendmail command but are not yet sent to the main Postfix queues by the pickup service sit around in the maildrop queue—you can send messages using the sendmail command, and they'll be added to the maildrop queue even when the Postfix system isn't running. The single-threaded pickup service scans the maildrop queue directory periodically or when notified of new message arrival by postdrop.

The rate at which the pickup service can inject messages into the primary queues is largely determined by disk access times, because it must commit the message to stable storage before finishing. The same is true of the postdrop program, which writes messages to the maildrop directory.

Because the pickup service is single-threaded, it can deliver only one message at a time, at an overall rate not exceeding the disk I/O latency (and CPU usage, if applicable) incurred by the cleanup service, because every mail that pickup processes needs to go through cleanup. As you remember, cleanup performs header_checks, body_checks, and so on, which can be very CPU intensive. cleanup then writes the message into a queuefile—and this is bounced by the disk I/O latency. If you have congestion in the maildrop queue, you probably have one of these two problems:

- Excessive local message submission rate
- Excessive CPU consumption in the cleanup service due to excessive body checks

However, keep in mind that when the active queue is full, the cleanup service attempts to slow down message injection by pausing for each message, according to the in_flow_delay parameter. In this case, congestion in the maildrop queue may be a result of further downstream congestion.

Don't try to deliver a lot of mail via the pickup service. If you have a high-volume site, you need to avoid using content filters that reinject scanned mail with sendmail and postdrop. Instead, use an SMTP connection for injection. There are plenty of programs that can do it for you, including mini_sendmail (http://www.acme.com/software/mini_sendmail).

If you've got a lot of locally submitted mail, you might have a forwarding loop or a runaway notification program. In addition, the postsuper -r command can place selected messages into the maildrop queue for reprocessing. Although this is useful for resetting stale content_filter settings, requeuing a large number of messages with postsuper -r can cause a spike in the size of the maildrop queue.

Deferred Queue Bottlenecks

When Postfix can't deliver a message to some of its recipients because of a temporary failure, it places the message in the deferred queue in hopes of delivering it later. The queue manager scans the deferred queue periodically at an interval specified by the queue_run_delay parameter. As mentioned in Chapter 5, the queue manager chooses messages from both the incoming and deferred queues in a round-robin fashion to prevent deferred mail from dominating the active queue.

Each deferred queue scan reinjects a fraction of the deferred queue back into the active queue for retrying, because each message in the deferred queue is assigned a cool-off time when it is deferred. Postfix does this by time-warping the modification times of the queue file into the future. A queue file is not eligible for retry if its modification time hasn't arrived.

The cool-off time is at least the value of `minimal_backoff_time` and at most `maximal_backoff_time`. Postfix sets the next retry time by doubling the message's age in the queue and adjusting the result to make sure that the time lies between these limits. The end result is that Postfix retries young messages more frequently.

If your high-volume site has a large deferred queue, you may want to tweak the `queue_run_delay`, `minimal_backoff_time`, and `maximal_backoff_time` parameters to provide short delays upon the first failure and perhaps causing longer delays after multiple failures. This will reduce the retransmission rate of old messages, reducing the quantity of previously deferred mail in the active queue.

CAUTION *One common reason for large deferred queues is a failure to validate recipients at the SMTP input stage. See the "Mail to Unknown Recipients" section in Chapter 8 for the reasons why you must do recipient validation.*

If a server with lots of deferred mail goes down for a while, it's possible for the entire deferred queue to reach the retry time simultaneously when the server comes back up. This can lead to a very busy active queue. Complicating this, the phenomenon will repeat itself approximately every `maximal_backoff_time` seconds if most of the messages are again deferred.

Ideally, to fix this problem, Postfix will include a random offset in addition to the standard retry time to reduce the chances of the entire deferred queue being repeatedly flushed at the same time.

Active Queue Bottlenecks

As described in Chapter 5, the queue manager is a delivery agent scheduler that tries to ensure fast and fair message delivery to all destinations within designated resource limits. Congestion in the active queue occurs when one or more destinations accept messages at a slower pace than the corresponding message input rate.

If the destination is down for some time, the queue manager will mark it as dead and immediately defer all mail for the destination without even bothering to assign it to a delivery agent. Therefore, these messages leave the active queue quickly, but they end up in the deferred queue. If the destination is just plain slow, or if there is a problem causing an excessive input rate, the active queue grows and becomes saturated by messages destined for the slow destination. There are only two ways to reduce the congestion:

- Reduce the input rate.
- Increase throughput.

Increasing throughput requires either increasing the concurrency (the number of simultaneous Postfix smtp processes that you run) or reducing the latency of deliveries (by getting on a better network, changing the map type, fixing a DNS slowdown, and the like). To increase concurrency, you can increase the number of the default_process_limit parameter in your main.cf file. However, if you want to do it on a per-destination basis, find the slow transport (such as a transport for content_filter) or destination (such as certain big freemail sites) that's dominating the active queue (qshape is great for this). After you zero in on the culprit, define a dedicated transport name and set name_destination_concurrency_limit. See "Configuring an Alternative Transport" in this chapter for more detailed information on how to do this.

Above all, keep in mind that the maximum number of processes used for any service is limited in master.cf and main.cf.

NOTE *Remember that your operating system must be able to handle the increased number of processes and open files. See "Running hundreds of processes" in the Postfix FAQ at http://www.postfix.org/faq.html.*

The latency can sometimes be lowered by speeding up DNS (see the section "Improving DNS Lookup Performance" in this chapter) and map lookups as mentioned in Chapter 5, in the section "Databases (MySQL, PostgreSQL, LDAP)." In addition, decreasing timeouts for busy sites with lots of MX hosts can help. However, none of this will help if the receiving system cannot keep up (for example, when you're sending to slow sites like certain freemail sites).

Another cause of congestion in the active queue is unwarranted flushing of the entire deferred queue. The deferred queue holds messages that probably won't be delivered, at least not in any random try. Furthermore, it's also likely that the failure leading to the deferral will take a long time, because Postfix will have to wait for a timeout.

CAUTION *The "flush the queue" instinct of some administrators for a large deferred queue will probably be counterproductive and make the problem worse. Don't flush the deferred queue unless you expect that most of the messages in there will actually make it to their destinations on the next try! So analyze first, fix the problem, then flush the queue!*

Finally, avoid reloading or restarting Postfix when possible. When the queue manager restarts, there may be messages in the active queue directory, but the true active queue (in memory) is empty. In order to recover the in-memory state, the queue manager moves all of the messages in the active queue back into the incoming queue and relies on the normal incoming queue scan to refill the active queue. The process of moving all the messages back and forth, redoing the transport table lookups, and re-importing the messages to memory is expensive.

CAUTION *The postfix reload command restarts the queue manager, so you should avoid fooling around with configuration files that require the postfix reload command for their changes to take effect on busy production servers.*

Asynchronous Bounce Queue Congestion Inequality

If the deferred queue is full of undeliverable bounces, Postfix is not to blame for the queue congestion. The congestion is a consequence of high average latency when you have a large backlog of undeliverable mail, because the smtp daemons trying to send the mail just time out. Victor Duchovni figured out the congestion inequality that will tell you if you're having problems like this.

In a queue with lots of bounces that will never be deliverable, the number of junk messages brought into the active queue by a queue run is determined by the following formula:

$$\frac{\text{size\_of\_the\_queue} \times \text{queue\_run\_delay}}{\text{maximal\_backoff\_time}}$$

The number of messages processed per queue run is at most:

$$\frac{\text{queue\_run\_delay} \times \text{default\_process\_limit}}{\text{smtp\_connect\_timeout} \times M}$$

When the process limit is exhausted, you can assume that the number of bounces in the queue is much larger than the process limit. (This is assuming that the default_process_limit applies to the smtp daemons. If you raised the entry in the maxproc column of master.cf, use that value in this equation instead.)

Putting these equations together, you get this result:

$$\frac{\text{size\_of\_the\_queue} \times \text{queue\_run\_delay}}{\text{maximal\_backoff\_time}} \geq \frac{\text{queue\_run\_delay} \times \text{default\_process\_limit}}{\text{smtp\_connect\_timeout} \times M}$$

When you multiply both sides by maximal_backoff_time / queue_run_delay, you get the congestion inequality:

$$P \times B \geq Q \times T \times M$$

The parameters are as follows:

P The smtp transport process limit, obtained by running this command:

```
# postconf default_process_limit
default_process_limit = 100
```

NOTE *Check the maxproc value of the smtp line in master.cf to see if there's an explicit smtp transport process limit.*

B The maximal backoff time, obtained with this command:

```
# postconf maximal_backoff_time
maximal_backoff_time = 4000s
```

Q The number of bounces in the queue (these bounces presumably go to at least P / destination_concurrency_limit distinct destinations).

T The smtp connection timeout, obtained with this command:

```
# postconf smtp_connect_timeout
smtp_connect_timeout = 30s
```

M The average MX IP address count. When a domain has more than one MX record, Postfix has to try each one. You don't need exact numbers; just estimate it, and use qshape to estimate the MX count for the dominant destinations.

NOTE *By default, each destination can consume at most 20 delivery agents (default_ destination_concurrency_limit = 20), so keep adding destinations until you reach the process limit.*

In practice, just estimate a range for M and perhaps cap it by setting smtp_mx_ address_limit (the upper limit for the number of MX addresses Postfix will try).

If you can't satisfy this inequality, you're in serious trouble. Do everything you can to lower the value of the right side and raise the left side.

When attempting to lower the value of the right side, keep these points in mind:

- You can't decrease Q short of deleting the bounces.
- You can decrease T by creating a dedicated smtp transport for the recipient domains of the bounces and lowering its SMTP connection timeout.
- You can't decrease M, because you don't run the recipient servers and DNS services.

Here are some suggestions for increasing the value of the left side:

- Increasing P is easy. Change the default process limit or edit master.cf to allow for more smtp processes.
- To increase B, increase the maximal backoff time.

Let's look at a couple of examples. The first is an installation of Postfix 1.*x* on Solaris with 2,000 junk messages in the queue.

In Postfix 1.*x*, the smtp_connection_timeout setting is the operating system's TCP connection timeout. This is about 180 seconds by default on Solaris, and much longer on Linux. If you're using the default_process_limit default of 50, you get the following result.

```
P * B >= Q * T
50 * 4000 >= 2000 * 180
200000 >= 360000
```

Here, the inequality does not hold, because the maximal_backoff_time of 4,000 seconds is too small, especially if junk destinations have multiple MX records.

Now let's consider the situation where we're using Postfix 1.1.11 (or later) with 2,000 junk messages in the queue.

For later versions of Postfix (at least 1.1.11-20020717), the connection timeout is 30 seconds on all platforms, and version 1.1.12-20021212 raised the default process limit to 100. This yields the following picture:

```
P * B >= Q * T
100 * 4000 >= 2000 * 30
400000 >= 60000
```

This time, the inequality holds true. Furthermore, because the default backoff is 4,000 seconds, this is well below the critical level, even if the typical junk destination MX host count is 4. Later Postfix versions can handle a much larger queue full of junk.

The critical queue size with a default_process_limit setting of 100 is approximately as follows:

```
100 * 4000 / 30 = 13000
```

It might be lower if the MX count is above one. With a process limit of 500, a timeout of 10 seconds, and a maximal_backoff_time of 4 hours, the critical queue size is this whopping number:

```
500 * 14400 / 10 = 720000
```

However, this absurd limit would keep 500 processes busy trying new messages every 10 seconds—in other words, 50 messages will be leaving and reentering the deferred queue every second.

Using Fallback Relays

If the primary queue is buckling under the load, it is worth the effort to set up a second server (or Postfix instance; multi-instance support is slated for version 2.2) to deal with retries. Therefore, you can tune the primary queue normally, perhaps with very short timeouts, and any messages that can't be delivered on the first attempt can be retried in a fallback queue or on the fallback relay with the special tuning described earlier in this chapter.

To set it up, set the following parameters in the `main.cf` file for your main Postfix server:

```
smtp_connect_timeout = 5s
smtp_mx_address_limit = 3
#fallback_relay = [127.0.0.1]:20025
# for multiple instances of Postfix on the same machine
fallback_relay = fallback.example.com
# for another instance on another host
```

Then, on the server specified by `fallback_relay`, set a high critical queue size. For example, use these parameters to set a limit of 720000:

```
smtp_connect_timeout = 10s
smtp_mx_address_limit = 5
default_process_limit = 500
bounce_queue_lifetime = 2d
maximal_backoff_time = 4h
```

NOTE   *You may want to increase* `smtp_connect_timeout` *by just a little. Some hosts and networks really are that slow.*

Tuning for Higher Throughput

If your machine relays a high volume of inbound mail, you can arrange to have a separate transport forward mail to the inbound domains. For the purposes of this section, let's call that transport "relay." In Postfix 2.x, you tune it like this:

1. Set `relay_destination_concurrency_limit` to a high number (for example, 50).
2. Set up the `master.cf` entry for relay so that it contains `-o smtp_connect_timeout=$relay_connect_timeout` (with no spaces around the equal sign).
3. Set `relay_connect_timeout` in `main.cf` to 5 or 1.

If you're doing content filtering for viruses with an SMTP-based `content_filter` (see Chapter 12), make sure the sending transport is configured with `-o disable_dns_lookups=yes`. This also helps when you're sending all mail to a fixed destination, and you don't have to look up MX records (for example, when using the `relayhost` feature).

Configuring an Alternative Transport

If you routinely send high volumes of mail to sites with a lot of mail exchangers (Hotmail is one notable example), there isn't much point in using the default timeouts. Postfix can probably deliver mail bound for these domains more quickly if it doesn't spend so much time on each broken mail exchanger. This section shows you how to do it.

First, define a new smtp transport called deadbeats in your master.cf file. To do this, copy the smtp transport line, rename it as deadbeats, and add a little tweak—a lower smtp_connect_timeout value:

```
deadbeats unix  -       -       -       -       -       smtp
    -o smtp_connect_timeout=$deadbeats_connect_timeout
```

The default timeout is 30 seconds, so give set this deadbeats_connect_timeout a value of five seconds in your main.cf file:

```
deadbeats_connect_timeout = 5
```

Now, still inside your main.cf file, instruct Postfix to use this special transport when sending mail to certain destination domains by setting the transport_maps parameter:

```
transport_maps = hash:/etc/postfix/transport
```

Create the /etc/postfix/transport map like this:

```
yahoo.com               deadbeats:
# yahoo.com has 3 MX host, with 9 A records in total
compuserve.com          deadbeats:
# compuserve.com has 3 MX hosts with 4 A records each
aol.com                 deadbeats:
# aol.com has 4 MX hosts with 18 A records in total
hotmail.com             deadbeats:
# hotmail.com has 4 MX hosts with 10 A records in total
hotmail.de              deadbeats:
# hotmail.de has no MX hosts, but 6 A records
```

To put it in place, run **postmap hash:/etc/postfix/transport**, and reload your configuration.

APPENDICES

The last part of *The Book of Postfix* is the appendices. The appendices should help you get started, help you troubleshoot problems when you experience them, and give you some references to have at hand while you are in the midst of configuring your server:

Installing Postfix

Appendix A contains instructions for installing Postfix from source code, as well as for the Debian and Red Hat Linux distributions.

Troubleshooting Postfix

Having trouble with something when you try to modify a configuration? Appendix B offers advice for the most frequent gotchas and gives some general tips for tracking down problems.

CIDR and SMTP Standards Reference

Not everyone can memorize subnets in CIDR notation or SMTP server response codes. We've put them together for you in Appendix C.

A

INSTALLING POSTFIX

 This appendix describes how to build Postfix from source code, as well as how to install, prepare, and build packages for Debian Linux and Red Hat Linux.

The Postfix Source Code

You can find links to the Postfix source code at http://www.postfix.org/download.html. There are several mirror sites; you should select the one closest to you for maximum speed.

Before you download the source code, you should know the difference between experimental (snapshot) and official releases. The official release does not change, except for bug fixes and portability patches. On the other hand, snapshot releases contain newer untested features. Code in snapshot versions that works (and stops changing) eventually becomes part of an official release.

Official Postfix releases are named postfix-*a.b.c*.tgz, where *a*, *b*, and *c* are as follows:

a Major release number (significant package restructuring)

b Minor release number (new features)

c Patch level (bug fixes)

Snapshot releases have names such as postfix-*a.b-yyyymmdd*.tgz, where *yyyymmdd* is the release date. The mail_release_date configuration parameter contains the release date for both official and snapshot releases.

When you apply an official patch, the patch level and release date change. However, a new snapshot has only a different release date, unless the snapshot includes the same bug fixes as a patch release.

Applying Patches

There are several special features that you can get by applying third-party patches. You can find a list of Postfix patches at http://www.postfix.org/ addon.html. (If you don't know how to apply a patch, you probably shouldn't be doing this.)

Patches have their own documentation, and because they can significantly alter the features and behavior of Postfix, you should carefully read the instructions.

Building and Installing from Source Code

After you unpack your source code package using tar xfz postfix-*a.b.c*.tgz, you will probably customize your build process depending on the features that you want. The README_FILES directory contains the documentation for features such as BerkeleyDB, PCRE, MySQL, and SASL (SMTP-AUTH) support. Each of the files in this directory gives instructions on how to set environment variables that alter the build process.

If you're looking for functionality described in this book that isn't in the default configuration, you will most likely find instructions on how to build Postfix with the feature at the beginning of the chapter that describes the feature. You can find a complete list of available options in the INSTALL file that comes with Postfix. The build procedure is always the same:

1. Set the AUXLIBS environment variable to a set of linker options.

2. Set the CCARGS environment variable to a set of compiler and preprocessor options.

3. Run **make makefiles** to create the Makefile.

For example, on an ancient HP-UX 10.20 machine, the following is the command to include BerkeleyDB support, where the library path is /users2/ local/BerkeleyDB-4.0.14/lib and the include path is /users2/local/BerkeleyDB-4.0.14/include).

```
$ AUXLIBS='-L/users2/local/BerkeleyDB-4.0.14/lib -ldb' \
  CCARGS='-DHAS_DB -I/users2/local/BerkeleyDB-4.0.14/include' \
  make makefiles
```

If you want to use CDB instead, apply the patch, install the CDB libraries, and run this command:

```
$ AUXLIBS='-L/usr/local/lib -lcdb' \
  CCARGS='-DHAS_CDB -I/usr/local/include' \
  make makefiles
```

Then, as a regular user, run `make`:

```
$ make
```

After compiling the package, you need to determine whether you're installing Postfix for the first time or just installing an upgrade. For a first-time installation, run this command as `root`:

```
# make install
```

This command asks several questions about installation paths.

However, if you are upgrading an existing installation, run these commands as `root` instead:

```
# postfix stop
# make upgrade
# postfix start
```

For upgrades, the installer extracts the paths of the existing Postfix installation from the `main.cf` file and reuses the paths and configuration files.

Starting and Stopping Postfix

As you have probably noticed, you can control Postfix with the `postfix` program. It understands the following parameters:

start   Starts the Postfix mail system. This also runs the configuration check described below.

stop   Performs an orderly shutdown of the mail system. Running processes terminate at their earliest convenience.

check   Verifies that the Postfix configuration is valid. This command warns you about bad directory or file ownership and permissions, and it creates missing directories.

Installing Postfix on Debian Linux

It's easy to install Postfix on a Debian Linux distribution with the apt-get command. Although Postfix versions may differ over time, the steps that you need to perform for installation and integration on Debian Linux are likely to remain the same for some time.

Installing Postfix

When you initially install your system with Debian, you can choose Postfix as a package. However, if you don't manually override the default choice for mail system, exim will be enabled as the default MTA after the initial boot. You can see whether Postfix is installed on your system with the dpkg command, which will print out the installed version if present. Use it like this:

```
$ dpkg -l 'postfix*'
Desired=Unknown/Install/Remove/Purge/Hold
| Status=Not/Installed/Config-files/Unpacked/Failed-config/Half-installed
|/ Err?=(none)/Hold/Reinst-required/X=both-problems (Status,Err:
uppercase=bad)
||/ Name              Version               Description
+++-=================-=====================-
==========================================================
ii  postfix           1.1.11.0-3            A high-performance mail
transport agent
un  postfix-dev       <none>               (no description available)
un  postfix-doc       <none>               (no description available)
ii  postfix-ldap      1.1.11.0-3            LDAP map support for Postfix
ii  postfix-mysql     1.1.11.0-3            MYSQL map support for Postfix
ii  postfix-pcre      1.1.11.0-3            PCRE map support for Postfix
un  postfix-snap      <none>               (no description available)
un  postfix-snap-dev  <none>               (no description available)
un  postfix-snap-doc  <none>               (no description available)
un  postfix-snap-ldap <none>               (no description available)
un  postfix-snap-mysql <none>              (no description available)
un  postfix-snap-pcre <none>               (no description available)
un  postfix-snap-tls  <none>               (no description available)
un  postfix-tls       <none>               (no description available)
```

As you can see, Postfix 1.1.11.0-3 is installed. This system also has support for ldap, mysql, and pcre maps. Not present are the postfix-tls package (the package that supports TLS and SASL) or one of the more experimental snapshot versions (postfix-snap).

If you'd like to try out a Postfix snapshot, run this command:

```
# apt-get install postfix-snap
Reading Package Lists... Done
Building Dependency Tree... Done
```

```
The following packages will be REMOVED:
  postfix postfix-ldap postfix-mysql postfix-pcre
The following NEW packages will be installed:
  postfix-snap
0 packages upgraded, 1 newly installed, 4 to remove and 0  not upgraded.
Need to get 567kB of archives. After unpacking 47.1kB will be freed.
Do you want to continue? [Y/n]
```

Debian's package management system removes any conflicting packages, such as exim and Sendmail before installing the postfix-snap package.

Starting and Stopping Postfix

Debian policy dictates that system daemons ship with startup and shutdown scripts that go into /etc/init.d. You can start Postfix manually with /etc/init.d/postfix start and stop it with /etc/init.d/postfix stop.

Installing an Update

Installing updates and upgrades on Debian also goes through the apt-get command. Here is an example of an update being performed:

```
# apt-get update
Hit http://marillat.free.fr unstable/main Packages
Hit http://marillat.free.fr unstable/main Release
Hit http://smarden.org woody/unofficial Packages
Ign http://smarden.org woody/unofficial Release
Hit http://smarden.org woody/pape Packages
...
Reading Package Lists... Done
Building Dependency Tree... Done
# apt-get upgrade
Reading Package Lists... Done
Building Dependency Tree... Done
0 packages upgraded, 0 newly installed, 0 to remove and 0  not upgraded.
```

Upgrades leave the current configuration intact unless there are some changes that are absolutely necessary, such as additions or changes to the master.cf file and changes to the queue directory.

Building from a Debian Source Package

If you want to build Postfix from a Debian source code package, first retrieve the source package:

```
# apt-get source postfix
Reading Package Lists... Done
Building Dependency Tree... Done
```

```
Need to get 2382kB of source archives.
Get:1 http://http.us.debian.org unstable/main postfix 2.1.3-1 (dsc) [832B]
Get:2 http://http.us.debian.org unstable/main postfix 2.1.3-1 (tar) [1972kB]
Get:3 http://http.us.debian.org unstable/main postfix 2.1.3-1 (diff) [409kB]
Fetched 1977kB in 9s (216kB/s)
dpkg-source: extracting postfix in postfix-2.1.3
```

After you get the source code on your system, you can modify debian/rules or other files in the debian directory if you want to change the build in any way. When you're happy with your configuration, you can try to build Postfix with these commands:

```
# cd postfix-2.1.3
# dpkg-buildpackage
```

Let's say you try this, but you get some error messages, like these:

```
dpkg-buildpackage: source package is postfix
dpkg-buildpackage: source version is 2.1.3-1
dpkg-buildpackage: source maintainer is LaMont Jones <lamont@debian.org>
dpkg-buildpackage: host architecture is i386
dpkg-checkbuilddeps: Unmet build dependencies: libdb4.2-dev libgdbm-dev
libldap2-dev (>= 2.1) libmysqlclient10-dev libsasl2-dev postgresql-dev
dpkg-buildpackage: Build dependencies/conflicts unsatisfied; aborting.
dpkg-buildpackage: (Use -d flag to override.)
```

This means that you're missing some packages required to build this particular Postfix source package. Install the packages like this:

```
# apt-get install libdb4.2-dev libgdbm-dev libldap2-dev libmysqlclient10-dev
libsasl2-dev postgresql-dev
...
```

Now, try it again. The build process should look like this:

```
# dpkg-buildpackage
dpkg-buildpackage: source package is postfix
dpkg-buildpackage: source version is 2.1.3-1
dpkg-buildpackage: source maintainer is LaMont Jones <lamont@debian.org>
dpkg-buildpackage: host architecture is i386
 debian/rules clean
test -f debian/rules
dh_clean build
...
dpkg-deb: building package `postfix-doc' in `../postfix-doc_2.1.3-1_all.deb'.
 dpkg-genchanges
dpkg-genchanges: including full source code in upload
dpkg-buildpackage: full upload (original source is included)
```

So far, so good, but you might want to make sure that the packages are there:

```
# cd ..
# ls -l *.deb
-rw-r--r--  1 root  src    97592 Jul  5 13:11 postfix-dev_2.1.3-1_all.deb
-rw-r--r--  1 root  src   662758 Jul  5 13:11 postfix-doc_2.1.3-1_all.deb
-rw-r--r--  1 root  src    33644 Jul  5 13:11 postfix-ldap_2.1.3-1_i386.deb
-rw-r--r--  1 root  src    29646 Jul  5 13:11 postfix-mysql_2.1.3-1_i386.deb
-rw-r--r--  1 root  src    29430 Jul  5 13:11 postfix-pcre_2.1.3-1_i386.deb
-rw-r--r--  1 root  src    29920 Jul  5 13:11 postfix-pgsql_2.1.3-1_i386.deb
-rw-r--r--  1 root  src   140110 Jul  5 13:11 postfix-tls_2.1.3-1_i386.deb
-rw-r--r--  1 root  src   763570 Jul  5 13:11 postfix_2.1.3-1_i386.deb
```

If everything looks good, install the packages with dpkg -i:

```
# dpkg -i postfix_2.1.3-1_i386.deb
```

Installing Postfix on Red Hat Linux

You can install Postfix on a Red Hat Linux distribution with the RPM (Red Hat Package Manager) system. As of Red Hat Linux version 7.3, you can even install Postfix in parallel with Sendmail. You can choose which MTA to run by switching between them using the alternatives system.

As with the Debian packages, although Postfix versions vary over time, the steps required to install Postfix on a Red Hat Linux system are unlikely to change for a long time.

Getting Postfix for Red Hat Linux

The Red Hat installer does not include Postfix by default when you install Red Hat Linux, but you can add it at installation time. To check whether Postfix is already on your system, query the package manager:

```
# rpm -q postfix
postfix-2.1.1-3.fc1
```

Here, the package manager printed the currently installed version. If you don't have Postfix on your system, you'll get something like this instead:

```
# rpm -q postfix
package postfix is not installed
```

NOTE   *RPM only lists software that was installed using RPM. It does not list applications that were compiled and installed from source code.*

Getting Postfix on CD

The most convenient way to get Postfix on your machine is to copy it from the Red Hat CDs to your hard disk and install the RPM. Insert the disc into your CD drive, and attach it to your system with a command such as this:

```
# mount /dev/cdrom /mnt/cdrom/
```

Copy the Postfix RPM to your hard disk with a command like this:

```
# rpm -ivh /mnt/cdrom/RedHat/RPMS/postfix-XX-xx.rpm
```

Downloading Postfix from the Red Hat Site

You can also download the Postfix package from the Red Hat FTP site or one of its mirrors. You'll find a list of the mirrors at `http://www.redhat.com/download/mirror.html`. After downloading the package, tell the package manager to retrieve the file and install it:

```
# rpm -ivh ftp://USER:PASSWORD@HOST:PORT/path/to/postfix-XX-xx.rpm
```

Keep in mind that Red Hat does not update these packages at the same rate as Postfix development advances. If you want to run a Postfix package with the newest features but don't want to build it from source code, have a look at the RPMs that Simon J. Mudd maintains.

Downloading Simon J. Mudd's Postfix RPMs

Simon's RPMs are usually more current than the ones that ship with the Red Hat distribution. You can download ready-made binaries for multiple platforms, including Linux on Alpha, Sparc, and IBM S390 (mainframe), or you can get the SRPM (RPM Source Package). The SRPMs provide support for building binary packages with several options listed on the website.

You'll find mirror sites for Simon's RPMs and SRPMs at `http://postfix.wl0.org/en/mirrors/`.

Downloading Postfix from rpmfind.net

Finally, you'll find that rpmfind.net has RPMs for many distributions. Point your browser at `http://www.rpmfind.net`, search for *postfix*, and download the RPM appropriate to your needs.

Building an RPM from an SRPM

For security reasons, you shouldn't build RPMs from SRPMs as root. However, building them as a non-root user requires some preparation. Specifically, RPM needs a certain directory structure to build RPMs from source code or from SRPMS. By default, these directories are under `/usr/src/redhat`.

Setting Up the Directory Structure and Environment Variables

When you build an RPM as a regular user, you cannot use the default location because only root is allowed to write to the default directories. Use the following script to create the required directory structure in your home directory, and set appropriate environment variables for RPM:

```
#!/bin/sh
# rpmuser Build user rpmbuild environment
# Author: Tuomo Soini <http://tis.foobar.fi>
#
# create directories
for i in SOURCES SPECS BUILD SRPMS RPMS/i386 RPMS/i486 RPMS/i586 RPMS/i686 \
RPMS/athlon RPMS/noarch
do
  mkdir -p $HOME/rpm/$i
done
unset i
# set environment variables
echo "%_topdir $HOME/rpm" >> $HOME/.rpmmacros
# EOF
```

Let's say that you create a user named rpmuser to build the RPM. After running rpm_prepare.sh, the user's home directory should have the following directories and subdirectories:

```
$ tree
.
|-- rpm
|   |-- BUILD
|   |-- RPMS
|   |   |-- athlon
|   |   |-- i386
|   |   |-- i486
|   |   |-- i586
|   |   |-- i686
|   |   `-- noarch
|   |-- SOURCES
|   |-- SPECS
|   `-- SRPMS
`-- rpm_prepare.sh
12 directories, 1 file
```

The script also sets the correct variables in the .rpmmacros file. You need to set the environment every time you log in and out as the user who builds the RPMs. Use the **echo "%_topdir $HOME/rpm" >> $HOME/.rpmmacros** command to do this.

NOTE   *If you want to get into more detail on building RPMs, have a look at the RPM HOWTO at http://rpm.org.*

Building and Installing an RPM

You can't query source packages for the options to build into the binary. The workaround is to install the source package with `rpm -ivh postfix-XX-xx.src.rpm` into the new rpm build directory; then take a look at the script that is used to build spec files:

```
$ less rpm/SOURCES/make-postfix.spec
...
# The following external variables if set to 1 affect the behaviour
#
# POSTFIX_MYSQL          include support for MySQL's MySQL packages
# POSTFIX_MYSQL_REDHAT   include support for RedHat's mysql packages
# POSTFIX_MYSQL_PATHS    include support for locally installed mysql binary,
#                        providing the colon seperated include and
#                        library paths ( /usr/include/mysql:/usr/lib/mysql )
# POSTFIX_MYSQL_QUERY    include support for writing full select statements
#                        in mysql maps
# POSTFIX_LDAP           include support for openldap packages
# POSTFIX_PCRE           include support for pcre maps
# POSTFIX_PGSQL          include support for PostGres database
# POSTFIX_SASL           include support for SASL (1, 2 or 0 to disable)
# POSTFIX_TLS            include support for TLS
# POSTFIX_IPV6           include support for IPv6
# POSTFIX_VDA            include support for Virtual Delivery Agent
...
# To rebuild the spec file, set the appropriate environment
# variables and do the following:
#
# cd `rpm --eval '%{_sourcedir}'`
# export POSTFIX_MYSQL=1       # for example
# sh make-postfix.spec
# cd `rpm --eval '%{_specdir}'`
# rpmbuild -ba postfix.spec
```

Follow the instructions in the script to set the appropriate environment variables and create your spec file. After you're satisfied with your spec file, build your RPM with this command:

```
$ rpmbuild -ba rpm/SPECS/postfix.spec
```

Upon successful completion, become root and install Postfix:

```
# rpm -ivh /path/to/postfix-XX-xx.rpm
```

Now all you need to do is tell your Red Hat server to use Postfix as its MTA.

Switching to Postfix

The default MTA for Red Hat servers is Sendmail. You can change this by using alternatives to switch to Postfix.

NOTE *As of Red Hat 7.3, the distribution comes with a Debian port called* alternatives. *This command makes it possible for several programs that perform identical or similar functions to be installed on a single system at the same time.*

Become root, invoke alternatives --config mta, and then specify Postfix as the default MTA:

```
# alternatives --config mta
There are 2 programs which provide 'mta'.
  Selection    Command
-----------------------------------------------
*+ 1           /usr/sbin/sendmail.sendmail
   2           /usr/sbin/sendmail.postfix
Enter to keep the default[*], or type selection number: 2
```

As the default MTA, Postfix will automatically be started by Red Hat at boot time. You can check the runlevels by running chkconfig:

```
# chkconfig --list postfix
postfix         0:off   1:off   2:on    3:on    4:on    5:on    6:off
```

Removing the Sendmail MTA

After you install Postfix, there's no reason to keep Sendmail hanging around, so remove it like this:

```
# rpm -e sendmail
```

Starting and Stopping Postfix in Red Hat Linux

Red Hat Linux RPMs usually ship with startup and shutdown scripts that go in /etc/init.d. You can start Postfix with /etc/init.d/postfix start and stop it with /etc/init.d/postfix stop.

B

TROUBLESHOOTING POSTFIX

This chapter contains tips for several different Postfix trouble areas, including the system logger, configuration issues, network oddities, and general system issues. As with any kind of troubleshooting, when you're having trouble with Postfix, you need to have an idea of where the problem is before you can fix it. This is especially true for Postfix, which has several separate subsystems.

Problems Starting Postfix and Viewing the Log

The most "obvious" reason for Postfix not to be processing your mail is that Postfix might not even be running. Postfix must be running, even if you're only submitting mail using the sendmail command. The easiest way to find out if Postfix is running is to run **postfix start**:

```
# postfix start
postfix/postfix-script: starting the Postfix mail system
```

If you see this message, it means that Postfix wasn't running, so the command tried to start it up. However, if Postfix is already running, you'll get this message:

```
# postfix start
postfix/postfix-script: fatal: the Postfix mail system is already running
```

When running this command, you should see similar messages in your mail log, such as these:

```
Jul  5 22:49:29 mail postfix/postfix-script: starting the Postfix mail system
Jul  5 22:49:29 mail postfix/master[14835]: daemon started -- version 2.1.3
```

If you don't see these messages, check your syslog configuration immediately. You want to make sure that it logs *mail.*; complete logs are essential for any kind of comprehensive troubleshooting.

We recommend consolidating all syslog entries for the mail facility (or whichever facility Postfix is configured for) into one log file. Some installations (such as the one in Debian GNU/Linux) split the log into multiple files, but this makes reading the log very tedious. To set it up for easy viewing, make sure your /etc/syslog.conf has an entry like this:

```
# (- Log all the mail messages to one place.)
mail.*                                              -/var/log/maillog
```

Let's say that you see the messages on the command line and log, but you still wonder if Postfix is actually running. Sometimes it pays to be paranoid, because Postfix can start and crash immediately afterward if there's a serious problem. Use ps and grep to see if the Postfix component daemons are really running. If they are running, the command execution should look like this:

```
# ps aux|grep postfix
root      5035  0.0  0.4  2476 1100 ?         S    09:29   0:00 /usr/lib/postfix/master
postfix   5036  0.0  0.3  2404  936 ?         S    09:29   0:00 pickup -l -t fifo -u -c
postfix   5037  0.0  0.3  2440  964 ?         S    09:29   0:00 qmgr -l -n qmgr -t fifo -u -c
```

In the preceding output, you can see that the Postfix master daemon is running as root, and the queue manager (qmgr) and pickup service are running as the postfix user, so the system is up and running.

There are several reasons why Postfix might fail to start, but the most common is that a Postfix daemon can't find a shared library. To approach this problem, first find the directories that Postfix uses with this command:

```
# postconf | grep directory
command_directory = /usr/sbin
config_directory = /etc/postfix
```

```
daemon_directory = /usr/lib/postfix
mail_spool_directory = /var/mail
manpage_directory = /usr/local/man
process_id_directory = pid
program_directory = /usr/sbin
queue_directory = /var/spool/postfix
readme_directory = no
require_home_directory = no
sample_directory = /etc/postfix
tls_random_exchange_name = ${config_directory}/prng_exch
```

You're looking for the path to daemon_directory. Find it and change to that directory. Look at the contents:

```
# cd /usr/lib/postfix
# ls -l
total 384
-rwxr-xr-x    1 root        root        16588 Sep 12 18:50 bounce
-rwxr-xr-x    1 root        root        22684 Sep 12 18:50 cleanup
-rwxr-xr-x    1 root        root         4248 Sep 12 18:50 error
-rwxr-xr-x    1 root        root        10344 Sep 12 18:50 flush
-rwxr-xr-x    1 root        root        20508 Sep 12 18:50 lmtp
-rwxr-xr-x    1 root        root        31956 Sep 12 18:50 local
-rwxr-xr-x    1 root        root        22388 Sep 12 18:50 master
-rwxr-xr-x    1 root        root        33084 Sep 12 18:50 nqmgr
-rwxr-xr-x    1 root        root         7248 Sep 12 18:50 pickup
-rwxr-xr-x    1 root        root        10496 Sep 12 18:50 pipe
-rwxr-xr-x    1 root        root        27424 Sep 12 18:50 qmgr
-rwxr-xr-x    1 root        root        12160 Sep 12 18:50 qmqpd
-rwxr-xr-x    1 root        root         7456 Sep 12 18:50 showq
-rwxr-xr-x    1 root        root        25000 Sep 12 18:50 smtp
-rwxr-xr-x    1 root        root        44712 Sep 12 18:50 smtpd
-rwxr-xr-x    1 root        root         5612 Sep 12 18:50 spawn
-rwxr-xr-x    1 root        root        10284 Sep 12 18:50 trivial-rewrite
-rwxr-xr-x    1 root        root        10400 Sep 12 18:50 virtual
```

The Postfix daemons from the command column in the /etc/postfix/master.cf file should be in this directory. You can inspect the shared library dependencies of a single program with the ldd command (this works on Linux, Solaris, and other common Unix variants; it may be a different command on other systems):

```
# ldd `postconf -h daemon_directory`/smtpd
        libpostfix-master.so.1 => /usr/lib/libpostfix-master.so.1 (0x4001d000)
        libpostfix-global.so.1 => /usr/lib/libpostfix-global.so.1 (0x40023000)
        libpostfix-dns.so.1 => /usr/lib/libpostfix-dns.so.1 (0x4003c000)
        libpostfix-util.so.1 => /usr/lib/libpostfix-util.so.1 (0x40040000)
        libdb3.so.3 => /usr/lib/libdb3.so.3 (0x4005d000)
        libnsl.so.1 => /lib/libnsl.so.1 (0x40105000)
```

```
libresolv.so.2 => /lib/libresolv.so.2 (0x40119000)
libgdbm.so.1 => /usr/lib/libgdbm.so.1 (0x4012a000)
libc.so.6 => /lib/libc.so.6 (0x40130000)
libdl.so.2 => /lib/libdl.so.2 (0x4024b000)
/lib/ld-linux.so.2 => /lib/ld-linux.so.2 (0x40000000)
```

The preceding output seems to indicate that everything is in order with the smtpd daemon because every library dependency resolves to an actual file. However, you might be unlucky enough to get this instead:

```
# ldd `postconf -h daemon_directory`/smtpd
        libpostfix-master.so.1 => /usr/lib/libpostfix-master.so.1 (0x4001d000)
        libpostfix-global.so.1 => /usr/lib/libpostfix-global.so.1 (0x40023000)
        libpostfix-dns.so.1 => /usr/lib/libpostfix-dns.so.1 (0x4003c000)
        libpostfix-util.so.1 => /usr/lib/libpostfix-util.so.1 (0x40040000)
        libdb3.so.3 => not found
        libnsl.so.1 => /lib/libnsl.so.1 (0x4005d000)
        libresolv.so.2 => /lib/libresolv.so.2 (0x40071000)
        libgdbm.so.1 => /usr/lib/libgdbm.so.1 (0x40082000)
        libc.so.6 => /lib/libc.so.6 (0x40088000)
        libdl.so.2 => /lib/libdl.so.2 (0x401a3000)
        /lib/ld-linux.so.2 => /lib/ld-linux.so.2 (0x40000000)
```

In this case, libdb3.so.3 is missing. A program that cannot find all of its shared libraries will not run. If you're running Linux, and you installed a Postfix package intended for another distribution (or even another version of your distribution), it's possible that you may discover this kind of problem only at run time. If this is the case, you need to make a decision.

The best solution is to find a Postfix package that fits your distribution or to compile Postfix from source code (see Appendix A). However, if you insist on trying to work with what you have, you can try to find libdb3.so.3 like this:

```
# find / -name libdb3.so.3
/usr/lib/libdb3.so.3
```

This command will probably take forever to finish (because it searches your whole filesystem), but if you're lucky enough to find the library, you can add its directory path to the /etc/ld.so.conf file and run ldconfig. Of course, this might invite library and symbol clashes. It's almost never a good idea to mess around with shared libraries unless you really know what you're doing.

The find command may not even help, because the library may not reside on your system. If this is the case, you might be able to find the package that contains the library. However, if you just can't seem to work it out, you need to make a tough decision. If finding a Postfix package that works seems out of the question, and compiling from source code seems daunting, you might consider switching operating systems or distributions.

Connecting to Postfix

If Postfix starts up fine but doesn't behave as expected, see if your server actually accepts connections on port 25. Connect to the SMTP port to find out. Here's how a successful connection plays out:

```
# telnet localhost 25
220 mail.example.com ESMTP Postfix
QUIT
221 Bye
```

You may be able to connect to the loopback interface, but this doesn't mean that the entire Internet can. Let's say that your machine is at 10.1.2.233. Try it again, this time connecting to that address:

```
# telnet 10.1.2.233 25
220 mail.example.com ESMTP Postfix
QUIT
221 Bye
```

If this doesn't work, the first thing to do is look in your `main.cf` file to see if `inet_interfaces` has been set but excludes the IP address that you're trying to reach. The default is to listen on all interfaces.

Checking the Network

If the Postfix configuration seems fine, and Postfix has been restarted, but you still can't establish a connection, check the firewall or IP filtering configuration of your network. It's possible that your system blocks the port by default. There are several places to look, because IP filtering can happen through an operating system firewall script (for example, something that calls `iptables` or `ipf`), or it can be performed outside of the machine by firewall appliances and routers.

You have to check everywhere.

If your configuration seems correct so far, you need to check outside of your local network. Your ISP can block incoming traffic to your port 25 (and, incidentally, outgoing traffic to port 25 on another machine). If you find that your ISP is refusing incoming traffic and it refuses to open up the port, your only recourse is to change ISPs.

To see if an outsider can reach you, run this command:

```
# telnet relay-test.mail-abuse.org
```

When you make this connection, relay-test.mail-abuse.org performs an online relay test of the machine that made the connection. If your ISP (or your own firewall) doesn't block incoming connections to your box on port 25, then you should see quite a few messages in your log file.

If you can't connect to the preceding host, you may be having name resolution problems. Test it with this command:

```
# host relay-test.mail-abuse.org
relay-test.mail-abuse.org is an alias for cygnus.mail-abuse.org.
cygnus.mail-abuse.org has address 168.61.4.13
```

You should see an IP address, as shown in the preceding output. If you don't, you can't resolve hostnames. Your /etc/resolv.conf or /etc/nsswitch.conf file (or both) could be incorrect. It could be even worse; your machine might not even be able to connect to the Internet. Try to ping something. A successful test looks like this (use CTRL-C to stop the test):

```
# ping 134.169.9.107
PING 134.169.9.107 (134.169.9.107): 56 data bytes
64 bytes from 134.169.9.107: icmp_seq=0 ttl=54 time=12.1 ms
64 bytes from 134.169.9.107: icmp_seq=1 ttl=54 time=12.1 ms
64 bytes from 134.169.9.107: icmp_seq=2 ttl=54 time=12.1 ms
--- 134.169.9.107 ping statistics ---
3 packets transmitted, 3 packets received, 0% packet loss
round-trip min/avg/max = 12.1/12.1/12.1 ms
```

Verifying the Listening Process

If Postfix is running and your network checks out, but your test connections still don't seem to work, see if Postfix is actually listening on port 25 with the netstat command:

```
# netstat -t -a | grep LISTEN
tcp        0      0 *:printer              *:*                LISTEN
tcp        0      0 localhost:domain       *:*                LISTEN
tcp        0      0 *:ssh                  *:*                LISTEN
tcp        0      0 *:smtp                 *:*                LISTEN
```

The preceding output shows that there are servers listening on the printer, domain, SSH, and SMTP ports (check /etc/services for the numerical counterparts of the names). You can see that something is listening on port 25 (smtp). However, is this Postfix or something else?

The lsof command can tell you. Try the command that follows. If the output includes sendmail listening on port 25, then your old sendmail binary is still active:

```
# lsof -i tcp:25
COMMAND    PID USER   FD   TYPE DEVICE SIZE NODE NAME
sendmail 25976 root    4u  IPv4 228618      TCP mail.example.com:smtp
(LISTEN)
```

Kill this process, and edit your system startup files so that it won't come back when you reboot (if at all possible, remove Sendmail from your system entirely, because you're supposed to run Postfix, remember?).

NOTE   *lsof is an extremely powerful tool that can show all open files (and the processes using the files), but it is very dependent on your kernel. Make sure that your* lsof *is up-to-date and matches your current kernel. An outdated* lsof *returns no output for Internet connections at all. Run* **lsof -i** *if you're not sure if it works.*

If you're using Postfix, the lsof output should include Postfix listening on port 25 with the master daemon:

```
# lsof -i tcp:25
COMMAND   PID USER   FD   TYPE DEVICE SIZE NODE NAME
master  26079 root   11u  IPv4 228828      TCP *:smtp (LISTEN)
```

Getting Postfix to Use Your Configuration Settings

The main.cf file is long and can be difficult to read. A configuration option can appear twice, or a typo can be hidden somewhere in a pile of comments. Use the postconf command to display the configuration that Postfix uses. You can see the difference just from line counts:

```
# cd /etc/postfix
# wc -l main.cf
# postconf -n | wc -l
```

The output of postconf -n lists all parameter settings in main.cf, even parameters that have the same value as the default. When changing main.cf, you should verify your changes with postconf to see if Postfix sees them.

You might prefer to use the command postconf -e *parameter=value* to edit the parameter in main.cf to *value* programmatically. This little trick allows you to make changes to the Postfix configuration with shell scripts or cron jobs.

If you're approaching a configuration issue, the postconf(5) manual page is worth reading.

Reporting Postfix Problems

When you are first starting out with Postfix, it can be difficult to judge the kind of information that should be reported to postfix-users@postfix.org. The postfinger program (by Simon J. Mudd) extracts most of the relevant information. To see what it does, mail the postfinger output, along with your own questions, to yourself like this:

```
# postfinger | /usr/sbin/sendmail youraddress@your.domain
```

Of course, this assumes that outgoing mail works on your system. When all else fails, you can transfer the output to another system.

If your problem is related to SMTP-AUTH and thus SASL, use Patrick's script saslfinger! saslfinger is a bash utility script that seeks to help you debug your SMTP AUTH setup. The saslfinger program gathers various information about Cyrus SASL and Postfix from your system and sends it to stdout. To see what it does, mail the saslfinger output, along with your own questions, to yourself like this:

```
# saslfinger -s | /usr/sbin/sendmail youraddress@your.domain
```

NOTE *Postfinger has been part of the source distribution of Postfix since version 2.1. You can also get it at ftp://ftp.wl0.org/sources/postfinger.*

saslfinger is not part of the source distribution of Postfix. You can get it at http://postfix.state-of-mind.de/patrick.koetter/saslfinger.

Getting More Logging Information

If you're having trouble zeroing in on problems with specific pieces of your Postfix installation, you can increase the amount of logging information on a per-daemon basis. Do this by appending -v to the daemon configuration entry in /etc/postfix/master.cf, as in this example for smtpd:

```
# ==========================================================================
# service type  private unpriv  chroot  wakeup  maxproc command + args
#               (yes)   (yes)   (yes)   (never) (50)
# ==========================================================================
smtp      inet n    -       -       -       -       smtpd -v
```

To make the change take effect, reload Postfix. The daemon should now be very verbose when it does its work. If this still isn't enough information, you can even add another -v to the entry, and you'll get even more output. Make sure that you set it back to normal after you're finished with debugging, because verbose logging generates lots of lines in your log file, hindering the overall system performance.

Client-Specific Logging

If you have a busy mail server, and increasing the log level for all clients will bury you in output, you can also selectively increase logging for certain clients with the debug_peer_list parameter. The following example shows how to make the smptd logging more verbose for only the clients at 10.0.0.1 and 10.0.0.4:

```
debug_peer_list = 10.0.0.1, 10.0.0.4
```

You can specify one or more hosts, domains, addresses, and networks as the value for this parameter. To make the change effective immediately, you need to run the **postfix reload** command.

Logging and qmgr

One common problem is that log output from the qmgr process is missing. The queue manager should emit log entries like this:

```
Aug  5 17:05:26 hostname postfix/qmgr[308]: A44F828C71:
  from=<bamm@example.com>, size=153136, nrcpt=1
(queue active)
```

If you're missing the log information, there are two possible causes:

libc problems

The libc implementation is broken (the syslog client does not reconnect when the syslogd server is restarted). If this is the case, you should upgrade your libc.

qmgr is running chrooted

The Postfix qmgr process is running chrooted (see master.cf), but there is no syslog socket inside the chroot jail. See the syslog(8) manual page for how to specify additional sockets and to specify one for the Postfix chroot jail.

Other Configuration Errors

There are three errors that seem to happen all of the time:

Problems opening files

If you have a problem opening a file that seems to exist, see if it's specified as a map in the configuration file (for example, if it starts with a hash: prefix). If this is the case, run **postmap** on the plaintext file that contains the map data to create an indexed version.

Also, verify that the permissions and ownership are correct. Don't forget executable access on the directory and all directories leading up to it.

Permissions problems

If you have permissions problems, you can see whether Postfix can fix them automatically with the post-install command:

```
# /etc/postfix/post-install set-permissions upgrade-configuration
```

This command edits main.cf and master.cf as appropriate, in addition to fixing permission problems, so you might want to make a backup of your configuration before doing this.

Comments

Any line whose first non-space character is a hash (#) is a comment. Postfix doesn't accept any other comment syntax. If postconf shows a parameter that seems unfamiliar, you may have a misplaced # somewhere in your configuration file.

Intricacies of the chroot Jail

All too often, the ability to run chrooted causes strange problems. A Postfix installation *never* runs chrooted by default. There are just too many things that can go wrong, so Wietse wisely chose *not* to chroot by default. Unfortunately, other package maintainers sometimes go a little crazy with security features.

Postfix daemons open all their maps before entering the jail. However, system files that are needed for DNS lookups, other host related lookups, network service lookup, timezone lookup, and other stuff that happens in libraries that are linked into Postfix must be in the chroot jail. The package maintainer needs to provide scripts that copy the necessary files from their original locations in the filesystem into the jail. You typically need /etc/resolv.conf and /etc/nsswitch.conf. The Postfix source distribution includes an examples/chroot-setup subdirectory that contains scripts for setting up a chroot jail under different operating systems. Matthias Andree wrote a LINUX2 script that sets things straight on Linux.

In theory, a package maintainer should include the mechanism to build the chroot jail correctly on your particular operating system or distribution. However, if you're just starting out, you could be overwhelmed. Instead of correcting your chroot jail, which you never knew existed at all, you should probably un-chroot Postfix's daemons until you get Postfix fully operational. Edit /etc/postfix/master.cf, and look at each entry:

```
# ==========================================================================
# service type  private unpriv  chroot  wakeup  maxproc command + args
#               (yes)   (yes)   (yes)   (never) (50)
# ==========================================================================
smtp      inet  n       -       -       -       -       smtpd
```

A hyphen in the chroot column indicates that smtpd *is* running chrooted. Set this to n, and reload Postfix. In addition, remember that not every Postfix daemon can run chrooted. Most of them can, but you're likely to encounter bizarre problems if you try to chroot the pipe, local, or virtual daemons.

You'll find a lot more information about the chroot process in Chapter 20.

Solving Filesystem Problems

Most modern Unix flavors offer journaling filesystems, but this may not protect you from occasional filesystem corruption, especially if you have bad hardware or are using a newfangled filesystem that hasn't been fully debugged. If there are very strange things happening, such as directories turning into files, consider an immediate reboot with a full forced fsck of all disks with a series of commands like this:

```
# touch /forcefsck
# sync
# reboot
```

Yes, you won't have a pretty uptime number, and users will complain, but you cannot fix filesystem problems without forcing fsck. We've successfully annoyed many users on Red Hat and Debian this way.

Library Hell

Postfix makes extensive use of shared libraries, such as the BerkeleyDB library. This particular library causes a lot of problems because there are so many different versions with different on-disk data formats. All mail service components, such as Postfix, POP-before-SMTP, dracd, postgrey, and other tools that access and alter hash: or btree: type maps need to use compatible BerkeleyDB libraries.

It gets even worse; on-disk formats for different versions of BerkeleyDB are incompatible, meaning that an application may not be able to read a map written by another application that uses a different version of BerkeleyDB.

To check the libraries that Postfix uses, use the ldd command as described in the section "Problems Starting Postfix and Viewing the Log":

```
# ldd `postconf -h daemon_directory`/smtpd
        libpcre.so.0 => /usr/local/lib/libpcre.so.0 (0x4001d000)
        libdb-3.1.so => /lib/libdb-3.1.so (0x40028000)
        libnsl.so.1 => /lib/libnsl.so.1 (0x400a1000)
        libresolv.so.2 => /lib/libresolv.so.2 (0x400b8000)
        libc.so.6 => /lib/libc.so.6 (0x400ca000)
        /lib/ld-linux.so.2 => /lib/ld-linux.so.2 (0x40000000)
```

In the preceding output, smtpd was linked against BerkeleyDB-3.1.*x*, so all other programs that need to share the Postfix hash: and btree: maps must use the same version of BerkeleyDB (or at least a version that has the same on-disk format).

Daemon Inconsistencies

If an upgrade of Postfix fails, or if you do it in a nonstandard way (such as installing from source over an RPM install instead of removing the old version first), strange things can happen. You may be mixing daemons from different versions of Postfix.

To find out the version of Postfix that a daemon belongs to, use `strings` on all daemon binaries, like this:

```
# strings /usr/libexec/postfix/smtpd | grep 2003
2.0.13-20030706
20030706
# strings /usr/libexec/postfix/cleanup | grep 2003
2.0.13-20030706
20030706
```

In this case, the versions (represented as dates) actually match. We've used 2003 as the year in this example, but you're using a version from another year, grep for that year instead.

Fork Hell

One common problem that is caused by mixing daemons from incompatible Postfix versions has to do with the `tlsmgr` daemon. The load appears to be incredibly high and process IDs are increasing constantly, but nothing's running, and there isn't even much mail traffic or queued mail.

You probably upgraded Postfix but kept an old `tlsmgr` and `master.cf` file that runs `tlsmgr`.

The problem is that the new Postfix spawns the old `tlsmgr`, but this daemon immediately exits with status 0 because it can't work with the new version of Postfix. Postfix logs nothing because an exit code of 0 is normal. However, Postfix immediately respawns `tlsmgr`, and the process repeats itself.

If this turns out to be the case, first comment out the `tlsmgr` line in `master.cf`, then reload Postfix to resume normal services. Then you can get a working upgrade with a compatible version of `tlsmgr`.

Stress-Testing Postfix

To find out how much mail traffic your installation can handle, you need to perform some kind of stress testing. To put an adequate load on the server, you need a fast mail generator. Postfix comes with a pair of testing programs named `smtp-source` and `smtp-sink` for just this purpose. Here's how they work:

`smtp-source`

This program connects to a host on a TCP port (port 25 by default) and sends one or more messages, either sequentially or in parallel. The program speaks both SMTP (the default) or LMTP, and it is meant to aid in measuring server performance.

`smtp-sink`

This test server listens on the named host (or address) and port. It receives messages from the network and throws them away. You can measure client and network performance with this program.

Let's start with `smtp-source` to stress-test your Postfix installation. The following example injects 100 total messages of size 5KB each in 20 parallel sessions to a Postfix server running on `localhost` port 25. Because you're also interested in how much time this takes, use the `time` command:

```
$ time ./smtp-source -s 20 ❶ -l 5120 ❷ -m 100 ❸ -c ❹ \
  -f sender@example.com ❺ -t recipient@example.com ❻ localhost:25 ❼
100
real    0m4.294s
user    0m0.060s
sys     0m0.030s
```

  ❶ 20 parallel sessions
  ❷ 5KB message size
  ❸ 100 total messages
  ❹ Display a counter
  ❺ Envelope sender
  ❻ Envelope recipient
  ❼ Target SMTP server

In this example, injection took 4.294 seconds. You also want to know how long actual delivery takes. Check your logs for this and to verify that every last message that arrived for `recipient@example.com` was received.

Now let's turn our attention to `smtp-sink` to find out how many messages per second your server can handle from your horrible mass-mailing software. Postfix has to process each outgoing message even if the server on the other side throws it away (so you can't use this to test the raw performance of your mass mailer unless you connect your mailer directly to `smtp-sink`).

The following example sets up an SMTP listener on port 25 of `localhost`:

```
$ ./smtp-sink -c localhost:25 1000
```

Now you can run your client tests.

If you want to get an idea of how much overhead the network imposes, and also run a controlled experiment to see what the theoretical maximum throughput is for your mail server, you can make `smtp-source` and `smtp-sink` talk to each other. Open two windows, and in the first, start up the dummy server like this:

```
# ./smtp-sink -c localhost:25 1000
100
```

With this in place, start throwing messages at this server with `smtp-source` in the other window:

```
$ time ./smtp-source -s 20 -l 5120 -m 100 -c \
  -f sender@example.com -t recipient@example.com localhost:25
100
real    0m0.239s
user    0m0.000s
sys     0m0.040s
```

This output shows that `smtp-sink` is much faster at accepting messages than Postfix. It took only 0.239 seconds to accept the messages, which is 18 times faster than the Postfix injection process. Now, wouldn't it be nice if you could throw away all incoming email like this?

Disk I/O

When you run your stress testing, you might encounter huge load averages on your machine that seem out of place. Assuming that you don't have any content filtering in place, Postfix is I/O bound, so your I/O subsystem could be saturated.

If the output of `top` shows a high load, such as `10.7`, but none of your processes are actually using the CPU, your load is probably coming from the kernel using most of the CPU for I/O and not letting processes run. Furthermore, the reason that the kernel is doing so much I/O is that many more processes have requested I/O operations (and are now waiting for them).

Linux 2.6 kernels support iowait status in the `top` command. To see if this is the case on 2.4.*x* kernels (which don't have a separate means of displaying the iowait status), you can add a kernel module. Oliver Wellnitz wrote just such a kernel module that you can download from `ftp://ftp.ibr.cs.tu-bs.de/os/linux/people/wellnitz/programming`. This module calculates the load differently and gives you an interface in the /proc filesystem that you can see, like this:

```
# cat /proc/loadavg-io
rq 0.30 0.23 0.14
io 0.08 0.31 0.27
```

In this example, `rq` is the number of processes that are in the state `TASK_RUNNING`, while `io` is the number of processes that are in the state `TASK_UNINTERRUPTIBLE` (waiting for I/O). The sum of those two is what the kernel usually calls load.

If you're having problems like this, you need faster disks, or even a solution such as an SSD (a solid state disk—basically a RAM disk with a battery backup) or a mirrored or striped RAID for the queue directory. See the section "Incoming Queue Bottlenecks" in Chapter 22 for more information.

One other solution that may or may not work is to remove the synchronous updates for the queue directory. If you're using an ext2 or ext3 filesystem, try this command:

```
# chattr -R -S /var/spool/postfix/
```

This setting is actually the default with recent Postfix installations.

Too Many Connections

When you set up your mail server, you may try to tackle too many problems at once. If you want a stable Postfix system, change one thing at a time. This especially holds true if you want to use LDAP or SQL. Try proceeding like this:

1. Build your system *without* LDAP maps (that is, use hash, btree or dbm maps).

2. Use appropriate ldapsearch commands to extract all the necessary data from your LDAP server. Use a scripting language, such as Perl or Python, to reformat the data into the Postfix map file input.

3. When your Postfix is working correctly without LDAP, replace one map at a time with a corresponding LDAP map. Test each LDAP map as user postfix, like this:

    ```
    $ postmap -q - ldap:mapname < keyfile
    ```

    keyfile contains a list of addresses (keys) to be queried. If the map returns sensible data, change a suitable _maps configuration parameter to have Postfix use the LDAP map.

4. To consolidate the number of open lookup tables, share one open table among multiple Postfix processes with the proxymap daemon, as described in the section titled "Postfix Daemons" in Chapter 5.

C

CIDR AND SMTP STANDARDS REFERENCE

 This first section in this chapter explains the Classless Inter Domain Routing (CIDR) notation that Postfix can use in cidr: type maps and for the mynetworks parameter. The second section cites possible SMTP server response codes from RFC 2821.

Subnets in CIDR Notation

In CIDR notation, an IP address is represented as A.B.C.D/n, where n is called the IP prefix or network prefix. The IP prefix identifies the number of significant bits used to identify a network. For example, 192.9.205.22 /18 means the first 18 bits are used to represent the network and the remaining 14 bits are used to identify hosts. Common prefixes are 8, 16, 24, and 32.

Even if you claim to have been fooling around with computers since you were 10, and to have been one of the first to get online (back when the word ARPANET meant something), you may still have trouble remembering subnet masks in CIDR notation. Table C-1 lists the subnet masks and their equivalents.

Table C-1: Subnets in CIDR Notation

CIDR Prefix	Netmask	Binary Value	Number of Networks
/1	128.0.0.0	10000000000000000000000000000000	128 Class A domains
/2	192.0.0.0	11000000000000000000000000000000	64 Class A domains
/3	224.0.0.0	11100000000000000000000000000000	32 Class A domains
/4	240.0.0.0	11110000000000000000000000000000	16 Class A domains
/5	248.0.0.0	11111000000000000000000000000000	8 Class A domains
/6	252.0.0.0	11111100000000000000000000000000	4 Class A domains
/7	254.0.0.0	11111110000000000000000000000000	2 Class A domains
/8	255.0.0.0	11111111000000000000000000000000	1 Class A domain
/9	255.128.0.0	11111111100000000000000000000000	128 Class B domains
/10	255.192.0.0	11111111110000000000000000000000	64 Class B domains
/11	255.224.0.0	11111111111000000000000000000000	32 Class B domains
/12	255.240.0.0	11111111111100000000000000000000	16 Class B domains
/13	255.248.0.0	11111111111110000000000000000000	8 Class B domains
/14	255.252.0.0	11111111111111000000000000000000	4 Class B domains
/15	255.254.0.0	11111111111111100000000000000000	2 Class B domains
/16	255.255.0.0	11111111111111110000000000000000	1 Class B domain
/17	255.255.128.0	11111111111111111000000000000000	128 Class C domains
/18	255.255.192.0	11111111111111111100000000000000	64 Class C domains
/19	255.255.224.0	11111111111111111110000000000000	32 Class C domains
/20	255.255.240.0	11111111111111111111000000000000	16 Class C domains
/21	255.255.248.0	11111111111111111111100000000000	8 Class C domains
/22	255.255.252.0	11111111111111111111110000000000	4 Class C domains
/23	255.255.254.0	11111111111111111111111000000000	2 Class C domains
/24	255.255.255.0	11111111111111111111111100000000	1 Class C domain
/25	255.255.255.128	11111111111111111111111110000000	128 hosts
/26	255.255.255.192	11111111111111111111111111000000	64 hosts
/27	255.255.255.224	11111111111111111111111111100000	32 hosts
/28	255.255.255.240	11111111111111111111111111110000	16 hosts
/29	255.255.255.248	11111111111111111111111111111000	8 hosts
/30	255.255.255.252	11111111111111111111111111111100	4 hosts
/31	255.255.255.254	11111111111111111111111111111110	2 hosts
/32	255.255.255.255	11111111111111111111111111111111	1 host

Server Response Codes

The following server response codes can help you to understand log messages or to set response codes that differ from Postfix's default settings. The codes are excerpts from RFC 2821, section 4.2.

4.2.1 Reply Code Severities and Theory

The three digits of the reply each have a special significance. The first digit denotes whether the response is good, bad or incomplete. An unsophisticated SMTP client, or one that receives an unexpected code, will be able to determine its next action (proceed as planned, redo, retrench, etc.) by examining this first digit. An SMTP client that wants to know approximately what kind of error occurred (e.g., mail system error, command syntax error) may examine the second digit. The third digit and any supplemental information that may be present is reserved for the finest gradation of information.

There are five values for the first digit of the reply code:

1yz Positive Preliminary reply
    The command has been accepted, but the requested action is being held in abeyance, pending confirmation of the information in this reply. The SMTP client should send another command specifying whether to continue or abort the action.

NOTE   *Unextended SMTP does not have any commands that allow this type of reply, so it does not have continue or abort commands.*

2yz Positive Completion reply
    The requested action has been successfully completed. A new request may be initiated.

3yz Positive Intermediate reply
    The command has been accepted, but the requested action is being held in abeyance, pending receipt of further information. The SMTP client should send another command specifying this information. This reply is used in command sequence groups (i.e., in DATA).

4yz Transient Negative Completion reply
    The command was not accepted, and the requested action did not occur. However, the error condition is temporary and the action may be requested again. The sender should return to the beginning of the command sequence (if any). It is difficult to assign a meaning to "transient" when two different sites (receiver- and sender-SMTP agents) must agree on the interpretation. Each reply in this category might have a different time value, but the SMTP client is encouraged to try again. A rule of thumb to determine whether a reply fits into the 4yz or the 5yz category (see below) is that replies are 4yz if they can be successful if repeated without any change in command form or in properties of the sender or receiver (that is, the command is repeated identically and the receiver does not put up a new implementation.)

5yz Permanent Negative Completion reply
The command was not accepted and the requested action did not occur.
The SMTP client is discouraged from repeating the exact request (in
the same sequence). Even some "permanent" error conditions can be
corrected, so the human user may want to direct the SMTP client to
reinitiate the command sequence by direct action at some point in
the future (e.g., after the spelling has been changed, or the user
has altered the account status).

[. . .]

4.2.3. Reply Codes in Numeric Order

211 System status, or system help reply

214 Help message
(Information on how to use the receiver or the meaning of a particular non-standard command; this reply is useful only to the human
user)

220 <domain> Service ready

221 <domain> Service closing transmission channel

250 Requested mail action okay, completed

251 User not local; will forward to <forward-path>
(See section 3.4) [ann.: in RFC 2821]

252 Cannot VRFY user, but will accept message and attempt delivery
(See section 3.5.3) [ann.: in RFC 2821]

354 Start mail input; end with <CRLF>.<CRLF>

421 <domain> Service not available, closing transmission channel
(This may be a reply to any command if the service knows it must
shut down)

450 Requested mail action not taken: mailbox unavailable
(e.g., mailbox busy)

451 Requested action aborted: local error in processing

452 Requested action not taken: insufficient system storage

500 Syntax error, command unrecognized
(This may include errors such as command line too long)

501 Syntax error in parameters or arguments

502 Command not implemented (see section 4.2.4) [ann.: in RFC 2821]

503 Bad sequence of commands

504 Command parameter not implemented

550 Requested action not taken: mailbox unavailable
(e.g., mailbox not found, no access, or command rejected for policy
reasons)

551 User not local; please try <forward-path>
(See section 3.4) [ann.: in RFC 2821]

552 Requested mail action aborted: exceeded storage allocation

553 Requested action not taken: mailbox name not allowed (e.g., mailbox syntax incorrect)

554 Transaction failed (Or, in the case of a connection-opening response, "No SMTP service here")

GLOSSARY

A

A record   In DNS, a record that maps a hostname to an IP address.

Active Directory   Microsoft's directory service. It is a centralized system to distribute data related to users, networks, and security settings. Think of it as LDAP with Kerberos, but with value-added non-conformance to standards.

Active Directory Service Interface (ADSI)   An API that enables programmers of scripts or C/C++ programs to easily query and manipulate the objects in the Active Directory.

attachment   A file within an email message.

B

base64 encoding   A data-encoding scheme that converts binary-encoded data to printable ASCII characters. It is one of the MIME content transfer encodings used in Internet email.

blind carbon copy   An email header, noted as bcc:, that lists addresses to which a message should be sent, not seen by the recipients. *See also* carbon copy.

Boolean   A variable holding a truth value, either true or false.

C

carbon copy   An email header, noted as cc:, that lists secondary addresses to which a message should be sent, visible to all recipients.

certificate   A file that holds information to prove the identity of a person or machine.

certification authority (CA)   An authority that issues and manages digital identities.

chroot   The chroot() system call specifies a new root directory for a process.

CNAME record In DNS, a CNAME record, also known as a canonical name, is a record that expands an alias. Depending on the DNS tree involved (forward or in-addr.arpa), a CNAME can refer to an A record or to a PTR record. *See also* A record *and* PTR record.

comment A note inside configuration files or source code that provides helpful information about bits of configuration or code.

D

daemon A process that runs and performs its services in the background of a computer.

DCF-77 An encoded time signal sent on the long-wave frequency 77.5 kHz. The Physikalisch-Technische Bundesanstalt (`http://www.ptb.de`) in Germany is the official source of this signal, which distributes the correct time for Germany. Anyone may use this signal to synchronize devices to the official time.

demilitarized zone A neutral zone between private and public networks that gives users from the public network controlled access to data provided by the private network. *See also* firewall.

dial-up user list (DUL) An RBL-style blacklist that contains IP addresses of known dial-up pools.

dictionary attack Refers to obtaining a recipient's address by running through a list of likely possibilities, often a list of words from a dictionary.

distribution An operating system set comprising a kernel, an operating system, assorted free software, and sometimes proprietary software. The term is most commonly used with respect to Linux.

domain A group of computers whose hostnames share a common suffix, the domain name. *See also* top-level domain, domain name service (DNS).

domain name service (DNS) A general purpose, distributed, and replicated data query service chiefly used on the Internet for translating hostnames into Internet addresses.

dynamic IP address An IP address that is assigned to a computer's network interface from a pool of IP addresses upon connecting to a network.

dynamic linking A program execution system where the operating system loads and links library code for an executable when the executable runs. *See also* library.

E

Extended Simple Mail Transfer Protocol (ESMTP) A set of extensions to the original SMTP protocol that enables a mail client to ask a mail server about its capabilities.

external application An application outside of Postfix, such as a virus scanner or a script.

F

false positive   Occurs when a test incorrectly reports a condition as true.

firewall   A gateway server that controls inbound and outbound connections between a private and public network. It can also provide controlled access from the outside to a demilitarized zone. *See also* demilitarized zone.

first-in, first-out (FIFO)   A system of handling requests or data. A queue is a FIFO; whatever goes in first is processed first. The idea is always to handle the oldest request first.

fully qualified domain name (FQDN)   The full name of a system, consisting of its local hostname and its domain name, including a top-level domain. For example, `mail` is a hostname and `mail.example.com` is an FQDN. An FQDN should be sufficient to determine a unique Internet address for any host on the Internet. This process (called *name resolution*) uses the domain name service (DNS).

G

groupware   A highly integrated application that consists of several programs that provide various services, such as email, time planning, address database, and news services.

H

hexadecimal   A base-16 numeral system, usually written using the symbols 0–9 and A–F or a–f.

I

include file   Include (header) files contain function prototypes, constant definitions, and macros necessary for compiling software. Most include files correspond to a library. *See also* library.

Internet Assigned Number Authority (IANA)   The central registry for various assigned numbers in the Internet Protocol, such as ports, protocols, enterprise numbers, options, codes, and types.

Internet Message Access Protocol (IMAP)   A protocol allowing a client to access and manipulate email messages on a server. It permits manipulation of remote message folders (mailboxes) in a way that is functionally equivalent to local mailboxes.

IMAP includes operations for creating, deleting, and renaming mailboxes; checking for new messages; permanently removing messages; searching; and selective fetching of message attributes, texts, and portions thereof. It does not specify a means of posting mail; this function is handled by a mail transfer protocol such as SMTP.

interprocess communication (IPC) An application programming interface (API) and underlying support that allows several running processes to talk to each other.

K

kernel The foundation of an operating system. A kernel is responsible for providing various computer programs with secure access to the machine's hardware.

L

left-hand side (LHS) In a map with two columns, the left-hand side is the left column. In Postfix, the left-hand side of an entry is called the key.

library A collection of precompiled machine code that can be linked to when compiling programs. Libraries serve as helper code for other programs. *See also* include file.

Lightweight Directory Access Protocol (LDAP) A protocol for accessing online directory services. It defines a relatively simple protocol for updating and searching directories running over TCP/IP.

Local Mail Transfer Protocol (LMTP) A derivative of SMTP, the Simple Mail Transfer Protocol. *See also* Simple Mail Transfer Protocol (SMTP).

M

macro A short instruction that expands into a set of larger instructions.

mail exchange record (MX record) A DNS resource record indicating the host that handles email for a hostname.

mail user agent (MUA) A program that allows a user to compose and read email messages. The MUA provides the interface between the user and the message transfer agent (MTA). Outgoing mail is eventually transmitted to an MTA for delivery, and incoming messages are picked up from where the mail delivery agent (MDA) left them.

malicious software (malware) A program or a file that is harmful to a computer.

man-in-the-middle attack Describes an attack where an attacker sits in between the communication of two parties. The attacker is able to read and modify the messages sent between the two parties without the parties knowing that the link between them has been compromised.

map A map in Postfix is a table of two columns, where each line represents an entry that associates a key with a value. The key and value are sometimes referred to as the left-hand side and the right-hand side. *See also* left-hand side (LHS), right-hand side (RHS).

mbox format   A file format used for holding email messages. All messages are concatenated in one file, separated by a From line at the beginning of each message and followed by a blank line at the end.

message transport agent (MTA)   A program responsible for receiving incoming email and/or delivering it to individual users. It may also transport nonlocal messages to their remote destinations. *See also* Internet Message Access Protocol (IMAP), Post Office Protocol (POP), and Simple Mail Transfer Protocol (SMTP).

Multipurpose Internet Mail Extensions (MIME)   An Internet standard for the format of email.

mumble   A word often used on the Postfix mailing list to describe a set of parameters that share the same name, but differ in some part. For example, `smtpd_mumble_restrictions` subsumes all `smtpd` restrictions such as `smtpd_client_restrictions`, `smtpd_sender_restrictions`, `smtpd_recipient_restrictions`, `smtpd_data_restrictions`, and so on.

N

name resolution   The process of resolving a hostname to an IP address.

network address translation (NAT)   Sometimes known as Network masquerading or IP masquerading, network address translation is a technique used in computer networking for allowing a private network to access a public network through a single point. It relies on rewriting IP addresses of network packets passing through a router or firewall.

Network Time Protocol (NTP)   An Internet protocol used to synchronize the clocks of computers to some time reference. NTP is an Internet standard protocol originally developed by Professor David L. Mills at the University of Delaware.

O

open proxy   A misconfigured proxy that processes connection requests from third parties. Open proxies can be used to submit mail to servers by means of that open proxy.

open relay   An SMTP server that forwards mail between third parties. A third-party message relay occurs when a mail server processes a mail message where neither the sender nor the recipient is a local user.

P

patch   A (temporary) addition to a piece of code, usually as a remedy to an existing bug or to provide a new feature.

port   A (network) port is an interface for communicating with a computer program over a network. Network ports are usually numbered, and a network implementation, such as TCP or UDP, attaches a port number to data it sends; the receiving implementation uses the attached port number to figure out which computer program to send the data to.

Post Office Protocol (POP)   A protocol for retrieving email from a server. Messages are downloaded immediately from the server. *See also* Internet Message Access Protocol (IMAP), Simple Mail Transfer Protocol (SMTP).

Pretty Good Privacy (PGP)   A computer program that provides cryptographic privacy and authentication.

proxy   A server that acts on behalf of another server, typically in a transparent manner.

PTR record   In DNS, a record that maps an IP address to a hostname.

Q

Quick Mail Queuing Protocol (QMQP)   QMQP provides a centralized mail queue within a cluster of hosts. One central server runs a message transfer agent. The other hosts do not have their own mail queues; they give each new message to the central server through QMQP. QMQP was invented by D.J. Bernstein, also the inventor of qmail.

R

redundant array of independent disks (RAID)   A method of storing data on multiple disks. All disks in a RAID system appear to the operating system as a single disk. A RAID system can balance I/O operations, thus increasing performance.

regular expression   A regular expression (abbreviated as regexp, regex, or regxp) is an advanced pattern-matching system that is actually the result of a nondeterministic finite-state automaton that accepts a particular language.

Request for Comments (RFC)   A formal document from the Internet Engineering Task Force (IETF). RFCs are either informational or meant to become Internet standards and provide for interoperability among networks and applications. Although one can't alter an RFC, it is possible to write a new RFC that supersedes an existing RFC.

right-hand side (RHS)   In a map with two columns, the right hand side is the last column. In Postfix, the right hand side of an entry is called the value.

root   *See* superuser.

router   A computer networking device that determines the next network point to which a data packet should be forwarded on its way toward its destination.

S

Secure Multipurpose Internet Mail Extensions (S/MIME) An Internet standard for a secure method of sending email. It describes how encryption information and a digital certificate can be included as part of the message body.

Secure Socket Layer (SSL) *See* Transport Layer Security (TLS).

Sendmail One of the oldest and most widely used MTAs on the Internet.

Simple Authentication and Security Layer (SASL) An authentication framework defined in RFC 2222 (`ftp://ftp.rfc-editor.org/in-notes/rfc2222.txt`) for applications that use connections based on protocols such as IMAP, LDAP, or SMTP. It provides authentication services to those applications and can look up user data in numerous data backends.

Simple Mail Transfer Protocol (SMTP) A protocol defined in STD 10, RFC 821, used to transfer email between computers. See `http://www.faqs.org/rfcs/std/std-index.html`.

Structured Query Language (SQL) A programming language used for interacting with databases.

superuser Aka `root`, the superuser is the user who has all rights and permissions in all modes (single-user or multi-user) on a Unix-style operating system.

T

tarpit A service on a computer system (usually a server) that delays incoming connections for as long as possible. A tarpit makes network abuses, such as spamming or dictionary attacks, less effective because it takes the attacker too long to process the attack. The name is an analogy to a tar pit, in which animals can get bogged down and slowly sink under the surface. Also known by the German name *teergrube*.

telnet A network protocol used on the Internet. It is also the name of a program used to invoke a telnet session to a remote host.

top-level domain The last and most significant component of an Internet fully qualified domain name, the part after the last dot. For example, the host `mail.example.com` is in the `com` top-level domain (which is for commercial bodies).

Transport Layer Security (TLS) TLS (formerly SSL) is a protocol for encrypting the communication layer between a client and a server. It should not be confused with email encryption technologies such as S/MIME and PGP, which encrypt content but not communication.

U

Unix   An operating system that originated at Bell Labs in 1969.

Unix domain socket   Unix domain sockets (the correct standard POSIX term is POSIX Local IPC Sockets) function primarily as a means for interprocess communication and are therefore also called IPC sockets. These connections are from the local computer to itself; they are not connections actually transmitted over a physical network.

Unix-to-Unix Copy Protocol (UUCP)   A Unix utility program and protocol that allows one Unix system to send files to another via a serial line, which may be a cable going directly from one machine's serial port to another's, or may involve a modem at each end of a telephone line.

Software is also available to allow UUCP to work over Ethernet, though there are better alternatives, such as scp for file transfer, SMTP for email, and NNTP for news.

unsolicited commercial email (UCE)   UCE is a more precise expression for spam. UCE must not be mistaken for commercial email that recipients subscribed for at their own will.

W

whitespace   A whitespace character is any character that takes up space but does not show up on a display.

INDEX

Special Characters

%d substitution, 329
%p macro, 238
%r macro, 238
%s substitution, 329
%u macro, 238
%u substitution, 329
%v macro, 238
*_checks parameter, 56
+ delimiter, 193

A

-a getpwent parameter, 234
A records, 13–14, 18, 31, 441
ACL (access control list), 356
Active Directory, exporting valid
        recipients from, 176–77
Active Directory Service Interface
        (ADSI), 441
active queue, 42, 397–99
additional_conditions parameter, 211
address rewriting, 131–32
address_verify_map parameter, 105
address_verify_negative_cache parameter,
        105
address_verify_sender parameter, 104
ADSI (Active Directory Service
        Interface), 441
aliases
    creating, 26
    defining, 319
allow_percent_hack restriction, 72
alterMIME program, 143–44
alternatives port, 417
amavisd-new, 149–50, 154, 164
    configuring Postfix to use, 157–60
    configuring Postfix to use with
        smtpd_proxy_filter, 164–65
    installing, 149–50

optimizing performance, 154–57
testing, 150–54, 160–63
ANONYMOUS mechanism, 223
antispam measures, 94–108
    bogus nameserver records, 95–97
    bounces to multiple recipients, 97–98
    overview, 94
    preventing obvious forgeries, 94–95
    restriction process order, 107–8
    using DNS blacklists, 98–103
    verifying sender, 103–7
anvil daemon, 41, 381
anvil log interval, changing, 381–82
apt-get command, 411
ASCII, 65
asynchronous bounce queue congestion
        inequality, 399–401
at service, 20
attachments, 65–68
AUTH for Postfix SMTP client, 260–62
AUTH parameter, 255
authldap.schema, 316–19
authmodulelist parameter, 344
auxiliary plug-ins (auxprop), 236–41
    overview, 236
    using sasldb2 plug-in, 236–38
    using sql plug-in, 238–41
AUXLIBS environment variable, 325, 408
auxprop service, 225, 237, 253

B

base64 MIME encoding, 65, 441
base64 string, 255–56
BCC (blind carbon copy), 441
BerkeleyDB library, 429
BIND distribution, 12
bind parameter, 357
bind_dn parameter, 357
bind_pw parameter, 357

blacklisted networks, blocking messages from, 391

blind carbon copy (BCC), 441

body filtering, 73

body of messages, 64–65, 126–27

body_checks parameter, 63, 113, 126–27

bogus nameserver records, 95–97

both choice option, 353

bottlenecks, finding, 392–402
  active queue bottlenecks, 397–99
  asynchronous bounce queue
      congestion inequality, 399–401
  deferred queue bottlenecks, 396–97
  incoming queue bottlenecks, 393–95
  maildrop queue bottlenecks, 395–96
  overview, 392–93
  using fallback relays, 401–2

bounce daemon, 37

bounces to multiple recipients, 97–98

broken_sasl_auth_clients parameter, 252

building mail server, 313–67
  adding authentication to servers,
      350–56
    applying ldapdb patch, 351–52
    configuring ldapdb, 352–54
    overview, 350–51
    testing ldapdb plug-in, 354–56
  conceptual overview, 314
  configuring Courier IMAP, 343–48
    configuring authentication
        backend, 344–45
    configuring Courier IMAP to use
        its LDAP authentication
        daemon, 344
    creating IMAP certificate, 345–46
    installing Courier IMAP, 343–44
    overview, 343
    testing IMAP server, 346–48
  configuring Courier maildrop, 333–43
    configuring Courier maildrop, 335
    creating Maildir mailboxes, 335–37
    creating mail filter, 337–39
    installing Courier maildrop, 334–35
    overview, 333
    preparing Maildir quotas, 339
    preparing your system, 334
    testing Courier maildrop, 339–43
  configuring Cyrus SASL, 321
  configuring OpenLDAP, 322–24
  configuring Postfix and LDAP, 325–33
    adding LDAP queries for local
        recipients, 327–30
    creating LDAP configuration
        directory, 327

delegating transport to Courier
    maildrop, 332–33
  LDAP lookups, 326–27
  overview, 325–26
  querying LDAP for mail aliases,
      330–32
  encrypting LDAP queries, 358–65
    configuring slapd to offer TLS, 360
    configuring TLS for LDAP clients,
        360–62
    configuring TLS for OpenLDAP,
        359–60
    overview, 358
    testing TLS, 362–65
  enforcing valid sender addresses,
      365–67
  expanding directory, 349–50
  LDAP directory structure, 315–21
    adding attributes for remaining
        servers, 320–21
    branch design, 317
    building user objects, 318–19
    choosing attributes in Postfix
        schema, 316–17
    creating list objects, 319–20
    overview, 315–16
  protecting directory data, 356–58

C

c_rehash program, 305

c_rehash utility, 360

CA (certification authority), 268–77, 441

ca-bundle.crt file, 285

cacert.pem, 272–73

cakey.pem, 272–73

cat command, 286

catchall address, 192

Cc header field, 64

CCARGS environment variable, 325, 408

certificates, 270–78
  creating CA certificate, 272–73
  creating server's certificate, 276–77
  distributing and installing CA
      certificate, 273–76
  overview, 271
  preparing certificates for use in
      Postfix, 278
  required information, 271–72
  signing server's certificate, 277–78

certification authority (CA), 268–77, 441

chatr command, 374

check parameter, 409

check_client_access parameter, 184

check_helo_access option, 95
check_recipient_access option, 94
check_recipient_access parameter, 92–93
check_sender_access option, 102
check_sender_mx_access option, 97, 107
checks, 111–27
  applying to separate message sections,
    112–14
  checking body, 126–27
  checking for checks support, 118
  checking headers, 120–24
    in attached messages, 125
    discarding messages, 122–23
    filtering messages, 123–24
    holding delivery, 122
    overview, 120
    redirecting messages, 123
    rejecting messages, 121
    removing headers, 122
  checking MIME headers, 124–25
  how checks work, 112
  overview, 111–12, 117–18
  safely implementing header or body
    filtering, 119–20
  when Postfix applies, 114
chkconfig command, 417
chmod command, 262
chown command, 262
chroot environment, 369–76
  how chroot affects Postfix, 371–75
    chroot libraries, configuration files,
      and other files, 374–75
    chrooted daemons, 372–74
    helper scripts for chroot, 372
    overview, 371–72
  overcoming chroot restrictions, 375–76
  overview, 369–70
chroot jail, 369–70
  how it works, 370–71
CIDR (Classless Inter-Domain Routing),
    27–28, 435
CIDR SMTP standards reference, 435–39
  overview, 435
  server response codes, 437–39
  subnets in CIDR notation, 435–36
class option, 27
Classless Inter-Domain Routing (CIDR),
    27–28, 435
cleanup daemon, 39, 41, 114
client_connection_rate_time_unit
    parameter, 382
client_connection_status_update_time
    parameter, 381

client-side SMTP authentication. See
    SMTP authentication, client-side
client-side Transport Layer Security.
    See Transport Layer Security,
    client-side
client-specific logging, 426–27
CNAME record, 15
command-line utilities, 48–52
  overview, 48
  postalias, 48
  postcat, 48
  postdrop, 49
  postfix, 48
  postkick, 49–50
  postlock, 50
  postlog, 50
  postmap, 48–49
  postqueue, 50–51
  postsuper, 51–52
Comprehensive Perl Archive Network
    (CPAN), 149–50
Compress::Zlib module, 150
configure command, 282, 343
./configure --help command, 233
CONNECT statement, 212
connectivity, 8–9
content control, 53–54
content filters. See external content filters
content types, 66–67
content_filter, 132–37
  basics of configuring, 135–37
  filter-delegation daemons, 134–35
  overview, 132–34
content_filter directive, 122
content_filter parameter, 145, 157–60
Content-type header field, 64
core.schema package, 316
corrupt queue, 42
Courier authentication daemon, 344
Courier IMAP, 314–19, 343–48, 362
  configuring authentication backend,
    344–45
  configuring to use its LDAP
    authentication daemon, 344
  creating IMAP certificate, 345–46
  installing, 343–44
  overview, 343
  testing IMAP server, 346–48
Courier maildrop, 314–15, 333–43
  configuring, 335
  creating Maildir mailboxes, 335–37
  creating mail filter, 337–39
  installing, 334–35

Courier maildrop, *continued*
   overview, 333
   preparing Maildir quotas, 339
   preparing your system, 334
   testing, 339–43
`CourierMailAccount` object, 318
`CourierMailAlias` object, 318–19
CPAN (Comprehensive Perl Archive
   Network), 149–50
CRAM-MD5 mechanism, 223–24
creating aliases query, 211–12
creating recipient query, 211
`crle` command, 282
`cron` service, 20
cryptographic signature, 303
`csvde export` command, 181
`csvde` tool, 176
customizable restrictions, 72–73
Cyrus IMAP project, 40, 351
Cyrus SASL, 217, 229–45, 321, 351, 356
   architecture and configuration of,
      218–21
   configuring, 229–31, 321
   configuring auxiliary plug-ins
      (auxprop), 236–41
     overview, 236
     using sasldb2 plug-in, 236–38
     using sql plug-in, 238–41
   configuring logging and log level, 231
   configuring saslauthd, 232–36
   creating Postfix application
      configuration file, 230–31
   installing, 229–30
   overview, 229
   selecting SMTP AUTH mechanisms,
      232
   setting password-verification service,
      231–32
   testing authentication, 242–45
     creating server configuration file,
      243
     overview, 242
     starting saslauthd, 242–43
     starting server program, 243
     testing with client program, 243–45

D

D flag, 332
-d option, 51
daemons, 37–42
`DATA` command, 58, 71, 139

database-driven virtual mailbox domains,
   203–15
   building Postfix to support MySQL
      maps, 205
   checking Postfix for MySQL map
      support, 204
   configuring database, 205–7
   configuring Postfix to use database,
      208–12
   overview, 203–4
   testing, 212–15
databases, 46–47
Date header field, 63
DCF-77, 442
`deadbeats` transport, 403
`deadbeats_connect_timeout` parameter, 403
Debian Linux, installing Postfix on,
   410–13
`debug_peer_list` parameter, 426
`debuglevel` parameter, 330
`default_process_limit` parameter, 398
`default_rbl_reply` restriction, 73
`defer` command, 71
`defer` daemon, 37
`defer_transports` parameter, 32–33
deferred queue, 42, 396–97
`delete-from-mailq` command, 51
delivery of message, triggering, 33
demilitarized zone (DMZ), 27, 175
denial-of-service attack, 41, 175
`/dev/random` generator, 287
`/dev/urandom` generator, 287
dial-up mail server for single domain,
   29–34
   adjusting relay permissions, 31–32
   configuring relay permission for relay
      host, 34
   deferring message transport, 32–33
   disabling DNS resolution, 31
   overview, 29–31
   setting relay host, 32
   triggering message delivery, 33
dial-up user list (DUL), 32, 299, 442
dictionary attack, 89
`dig` command, 12–13, 389
DIGEST-MD5 mechanism, 223–24
`disable_dns_lookups` parameter, 159
`disable_vrfy_command` restriction, 72
`DISCARD` action, 115, 120, 122
discarding messages, 122–23
DMZ (demilitarized zone), 27, 175
DNS blacklists, 98–103

DNS (domain name service), 8, 11, 31, 442
DNS for mail servers, 13–15
DNS lookups, speeding up, 388–89
DNS resolution, disabling, 31
DNSBL (DNS-based Blackhole List), 47, 99, 299
domain name service (DNS), 8, 11, 31, 442
double_bounce_recipient parameter, 390
downloading
    Postfix, from rpmfind.net, 414
    Simon J. Mudd's Postfix RPMs, 414
dpkg command, 410
DUL (dial-up user list), 32, 299, 442
DUNNO action, 76

E

egrep command, 112, 306, 310
EHLO command, 58–59, 85–86, 153, 222, 255
EICAR, 162
--enable-maildirquota option, 334
--enable-maildropldap option, 334
encoding processor, 65–66
encoding structure, 67–68
envelope recipient, restricting, 88–91
envelope sender
    empty, 92
    restricting, 87–88
envelope (SMTP communication), controlling, 57–60
error daemon, 39
ESMTP (Extended Simple Mail Transfer Protocol), 139, 153, 159, 442
/etc/resolv.conf file, 12
/etc/syslog.conf file, 10–11
ETRN command restrictions, 73
ETRN (SMTP Extended Turn), 39
Exchange Server. See Microsoft Exchange Server, using Postfix with
export_valid_recipients.bat file, 181
Extended Simple Mail Transfer Protocol (ESMTP), 138, 153, 159, 442
external content filters, 129–65
    amavisd-new
        configuring Postfix to use, 157–60
        configuring Postfix to use with smtpd_proxy_filter, 164–65
        installing, 149–50
        optimizing performance, 154–57
        testing, 150–54, 160–63
    appending disclaimers to messages with a script, 142–48

configuring Postfix for disclaimer script, 145–46
installing alterMIME and creating filter script, 143–45
overview, 142–43
testing filter, 146–48
best moment to filter content, 130–32
content_filter, 132–37
    basics of configuring, 135–37
    filter-delegation daemons, 134–35
    overview, 132–34
overview, 129–30, 141, 163–64
smtpd_proxy_filter, 137–40
    basics of configuring, 139–40
    overview, 137–38
EXTERNAL mechanism, 224
external sources, 47
extract_valid_recipients command, 182

F

-f option, 8
fallback relays, 401–2
fallback_relay parameter, 392, 402
fetchmail utility, 34
FILTER action, 115, 123
filtering messages, 123–24
filters. See checks; external content filters
find command, 281
flush daemon, 39
forgery prevention, 94–95
FQDN (fully qualified domain name), 8, 19, 85–86, 186, 443
from choice, 353
From header field, 63
fully qualified domain name (FQDN), 8, 19, 85–86, 186, 443
fuzzy program, 193

G

gateways. See mail gateways
generic network relay permissions, 27
generic restrictions, 71–72
gethostbyname() method, 31
GID (group ID), 196, 210–11
GID mapping, 201
gidNumber attribute, 334
GnuPG tool, 269
GRANT command, 207
grep command, 156, 264, 280, 394, 420
group ID (GID), 196, 210–11
GSSAPI mechanism, 224

H

h flag, 332
-h option, 51
-H option, 51
hash keyword, 209
Header filtering, 73
header_checks linear map, 45, 63, 113
headers
    checking, 120–25
        in attached messages, 125
        discarding messages, 122–23
        filtering messages, 123–24
        holding delivery, 122
        MIME headers, 124–25
        overview, 120
        redirecting messages, 123
        rejecting messages, 121
        removing headers, 122
    optional (X-headers), 64
    recommended, 63–64
    required, 63
HELO command, 58–59
HELO/EHLO, restricting hostname in, 85–87
HOLD action, 115, 122
hold queue, 42
holding delivery, 122
homeDirectories attribute, 335
homeDirectory attribute, 321
host and environment preparation, 7–15
    connectivity, 8–9
    DNS for mail servers, 13–15
    hostname, 8
    name resolution (DNS), 11–13
    overview, 7–8
    syslog, 10–11
    system time and timestamps, 9–10
host command, 12, 97
host option, 27
hostname, 8, 85–87

I

-I flag, 118
IANA (Internet Assigned Number
        Authority), 9, 65, 443
ifconfig command, 27
IGNORE action, 115, 122
IMAP (Internet Message Access
        Protocol), 1, 225, 235, 443
imapd certificate, 345
imapd-ssl tool, 345
imtest utility, 265
in_flow_delay parameter, 394

incoming queue, 42, 393–95
indexed maps, 44–45
individual relay permissions, 28
inetd server, 37
inetOrgPerson object, 318
installing Cyrus SASL, 229–30
installing Postfix, 407–17
    building an RPM from an SRPM,
        414–16
    on Debian Linux, 410–13
    overview, 407
    Postfix source code, 407–9
    on Red Hat Linux, 413–14
    removing Sendmail MTA, 417
    starting and stopping Postfix in Red
        Hat Linux, 417
    switching to Postfix, 417
Internet Assigned Number Authority
        (IANA), 9, 65, 443
Internet Message Access Protocol
        (IMAP), 1, 225, 235, 443
Internet service provider (ISP), 8, 9, 30,
        32, 423
interprocess communication (IPC), 49,
        382, 394, 444, 448
introduction to Postfix, 1–4
IPC (interprocess communication), 444
ISP (Internet service provider), 8, 9, 30,
        32, 423

K

KERBEROS_V4 mechanism, 224
ktrace program, 374

L

LDA (local delivery agent), 21, 40, 194,
        320
    testing, 333
LDAP Data Interchange Format (LDIF),
        315
LDAP (Lightweight Directory Access
        Protocol), 174–175, 325–33
    adding LDAP queries for local
        recipients, 327–30
    bind, disabling, 327
    creating LDAP configuration
        directory, 327
    delegating transport to Courier
        maildrop, 332–33
    directory structure
        adding attributes for remaining
            servers, 320–21

LDAP; directory structure, *continued*
  branch design, 317
  building user objects, 318–19
  choosing attributes in Postfix
    schema, 316–17
  creating list objects, 319–20
  overview, 315–16
  lookups, 326–27
  overview, 325–26
  querying for mail aliases, 330–32
ldapdb plug-in, 321, 350–51
ldapdb_id parameter, 353
ldapdb_pw parameter, 353
ldapmodify utility, 342
ldapsearch command, 324, 354, 364
ldapwhoami command, 354
ldconfig command, 282
ldd command, 283, 359, 374, 421, 429
LDIF (LDAP Data Interchange Format),
  315
LHLO command, 154
libsasldb.so, 261
libssl.a file, 281
libssl.so file, 281
linear maps, 45–46
Linux
  Debian, 410–13
  Red Hat, 413–14, 417
lmtp client, 40, 265
lmtp daemon, 134, 259
LMTP (Local Mail Transfer Protocol),
  40, 153–54, 444
lmtp_passwd file, 265
lmtp_sasl_security_options parameter, 265
local daemon, 40, 46, 174, 373
local delivery agent (LDA), 21, 40,
  194, 320
Local Mail Transfer Protocol (LMTP),
  40, 153–54, 444
local_destination_recipient_limit
  parameter, 333
local_recipient_maps parameter, 90, 173,
  329, 391
local_transport parameter, 173
locate command, 285
log_level parameter, 231
logging and qmgr, 427
loghost command, 11
LOGIN mechanism, 223–26
lookup tables, 36
lsof command, 424

M
-m 10 option, 385
-m command-line option, 243
-m dir option, 234
-m option, 376
mail attribute, 318
mail command, 24
MAIL command, 58
MAIL FROM command, 73, 88, 139
mail gateways, 169–88
  advanced gateway setup, 172–87
    See also Microsoft Exchange Server
    improving security on mail gateway,
      173–74
    overview, 172
  basic setup, 170–72
  NAT setup, 187–88
  overview, 169–70
mail server, building. *See* building mail
  server
mail user agent (MUA), 1, 444
mail_release_date configuration
  parameter, 408
mailbox attribute, 320
Maildir format, 343
Maildir quotas, 339
maildirmake utility, 335–36, 338
maildrop agent, 21, 40
maildrop attribute, 319, 330, 365
maildrop command, 340
maildrop directory, 49
maildrop queue, 41, 42, 50, 395–96
maildrop transport, 332
maildrop.log file, 342
mailq command, 39, 48, 392
main.cf file, 32
make command, 143, 230, 249
make install command, 143, 230, 249
make makefiles command, 249
make upgrade command, 249
maps, 43–47
  overview, 43–44
  querying, 47
  types of, 44–47
_maps configuration parameter, 433
master daemon, 37, 174, 195, 371–73, 425
master.cf file, 171
maximal_backoff_time parameter, 392, 397
maximal_queue_lifetime parameter, 43, 382
MAY policy, 307
mech_list parameter, 232

message content, controlling, 61–68
  attachments, 65–68
  body, 64–65
  headers, 63–64
  overview, 61–63
message delivery, triggering, 33
message transfer restrictions, 69–109
  antispam measures, 94–108
    bogus nameserver records, 95–97
    bounces to multiple recipients,
      97–98
    overview, 94
    preventing obvious forgeries, 94–95
    restriction process order, 107–8
    using DNS blacklists, 98–103
    verifying sender, 103–7
  building, 74–83
    influence of actions on restriction
      evaluation, 75–77
    moment of evaluation, 75
    notation, 74–75
    overview, 74
    slowing down bad clients, 77–78
  classes, 79
  defaults, 84
  maintaining RFC conformance, 91–93
    empty envelope sender, 92
    overview, 91
    special role accounts, 92–93
  overview, 69, 81
  processing order for RFC restrictions,
    93–94
  requiring RFC conformance, 84–91
    overview, 84
    restricting envelope recipient, 88–91
    restricting envelope sender, 87–88
    restricting hostname in HELO/EHLO,
      85–87
  testing
    making restrictions effective
      immediately, 83
    overview, 81–82
    simulating impact of restrictions,
      82–83
  triggers, 70–71
  types of, 71–74
    additional UCE control
      parameters, 73
    application ranges, 74
    customizable restrictions, 72–73
    generic restrictions, 71–72
    overview, 71
    switchable restrictions, 72
  uses for restriction classes, 108–9

message transport
  deferring, 32–33
  overview, 55–57
message transport agent (MTA), 1–2, 11,
  35, 445
Message-Id header field, 63
message/rfc822 MIME type, 66
messages to nonexistent users, refusing,
  390–91
Microsoft Exchange Server, using Postfix
  with, 174–85
  automating map-building process,
    184–85
  building recipient map, 181–83
  building sender access map, 183–84
  configuring Exchange and Postfix
    communication, 185–87
  exporting valid recipients from Active
    Directory, 176–77
  overview, 174–75
  sending recipient list to mail relay,
    177–81
    adding public key to authorized
      key list, 178–79
    converting SSH key to PuTTY key
      format, 179–80
    copying list of recipients to
      smarthost, 181
    copying private key to Windows,
      179
    creating authentication keys, 178
    creating copy user on smarthost,
      178
    getting secure copy client for
      Windows, 177–78
Microsoft Management Console (MMC),
  176
Microsoft Outlook, 85, 252
MIME encodings, 65
MIME headers, 124–25
MIME (Multipurpose Internet Mail
  Extensions), 65, 445
mime_header_checks, 63, 113, 124
MIME-Version header field, 64
minimal_backoff_time parameter, 397
misc/CA.pl program, 272
mkimapdcert utility, 345
MMC (Microsoft Management Console),
  176
mod_ssl module, 285
mpack utility, 65
MTA (message transport agent), 1–2, 11,
  35, 445
MUA (mail user agent), 1, 444

multipart/alternative MIME type, 67
multipart/mixed MIME type, 66
multiple domains, 189–215
   database-driven virtual mailbox
      domains, 203–15
      building Postfix to support MySQL
         maps, 205
      checking Postfix for MySQL map
         support, 204
      configuring database, 205–7
      configuring Postfix to use database,
         208–12
      overview, 203–4
      testing, 212–15
   overview, 189
   virtual alias domains, 189–94
      advanced mappings, 192–94
      configuring Postfix to receive mail
         for, 191
      creating recipient address map,
         190–91
      overview, 189–90
      setting name, 190
      testing settings, 191–92
   virtual mailbox domains, 194–203
      advanced configuration, 199–203
      basic configuration, 195–98
      checking Postfix for virtual
         delivery agent support, 195
      overview, 194–95
multiple recipients, bounces to, 97–98
Multipurpose Internet Mail Extensions
    (MIME), 65, 445
munpack utility, 65
MUST policy, 307
must_be_valid_sender restriction, 184
MUST_NOPEERMATCH policy, 307
mutual_auth setting, 251
MX records, 12–13, 15, 31, 171
mydestination parameter, 19, 173, 189–90
mydomain, setting, 19
myhostname, setting, 19
mynetworks parameter, 170, 249, 256,
    389, 435
myorigin parameter, 174
MySQL, 203–9, 238–40
mysql socket, 372

N

n chroot option, 372
nameserver records, bogus, 95–97
NAT gateway, 187–88
NAT (network address translation), 445

nested_header_checks, 113, 125
Netscape Mail, 252
network address translation (NAT), 445
Network Time Protocol (NTP), 9–10, 445
newaliases command, 22, 44
nis.schema, 318
noactive setting, 251
noanonymous setting, 251
nodictionary setting, 251
none choice, 353
NONE policy, 307
nonexistent users, refusing messages to,
    390–91
noplaintext setting, 251
nqmgr daemon, 83
nslookup command, 12
NTLM mechanism, 224
NTP (Network Time Protocol), 9–10, 445

O

OK action, 76
one-time pad (OTP) mechanism, 224
open relays, 26, 389
OpenLDAP, 235, 313–14, 322–24, 361
OpenSSL, 272–73
openssl s_client option, 289, 293, 296
openssl-dev package, 281
openssl-devel package, 281
organizationalUnit object, 317
OTP (one-time pad) mechanism, 224

P

-p option, 51
PAM (Pluggable Authentication
    Modules), 225
passwd command, 178
passwd/shadow authentication backend,
    226
patch command, 283
PCRE map support, 118
PCRE (Perl-compatible regular
    expression), 45, 117–18
performance tuning, 387–403
   basic enhancements, 387–92
      blocking messages from blacklisted
         networks, 391
      confirming that server is not listed
         as open relay, 389
      overview, 387
      reducing retransmission attempt
         frequency, 392
      refusing messages from unknown
         sender domains, 391–92

performance tuning; basic enhancements, *continued*
    refusing messages to nonexistent users, 390–91
    speeding up DNS lookups, 388–89
  configuring alternative transport, 403
  finding bottlenecks, 392–402
    active queue bottlenecks, 397–99
    asynchronous bounce queue congestion inequality, 399–401
    deferred queue bottlenecks, 396–97
    incoming queue bottlenecks, 393–95
    maildrop queue bottlenecks, 395–96
    overview, 392–93
    using fallback relays, 401–2
  overview, 387
  tuning for higher throughput, 402
Perl-compatible regular expression (PCRE), 45, 117–18
PERMIT action, 76
permit command, 71
permit option, 94
permit_mx_backup_networks restriction, 73
permit_mynetworks option, 93, 97
permit_sasl_authenticated parameter, 253
permit_tls_all_clientcerts parameter, 301
permit_tls_clientcerts parameter, 301
PGP (Pretty Good Privacy), 446
PGP tool, 269
pickup daemon, 41
pipe daemon, 41, 134, 146–47, 334–35, 373
PKI, 271
PLAIN mechanism, 223–26
Pluggable Authentication Modules (PAM), 225
POP (Post Office Protocol), 446
POP-before-SMTP, 34
Post Office Protocol (POP), 446
postalias command, 22, 44–45, 48
postcat command, 43, 48, 122
postconf command, 425
postconf -m command, 44, 118, 204
postdrop command, 49, 395–396
postdrop program, 42, 396
postfinger program, 425
postfix command, 48
postfix reload command, 22, 32, 45, 83, 427
Postfix source code, 407–9
postfix start command, 22, 419
postfix-snap package, 411
PostgreSQL, 209, 226, 238
post-install command, 427
postkick command, 49–50

postlock command, 50
postlog command, 50
postmap command, 44, 48–49, 97, 109, 183, 214–15, 258, 308, 330, 331, 364, 366
postmap -q command, 48
postqueue command, 50–51
postsuper command, 43, 51–52
postsuper -d command, 122
postsuper -d queueid command, 51
postsuper -H command, 122
postsuper -r - command, 49
postsuper -r command, 396
Pretty Good Privacy (PGP), 446
procmail agent, 21
procmail LDA, 40
Project Cyrus, 221
proxyAddresses attribute, 176
proxymap daemon, 40, 46, 198, 329–30, 373–74, 433
ps command, 10, 345, 394, 420
pscp.exe utility, 178–79, 181
PTR records, 13–14
PuTTY key format, converting SSH key to, 179–80
puttygen.exe utility, 178–79
pwcheck_method parameter, 231

Q

q flag, 146
qmgr daemon, 39, 83, 420, 427
qmgr process, 427
QMQP (Quick Mail Queuing Protocol), 41, 446
qshape utility, 392–93
query_filter parameter, 328, 330
queue manager, 37
queue_directory parameter, 41
queue_run_delay parameter, 43, 396–97
queues, 42–43
Quick Mail Queuing Protocol (QMQP), 41, 446
QUIT command, 139
quota attribute, 320
quoted-printable MIME encoding, 65

R

R flag, 146, 332
-r option, 51
RAID (redundant array of independent disks), 395, 433, 446
rbl_reply_maps restriction, 73

RCPT command, 58
RCPT TO command, 72, 139
Received header field, 64
recipient address restrictions, 73
recipient domains query, 209–10
recipient_delimiter parameter, 193
Red Hat Linux
    installing Postfix on, 413–14
    starting and stopping Postfix in, 417
Red Hat Package Manager (RPM), 413
REDIRECT action, 115, 123
redirecting messages, 123
reducing retransmission attempt
        frequency, 392
redundant array of independent disks
        (RAID), 446
refusing messages from unknown sender
        domains, 391–92
Register of Known Spam Operations
        (ROKSO), 96
REJECT action, 76, 115, 120, 121
reject command, 71
reject_authenticated_sender_login_mismatch
        parameter, 366
reject_authenticated_sender_login_mismatch
        restriction, 365
reject_multi_recipient_bounce option, 97
reject_non_fqdn_hostname option, 85
reject_non_fqdn_sender option, 87
reject_rbl_client option, 99
reject_rhsbl_sender option, 101
reject_sender_login_mismatch restriction,
        259
reject_unauth_destination option, 94
reject_unauth_pipelining command, 72
reject_unauthenticated_sender_login_
        mismatch restriction, 259
reject_unknown_recipient_domain option,
        89, 96
reject_unknown_sender_domain option, 88, 96
reject_unverified_sender option, 104
reject_unverified_sender parameter, 105
rejecting messages, 121
relay host, setting, 32
relay permissions
    adjusting, 31–32
    configuring for relay host, 34
    generic network, 27
    individual, 28
relay_connect_timeout parameter, 402
relay_destination_concurrency_limit
        parameter, 402
relay_domains parameter, 171
relay_domains restriction, 73

relay_recipient_maps parameter, 90,
        172, 391
relayhost feature, 402
relayhost parameter, 32
reload command, 399
remote client concurrency and request
        rate limiting, 379–86
    basics of rate limiting, 379–80
    exempting clients from limits, 386
    gathering rate statistics, 380–82
    limiting client-connection frequency,
        382–84
    overview, 379
    restricting simultaneous client
        connections, 384–85
removing
    headers, 122
    Sendmail MTA, 417
Reply-To header field, 64
Request for Comments. *See* RFC
request rate limiting. *See* remote client
        concurrency and request rate
        limiting
restrictions. *See* message transfer
        restrictions
result_attribute parameter, 329, 330
result_filter parameter, 329
retransmission attempt frequency,
        reducing, 392
Return-Path header field, 64
Return-Path message header, 146
RFC conformance
    maintaining, 91–93
        empty envelope sender, 92
        overview, 91
        special role accounts, 92–93
    requiring
        overview, 84
        restricting envelope recipient,
            88–91
        restricting envelope sender, 87–88
        restricting hostname in HELO/EHLO,
            85–87
RFC (Request for Comments), 446
RFC restrictions, 93–94
RHSBL (right-hand-side blacklist), 47,
        100–101
ROKSO (Register of Known Spam
        Operations), 96
role accounts, special, 92–93
RPM (Red Hat Package Manager), 413
RPM Source Package (SRPM), 414
rpmfind.net, downloading Postfix from,
        414

S

-s 10 option, 385
-s option, 51
s_client utility, 347, 362
SASL (Simple Authentication and Security Layer), 221–26, 447
  See also Cyrus SASL
  authentication backends, 225–26
  authentication interface, 222–23
  authentication methods (password-verification services), 225
  overview, 221–22
  SMTP AUTH mechanisms, 223–24
SASL socket, 372
sasl_passwd file, 262
saslauthd, 225, 232–36, 242–43, 244, 253
saslauthd_path parameter, 234, 376
saslauthz-policy parameter, 353
saslAuthzTo attribute, 350
sasld daemon, 245
sasldb plug-in, 242
sasldb2 plug-in, 226, 236–38
sasldblistusers2 utility, 236
saslfinger program, 426
saslpasswd2 utility, 236–37
sasl-regexp filter, 354
ScanMail application, 121
scp utility, 177
search_base parameter, 328
Secure Multipurpose Internet Mail Extensions (S/MIME), 447
Secure Sockets Layer (SSL), 280, 447
SELECT statement, 207–12
sender address restrictions, 73
sender, verifying, 103–7
sendmail binary, 340
sendmail command, 50, 94, 395–96, 419
Sendmail MTA, removing, 417
sendmail utility, 23
server_host parameter, 328
server_port parameter, 328
server-side SMTP authentication, 249–59
  advanced server settings, 258–59
  enabling and configuring server, 250–54
  overview, 249–50
  testing server-side SMTP AUTH, 254–58
server-side Transport Layer Security. *See* Transport Layer Security, server-side
showq daemon, 39

Simon J. Mudd's Postfix RPMs, downloading, 414
Simple Authentication and Security Layer. *See* SASL
Simple Mail Transfer Protocol (SMTP), 1, 5, 9, 447
single domain
  configuration, 17–28
    mapping email addresses to usernames, 25–26
    mapping mail sent to root to different mailbox, 21–22
    minimum configuration, 17–18
    overview, 17–18
    setting domain mail is accepted for, 19–20
    setting domain to be appended to outgoing messages, 20–21
    setting hostname in smtpd banner, 18–19
    setting permissions to make Postfix relay email from network, 26–28
    starting Postfix and testing mail delivery to root, 22–25
  dial-up mail server for, 29–34
    adjusting relay permissions, 31–32
    configuring relay permissions for relay host, 34
    deferring message transport, 32–33
    disabling DNS resolution, 31
    overview, 29–31
    setting relay host, 32
    triggering message delivery, 33
slapadd utility, 323, 339–43
slapd server, 322–24
slapd.conf file, 322–23
smarthost, 169
S/MIME (Secure Multipurpose Internet Mail Extensions), 447
S/MIME tool, 269
SMTP authentication, 34, 217–65
  adding SMTP AUTH support to Postfix, 248–49
  checking Postfix for SMTP AUTH support, 247–48
  client-side, 259–65
    AUTH for Postfix SMTP client, 260–62
    lmtp client, 265
    overview, 259–60
  future of SMTP AUTH, 245–46
  overview, 217, 247

SMTP authentication, *continued*
SASL (Simple Authentication and
Security Layer), 221–26
authentication backends, 225–26
authentication interface, 222–23
authentication methods (password-
verification services), 225
overview, 221–22
SMTP AUTH mechanisms, 223–24
server-side, 249–59
advanced server settings, 258–59
enabling and configuring server,
250–54
overview, 249–50
planning, 226–28
testing server-side SMTP AUTH,
254–58
SMTP communication (envelope),
controlling, 57–60
smtp daemon, 40, 46, 134, 147, 259,
263–64, 273
SMTP Extended Turn (ETRN), 39
SMTP (Simple Mail Transfer Protocol),
1, 5, 9, 447
smtp_connection_timeout setting, 400
smtp_data_done_timeout parameter, 130, 159
smtp_enforce_tls parameter, 311
smtp_sasl_auth_enable parameter, 261
smtp_sasl_password_maps parameter, 262
smtp_sasl_security_options parameter,
262, 309
smtp_sasl_tls_security_options parameter,
309
smtp_tls_CAfile parameter, 304
smtp_tls_CApath parameter, 305
smtp_tls_cert_file parameter, 309
smtp_tls_enforce_peername parameter, 311
smtp_tls_key_file parameter, 309
smtp_tls_loglevel parameter, 306
smtp_tls_note_starttls_offer parameter,
308
smtp_tls_per_site parameter, 307
smtp_tls_session_cache_database
parameter, 308
smtp_tls_session_cache_timeout parameter,
308
SMTP-after-IMAP, 218
SMTP-after-POP, 218
smtpd command, 254
smtpd daemon, 41, 46, 70, 131–32, 244–45,
273, 351, 377, 380, 422
smtpd restriction, 366–67
smtpd utility, 333

smtpd_*_restrictions parameter, 56, 60
smtpd_authorized_xforward_hosts
parameter, 165
smtpd_client_connection_count_limit
parameter, 384–85
smtpd_client_connection_limit_exceptions
parameter, 386
smtpd_client_connection_rate_limit
parameter, 382–83
smtpd_client_restrictions trigger, 70
smtpd_data_restrictions trigger, 71
smtpd_delay_reject parameter, 75
smtpd_enforce_tls parameter, 302
smtpd_error_sleep_time parameter, 78
smtpd_etrn_restrictions trigger, 70
smtpd_hard_error_limit parameter, 78
smtpd_helo_required parameter, 85
smtpd_helo_required restriction, 72
smtpd_helo_restrictions trigger, 70
smtpd_proxy_filter, 130–31, 137–40
basics of configuring, 139–40
configuring Postfix to use amavisd-
new with, 164–65
overview, 137–38
smtpd_proxy_filter parameter, 139
smtpd_recipient_restrictions parameter,
91, 95, 104, 299, 367
smtpd_recipient_restrictions trigger, 71
smtpd_sasl_auth_enable parameter, 251
smtpd_sasl_exceptions_networks parameter,
258
smtpd_sasl_local_domain parameter, 237,
253
smtpd_sasl_security_options parameter,
251–52, 295
smtpd_sasl_tls_security_options
parameter, 295
smtpd_sender_login_maps parameter, 258,
366
smtpd_sender_login_maps restriction, 73
smtpd_sender_restrictions trigger, 70
smtpd_soft_error_limit parameter, 78
smtpd_tls_ask_ccert parameter, 299
smtpd_tls_auth_only parameter, 292
smtpd_tls_CAfile parameter, 286, 301
smtpd_tls_CApath parameter, 286
smtpd_tls_loglevel parameter, 287
smtpd_tls_received_header parameter,
287, 310
smtpd_tls_req_ccert parameter, 302
smtpd_tls_session_cache_database
parameter, 291

smtpd_tls_session_cache_timeout
      parameter, 291
smtpd_use_tls parameter, 284
smtp-sink program, 430–32
smtp-source command, 383–85
smtp-source program, 430–31
spam, 32, 94, 96, 100, 121, 126, 148, 380.
      See also unsolicited commercial
      email (UCE)
SpamAssassin, 148, 151
spawn daemon, 40
special role accounts, 92–93
sql plug-in, 238–41
SQL (Structured Query Language), 226,
      447
sql_database parameter, 238
sql_engine parameter, 238
sql_hostnames parameter, 238
sql_insert parameter, 238
sql_passwd parameter, 238
sql_select parameter, 238
sql_update parameter, 238
sql_user parameter, 238
sql_usessl parameter, 238
SquirrelMail software, 122
SRP mechanism, 224
SRPM (RPM Source Package), 414
SSH key, converting to PuTTY key
      format, 179–80
SSH server, 178–79
sshkeygen command, 178
SSL (Secure Sockets Layer), 280, 447
ssl.h file, 281
start parameter, 409
start_tls parameter, 361
starting Postfix in Red Hat Linux, 417
STARTTLS keyword, 269, 284, 288
stop parameter, 409
stopping Postfix in Red Hat Linux, 417
strace program, 374
stress-testing Postfix, 430–33
      disk I/O, 432–33
      overview, 430–32
      too many connections, 433
strict_rfc821_envelopes restriction, 72
Structured Query Language (SQL), 226,
      447
Subject header field, 64
subnet option, 27
swap_bangpath restriction, 72
switchable restrictions, 72
syslog, 10–11
syslogd utility, 10

system time, 9–10
SystemMailbox, 181

T

TCP, 8
TCP port 25, 8–9
telnet session, sending mail through, 28
testing
      amavisd-new, 150–54, 160–63
      authentication, Cyrus SASL, 242–45
            creating server configuration file,
                  243
            overview, 242
            starting saslauthd, 242–43
            starting server program, 243
            testing with client program, 243–45
      Courier maildrop, 339–43
      database-driven virtual mailbox
            domains, 212–15
      IMAP server, 346–48
      LDA, 333
      ldapdb plug-in, 354–56
      message transfer restrictions
            making restrictions effective
                  immediately, 83
            overview, 81–82
            simulating impact of restrictions,
                  82–83
      server-side SMTP AUTH, 254–58
      stress-testing Postfix, 430–33
            disk I/O, 432–33
            overview, 430–32
            too many connections, 433
      TLS, 362–65
      virtual alias domain settings, 191–92
text/plain MIME type, 66
timestamps, 9–10
TLD (top level domain), 86
TLS. *See* Transport Layer Security
TLS client certificate, 219
tls_ca_cert_file parameter, 361
TLS_CACERT parameter, 361
tls_cert parameter, 361
TLS_CERT parameter, 361
tls_key parameter, 361
TLS_KEY parameter, 362
tls_random_source parameter, 287, 305
TLS_REQCERT parameter, 362
TLSCACertificateFile parameter, 360
tlsmgr daemon, 291–92, 308, 430
TLSVerifyClient parameter, 360
tmpfs, sizing, 155

To header field, 63
top command, 432
top level domain (TLD), 86
transfer restrictions. *See* message transfer
    restrictions
Transport Layer Security (TLS), 267–311
    building Postfix with TLS support,
        281–83
        building and installing OpenSSL
            from source code, 282
        overview, 281
    certificates, 270–78
        creating CA certificate, 272–73
        creating server's certificate, 276–77
        distributing and installing CA
            certificate, 273–76
        overview, 271
        preparing certificates for use in
            Postfix, 278
        required information, 271–72
        signing server's certificate, 277–78
    checking Postfix for TLS support,
        279–81
    overview, 267–70, 279
Transport Layer Security, client-side,
    302–11
    basic client configuration, 303–6
    client performance tuning, 308
    client-side certificate-based relaying,
        309–11
    overview, 302–3
    securing client SMTP AUTH, 309
    selective use, 307–8
    tightening, 311
Transport Layer Security, server-side,
    283–98
    basic server configuration, 284–90
        adding information to mail
            headers, 287–88
        connecting Postfix to random
            source generator, 286–87
        enabling server-side TLS, 284
        increasing TLS log level, 287
        overview, 284
        setting certificate paths, 285–86
        testing, 288–90
    overview, 283–84
    server performance tuning, 290–92
    server-side certificate-based relaying,
        298–301
        configuring Postfix to ask for client
            certificates, 299

        configuring Postfix to permit
            relaying for client certificates,
            299–301
        overview, 298–99
    server-side measures to secure SMTP
        AUTH handshake, 292–98
        controlling SASL mechanisms in
            TLS, 295
        offering SMTP AUTH with TLS
            only, 292–95
        overview, 292
    tightening TLS server, 302
transport_maps parameter, 171, 403
trivial-rewrite daemon, 39
trivial-rewrite service, 394–95
troubleshooting Postfix, 419–33
    connecting to Postfix, 423–25
        checking network, 423–24
        overview, 423
        verifying listening process, 424–25
    daemon inconsistencies, 429–30
    getting more logging information,
        426–27
    getting Postfix to use your
        configuration settings, 425
    intricacies of chroot jail, 428
    libraries, 429
    overview, 419
    problems starting Postfix and viewing
        log, 419–22
    reporting problems, 425–26
    solving filesystem problems, 428–29
    stress-testing Postfix, 430–33
        disk I/O, 432–33
        overview, 430–32
        too many connections, 433
truss program, 374

U

u flag, 332
UCE (unsolicited commercial email), 41,
    448
UDP (User Datagram Protocol), 10
uid attribute, 318–19
UID mapping, 201
UID (user ID), 196, 210–11
uidNumber attribute, 334
uname -n command, 19
undisclosed_recipients_header parameter,
    63
Unix operating system, 7

Unix-to-Unix Copy Protocol (UUCP), 33, 448
unknown sender domains, refusing messages from, 391–92
unsolicited commercial email (UCE), 41, 448
User Datagram Protocol (UDP), 10
user flag, 332
user ID (UID), 196, 210–11
useradd command, 196
usermod -L command, 181
userPassword attribute, 319, 348
uses for restriction classes, 108–9
UUCP (Unix-to-Unix Copy Protocol), 33, 448
uudeview utility, 65

V

-v parameter, 331
verifying sender, 103–7
VeriSign, 96
version parameter, 344, 361
virtual alias domains, 189–94
    advanced mappings, 192–94
    configuring Postfix to receive mail for, 191
    creating recipient address map, 190–91
    overview, 189–90
    setting name, 190
    testing settings, 191–92
virtual daemon, 40, 195, 373
virtual delivery agent, 40, 194–97
virtual mailbox domains, 194–203
    advanced configuration, 199–203
    basic configuration, 195–98
    checking Postfix for virtual delivery agent support, 195
    overview, 194–95
virtual private network (VPN), 218, 220
virtual_alias_domains parameter, 190–92
virtual_alias_maps parameter, 173, 191–94, 198, 211, 331
virtual_gid_maps parameter, 196
virtual_mailbox_base parameter, 197, 199
virtual_mailbox_domains parameter, 195, 199
virtual_mailbox_domains.cf file, 214
virtual_mailbox_maps parameter, 197, 200, 211
virtual_uid_maps parameter, 196, 201
vmail group, 334
VPN (virtual private network), 218, 220
VRFY command, 72

W

-w flag, 332
WARN action, 82, 115, 119
warn_if_reject command, 71
warn_if_reject parameter, 82–83
WHERE clause, 213
wildcard MTA, 96
--with-redhat option, 344
--with-trashquota, 334

X

X509 certificates, 339–43, 359
XFORWARD command, 165
X-headers, 64

Y

y chroot option, 372

Z

-ZZ option, 364

Electronic Frontier Foundation

Defending Freedom in the Digital World

Free Speech. Privacy. Innovation. Fair Use. Reverse Engineering. If you care about these rights in the digital world, then you should join the Electronic Frontier Foundation (EFF). EFF was founded in 1990 to protect the rights of users and developers of technology. EFF is the first to identify threats to basic rights online and to advocate on behalf of free expression in the digital age.

The Electronic Frontier Foundation Defends Your Rights!
Become a Member Today!
http://www.eff.org/support/

Current EFF projects include:

Protecting your fundamental right to vote. Widely publicized security flaws in computerized voting machines show that, though filled with potential, this technology is far from perfect. EFF is defending the open discussion of e-voting problems and is coordinating a national litigation strategy addressing issues arising from use of poorly developed and tested computerized voting machines.

Ensuring that you are not traceable through your things. Libraries, schools, the government and private sector businesses are adopting radio frequency identification tags, or RFIDs – a technology capable of pinpointing the physical location of whatever item the tags are embedded in. While this may seem like a convenient way to track items, it's also a convenient way to do something less benign: track people and their activities through their belongings. EFF is working to ensure that embrace of this technology does not erode your right to privacy.

Defending your right to listen to and copy digital music and movies. The entertainment industry has been overzealous in trying to protect its copyrights, often decimating fair use rights in the process. EFF is standing up to the movie and music industries on several fronts.

Stopping the FBI from creating surveillance backdoors on the Internet. EFF is part of a coalition opposing the FBI's expansion of the Communications Assistance for Law Enforcement Act (CALEA), which would require that the wiretap capabilities built into the phone system be extended to the Internet, forcing ISPs to build backdoors for law enforcement.

Providing you with a means by which you can contact key decision-makers on cyber-liberties issues. EFF maintains an action center that provides alerts on technology, civil liberties issues and pending legislation to more than 50,000 subscribers. EFF also generates a weekly online newsletter, EFFector, and a blog that provides up-to-the minute information and commentary.

Check out all of the things we're working on at http://www.eff.org and join today or make a donation to support the fight to defend freedom online.

ELECTRONIC FRONTIER FOUNDATION · 454 SHOTWELL STREET · SAN FRANCISCO, CA 94110 · 415.436.9333

THE LINUX COOKBOOK 2ND EDITION

Tips and Techniques for Everyday Use

by MICHAEL STUTZ

The Linux Cookbook 2nd Edition is nearly 50 percent larger than the first and will help new and existing users get the most out of Linux. It includes hundreds of new recipes and is also distribution neutral, covering all flavors of Linux, including Red Hat, SuSE, and Debian. The 2nd edition includes new sections on package management, file conversion, multimedia, working with sound files (including OGG and MP3), Vi text editing, and advanced text manipulation. And, just to show what level of text manipulation Linux is capable of, Stutz designed and typeset his book using only Linux.

AUGUST 2004, 824 PP., $39.95 ($55.95 CAN)

ISBN 1-59327-031-3

HOW LINUX WORKS

What Every Superuser Should Know

by BRIAN WARD

How Linux Works describes the inside of the Linux system for systems administrators, whether they're tasked with maintaining an extensive network in the office or one Linux box at home. Some books try to give you copy-and-paste instructions for how to deal with every single system issue that may arise, but *How Linux Works* actually shows you how the Linux system functions, so you can come up with your own solutions. After a guided tour of filesystems, the boot sequence, system management basics, and networking, author Brian Ward delves into open-ended topics such as development tools, custom kernels and buying hardware, all from an administrator's point of view. With a mixture of background theory and real-world examples, this book shows both "how" to administer Linux, and "why" each particular technique works, so that you will know how to make Linux work for you.

MAY 2004, 368 PP., $37.95 ($55.95 CAN)

ISBN 1-59327-035-6

PHONE:
800.420.7240 OR
415.863.9900
MONDAY THROUGH FRIDAY,
9 A.M. TO 5 P.M. (PST)

FAX:
415.863.9950
24 HOURS A DAY,
7 DAYS A WEEK

EMAIL:
SALES@NOSTARCH.COM

WEB:
HTTP://WWW.NOSTARCH.COM

MAIL:
NO STARCH PRESS
555 DE HARO ST, SUITE 250
SAN FRANCISCO, CA 94107
USA

UPDATES

Visit http://www.postfix-book.com for updates, errata, and other information.